Thank you, God
for your presence
in my life.

Nihil Obstat	Imprimatur	The Ad Hoc Committee to Oversee the Use of the Catechism, United States Conference of Catholic Bishops, has found this catechetical series, copyright 2007, to be in conformity with the *Catechism of the Catholic Church*.
Reverend John G. Lodge, S.S.L., S.T.D. Censor Deputatus July 5, 2006	Reverend John F. Canary, D.Min. Vicar General Archdiocese of Chicago July 7, 2006	

The *Nihil Obstat* and *Imprimatur* are official declarations that a book is free of doctrinal and moral error. No implication is contained therein that those who have granted the *Nihil Obstat* and *Imprimatur* agree with the content, opinions, or statements expressed. Nor do they assume any legal responsibility associated with publication.

Finding God: Our Response to God's Gifts is an expression of the work of Loyola Press, an apostolate of the Chicago Province of the Society of Jesus.

Senior Consultants

Jane Regan, Ph.D.
Richard Hauser, S.J., Ph.D., S.T.L.
Robert Fabing, S.J., D.Min.

Advisors

Most Reverend Gordon D. Bennett, S.J., D.D.
George A. Aschenbrenner, S.J., S.T.L.
Paul H. Colloton, O.P., D.Min.
Eugene LaVerdiere, S.S.S., Ph.D., S.T.L.

Gerald Darring, M.A.
Thomas J. McGrath
Joanne Paprocki, M.A.

Catechetical Staff

Jeanette L. Graham, M.A.
Marlene Halpin, O.P., Ph.D.
Jean Hopman, O.S.U., M.A.

Thomas McLaughlin, M.A.
Joseph Paprocki, M.A.
Julie Vieira, I.H.M., M.A.

Cover and Interior Design

Mia Basile, Kathy Greenholdt, Judine O'Shea/Loyola Press

Grateful acknowledgment is given to authors, publishers, photographers, museums, and agents for permission to reprint the following copyrighted material. Every effort has been made to determine copyright owners. In the case of any omissions, the publisher will be pleased to make suitable acknowledgments in future editions. Continued on page 399.

ISBN 10: 0-8294-2162-9, ISBN 13: 978-0-8294-2162-0

Manufactured in the United States of America.

LOYOLAPRESS.

3441 N. ASHLAND AVENUE
CHICAGO, ILLINOIS 60657
(800) 621-1008
www.LoyolaPress.org
www.FindingGod.org

08 09 10 11 12 13 Banta 10 9 8 7 6 5 4 3 2

FINDING GOD
Following Jesus

Barbara F. Campbell, M.Div., D.Min.

James P. Campbell, M.A., D.Min.

LOYOLAPRESS.

CHICAGO

Contents

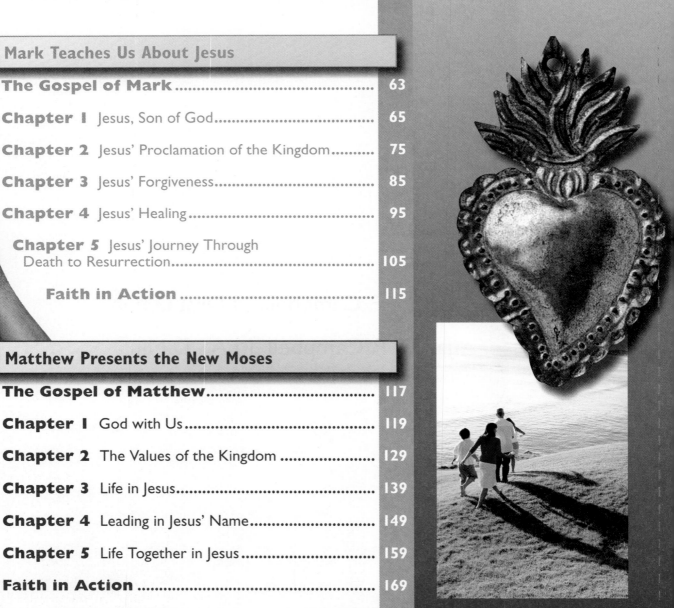

The Year in Our Church

Prayers and Practices of Our Faith

Understanding the Words of Our Faith:

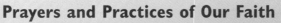

John Explores the Mystery of God

THE GOSPEL OF JOHN

The Gospel of John was written between 90 and 100. This was 50 to 60 years after Jesus' life, death, and Resurrection. Although this Gospel has been attributed to the apostle John, it is more likely to have been written by a few members of the early Christian community. It was common practice at that time to write in the name of a person admired by the community so that people would pay attention to your writing. Since the Gospel was written nearly two generations after Jesus walked the earth, the writer was able to reflect on what had already been written and taught about Jesus.

John 1:1–18 is an excellent prologue that introduces the main theme of the Gospel. The writer sketches out the whole plan of God's Revelation. He explains that the Word was with God from the beginning and that the Word of God become man is Jesus. Jesus in turn reveals the Father and his intentions and love for us.

The presence of God is fully in the man Jesus. Reborn in Baptism through the power of the Holy Spirit we participate in the divine nature of Jesus Christ. Because of this, God dwells in us. We ourselves become witnesses to God's presence in the world. He is fully revealed in his Word. In Jesus, God's glory is revealed as a sign of his everlasting love.

THE BOOK OF SIGNS

John's Gospel is divided into two major sections—the Book of Signs and the Book of Glory. The Book of Signs, John 1:19 through 12:50, recounts the wondrous deeds of Jesus. Each of these deeds is interpreted by the writer so that the deeper meaning of the story is understood. For example, the story of the transformation of the water into wine at Cana in John 2:1–11 is not only about Jesus saving his friends the embarrassment of having run out of wine at the wedding feast. The abundance of wine that Jesus provides is a sign that the kingdom has come in the person of Jesus.

Another important story concerning the identity of Jesus is told in John 3. The Jewish leader Nicodemus comes in the night to speak with Jesus. He does not want to be recognized by his peers. John shows that Nicodemus is coming out of the darkness and into the light of Jesus. Jesus speaks to Nicodemus about the importance of faith and baptism. Jesus also tells Nicodemus in John 3:16 that he has come because of the Father's great love for the world. Jesus has come to save the world. We participate in that salvation by believing in Jesus.

THE BOOK OF GLORY

The second major section of John's Gospel, John 13:1 through 20:31, is known as the Book of Glory. These chapters recount the Last Supper and Jesus' passion and death. Here John shows how Jesus reverses the values of the world. Crucifixion is a Roman punishment, a horrible, slow death inflicted on those despised by the government. Throughout his Gospel, John presents Jesus' death on the cross not as a sign of shame, but as a sign of glory. In what looks like a shameful death, the Glory of God is revealed and we finally realize how far God will go so that we might be saved.

Jesus tells his disciples to be hopeful after he returns to the Father. Jesus promises not to leave them alone in the world. He would send an Advocate, the Holy Spirit, to be with them and to guide them. The disciples would later experience the glory of Jesus' presence, especially in those times when they were persecuted for proclaiming the Good News. Jesus does not leave them orphans, and neither does he leave us orphans.

JOHN IN THIS UNIT

The stories from the Gospel of John give us many opportunities to discover that Jesus is the Son of God made man and that he came to save us. John presents Jesus as a person totally confident in his relationship with the Father. Jesus understood what he was asked to do by the Father—to proclaim how deeply the Father cares for all of us.

John presents Jesus as knowing all the Father's intentions for us. In Jesus these intentions are fulfilled, so that we may all live an abundant life. Not everyone in Jesus' time wanted to hear that message. So Jesus warns his disciples that the road to faithfulness will be difficult. But we also learn in John's Gospel that we are not left alone.

In this unit, with John's help, we will explore the wonderful mystery of the relationship between the Father, the Son, and the Holy Spirit. They want only for us to understand how much they love us and how much they are willing to do for us.

WORD OF Mouth

Did you ever wonder how people learned about history before textbooks, museums, or the Internet? Stories about the past were often handed down from one generation to the next by word of mouth. A good storyteller made history come alive. If you asked one of your grandparents or an older family member what history-making things happened when he or she was your age, what would he or she have to say?

First Rate

Today there are many different ways that we can learn things. Rate on a scale of 1 to 6 the ways you learn best.

- [ ] researching on the Internet
- [ ] asking someone
- [ ] watching someone

- [ ] reading a book
- [ ] experiencing something yourself
- [ ] using an audiovisual resource like a DVD

A Personal Message *from* God

You probably read many things on any given day. You might read a few pages of your history text-book for homework. You probably scan through a lot of pop-up ads and spam that find their way onto your computer screen. Perhaps you have to read an article from an encyclopedia for a school project. If it's your lucky day, you might get a personal letter or an e-mail from a friend you've been dying to hear from. It would be an easy choice if you had to choose between reading a personal letter or a pop-up ad.

When you read a personal message from a friend, you read it in an entirely different way than you read any other kind of writing. Whereas you might quickly skim through junk mail or information from a reference book, you read a personal message slowly. Perhaps you even reread certain lines to get a better understanding of what your friend is truly saying. A personal message from a friend reveals something about that person. It helps you to get to know that person more deeply.

Imagine receiving a personal message from God. Wouldn't it be wonderful to be able to read something directly from God that reveals something about him so that we can know him more deeply? The fact is, we already have such a personal message from God—the Bible. However, the Bible is more than simply a letter from God; it is more like a library filled with stories, poems, and letters. As in many good books, there are villains and heroes in the Bible. We see how God works in the world, mostly through the everyday experiences of his people.

THE GOSPEL OF JOHN

About 60 years after Jesus' life, death, and Resurrection, a man named John studied the Scriptures, the Revelation of God that had taken place over a long period of time. The Scriptures available to him were what we know today as the Old Testament. John read what the people had learned about God. He then meditated on what the stories in the Scriptures meant. He also meditated on the hymns that were used in his community to celebrate God. He adapted one of these hymns to begin his Gospel.

The Bible begins in Genesis 1:1 with the words, "In the beginning, when

IT'S LIKE THIS

The Old Testament, the first part of our Bible, was originally written for the Jews. Since Jesus and many of his disciples were Jewish, they would have read or heard these writings in light of their covenant with God—their binding sacred agreement. The early Christians began to refer to these writings as the old covenant, or old testament, as they began to understand that God was forming a new relationship with them through Jesus—the new covenant.

God created the heavens and the earth, . . ." Meditating on the meaning of these words in the light of the risen Jesus Christ, John wrote,

> **In the beginning was the Word,**
> **and the Word was with God,**
> **and the Word was God.**
> **He was in the beginning with God.**
> **(John 1:1–2)**

This is the way John showed the connection between Jesus and the creation of the world, which is recorded at the very beginning of the Old Testament. When John was writing about Jesus, he was writing about God—the same God who created the world. In teaching the importance of understanding who Jesus Christ is in relation to the created world, John wrote,

> **All things came to be through him,**
> **and without him nothing came to be.**
> **What came to be through him was life,**
> **and this life was the light of the human race.**
> **(John 1:3–4)**

OLD TESTAMENT

The Old Testament tells the story of how God chose a man named Abraham and made a Covenant with him and his descendants. By forming this special friendship with the Hebrews, the descendants of Abraham, God made them his people. He then revealed his Law to them through Moses. God spoke to his people through prophets so that they would be prepared to accept the salvation that he was going to bring for all people.

These are the things that we read about in the Old Testament. It is an essential part of the Bible because it gives us the history of the Jewish people and reveals God to us through that history.

continued on page 14 ▶

Reading the Bible with Confidence

In John's Gospel, there seems to be a great deal of misunderstanding. When Jesus spoke about the temple of his body being destroyed and rebuilt in three days, some people thought he was talking about the Jerusalem temple. When Jesus told Nicodemus that he must be born again, Nicodemus asked how someone can re-enter his mother's womb. When Jesus said Lazarus was asleep, he meant that he was dead. However, some of his disciples thought Jesus meant that Lazarus was taking a nap. John uses these occasions of misunderstanding to show that, unless we pay close attention to what Jesus is saying, we too will misunderstand his message.

The Catholic Church wants to be sure that we have no misunderstanding when we read the Bible. With that in mind, in 1943, Pope Pius XII promoted the idea of modern translations of the Bible from Hebrew and Greek. In response, the United States bishops invited around 50 biblical scholars to take on the task. A few decades of work led to the publication of *The New American Bible* in 1970. This is the official translation of the Bible into English published by the bishops of the United States. The translation has been updated in 1986 and 1991. *The New American Bible* offers us a translation we can trust for personal reading or study. It is also the translation used in the Mass and the Liturgy of the Hours.

LEFT: This 15th-century illustration depicts the Book of Exodus passage in which Bezalel and Oholiab build the Ark of the Covenant, a sacred chest containing the tablets of the law.

The Two Testaments

When Jesus talked about the Scriptures, what do you think he was referring to? It could not have been the Bible we have today because the New Testament had not been written yet. For Jesus and for his Jewish followers, the Scriptures were what we call the Old Testament.

In John's Gospel, Jesus makes it very clear that he is equal to the Father. In fact, once when speaking to a group of Jewish people, Jesus said, "before Abraham came to be, I AM." (John 8:58) The Jewish people listening to Jesus would recognize the reference to God telling Moses in the Old Testament, "I am who am." (Exodus 3:14) In other words, it is important for us to know the Old Testament if we are to fully understand the New Testament. Strangely enough, after the New Testament was written, there were a few Christians who wanted to get rid of the Old Testament. The Church disagreed. It kept the Old Testament in the Bible because the Old Testament is God's Word just as much as the New Testament is. The Church accepts and venerates as inspired both the 46 books of the Old Testament and the 27 books of the New Testament.

Saint Augustine (pictured above) explained the Bible well. He said that the "New Testament lies hidden in the Old and the Old Testament is unveiled in the New." In other words, the Old Testament prepares us to understand the message of the New Testament, and the New Testament helps us to fully understand the Old Testament.

▶ *continued from page 13*

FULFILLED IN JESUS

John knew that the revelation of God found in the Old Testament is fulfilled in Jesus. In other words, God completed everything he wanted to say about himself by sending his own Son and by establishing in him a new covenant with us. Because Jesus is the fullness of God's Word to us, nothing more needs to be revealed. Through Jesus, God has now told us everything that we need to know about our salvation. Jesus is the true light who completely enlightens us about the Father's intentions for the whole human family:

> **And the Word became flesh**
> **and made his dwelling among us,**
> **and we saw his glory,**
> **the glory as of the Father's only Son,**
> **full of grace and truth. . . .**
> **From his fullness we have all received, grace in place**
> **of grace, because while the law was given through**
> **Moses, grace and truth came through Jesus Christ.**
> **No one has ever seen God. The only Son, God, who**
> **is at the Father's side, has revealed him.**
> **(John 1:14,16–18)**

So this is God's personal message to us. We participate in God's great plan for the human family. Both the Old Testament and New Testament tell a single story of God's love for us. The Old Testament records how God revealed this plan through Abraham and his descendants. The New Testament tells us how this plan came to completion in Jesus Christ. Everything we need to know about what it means to live in relationship with God our Father is revealed in Jesus. FG

10 Fun Facts about the Bible

The Bible . . .

- was written over a period of about 1600 years.
- was written by more than 40 people including kings, fishermen, poets, government officials, teachers, and prophets.
- has been translated into about 3000 different languages.
- is not one book, but a collection of 73 books.
- includes poetry, history, prophecy, law, prayers, hymns, stories, and letters.
- includes letters that were written from prison to early Christian groups.
- never says that Adam and Eve ate an apple.
- contains the expression "apple of your eye". (Proverbs 7:2)
- tops the bestseller list every year.
- has worldwide sales of over 100 million copies each year.

Discovering the Truth in the Bible

When you think of interpreting something, what comes to mind? You might have had the experience of interpreting the directions of your teacher. What exactly does your teacher want you to do to get a good grade on a project? You might also think of a person working as a translator for a diplomat in a foreign country. Or you might think of an archaeologist holding a torch up to the wall of an ancient tomb in Egypt. The archaeologist attempts to interpret the clues in the hieroglyphics that will unlock the treasure of the tomb. Sometimes the archaeologist asks an expert in hieroglyphics to help translate the symbols into a modern language.

When you read and try to understand the Bible, you want to make sure that you get it right. Like the archaeologist, you want to unlock the secrets to a treasure. However, you might need help with the discovery.

Jesus wanted his disciples to know the truth about what it means to live in relationship with God his Father. So he devoted his public life to teaching the apostles the truth about God and about salvation. The apostles were so excited about what they had learned that after the coming of the Holy Spirit at Pentecost, they proclaimed it as loudly as they could. Later their stories and teachings were written down in what we now know as the New Testament. Through the ministry of the Church the stories were copied by hand for generations. Since the 1400s they have been printed in books for all to read. The same Holy Spirit who inspired the apostles and biblical writers continues to guide the Church today. Because of this inspiration,

the most important truths we need to know are given to us without error in the Bible and in the Church. However, we need help understanding these important truths. We know that the Bible teaches us the truths we need to know because it is inspired by God.

> **"If you remain in my word, you will truly be my disciples, and you will know the truth, and the truth will set you free."**
> (John 8:31–32)

INSPIRATION

But what is the meaning of inspiration in terms of the Bible? Inspiration means that God is the author of the Bible. While he did not actually sit down and write it, the Holy Spirit enlightened the minds of the authors while they were writing. By acting through the authors, the Holy Spirit made sure that they would teach the truth without any error.

INERRANCY

Inerrancy is the term we use to describe that the Bible teaches the truth without error. Inerrancy means that when the Bible tells us the religious truth about God,

continued on page 16 ▶

Copy, Copy, Copy

At the end of John's Gospel, we are told that it was the beloved disciple, John, who has written it. Does that mean that John actually wrote the Gospel in his own hand? Probably not. The Gospels were proclaimed orally for many years before they were eventually written by hand.

Imagine copying the entire Bible by hand! Well, until 1455, with the invention of the printing press, the Bible was always copied by hand. Monks and nuns working in monasteries copied the Bible by hand for centuries. If a monk started making a copy of the Bible when your school year started, he would finish copying the Bible right after your school year ended. He would try very hard not to make mistakes and he would have a companion check all his work. But mistakes were still made, and scholars still have a hard time figuring out the intended meaning of some letters and words. And yet those copyists did a fantastic job.

Although we do not have a single original copy of any book of the Bible, the text we have is very accurate. We know this because samples that were copied in different centuries were checked against each other and found to be the same. Thanks to a lot of hard work, the Bible was saved for us so that today we can learn from God's Word the things we need to know for our salvation.

▶ *continued from page 15*

about the world, and about our relationship with him and each other, it is telling us the truth without getting it wrong. But it's important that we understand what the Church means by religious truth. Religious truth is what we need to know for our salvation. The Bible is not wrong when teaching us about God and salvation. Does that mean that everything we read in the Bible is scientifically and historically accurate? No. Inerrancy does not address historical details and scientific facts. There can be errors in those areas because they are not things we need to know for our salvation.

INTERPRETATION

So if the Bible is inspired by God and teaches religious truth without error, why do there seem to be so many different explanations as to what it means? Imagine if your teacher asked several students to write book reports on the same book. Each student would take away something different from the experience. The same thing happens with the Bible. Everyone's experience of reading the Bible is different, and people will discover that they can have different interpretations about what is important even when reading the same story.

So the Bible has to be interpreted. *Interpretation* means deciding what the Bible means. To interpret the Bible correctly, we need to understand how people lived, thought, and wrote back in the days when it was written. The biblical writers were masters at writing epic stories, love poems, hymns, prayers, gospels, and epistles.

When you read a story in the Bible about a flood, a miraculous healing, or a wedding, you want to know what God is trying to tell you through that story. You want to know more than what the story says—you want to know what it means. And here is where we all need some guidance.

When you pick up the Bible and see all the ways that the story of our salvation is written, it can be intimidating. How do you find a path through this material? Who can help you discover what it means?

The pope, and the bishops in union with him, keep the Church on track when interpreting the Bible. They are the official teachers of the Church. They make sure that Catholics interpret the Bible correctly by helping us understand what is essential for us to know for the sake of our salvation. The pope and bishops, guided by the Holy Spirit, help us interpret the words that were written many centuries ago under the guidance of the same Holy Spirit. FG

Well now, isn't THAT an eye-opener! Not to puff my chest, but all season I thought inerrancy meant I was a sure thing for the Golden fin award.

And the Word Was God

RESPECT FOR THE BIBLE

In the first creation account in Genesis, God only needs to speak and the world is created. God's Word is powerful and creative. Because the Bible is the Word of God, it has always been treated with respect. The scrolls of the Torah and the other books of the Jewish scriptures are kept in a special container in the synagogue. When they are read aloud, a special pointer is often used so the reader does not touch the sacred text with his or her finger.

In the Catholic Church there developed the tradition of adding elaborate illuminations to the sacred text. These illuminations were beautiful illustrations of the story or the theme of the sacred text. Respect for the Word of God continues today.

Bibles are not always expensive and filled with art. Today there are many simply produced and inexpensive editions available. It is good to remember, however, that the Bible should still be treated with respect. The *Dogmatic Constitution on Divine Revelation* of the Second Vatican Council stated "The Church has always venerated the divine Scriptures just as she venerates the body of the Lord."

LEFT: illustration of Christ with the four Evangelists, from *The Bible of Alcuin,* 9th Century

Leader: Each time we open the Bible can be an opportunity to meet God in a new way. This year we'll focus our attention on Jesus, the Word of God. As a sign of our openness to receive the Word and allow it to form us, let's join in procession carrying the Bible and then listen attentively to the proclamation of the Gospel.

After processing to the prayer center, the reader opens the Bible and proclaims the following reading.

Reader 1: A reading from the Gospel according to John.

> In the beginning was the Word,
> and the Word was with God,
> and the Word was God.
> He was in the beginning with God.
>   All things came to be through him,
>   and without him nothing came to be.
> What came to be through him was life,
>   and this life was the light of the human race;
>   the light shines in the darkness,
>   and the darkness has not overcome it.
>
> (John 1:1-5)

The Gospel of the Lord.

All: Praise to you, Lord Jesus Christ.

Leader: The Word of God is like a light that shines in the darkness. It shows us the way to God by teaching us to live as followers of his Son, Jesus. Let's offer our prayers to God in thanksgiving for this gift of light.

Reader 2: God of all creation, through your word, all things came to be. Through our study of Scripture, help us to grow closer to Jesus, your Word. Let us pray to the Lord.

All: Lord, hear our prayer.

Reader 3: God of love, in Scripture you reveal how close you are to us. Through our study of Scripture, open our hearts to accept your friendship with us. Let us pray to the Lord.

All: Lord, hear our prayer.

Reader 4: God of all truth, in Scripture you teach us all we need to know for our salvation. Through our study of Scripture, guide us along your path of truth. Let us pray to the Lord.

All: Lord, hear our prayer.

Leader: And now let us pray in the words that Jesus taught us.

All: Our Father . . .

Leader: Your Word, O God, became flesh and made his dwelling among us. We thank you for the gift of your Word. Help us to recognize your presence in the Scripture we study. We ask this through Christ, our Lord. Amen.

Saint John the Evangelist, Berto di Giovanni, 1461–62

What's **WHAT?**

■ Main points from this chapter are listed below. Complete each sentence. Refer to the articles and sidebars for help.

- Reading the Bible is like a receiving a personal

  message from God.

- The Gospel of John shows that God completed everything he wanted to say about himself by

  sending his own son and establishing a new law.

- The official translation of the Bible into English is

  the New American Bible

- Both the Old and the New Testaments are

  the word of God.

- The most important truths we need to know given to us in the Bible and in the Church are

  with out error

Say **WHAT?**

Abraham • Catholic Social Teaching
Covenant • inerrancy • Revelation

equals w/out error Abraham - 2000 BC (Father of Jews)

So **WHAT?**

■ The Bible is a personal message from God. *Think about it. Pray about it.*

Now **WHAT?**

■ What will you do this week to grow more familiar with God's message in the Bible?

Here's **WHAT** the Catholic Church Teaches

Taking action to create a more just world is an essential part of living the Gospel. The major development of the social doctrine of the Church began in the 19th century when the Gospel encountered modern industrial society. Industrialism changed the world. There were new structures for the production of consumer goods, new concepts of society and the authority of the state, and new forms of labor and ownership. Since the start of industrialism, the Church has been applying the teaching of the Gospels to the economic and social matters that relate to the basic rights of people and their communities.

Catholic Social Teaching is a rich treasure of wisdom about how to build a just society and how to live holy lives amid the challenges of the modern world. The bishops of the United States have defined seven areas of social concern:

- Life and Dignity of the Human Person
- Call to Family, Community, and Participation
- Rights and Responsibilities
- Option for the Poor and Vulnerable
- The Dignity of Work and the Rights of Workers
- Solidarity
- Care for God's Creation

The feature **Here's What** explores these as well as other aspects of social teaching as they relate to the faith topics explored in each chapter.

Paired Interview

Your name _____

Your partner's name _____

Title of article read by your partner _____

_____

Q&A

Ask your partner the following questions about the article he or she read and record his or her answers in the space provided.

1. Explain what your article was about in a few sentences.	
2. What is one quote (sentence) from your article that you would put on a poster to inspire the group? Why?	
3. What are some specific things your article helped you to learn or realize about the Catholic faith?	
4. Based on your article, name some specific things we, as Catholics, need to know, do, or believe in order to live as followers of Jesus.	

TRACING OUR

Roots

People have a natural curiosity to know where they came from and how they are related to others. The more we learn about our families, the more we learn about ourselves. Think about how exciting it would be to find a dusty old notebook under the wooden floorboards in your great-grand-mother's attic. What would you want to know about her?

For Your Eyes Only

If you were to write your autobiography, what would you want your great-grandchildren to know about you?

Jesus is the Center

art • i • fact
Christ in Benediction,
10th century, Byzantine,
cloisonné enamel plaque. The
Greek letters on either side
of the image are the first two
letters of Jesus and Christ.

When we read a biography about a historical person, we sometimes check to see if the author supported the facts. To do this we might read the footnotes at the bottom of the page or the endnotes at the back of the book. If we are really interested in the historical person, we might read the sources that the author used to research the facts. We do this so that we can be somewhat confident that the information we are learning about the person is accurate and truthful.

AUTHORS OF THE GOSPELS

It is easy to think that when we are reading the Gospels we are reading a biography of Jesus. But the authors of the four Gospels were not writing to tell us everything they knew about Jesus. They were writing to help us realize how important Jesus is for our salvation.

The Gospels are special to us because they tell us the most important things we should know about Jesus as Savior and Redeemer. The authors of the Gospels were inspired by the Holy Spirit to record the faith of the early Church, a faith that has been passed down to us. The Gospels are at the center of our faith because Jesus Christ is the center of the Gospels. One way of understanding what the authors of the Gospels did is to compare the different ways Jesus is depicted in the paintings and drawings in this book.

> If all the stories about Jesus were told, there would not be enough books to record them.

The paintings or drawings show Jesus in the way he was seen by different artists at different times and from different cultures. Each portrait is unique. But each one communicates to us how important Jesus is. The Gospels were written in the same way. Each author tells us what is important about Jesus, but each one does it in a unique way.

FORMATION OF THE GOSPELS

The Gospels didn't appear overnight. In fact, there were three different stages in the formation of the Gospels that we know today. The first stage was the life of Jesus, his birth and his life in Nazareth, his public ministry in Galilee, and finally his death, Resurrection, and Ascension. From the time Jesus entered into public life, he was accompanied by a number of disciples, some of whom he chose to be apostles. They saw the way he lived his life, they watched him care for others, and they listened carefully to his teachings. They also spoke to Jesus after his Resurrection.

The second stage in the formation of the Gospels was the preaching of the good news of the salvation of Jesus Christ. The apostles and other disciples of Jesus went out and told people about Jesus. The followers had been filled with the Holy Spirit, so they had a better understanding of who Jesus was and what his teachings meant. They shared their knowledge and understanding with anyone who would listen. They taught others the way Jesus had taught them. This passing on by the apostles of what they received from Jesus' teaching and example and what they learned from the Holy Spirit is called tradition. It is passed on to us today by the apostles' successors, the bishops, along with the pope.

The final stage was the actual writing of the Gospels. The writers collected stories about Jesus and sayings of Jesus that they remembered or had been told. Each of the four Gospel writers, known as the Evangelists, composed his own account of the life of Jesus. In each case they wanted to show what Jesus meant to them and to the others living in their communities.

All three of these stages took place under the guidance of the Holy Spirit. The authors were doing what Jesus wanted them to do. He had told them to preach the Gospel to others, but he had not directed them to write

continued on page 24 ▶

Why Four Gospels?

We usually think of John's Gospel as the "Fourth Gospel." Indeed, of the 4 Gospels in the Bible, John's Gospel was the last one written, probably some 60 to 70 years after Jesus' death and resurrection. However, at the time there were a number of manuscripts in circulation that were said to tell the real story of Jesus. Some of these manuscripts told of a Jesus who did not come to save everyone. In response, Church leaders established some rules to help them choose which writings would be considered inspired by the Holy Spirit. First, they asked whether the writings were of apostolic origin. Could they be linked to the teachings of one of the apostles? Second, they asked if the writings came from an authentic Christian community. For example, in about the year 180 Saint Irenaeus wrote that he accepted the writings found in the New Testament because he had received them from the Church in Rome. The importance and trustworthiness of the Church in Rome, the Church founded by Peter, was a sure sign for Irenaeus that the writings were inspired by God. Third, the Church leaders asked if the writings conformed to the "rule of faith." That is, did the writings reflect the authentic faith that had been learned from the apostles? Did the writings teach that Jesus Christ was Lord and Savior and had come to save the world? The writings we have today in the Gospels do all of these things and are the only Gospels accepted by the Church as truly inspired by the Holy Spirit as teaching the truth about Jesus Christ. There will be no other Gospels added to the Bible that will teach us anything new about Jesus Christ.

The New Testament

The author of John's Gospel refers to himself as an eyewitness (John 19:35). We need to remember, however, that there were no reporters present taking down his account. In fact, for about 25 years after Jesus' death and Resurrection, just about everything we know about Jesus was passed on through word of mouth. The apostles and the other disciples preached the gospel, and the followers of Jesus gathered in their homes to worship God. Then around the year 55 the apostle Paul began writing letters to communities of Christians in different parts of the Roman Empire. About a decade later the first Gospel was put together by Mark, and within 25 years the other three Gospels had been written by Matthew, Luke, and John. In the meantime, other letters were written by James, John, and Jude. Letters to the Hebrews, Colossians, Ephesians, and Timothy were written. The Book of Revelation was written near the very end of the first century. It was placed at the end of the New Testament. In its final form, the New Testament is made up of the four Gospels, followed by the Acts of the Apostles, all the letters by Paul and by the others, and finally the Book of Revelation.

▶ *continued from page 23*

anything down. However, the writers knew that they would not live forever. They wanted to preserve the teachings of Jesus accurately so that future generations, like our own, could read the Good News that they preached. Their inspiration came from the Holy Spirit. The Gospels that they wrote tell about God's gifts to everyone. They are the source of all truth and understanding about how we are to live our lives.

"Whoever belongs to God hears the words of God."
(John 8:47)

THE FOUR GOSPELS

We have four gospels—Matthew, Mark, Luke, and John. Even though each of the Gospels give us a unique portrait of Jesus, they all teach the essential truth that Jesus is the Son of God become man, sent by the Father for the sake of our salvation. At the end of the Gospel of John we are told that if all the stories about Jesus were told, there would not be enough books to record them. What we do have is a special treasure, helping us to know Jesus as Lord, Savior, and friend.

That sounds like a lot of writing. It makes my fins sore just thinking about it.

art • i • fact

St. John the Evangelist, Byzantine mosaic, San Vitale, Ravenna, Italy. The eagle behind John is his symbol.

Walkin' the Talk

John was called to be an apostle in the first year of Jesus' public ministry. He is often referred to as the "beloved disciple" and is the only one of the twelve apostles who did not abandon Jesus at the time of his Passion. John not only preached the Good News but is also credited with writing the fourth Gospel and three epistles. The Book of Revelation is also attributed to him, although his authorship is not certain. According to tradition, John was cast into a cauldron of boiling oil by order of the Roman emperor Dometian. He emerged unhurt and was banished to the island of Patmos for a year. John outlived the other apostles—he died of old age in Ephesus around the year 100.

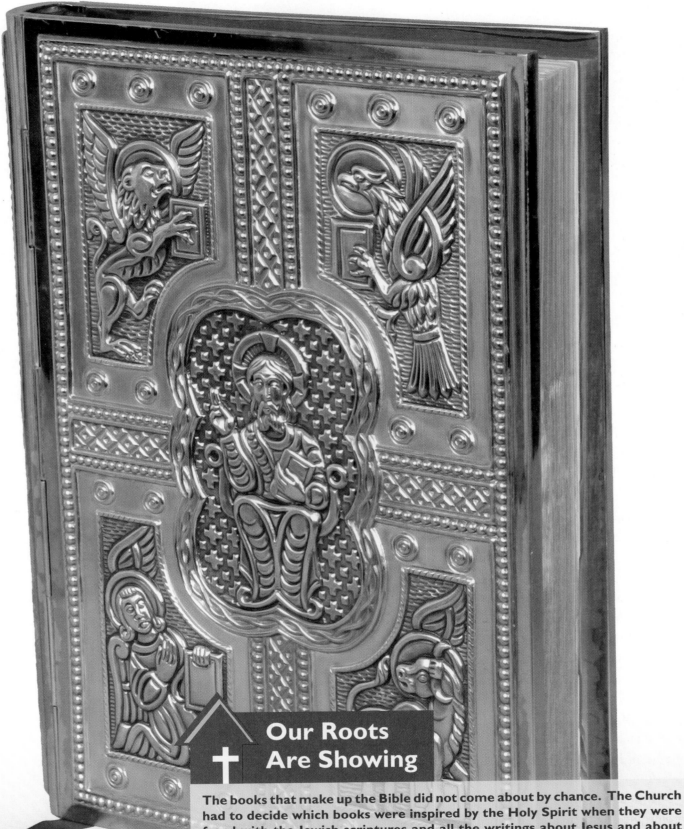

Our Roots Are Showing

The books that make up the Bible did not come about by chance. The Church had to decide which books were inspired by the Holy Spirit when they were faced with the Jewish scriptures and all the writings about Jesus and about living the Christian life. After several centuries, the Church established the official list of the 73 books that comprise the Old and New Testaments of the Bible. This official list is called the *canon*, which comes from a Greek word meaning "measuring stick" or "rule," because the writings contained within the Bible are our rule of faith.

Model of Faith

As Catholics we honor Mary, the mother of Jesus, as the model of our faith. Of all the Gospel writers, John points this out the most clearly. To understand John's message about Mary, let's look at two stories as John tells them—one from the beginning and one from the end of Jesus' public life.

WEDDING FEAST AT CANA

In John 2:1–12, Jesus is about 30 years old. Although he has disciples, he has not yet begun his public ministry. Jesus, Mary, and the disciples are invited to a wedding feast in the town of Cana, in Galilee. Wedding feasts at that time lasted a long time, sometimes even days. At this particular wedding, the hosts run out of wine. This is embarrassing for the family because they may have to cut the feast short and send everyone home.

Mary sees that the hosts have run out of wine and she tells Jesus about it. Jesus does not believe that it is his concern. He tells Mary that it is not yet his time to begin his public acts. However Mary tells the waiters, "Do whatever he tells you." She is confident and has faith that her son will solve the problem. It is interesting to note that these are the last words we hear Mary speak in the Gospel of John.

Although he was not planning on doing anything, Jesus does not disappoint. Nearby there are six empty water jars that, when filled, are going to be used for washing the hands and feet of the guests. Jesus tells the waiters to fill the large jars with water. Then he tells one of the waiters to pour out some of that water and take it to the headwaiter. By the time the headwaiter tastes the water it has been transformed into wine. In fact, all of the water

Do whatever he tells you.

in the jars have been transformed. The headwaiter is amazed that the hosts have saved such wonderful wine for the end of the feast. This did not often happen, as the best wine was usually served first. To have better wine later in the celebration is a great surprise for all who are there.

When John told this story, he wanted his readers to see that just as the people at the feast were given all the wine they desired, so the people of the world have been given all they need through the coming of the Messiah, Jesus Christ.

Mary had faith in Jesus. Her faith-filled action at the wedding feast set the stage for Jesus' glory to be revealed to his disciples. They saw this sign of Jesus' glory, and they came to believe in Jesus. The disciples' faith, then, followed upon Mary's faith, and that is what John wants us to know about her.

AT THE FOOT OF THE CROSS

The second story comes from the end of Jesus' public ministry. In John 19:26–27 Mary is once again with him at a pivotal moment. As Jesus hangs on the cross, Mary and the beloved disciple stand by. Jesus tells Mary that the beloved disciple is her son, and then he tells the beloved disciple that Mary is his mother.

The Gospel of John gives us these words, but what do they mean? As Christians have reflected on the words, they have come to understand how important Mary is in the story of our salvation. She is not our physical mother; however, she is the spiritual mother of everyone who believes in Jesus. We are her children in faith—that is, our faith in Jesus is modeled after Mary's faith. Like any good mother, she points us in the right direction.

Our faith tells us to have the same trust in Jesus that Mary showed at Cana and at the foot of the cross. Mary is our model of faith. That is what John shows in his Gospel. FG

IT OUT

Mary is a model of faith for people today, but especially for those who experience violence and poverty. Think about it—Mary lived in Nazareth, part of an occupied state under the heel of imperial Rome. She lived with the constant threat of violence. She gave birth while she and Joseph were homeless, and they had to flee like refugees to a strange land to escape being killed by a jealous king. We can turn to Mary when we experience tough times because she's experienced them too.

Signs

In the Gospels of Matthew, Mark, and Luke, there are many stories about Jesus performing miracles of healing, of feeding crowds of people, and of doing such things as walking on water. John's Gospel is somewhat different. There are fewer stories of miracles, of "signs" as John calls them, and they are told to reveal who Jesus is. The wedding at Cana illustrates the significant role of Mary in Jesus' ministry. With the sign of the changing of the water to the wine, Jesus' disciples place their faith in him as he showed he was the one who fulfilled God's promises with abundance. The miracle of the loaves and fishes provides a context for Jesus to proclaim that he is the bread of life. In the later chapters of John, the cure of the blind man in Chapter 8 and the bringing of Lazarus back from the dead in Chapter 11 show more clearly how Jesus is the one sent by God. But instead of inspiring faith in his adversaries, Jesus' signs lead them to hate him even more and to plot his murder. This leads to his greatest sign of love, his crucifixion for the sake of our salvation.

Filling Our Water Jars

LECTIO DIVINA

Lectio divina, Latin for "sacred reading," is an ancient form of Christian prayer. It is a way of spending time with the Word of God by using a special form of reading. However, it is more than just reading the Word of God—it is conversation with God.

This is how to prepare yourself for lectio divina. Begin by quieting your thoughts, perhaps by concentrating only on breathing in and out.

Read

The first step is reading slowly a brief passage of scripture.

Meditate

The second step is meditation—let the words sink in and echo within you. Reflect on what God might be saying to you. Which words speak the most to you? Repeat them a few times.

Pray

The third step is prayer. God speaks to you and you respond with your own words or with some words of the text.

Contemplate

The final step is contemplation, sitting quietly with God, beyond words and feelings.

If we want to grow closer to God, we have to spend time with him. Praying with Scripture is a way we get to know God and become aware of being filled with his love. Think of yourself as a water jar and think of God as the water overflowing within you.

Here's one way to pray with Scripture that we'll use throughout the year. Begin by focusing your attention on your breath. Be aware of your breath as it flows in and out. Let go of any distracting thoughts. Open yourself to receive the Word of God.

Read: John 2:1–12 (The Wedding Feast at Cana)

Meditate: Imagine yourself at the wedding with Jesus, Mary, and the other guests.

Read a second time: John 2:1–12 (The Wedding Feast at Cana)

Meditate: Use the space below to write down any words or phrases that stand out to you.

_____

_____

_____

Pray: Share your reflections with God in your own words. Ask him if there is anything else in this story he'd like you to notice. Then thank him for this time of prayer.

Contemplate: Spend a few moments in prayerful silence with God.

Let us close by praying together: Loving God, thank you for giving us an abundance of your life and love. Help us to be like Mary and to place our trust and love in Jesus, your Son. We ask this in his name. Amen.

What's WHAT?

■ Look over the main points of this chapter. What is one additional important insight you would add to this list? Write it on the lines below.

- Each of the four evangelists—Matthew, Mark, Luke, and John—wrote their own account of the life of Jesus. *True*
- There were three stages that had to happen before the Gospels were finished and in the form we know today. *True (Life of Jesus, Tradition, Writing)*
- The Gospels are at the center of our faith because Jesus Christ is at the center of the Gospels. *True*
- Mary, the Mother of Jesus, is the model of our faith. *True*
- Jesus' first miracle took place at a wedding feast in Cana. *True (John)*
- In the Gospel of John, Jesus' miracles are *Book of Signs + Book of Miricales* referred to as signs which reveal who Jesus is.
- _____
  _____
  _____

So WHAT?

■ How can reading the Gospels help you to get to know Jesus better?

_____
_____
_____

Say WHAT?

Evangelist • Gospel • lectio divina *Good News*
rights and responsibilities • tradition
Gospels Writer

Now WHAT?

What is one thing you will do this week to become more familiar with the Bible?

_____
_____
_____
_____
_____
_____

Here's WHAT the Catholic Church Teaches

One principle of Catholic Social Teaching is that we as human beings have both rights and responsibilities. We have intelligence and free will. We have a fundamental right to life, and the right to things we need to live such as food, shelter, employment, health care, and education. Along with these rights we have corresponding responsibilities to respect the rights of all people.

Our rights and responsibilities are universal and inviolable. This means that they cannot be taken from us and we cannot give them away. We cannot claim our rights while neglecting our duties to protect these rights for others. In 1963 Pope John XXIII wrote in his encyclical *Peace on Earth*: "Those, therefore, who claim their own rights, yet altogether forget or neglect to carry out their respective duties, are people who build with one hand and destroy with the other."

Making Connections

1. Read the article assigned to your group.

2. Note the main points from your article in the appropriate column below.

3. Join your group with a group who read the other article.

4. Record the main points in the appropriate column below.

5. Work together to complete the "Connect" section to show how the two articles connect.

Connect

How do these two articles connect?

NOTES FROM ARTICLE 1

JESUS IS THE CENTER

NOTES FROM ARTICLE 2

MODEL OF FAITH

IT'S A Mystery

Mysteries intrigue us. They tease us into looking for clues. They prod us to search for solutions. They engage us in moving beyond the obvious. Some mysteries can be solved; others remain forever beyond our understanding. Share with the group something that is a mystery to you.

IT OUT

There are all kinds of mysteries. Match the "mystery" with its explanation.

___ mystery of faith	1. a fictional story where problems are solved to explain the unknown
___ air of mystery	2. the quality of being unexplainable
___ mystery novel	3. one of 20 events in the lives of Jesus and Mary
___ mystery play	4. medieval drama based on a Bible story
___ mystery of the Rosary	5. inexplicable theological truth

Nicodemus
Seeks an Answer

Nicodemus carried a lantern as he walked the dark streets of Jerusalem. People usually stayed indoors after sunset. They did not want to face the dangers of unlit streets. But Nicodemus was on a personal mission. He was a Pharisee and a member of the ruling council, who was intrigued by what he had heard of the teachings of Jesus. But he did not want to be seen by his colleagues as being too interested in the new teacher. So he took the risk of walking in the dark of night to meet with Jesus.

As a faithful Jew, Nicodemus believed in the one God, he who had given his people the Torah—the law by which a believer could follow God. Nicodemus knew that his people loved God. But now this new teacher,

Jesus, was speaking about a new relationship with God. John 3:1–17 not only tells the story of Nicodemus but also explains the meaning of this event. Nicodemus was living in a world of darkness and sin. In the middle of the night he came into the presence of Jesus, the true light of the world.

FATHER AND SON

As a leader, Nicodemus might have expected that he would direct the conversation with Jesus. Instead Jesus immediately asserted his own authority. Jesus told Nicodemus that no one can ever really know God unless he or she is born of the water and the Holy Spirit. Nicodemus was confused, but Jesus continued. He taught that only he who has come down from heaven can truly tell what God is really like and how much God cares for us. Referring to his coming crucifixion and death, Jesus explained that he would be lifted up so that those who believe in him will have eternal life. He

My dad loved his kids unconditionally— even when the dentist said all 726 of us needed braces.

told Nicodemus that all of this would be done to show how much God loves the world:

"For God so loved the world that he gave his only Son, so that everyone who believes in him might not perish but might have eternal life. For God did not send his Son into the world to condemn the world, but that the world might be saved through him." (John 3:16–17)

> Jesus' teaching is not just for Nicodemus. It is for all of us.

Jesus' teaching is not just for Nicodemus. It is for all of us. What Jesus is telling us is that God loves us as a Father. God the Father is concerned about us and cares for us the way parents do their children. Jesus is telling us to remember the Scriptures where God is described as taking care of his people like one who "raises an infant to his cheeks." (Hosea 11:4)

A FATHER WHO LOVES US

Later in John's Gospel, Jesus speaks to his disciples on the evening before he dies. Jesus prays to his Father for his disciples, as he is about to send them into the world to proclaim what they had learned through him. He has already promised them that the Holy Spirit, the Advocate, will be with them always.

In his prayer Jesus is telling his disciples that his entire message about God the Father was wrapped up in love. God the Father loves his only Son. Together they love the world they created. Then to save the world, the Father sent his only Son to the world to bring his message of love.

Jesus asks that his disciples be consecrated in the truth. The disciples have the mission to proclaim the truth that Jesus came to save us. Jesus prays to his Father, "As you sent me

continued on page 34 ▶

The Best of Fathers

In John's Gospel, we easily recognize the loving and intimate relationship that Jesus has with his Father. Their relationship is especially evident in some of the long discourses of Jesus where he speaks at great length to and about his heavenly Father.

What kind of father is God? Jesus tried to help us understand the kind of father we have in God. He told us to go to God the Father for everything we need, for he is a Father who will take care of us. And suppose we turn our backs on our Father and run away from him; will he take us back in? Yes, Jesus taught us, our Father will spot us coming home, run out to greet us, throw his arms around us, and welcome us back. God is the best of fathers, loving us no matter what and caring for us more than we will ever be able to understand. God regards us as his children. There are many good fathers on earth and from them we have a hint of the immense love God has for us.

ABOVE: detail of the Father from a Ukranian image of the Holy Trinity (Manitoba, Canada)

For Your Eyes Only

John tells us that Nicodemus went to Jesus in the middle of the night. Nicodemus, an important Jewish leader, probably did not want anyone to see him searching out Jesus, a so-called miracle worker. But Nicodemus felt an urgency to talk with and question Jesus. Sometimes we are hesitant to ask our questions in front of a group. If you had a private meeting with Jesus, what might you want to ask him?

▶ *continued from page 33*

into the world, so I sent them into the world." (John 17:18) Think about it for a moment. God the Father loves us so much he sent us his Son, Jesus. Jesus wants us to know how much our Father loves us. So Jesus Christ and the Father send the Holy Spirit to teach us and to give us the grace to live as Jesus did. People today will know how much God loves them by seeing the way we model our lives on the example of Jesus Christ by serving others.

NICODEMUS, FRIEND OF JESUS

Nicodemus became a friend to Jesus. In John 7:50–52 we learn that Nicodemus defended Jesus against his accusers. Nicodemus asks those who were ready to condemn Jesus without a hearing, "'Does our law condemn a person before it first hears him and finds out what he is doing?'" The rest of the rulers brushed aside his question, and belittled Jesus for having come from Galilee, an insignificant region they could not imagine any important person coming from.

After Jesus was crucified, Nicodemus showed he was a friend by bringing an enormous amount of spices, about a hundred pounds, to help prepare Jesus' body for burial (John 19: 39–40). This is the last time Nicodemus is mentioned in the New Testament. In some of the legendary stories written decades later, Nicodemus is described as someone who defends Jesus in his trial. He is thrown out of the ruling body, becomes a Christian, and dies a martyr. While we do not know if any of these stories are true, the Gospels remember Nicodemus as a friend of Jesus, a man who first heard from Jesus of the Father's great love for us in sending his Son to save us from our sins. FG

> **IM** "The Father and I are one."
> (John 10:30)

A hooded Nicodemus mourns Jesus in Michelangelo's *Pieta* (1547–55).

One God in Three Persons

19th-century Mexican painting of the Holy Trinity with Mary

***Mystery* can be a tricky word.** It can mean a crime to be solved or a puzzle to be figured out. When we talk about the mystery of the Trinity, we do not mean either of those things.

The Trinity is a mystery; in fact, it is the most important mystery of our Christian faith and life. We would never know about the Trinity if God had not revealed it to us in the New Testament. You can state this mystery in just a few words—three Persons in one God. But even after a lifetime of studying this mystery, you will never be able to completely understand it. The point is that God is not a mystery to be solved. But he is a mystery you can explore. This exploration might help you see the meaning of God in your own life.

WHAT WE CAN KNOW FOR OURSELVES

As you grow up, you figure out some things for yourself and other things you have to be told by others. For example, you have to figure out for yourself who your friends are. On the other hand, you have to be told by astronomers what the universe is like because that is not something you can figure out for yourself without the proper education and equipment.

People throughout the ages and from different cultures have figured out that there is a God. They have had a harder time figuring out what he is like, however. It is difficult because God is so different from us. So we need God to tell us about himself. God has done this in the Old Testament and throughout history. But it is Jesus who especially tells us about God and who is the best example of God's love and concern.

ONE GOD

God made it very clear to us in the Old Testament that there is only one God. There are not many gods,

continued on page 36 ▶

footnote

We sometimes compare people's traits or abilities to those of animals. It's not uncommon to hear an expression such as "He's strong as an ox." Christianity does this when referring to the four Evangelists—the writers of the Gospels. John uses figurative language to explore the mystery of Jesus Christ. He is described as "the Word," the "light of the world," "Lamb of God," and "the bread of life." Meditating on John's Gospel helps the believer to soar with the words. The Gospel of John is represented by an eagle, symbolizing its soaring and lofty style.

Trinitarians

▶ *continued from page 35*

John's Gospel reveals that Jesus and his followers often came into conflict with some of the Jewish leaders. John makes it clear

that conflict is often a part of being a follower of Jesus. Since that time, Christians have been no strangers to conflict. One example occurred in the 13th century, at a time when wars in the lands surrounding the Mediterranean Sea led to a great number of Christian men and women being captured and held for ransom in non-Christian countries. In response, John de Matha (pictured above) founded a religious community to help people too poor to ransom themselves. The community he founded, the Order of the Most Holy Trinity, or Trinitarians, raised money, traveled to the places where people were held for ransom and negotiated their release. After the captives were released, the Trinitarians returned the captives to their homes and helped them readjust to society. Today the Trinitarians are active in service to the poor and still work for the release of people imprisoned for their religious beliefs.

as some people believed, only One. The God who created the world and sustains it is the same God who chose Abraham and his descendants to be his special people. He is the same God who liberated the Hebrews from the slavery of Egypt. He is the God who spoke through the prophets. And he is the God who sent his Son to be born of the Virgin Mary. These are not all different gods. There is only one God.

TRINITY

In the New Testament God is revealed as Three Persons in one God. This is something we could never figure out for ourselves, nor is it revealed in the Old Testament. The Three Persons in one God is called the Trinity, which means "three-in-one." The first Person of the Trinity is God the Father. God the Son is begotten of the Father but he is not created, because they both exist from before time. God the Holy Spirit proceeds from the

RIGHT: *Old Testament Trinity*, Andrei Rublev, ca 1410, Russia

IT'S LIKE THIS

Just look around you—*in the classroom, on the city bus, in public buildings–there is artwork everywhere. In the Church, icons are a form of art used for prayer. They are sacred symbols that help us enter into the mystery of what they portray.*

From the earliest times, the idea of the Trinity was difficult to understand. In trying to portray the Trinity, iconographers turned to the story of the hospitality of Abraham when he was visited by three wanderers. In Old Testament Trinity *(ca 1410), iconographer Andrei Rublev chose to represent through the three haloed figures that visited Abraham the unique nature of the Trinity and the symbol of the Eucharist as an image of unity and divine love. The symbols, drawing techniques, and colors used in this icon all come together to create a beautiful image, a wordless way to appreciate the mystery of the Trinity.*

Father and the Son, but he is not created either, because like the Father and the Son, the Holy Spirit exists from before time.

Each Person of the Trinity is God. The Father is not a "part" of God; the Father is God. The same is true of the Son and the Holy Spirit. They are each God, not a "part" of God. The Father, the Son, and the Holy Spirit are each God, but there is only one God.

In teaching us about the Trinity, God has told us that each Person of the Trinity is distinct from the others. In other words, the Father is not the Son, the Son is not the Holy Spirit, and the Holy Spirit is not the Father. They are distinct Persons, equally God, and there is only one God.

ACTING AS ONE

The Church, reflecting on God's word in the New Testament, realized that the three Persons of the Trinity have a single purpose in mind for the human family. The Father, Son, and Holy Spirit within a single divine operation is revealed in a way proper to each person. The actions of the Father, the Son, and the Holy Spirit are all for our benefit. The Father is our loving Creator. The Son, the second Person of the Trinity, became man so we could know and love God as our Father. The Holy Spirit was sent by the Father and the Son to give us the grace to understand how much we are loved. The Father, Son, and Holy Spirit then are inseperable in who they are and inseperable in what they do. While the work of creation is attributed to the Father, it is also true that the work of creation is the work of the Father, Son, and Holy Spirit and the one indivisible principle of creation.

Through the life, death, and Resurrection of Jesus Christ we are brought into God's own life. We are baptized into Christ so that we can join him in the praise of the Father. We are filled with the Holy Spirit so that the life and love of the Father and the Son breathe within us. The gift of the Spirit opens us up to faith in Jesus, who takes us to his Father.

So the mystery of God is not a puzzle to be solved, but an opportunity to explore the meaning of who God is in our lives and the life of the world. FG

Creation, the First Gift of Love

When we are awed by a sunset or a full moon, we can be moved to give God a prayer of thanks. The created world around us is God's first gift of love to us. The world was not created as an afterthought or by a God who ignores the universe, but by a God who shares his truth, goodness, and beauty. All that we see and experience in the created world is an expression of God's love for us.

The author of John's Gospel knew the story of creation and that God's first words of creation were, "Let there be light." (Genesis 1:3) He proceeded to use the image of light throughout his Gospel to describe Jesus' presence. John wanted to show that God was still present in the world through Jesus.

God continues to be intimately involved in the world through the Holy Spirit. The Father and the Son sent the Holy Spirit to make it possible for us to live in love and happiness in this world and the next. Since we are blessed by God through his gifts, we in turn can bless God who redeems and saves us.

Signs of Love

THE SIGN OF THE CROSS

As Christians, we begin our day and our prayers with the Sign of the Cross. It's a reminder that our whole life is lived under the sign that saved us, the cross of Jesus, by the power of the one God who is Father, Son, and Holy Spirit. It is an important sign that places before us and on us the shape of the cross that saves us. It is the sign made over us when we become a Christian in Baptism, and it is made over us in death as we complete our Christian life. The Jewish tradition of prayer always approaches God as one who blesses. When we bless ourselves with the Sign of the Cross we remember God who blesses us: Father, Son, and Holy Spirit. The Sign of the Cross is a mark of discipleship. Jesus says in Luke 9:23 that anyone who wishes to come after him must take up his cross daily and follow him.

Do you remember learning to make the Sign of the Cross? Perhaps the hardest part was learning to connect the words with the gestures in the right order. Though short and simple, the Sign of the Cross touches the very heart of our lives.

Look for a moment at the cross on this page. Then close your eyes and silently trace a cross on your forehead. Pause for a moment and reflect on the ways you use your mind to know and understand God better. When you are finished, open your eyes and pray:

All: *Faithful God, you created us with a mind that we might seek and know you. Help us to recognize you in all the people and events of our lives.*

Next, silently trace a cross on your chest. Pause for a moment to thank God for all of the ways he has shown you how much he loves you. Then pray together:

All: *God of Love, thank you for the gift of your Son, Jesus, who died on the cross for love of us. Help us to know how to love others the way you love us.*

Now slowly trace a cross on each of your shoulders. Take a moment to reflect on anything in your life that feels heavy to you or on a burden that you could use help carrying. When you are ready, pray together:

All: *Merciful God, your Son bore the weight of our human suffering on his shoulders. Help us to take up our cross each day and follow you. Inspire us to be generous in offering help to others who carry heavy burdens.*

End by praying the Sign of the Cross aloud.

What's **WHAT**?

■ Review the main points of the chapter. Which point was most important to you? Write your reasons on the lines below.

- God loves us like a Father and sent us his only Son, Jesus.
- The Holy Spirit was sent by Jesus and the Father to teach us and give us the grace to live as Jesus did.
- The Trinity is the mystery of Three Persons in One God.
- Creation is the first sign of God's love for us.

The Holy Trinity is the concept of 3 Gods

Say **WHAT**?

mystery • Pharisee — _Policical Party = Believe in strict law._ Nicodemus,

So **WHAT**? _Joseph, Saul_

■ What are some ways that I experience God's love in my everyday life?

Now **WHAT**?

■ What can you do this week at home to deepen your relationship with members of your family?

Here's **WHAT** the Catholic Church Teaches

The unity that we see among the three Persons of the Trinity can be reflected in the sharing that characterizes family life. In _On the Role of the Christian Family in the Modern World_ Pope John Paul II pointed out that the family is the first and most essential school for social life that a person will attend. The family helps each of its members learn a true and mature way of expressing unity with others.

The family is an example that can be used for building broader community relationships filled with respect, justice, communication, and love. It takes people out of anonymity, keeps them conscious of their personal dignity, and enriches them with a deep humanity.

The social role of the family does not stop with having and educating children. As their children grow, families should devote themselves to a variety of social service activities. "In particular," Pope John Paul II wrote, "note must be taken of the ever greater importance in our society of hospitality in all its forms, from opening the doors of one's home and still more of one's heart to the pleas of one's brothers and sisters." _(On the Role of the Christian Family in the Modern World)_

Cornerstones

1. As the two articles are read, note the cornerstones (main points) from each article in the appropriate column below.
2. With your group, share one cornerstone you identified from your group's assigned article. Keep sharing cornerstones until you have no new ones to share. Say "pass" if you have nothing new to add.

CORNERSTONES — ARTICLE 1	CORNERSTONES — ARTICLE 2
Nicodemus Seeks an Answer	One God in Three Persons

SEEK AND Find

Some games involve finding something or someone hidden. An interesting twist can be added to the game by blindfolding or spinning until dizzy the person who is "it." Playing the game in the dark adds another challenge. At times the person who is "it" needs help from friends who give hints like "hot" or "cold." Are there any games in which you depend on clues from others in order to find the person or object you're searching for?

10 games to match with their descriptions.

1.	Blind Man's Bluff	playing Hide and Seek at night
2.	Hot Potato	tossing a stone onto a square and hopping on one foot
3.	Duck Duck Goose	running into a chain of linked arms
4.	Ghost in the Graveyard	avoiding being hit by a ball
5.	Hot Box	trying to beat the person who tagged you on the head to his or her spot in the circle
6.	Hopscotch	following the leader's instructions
7.	Red Rover	trying to tag others while blindfolded after being spun around
8.	Dodgeball	trying to tag others in a swimming pool
9.	Simon Says	running between two bases without being tagged
10.	Marco Polo	passing an object around quickly so you don't get stuck with it

Removing the Blindness

The party game Blind Man's Bluff can be a disorienting experience when you are "it." A blindfold is put on your eyes, and you reach out your hand to find other people playing the game to tag as "it." It is a relief when the blindfold is taken off and you can see where people are.

John 9:1–38 tells the story of a man born blind who is cured by Jesus. One of the reasons that John tells the story is because he wants to contrast seeing with the eyes of faith with being blind to the truth of God. Sometimes people who can physically see are really blind, but people who are blind, yet receive the gift of faith from God, can really see. This story is not only about Jesus curing physical blindness. It is about spiritual blindness as well. Some people choose to be spiritually blind even if they can see with their eyes.

Healing of the Blind Man,
Corrine Vonaesch, 2001, French

AN EXPERIENCE OF JESUS

John tells us that Jesus met a man in Jerusalem who had been born blind. Jesus put some clay on the man's eyes and told him to go wash in the pool of Siloam. After the man had done this, he could see for the first time in his life. Imagine how this man felt when he could see for the first time!

You would think that everyone would be happy for the man. However, they were not. People asked him what happened. He could not explain it, and he could not tell them where Jesus was or what he looked like, as he had never seen him.

A CHALLENGE TO FAITH

The man whose blindness was cured was taken to the religious authorities, who questioned him sharply. These were the people who were supposed to know God and what he wants for us. "Who is this man who cured you?" they asked him. The man thinks about it and tells them that it was Jesus. He continues by saying that Jesus must be a prophet, one sent from God.

The authorities were not happy to hear this so they went to the man's parents for an explanation. The parents, afraid of being thrown out of the synagogue if they acknowledged Jesus, told the authorities to speak to their son themselves. He's an adult, they said, so ask him.

The authorities questioned the man even more sharply. They accused the man of not being a faithful Jew because he said that Jesus did such a miraculous thing for him. Eventually the authorities lost patience with the man and threw him out of the Temple.

The man was undoubtedly confused and disoriented. Why would people be so angry because of the astonishing thing that had happened to him? Why couldn't they see Jesus as the wonderful man that he was?

REMAINING FAITHFUL

What if something miraculous happened in your life and people criticized you for it? This is something like what the authorities were doing to the man who could now see. He had faith in Jesus, but they wanted him to pretend that Jesus' cure never happened. They didn't want him to see Jesus as the Messiah.

Jesus heard of the man's problems, and sought him out. Jesus asked the man if he believed. The man, seeing Jesus physically for the first time, also saw him with eyes of faith. The person in the story who had been born blind is the person who can really see. He recognized Jesus for who he was and worshipped him.

There will be situations where people will challenge us when we speak about our faith in Jesus. But if we remain faithful, we will be able to see with the eyes of faith. FG

Ok, now I can see, but I can't *smell* a thing!

Loving, Helping, and Serving

Some people talk about faith as if it were something you do with your mind. For them, faith is knowing certain things and thinking in certain ways. Jesus challenged us to live and experience a different kind of faith. He wanted us to show faith with our lives. Faith is to be lived and loved. Nowhere is this made clearer than in John's Gospel when on the night before Jesus died, he washed the feet of his disciples. He wanted to show that faith means giving yourself over to others. It might even mean giving up your life for them. Our love needs to be that strong if we claim to have faith in Jesus. You have to live that faith by loving, helping, and serving all the people in your life.

✝ Our Roots Are Showing

The archangel Raphael is the patron of people who are blind, travelers and others who need guidance. He appears in the Book of Tobit, in which Raphael travels with and protects Tobit's young son Tobiah. Tobit, who was deprived of his sight, doesn't realize the true identity of the man who has been helping his son. At the end of their journey, when Tobiah is returned unharmed to his parents, Raphael reveals himself to be an angel of God. Tobit, through the intercession of Raphael, has his sight restored. The name Raphael means "God's remedy" or "God has healed." The Church celebrates his feast day on September 29.

Augustine's Search for Truth

Saint Augustine grew up in northern Africa many centuries ago. His mother was a Christian and his father was a pagan. Augustine was quite intelligent, but this did not stop him from doing stupid things with his friends. They stole a bunch of pears from a farm, not because they were hungry, but for the sake of doing it. Augustine later wrote of this incident with regret. Why did he and his friends do such thoughtless things that hurt others?

As a young man Augustine became attached to a religious group that seemed to have the answers that he was looking for on the meaning of life. Eventually he became disappointed in what they taught. He tried reading the Old Testament, but thought it was too simplistic to be telling a real story about God and how he relates to us. Following the custom of his time, Augustine put off being baptized until he figured out what he believed. Throughout it all, his mother, Saint Monica, prayed for him and encouraged him in his search for the true faith.

Eventually Augustine developed some important friendships, especially with Saint Ambrose, bishop of Milan, Italy. These connections, as well as a series of strong personal experiences, helped Augustine to learn

art • i • fact
Saint Augustine, Benozzo Gozzoli, 1420–1497, San Agositino, San Gimignano, Italy. The child in this painting is the same as the one mentioned in the Footnote on page 45.

about Jesus and his revelation of the Father. Augustine's faith in Jesus and in the Church blossomed, and eventually he was baptized. He became a famous theologian and spiritual writer. The people of Hippo in northern Africa made him their bishop.

GIFT OF FAITH
Augustine's faith journey opened his eyes to what faith is. Because of his experiences and those of other saints, the Church has come to understand that faith means holding on to God with all that we have. Jesus has sent the Holy Spirit to teach us the truth that God has revealed about himself through what he has done for us and what he has told us in Scripture.

"I came into the world as light, so that everyone who believes in me might not remain in darkness."

(John 12:46)

But God doesn't force us to believe. Responding to God is a free human choice. How we express our faith may differ across cultures, but however we respond, we are responding to the same gift from God. This gift is called grace. Grace that helps us make choices to live as God wants us to is called actual grace.

Faith is a gift from God. It is a help received from the Holy Spirit, and without that grace we would not be able to believe. But for that faith to be complete, there has to be a response on our part. Faith, then, means saying yes to God when he reveals himself and gives himself to us.

GOD OF TRUTH AND LOVE

When Augustine turned to philosophy to look for answers about God, he was doing a good thing. We can use our minds to figure out that there is one God who made everything and supports the universe. But there are many things about God and our salvation that we can only know through God's revelation. To learn those things we must have faith, and our faith must be connected to the faith community. It is in the Church that our faith is born, supported, and nourished.

The faith that the Church passes on to us is a faith in one God. There are other religions that believe in many gods. We believe as it was declared in the Book of Deuteronomy and what Jesus called the greatest commandment: "Hear, O Israel! The Lord is our God, the Lord alone!" In faith we

continued on page 46 ▶

ⓕⓞⓞⓣⓝⓞⓣⓔ

Sometimes spiritual insights come to us at times and in places that we least expect. According to a legend popular since the 15th century, that is what happened to Augustine as he was reflecting on the mystery of the Trinity. While walking along the seashore, he spotted a child who had dug a pit in the sand. Patiently, the child drew water out of the sea with a seashell and poured it into the pit. When Augustine asked the child what he was doing, the child answered that he was emptying the sea into the pit. Augustine commented that such a task was impossible. The child responded that so too is it impossible for the human mind to understand the mystery of the most holy Trinity. And then the child vanished.

Necessary Faith

One of the keys to John's Gospel is the need for people to place their faith in Jesus. John (pictured above) makes it very clear that we have to believe in Jesus and in God who sent him. The Church teaches us that, if God has called you to know the fullness of the truth about Jesus and his Church, you will not be saved if you refuse to believe. As Jesus said, "He who believes and is baptized will be saved; whoever does not believe will be condemned" (Mark 16:16). This does not mean that people who are not Christians will be condemned. People who search for the truth honestly and with a sincere heart, even if they are not called by God to the fullness of faith in Jesus, can be saved. But for us who are called, believing in Jesus Christ and in the One who sent him is necessary for our salvation.

Spiritual Thirst

When Jesus met *a Samaritan woman at the well, John's Gospel tells us that he offered her "living water." Jesus was not talking about water to satisfy a physical thirst but rather a spiritual thirst. We use the word thirst to describe our desire for God. While many people do not think about the issue of God's existence as deeply as Augustine did, the evidence of God's existence is around for all to see. It's probably most prevalent in the emptiness, the spiritual thirst, that we all feel when we realize that no matter what we may accomplish, there is always something compelling us to look for more. The way Augustine put it was, "You have made us for yourself, O Lord, and our hearts are restless till they find their rest in you." After Augustine discovered that God had been seeking him out all along he wrote, "When I am completely united to you, there will be no more sorrow or trials; entirely full of you, my life will be complete."*

▶ *continued from page 45*

turn to that one God, who gave us all that we have. He is the God who is our final goal, the most important value in our lives. In faith we begin to experience the wonderful things that await us at the end of our journey on earth.

In faith we discover God's revelation of himself as Truth and Love. We are always trying to understand God better, and yet there is always more to learn about him. This is why we call God a mystery, because even when God tells us about himself, we don't completely understand. We find it hard to put God into words.

> Augustine's faith journey opened his eyes to what faith is.

JESUS THE KEY

To help us, God revealed himself in the Word, his only Son, Jesus, whom he sent to us for our salvation. This was the key to Augustine's growth in faith. He realized that to have faith in God, you must have faith in Jesus Christ, the one that God sent. Once Augustine learned that, he was able to open up to the full treasure of the faith of the Church. The Scriptures became clear to him, and he was able to live as a truly happy person, at peace with himself and with the world. FG

TO LEARN MORE about Pope Benedict XVI, visit www.FindingGod.org/teens.

IT OUT

Joseph Cardinal Ratzinger chose a seashell as part of his coat of arms when he was appointed the archbishop of Munich-Freising in 1977. The seashell symbolized the one in the story of Saint Augustine and the child playing at the seashore. The incident revealed to Augustine that the human mind can no more fully understand the mystery of the Trinity than a seashell can empty out the sea. When elected pope in 2005, Ratzinger, now Pope Benedict XVI, had seashells embroidered on the vestments he wore at his installation Mass.

Believing Is Seeing

FAITH AND PRAYER

Prayer arises from faith and through prayer faith is strengthened. Jesus tells us that "all that you ask for in prayer, believe that you will receive it and it shall be yours." (Mark 11:24) Such is the power of prayer and of faith that does not doubt. Whether healing infirmities or forgiving sins, Jesus always responds to a prayer offered in faith. The prayer of faith consists not only in saying "Lord, Lord," but in allowing our hearts to do God's will. Jesus calls us as his disciples to bring this concern for cooperating with God's plan into our prayer. Through conversion of heart and by cooperating more and more with the will of the Father, we learn to pray in faith. It's not so much the words but the intention in our heart that counts in prayer.

Believing Is Seeing

What do the man born blind, the disciples who had their feet washed, and Saint Augustine have in common? They were touched in some way by Jesus. And each encounter opened their eyes to greater faith in him.

The man born blind was forced to beg. He was invisible to those people who believed that blindness was a result of sin. Jesus knew the man's distress. With a small amount of mud and a loving gesture, he opened the man's eyes, and the man's faith in Jesus was born.

What are the things you see differently because of your belief in Jesus?

When the disciples gathered for the Passover with Jesus, they didn't know it would be their last time together. Nor did they expect to see Jesus stand up, tie a towel around his waist, and perform the work of a slave. As Jesus stood before each one with water for their feet, we can only imagine what thoughts came to their minds. Without a doubt, their eyes were opened to see Jesus in a new way, as he invited them into a more intimate relationship with him and his Father.

What are the things you do differently because of your belief in Jesus?

Saint Augustine was an intelligent young man. His desire to experience everything life had to offer led him to make the wrong choices sometimes. Augustine's search for meaning in life caused him to become interested in the Scriptures. His intellectual curiosity brought him to develop friendships with influential Christians like Saint Ambrose, by whom he was later baptized. God worked through Augustine's faith journey and intellectual pursuits to open his eyes to what faith is.

What things might you think differently about because of your belief in Jesus?

Spend a few minutes with Jesus and share with him silently anything else that may be on your mind. Conclude with the following prayer of Saint Augustine:

You have made us for yourself, O Lord, And our hearts are restless till they find their rest in you.

art • i • fact
The Healing of the Blind Man, 1811, tempera and gold leaf on panel, Rila Monastery National Museum, Bulgaria

What's WHAT?

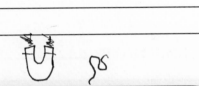

■ Review the main points of the chapter. Choose one that's most inspiring to you and write your reasons on the lines below.

- One reason why John tells the story of Jesus healing the man born blind is to help people understand what it means to live without faith in Jesus.

- Faith is a gift from God that helps us to see God more clearly.

- Faith is a free human choice that needs to be lived by loving and serving others.

- Saint Augustine's search for truth eventually led him to be baptized as an adult.

- It is in the Church that our faith is born, supported, and nourished.

- Believing in Jesus Christ and in the One who sent him is necessary for our salvation.

  Believing in Christ & the One
  who sent him: Foundation
  of Christianity.

Say WHAT?

actual grace • grace • synagogue

So WHAT?

■ How does participation in the Church support and nourish our faith?

_____

_____

_____

Now WHAT?

■ Faith is shown through loving, helping, and serving the people in our lives.

What is something you can do this week to show you are a person of faith?

_____

_____

_____

_____

Here's WHAT the Catholic Church Teaches

As we grow in faith in God, who is Truth and Love, we grow in solidarity with people all over the world. Faith does not isolate us or divide us. It makes us more aware of the interdependence among individuals and among nations. We are affected personally by the injustices and violations of human rights committed in distant countries, even if we never visit those countries. Pope John Paul II, in his encyclical letter *On Social Concern*, speaks of solidarity this way: "Solidarity helps us to see the "other"—whether a person, people or nation—not just as some kind of instrument, with a work capacity and physical strength to be exploited at low cost and then discarded when no longer useful, but as our "neighbor," a "helper," to be made a sharer, on a par with ourselves, in the banquet of life to which all are equally invited by God."

We Can Change the World

1. Read both articles silently.

2. In your group of four, decide which article each pair will work on.

3. With your partner, complete the "Something to Think About..." section below, listing the important ideas presented in your article.

4. Exchange worksheets with the other pair in your group and complete the "How It Can Change the World" section below.

5. With your partner, select one "Something to Think About...Change the World" idea and explain how and why this idea can make the world a better place.

6. With your partner, think of a role model you feel has changed the world in this way.

ARTICLE NAME _____

SOMETHING TO THINK ABOUT	HOW IT CAN CHANGE THE WORLD

PROMISES, Promises

Making promises is easy—keeping them is the difficult part. Sometimes they are simple things like promising to take the garbage out or promising to do our homework right away. Some promises require more effort and time, like promising to take care of a little brother or sister for the evening or promising to volunteer several hours each Saturday at the local animal shelter. What makes some promises difficult to keep?

First Rate

Match the brand name to the description used to promote the product. Then based on your experience, observation, or a good guess, rate the "promises" made by the brands in the following manner: 1–always true, 2–sometimes true, 3–can't possibly be true.

A. Diet Dr. Pepper   Have it your way.

B. M&Ms   Once you pop, you can't stop.

C. Pringles   Tastes like regular.

D. Burger King   Melt in your mouth, not in your hand.

E. Wheaties   The Breakfast of Champions

The Spirit of Truth

Picture this scene from the Gospel of John. Jesus and the apostles are gathered around the food that has been laid out for them. The apostles seem somewhat stirred up. Peter and Philip are engaged in a lively conversation, and Matthew is saying something excitedly to Andrew. Questions are flying around the room. The apostles have been swept off their feet by Jesus.

Throughout his ministry Jesus had challenged the apostles, taught them, and given them an example of how to live. They had watched him do wonderful things like feed huge crowds, cure people, and walk on water. But now it seemed to be coming to an end. Jesus was talking more and more about his death, and the authorities were closing in on him.

PASSOVER MEAL

The apostles knew that this Passover meal with Jesus was special. It could very well be one of the last times they would eat with him. So they were concerned about the future. What would it be like without Jesus around to lead them? Would they be able to stay together? Would they continue learning about God? Most importantly, perhaps, would Jesus be completely gone from their lives after his death and remain only a memory?

THE SPIRIT

John 14:15–27 tells us how Jesus spoke to the apostles and calmed them down considerably. He was not going to abandon them like orphans, he said. The Father would send them the Advocate, the Holy Spirit of truth in Jesus' name. The Holy Spirit would help them and guide them. Through the Spirit, Jesus would remain with them. And he would remain with all of them, not just a chosen few. His whole Church would be filled with the Spirit. This gift of the Holy Spirit would be another sign of the Father's love for them, just as the gift of his Son had been.

Gifts of the Spirit

HOLY SPIRIT AND PRAYER

We can quickly become discouraged when praying if we think that we alone are responsible for our prayer. But Jesus has sent us the Holy Spirit to help and guide us. Prayer comes from the Holy Spirit, not just from us. John tells us that the Advocate will teach us what we need to know. Every time we pray, it is the Holy Spirit who teaches us the way. The Holy Spirit is present in our prayer and makes it not just human prayer but divine prayer. We have an emptiness in us that comes from God and that only God can fill with the Holy Spirit. The Holy Spirit is the living breath of our prayer and is given to the Church so that through his power, the whole community of the People of God, though living in diverse circumstances all over the world, might persevere in the hope in which we have been saved.

LEFT: Detail of a metal-and-glass sanctuary wall decoration at Holy Spirit Church in Virginia, Minnesota

Gifts of the Spirit

Do you remember the advice Saint John Vianney gave his parishioners? He encouraged them to pray the short prayer below. His advice is good for us to follow too. And so we pray:

O God, send me your Spirit, to teach me what I am and who you are.

O God, send me your Spirit of Wisdom . . .
to teach me to see the world as you see it and to know that you are the God who guides me.

O God, send me your Spirit of Understanding . . .
to teach me to perceive your ways and to recognize that you are the God of Truth.

O God, send me your Spirit of Counsel . . .
to teach me to seek advice and be open to your will and to believe that you are the God who calls me.

O God, send me your Spirit of Knowledge . . .
to teach me to understand the truths of the universe and to know that you are the God who always stands ready to help me.

O God, send me your Spirit of Fortitude . . .
to teach me to do what is right in the face of difficulties and to know that you are the God who strengthens me.

O God, send me your Spirit of Piety . . .
to teach me to love and worship you and all that you created and to know that you are the God who is always present.

O God, send me your Spirit of Fear of the Lord . . .
to teach me to recognize your glory and my dependence on you and to know you as the God of love.

Conclude with Saint Augustine's *Prayer to the Holy Spirit:*

> **Breathe into me, Holy Spirit,**
> **That my thoughts may all be holy.**
> **Move in me, Holy Spirit,**
> **That my work, too, may be holy.**
> **Attract my heart, Holy Spirit,**
> **That I may love only what is holy.**
> **Strengthen me, Holy Spirit,**
> **That I may defend all that is holy.**
> **Protect me, Holy Spirit,**
> **That I always may be holy.**
> **Amen.**

What's **WHAT**?

■ Review the main points of the chapter. Which point was least familiar to you? Write your new insights on the lines below.

• Jesus and the Father sent the Holy Spirit to guide and teach us.

• Under the inspiration of the Holy Spirit, the bishops of the Church continue spreading the Good News through their preaching, writing, and actions.

• Saint Jean Vianney recognized that the Holy Spirit was at the center of his life and motivated all of his actions.

• Truth refers to the reliability of the person speaking as well as the reliability of the person's message.

• When we are open to the Holy Spirit we allow him to enter our lives, lead us, and guide us.

_____

_____

_____

Say **WHAT**?

Advocate • option for the poor

So **WHAT**?

■ Where in my life do I need the help of the Holy Spirit?

_____

_____

_____

Now **WHAT**?

■ What is one way you can help spread the Good News of Jesus this week at school or at home?

_____

_____

_____

_____

_____

_____

Here's **WHAT** the Catholic Church Teaches

Jesus promised not to leave us orphans but to send us the Holy Spirit to be our helper. The same Spirit of the Lord that was upon Jesus and sent him "to bring glad tidings to the poor" (Luke 4:18) has been sent to us and commits us to have a special concern for the poor. The United States bishops, in their 1986 pastoral letter *Economic Justice for All* stated it this way: "As followers of Christ, we are challenged to make a fundamental **'option for the poor'**—to speak for the voiceless, to defend the defenseless, to assess lifestyles, policies, and social institutions in terms of their impact on the poor. This 'option for the poor' does not mean pitting one group against another, but rather, strengthening the whole community by assisting those who are most vulnerable. As Christians, we are called to respond to the needs of *all* our brothers and sisters, but those with the greatest needs require the greatest response."

If . . . Then . . .

1. Read the first article.
2. Identify the main ideas about our Catholic faith from the article and note them in the "If we believe . . ." column below.
3. In your group, work together to complete the "Then we are called to . . ." column.
4. Repeat the process for the second article.

Article 1: The Spirit of Truth		Article 2: Saint John Vianney Teaches Us About the Holy Spirit	
IF we believe . . .	THEN we are called to . . .	IF we believe . . .	THEN we are called to . . .

Faith in Action

Faith is alive when we put it into action every day of our lives. It is expressed in the attitudes and values we hold and in the ways we relate to the people and the world around us. Taking action to create a more just world is an essential part of living the Gospel. Jesus preached not only with words but how he lived his life. We are called to do the same.

In this unit we explored the mystery of God through the lens of the Gospel of John. We were also introduced to the Church's rich tradition of Catholic Social Teaching. The Church calls us to put the needs of people who are poor and vulnerable first. Here are some ideas of how you can do this.

Become Gleaners

Purpose:

Learn about the practice of gleaning as a way for people who are poor and hungry to get food; become a gleaner by collecting food and distributing it to those in need.

Background:

The Gleaners is a famous painting by the French artist Jean-François Millet. It portrays peasants of the 19th century scavenging a harvested wheat field. Life was rough for people at the time, and they often resorted to gleaning, or collecting crops leftover in farmers' fields after a harvest. Today mechanical harvesting often leaves behind crops that would normally go to waste. With the farmers' permission, humanitarian groups practice gleaning in these fields so that they can distribute the food to those who are poor and hungry.

Steps:

a. Read Leviticus 23:22. What do you learn about God from this passage? What is God's message to you in this passage?

continued on page 62 ▶

> "It is an eternal obligation toward the human being not to let him suffer from hunger when one has a chance of coming to his assistance."
>
> —Simone Weil, French philosopher

Faith in Action

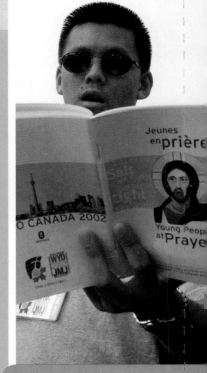

▶ *continued from page 61*

b. Contact local bakeries, grocery stores, and restaurants to see if they will donate unused food for people who are in need.

c. Organize your gleaning by getting volunteers to pick up the food on a regular schedule, sort the food, and store it.

d. Find local shelters and soup kitchens that could use the food.

What a Relief!

Purpose:

Identify areas where people who are homeless live in your community; work with your community to provide basic necessities to people in need.

Background:

Many communities provide services for people who are homeless. But some homeless people do not want to or are unable to go to shelters or soup kitchens. There are many understandable reasons for this. Some people are afraid that they'll get attacked or that what few possessions and dignity they have will be stolen from them. Some people may suffer from a physical or mental disease that makes them unable to seek help. And some people have simply lost hope. People who can't get to shelters or soup kitchens are often without basic necessities.

Steps:

a. Mobilize a group to collect basic necessities for people who are homeless. There are many ways to do this, such as having a food drive, collecting financial donations and then purchasing items, or getting businesses to donate items.

b. Contact the police department or local agencies that deal with homelessness in your community. Ask them where people who are homeless stay. They may also be able to tell you the best time to deliver food and other goods.

c. Design a plan to distribute the goods that you have collected.

d. Ask adults in your school or parish to be responsible for making the deliveries. You may want to provide them with some background information on homelessness in your area and explain how your faith is the basis for what you are doing.

> **"We need one great heave to deliver the relief supplies, find the missing, rescue the isolated, feed the hungry and shelter the homeless."**
>
> —Gloria Macapagal Arroyo, president of the Philippines

Mark Teaches Us about Jesus

Teaches
Teaches

THE GOSPEL OF MARK

The Gospel of Mark was most likely written between the years 65 and 70. These were troublesome years for both Jews and for the first Christians in the Mediterranean world. The Church in Rome had just suffered the first large-scale persecution at the hands of the Roman government. The Church in Palestine, still close to its Jewish roots, watched as Roman armies invaded to crush a Jewish uprising. This invasion ended with the conquest of Jerusalem and the destruction of the Temple in the year 70. Early Christians who had been converted and who had embraced Jesus with a great spirit of hope and expectation discovered that they now lived in the midst of suffering and destruction.

In the midst of these times of trouble, what message of comfort and hope could be given to Christians? Mark responded by writing the first Gospel. In it he proclaimed Jesus as the Son of God sent by the Father to save the human family through his service and the sacrifice of his life.

WRITING THE GOSPEL

From his vantage point of being Peter's companion in Rome, Mark collected the stories and preaching about Jesus, Jesus' teachings and sayings, and the stories of the events of the Last Supper and Jesus' death on the cross. He then shaped these stories into a larger story to help Christians recognize that Jesus was the Son of God. The Gospel of Mark was written in everyday Greek so it could be read by the mostly Greek-speaking audience. Mark presents Jesus as a dynamic figure who was always on the move, proclaiming the Kingdom of God to all who would listen. Mark's was the first written Gospel, and his work strongly influenced the Gospels of Matthew and Luke.

JESUS AS HEALER AND TEACHER

Mark 1–8 presents Jesus as a powerful healer and preacher. Even as he performs a number of miracles and explains the meaning of his parables, his disciples don't seem to understand the meaning of who he is. (Mark 4:13) After he performs miracles, he orders his disciples not to talk about it, but they continue to anyway. (Mark 7:36) The disciples don't understand that the real meaning of Jesus is not in his miracles and parables. The consistent theme in Mark is that it is not simply the miracles that reveal Jesus' true nature. It is Jesus' willingness to face the cross that defines who he is for us. And if we are to be his disciples, we must face the same difficulties. "Whoever wishes to come after me must deny himself, take up his cross, and follow me." (Mark 8:34)

Mark 9–15 tells the story of Jesus' passion and death. In these chapters Jesus reveals the nature of true discipleship. Jesus tells his followers that life in service to him is a life in service to others.

> "Rather, whoever wishes to be great among you will be your servant; whoever wishes to be first among you, will be the slave of all. For the Son of Man did not come to be served but to serve and to give his life as a ransom for many." (Mark 10:43–44)

The Gospel then describes the Crucifixion and death of Jesus. Jesus is recognized as the Son of God by a Roman centurion who witnesses his death. Mark is telling us that we look to the cross to understand the depth of God's love for us.

MARK IN THIS UNIT

In this unit the Gospel of Mark helps us to explore the mystery of Jesus and who he is in our life. Jesus is proclaimed at the beginning of the Gospel as the Son of God. This is how he is identified after he is baptized by John the Baptist. Jesus proclaims the Kingdom of God has come, and he shows God's care for those in need. He acts to address these needs in his works of healing and in his forgiveness of sins. We celebrate the healing ministry of Jesus today in the Sacraments of Penance and Anointing of the Sick. Jesus finally shows the depths of his love through the sacrifice of his life on the cross for the sake of our salvation. But the story is not over. The women who come to minister to Jesus' body discover an empty tomb and hear the message of his Resurrection. They are then sent to tell Peter and the disciples that Jesus would meet them in Galilee.

INTERESTING ID etails

When we go through security at an airport or apply for library cards, we are often asked to show identification. People want to make sure we are who we say we are. Name some other situations when you might be asked to show identification.

For Your Eyes Only

Create an ID card for yourself that tells more about you than just your vital statistics.

NAME:

Hobbies:

Favorite book:

Favorite music:

Favorite class:

Who Is This Man?

Crucifixion, Victor Joseph Gatto, 20th Century, New York

When we read the stories of the heroes in the Old Testament, we discover that people who seem ordinary sometimes do extraordinary things. They have unexpected talents or depths of character that are revealed during a crisis. Joseph is sold by his brothers into slavery, and he is later thrown into prison in Egypt. It is then revealed that he is an interpreter of dreams, which leads to his becoming pharaoh's most important representative. The boy David lives as an ordinary shepherd until he defeats the mighty Goliath and is revealed as a faithful warrior for God. Later, as King David, he is known as a musician and is credited with writing some of the psalms. Esther is a young Jewish woman who lost her parents and was adopted by her uncle Mordecai. She wins the favor of the Persian king and is made Queen of Persia. When she discovers the king's plan to execute all the Jews in Persia, Esther risks her life to prevent the tragedy.

> Jesus is God living among us.

MESSIAH

The Gospel of Mark begins with the proclamation that Jesus Christ is the Son of God. As he continues writing, Mark gradually tells us what this means. In the early part of Mark's Gospel, Jesus heals a number of people and then tells his disciples not to speak of it. Mark is telling us that Jesus did wonderful deeds, but we should not let ourselves be distracted by them. There is more to Jesus than being a miraculous healer. As you continue to read the Gospel, Mark presents Jesus as a mystery to be further explored. Like the hidden strengths of the heroes of the Old Testament, there are things about Jesus that are revealed gradually.

In Mark 8:27 Jesus himself asks the question, "Who do people say that I am?" Peter speaks up and answers for all the apostles. He says that Jesus is the Messiah, the Son of the living God. Jesus cautions the apostles not to tell anyone. He knows that the people have many ideas about who the expected Messiah should be and how he should act. Some thought the Messiah would be a liberator who would lead the people against their enemies. In Mark it is clear that Jesus doesn't want people to see him in this way.

Jesus' Crucifixion revealed the real meaning of who he is. Looking at the bruised and battered Jesus on the cross, the Roman centurion recognizes that Jesus is the Son of God. (Mark 15:39) It is at this point in Mark's Gospel that we too recognize that Jesus is much more than a miracle worker; he is the Messiah, the anointed one, the Christ. Over the centuries the Church has continued to reflect on who Jesus is and who he is for us.

HUMAN

God wanted us to share in his divine nature, so the Son of God became man. Jesus is human like us in every way except sin. He assumed human nature without losing his divine nature. People could see and hear him, and he could touch them with human hands.

GOD

Jesus is God living among us. Jesus is man, but he never stopped being God, so that means that God is one of us. We look at Jesus, and we know that our God is not someone who is set apart from us on a distant mighty throne. Our God walks and talks with us. He knows our thoughts and feelings because he had human thoughts and feelings. That is why he can save us from ourselves and from our sinful nature. That is why his name is *Jesus,* which means "God saves."

art • i • fact
Antique Russian icon depicting Saint Mark the Evangelist

continued on page 68 ▶

They Just Don't Get It

Mark tells many stories about Jesus performing miracles, but his Gospel is not primarily about miracles. He also tells stories about Jesus teaching people things they need to know about God, but his Gospel is not primarily about what Jesus taught. What is his Gospel about?

Mark's Gospel is about being a disciple of Jesus. Mark knew that the disciples had a hard time understanding what it means to follow Jesus. In his Gospel he showed how they struggled to follow Jesus, and only understood what it meant after he had been crucified and raised from the dead. The disciples thought that following Jesus would mean that they would have power and fame in this world. Jesus' Crucifixion taught them that being his disciple means serving the kingdom. Along the way the disciples will suffer, as people will reject them and even be hostile towards them. In the midst of this journey, Jesus will be with them, sharing the load of the cross. (Mark 8:34–35)

This Way Out

► *continued from page 67*

In Jesus' time a Jewish student became a disciple by choosing a rabbi (or teacher) and spending time with him. The student would learn the rabbi's teaching and do his best to imitate the rabbi's life. Eventually when the student had learned all that he could, he could become a rabbi himself. In contrast, Jesus' disciples did not choose him but were chosen by him. The goal of the Christian disciple is to grow into a close relationship with Jesus and follow him by proclaiming the Kingdom of God. Becoming a disciple of Jesus means answering his call to discover his presence in everyday life.

I really need to have someone from the phone company swim out and check my line. Whenever Jesus calls me to be a disciple, he sounds like he's under water.

SON OF GOD

Jesus is the Son of God, the second Person of the Blessed Trinity. Mark calls our attention to this at the beginning of his Gospel, when Jesus is revealed to be the Son of God after his baptism by John the Baptist. Mark wrote, "On coming up out of the water [Jesus] saw the heavens being torn open and the Spirit, like a dove, descending upon him. And a voice came from the heavens, 'You are my beloved Son; with you I am well pleased.'" (Mark 1:9–11)

IM "Truly this man was the Son of God!" (Mark 15:39)

Jesus is God's Son. Because he is God the Father's Son, he reveals the Father to us and shows us how much the Father loves us.

GOD AND MAN

Jesus, then, is true God and true man. He is one divine person with a divine and human nature. He is the only one who bridges the gap between God and us. Jesus, the God-man, is the only mediator, the only one who can reconcile us with God after the break caused by human sinfulness.

LORD

For all these reasons, Jesus is Lord. He is the one who rules our lives. When we call Jesus Lord, we are saying that he is God. We can recognize this because it has been revealed to us through the Holy Spirit.

"Who do people say that I am?" Jesus asked his disciples this question, but he also asks us that same question every day. Who do we say that he is? As Christians each of us is called to be open to the Holy Spirit, who helps us understand how Jesus, God and man, Lord and Savior, is calling us. FG

Is He for Real?

A *Jesus Image*, Fr. Jim Hasse, S.J., Cincinnati, Ohio

It was not hard for the people who followed Jesus in Palestine to see that he was a man. They looked into his eyes. They heard his voice. They heard his laughter when a joke was told. They felt his comforting touch on their shoulders. He was a man. What else were they supposed to think?

As time passed and people who had never met Jesus learned about him through the preaching of the disciples and from the Gospels, some people were less inclined to believe that Jesus was man. The Gospel of Matthew describes that when Jesus was born a special star appeared in the sky. When he died, there was an earthquake. During his life Jesus did amazing things. He touched lepers and cured them without catching the disease himself. The Gospel of John tells the story of how Jesus brought Lazarus back from the dead after he had been buried for four days. He fed thousands of people with only the amount of food that would fit in a grocery bag today. He walked on water. At the Transfiguration his face shone like the sun. Three days after he died, his disciples discovered an empty tomb, and later Jesus appeared and spoke to them.

You can understand why some early Christians decided that Jesus was God and not a man. They thought that he was something like what today we would consider a hologram. We see examples of holograms in science-fiction films and TV shows. Holograms are images of people in three dimensions, in which we see

continued on page 70 ▶

Where's the Baby? ↑

When Matthew and Luke wrote their Gospels, they started with stories about Jesus' birth and infancy. They used those stories to teach us how from his infancy, Jesus was recognized as a special person, Emmanuel, God with us, who would save us from our sins. Mark, on the other hand, didn't write anything about Jesus' childhood. Mark starts his Gospel with Jesus as an adult, ready to teach people the Good News. Mark does this so that he can devote his attention to the Incarnation and its meaning for us. The word *Incarnation* means that Jesus is one person who is both God and man. *Incarnate* means "made flesh." Jesus is God made flesh. Mark wanted to show that in Jesus, God became one of us and gave his life for us. So that's why Mark doesn't write about Jesus' birth and childhood. He is anxious to get to the main message about Jesus' life, death, and Resurrection for our salvation.

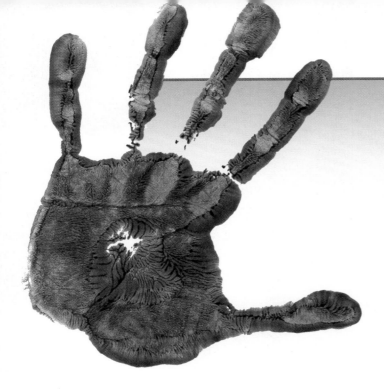

The Gospel of Mark especially highlights many of the human qualities of Jesus.

▶ *continued from page 69*

what looks like a real person standing before us. The hologram is not a real person, just light. This is how some people in early Christianity thought of Jesus. Instead of saying he was a real man, they pictured him as we would a hologram, seeming to have the physical appearance of a man, but not actually being human.

BORN AND RAISED A JEW

In response, the early Church stressed that Jesus was human in the same way that we are except for sin. His mother was a Jewish woman named Mary, and his foster father was a Jewish man named Joseph. Jesus was born in the Jewish province of the Roman empire and was raised in the Jewish culture and religion.

Jesus grew up in the town of Nazareth, a small town in the part of Israel known as Galilee. He helped his dad in his carpentry business. He was intelligent and learned about his Jewish religious heritage. By the time he was about 30 years old, he was ready to start his work as a traveling teacher.

The Gospel of Mark especially highlights many of the human qualities of Jesus. Mark tells how Jesus experienced joy at social gatherings, impatience when his disciples didn't get the point he was making, and compassion for sinners and for the sick. Mark also vividly describes the pain and suffering Jesus endured as he faced his passion and death.

Sister Marie of the Incarnation

Marie Guyart (1599–1672)—wife, mother, missionary, and mystic—was born in Tours, France. In her youth she considered becoming a nun, but her parents arranged for her to marry a man named Claude Martin. She married, had a son, and at age 19 was left a widow. Throughout this time, her desire to enter religious life never left her.

At the age of 30, Marie joined the Ursuline nuns in Tours and took the name Sister Marie of the Incarnation. Feeling called to a missionary life, Marie made the four-month journey to Canada, arriving in Quebec in 1639. For the next 30 years, Marie dedicated herself to the native people of Canada, learning the Algonquin and Iroquois languages and writing dictionaries for them.

Why would Marie Guyart choose to name herself after the Incarnation? Perhaps it was because Jesus was the inspiration for her work. Just as God sought to save us by becoming one of us in the Incarnation, so Sister Marie sought to be the hands, feet, and voice of God for the native peoples of Canada.

St. Joseph the Worker, Michael D. O'Brien, Canada

JOY AND SUFFERING

Jesus knew happiness. He experienced the joy of being loved by his parents. He went to parties and celebrations, and he enjoyed eating and drinking like the rest of us. He had close friends and enjoyed spending time with them. Jesus also knew unhappiness. He lived in a country that was controlled by the Romans. In his lifetime many Jewish men were crucified, and their bodies were hung on country roads to warn people of the consequences of rebellion against Rome. Jesus faced rejection, not only by strangers but also by friends and relatives. He was saddened by the suffering he saw in the world. In the days leading up to the end of his life, he experienced great suffering. Before his death he was arrested, tortured, and subjected to a form of execution that the Romans reserved for the people they despised the most—crucifixion.

OUR RISEN LORD

Jesus suffered and died for our sins, was resurrected by the Father, ascended into heaven, and now sits at the right hand of the Father in heaven. From there Jesus intercedes for us. In heaven Jesus' human nature is transformed and glorified; as the firstborn of the dead, he has traced the path to the Father that we all will follow.

TEACHER

We also can't forget that one reason Jesus lived his life on earth was to teach us how to be fully human and how to love God. Everything he did—his miracles, his actions, his prayer, his loving treatment of people, his special care for children, the elderly, and the poor, and his acceptance of the cross—all of these were done to help us learn how to live as God wants us to live. FG

IT'S LIKE THIS

Although Matthew points out that Joseph was a carpenter, Mark is the only one who suggests that Jesus himself was a carpenter. (Mark 6:3) Throughout the history of Christianity, many people have assumed that Jesus worked as a carpenter before he began traveling and teaching. Even today we might see a bumper sticker that says "My boss is a Jewish carpenter." This would have been a safe assumption because in Jesus' time, a son learned a trade from his father and went into the family business. Although Jesus probably did learn some tricks of the trade from his foster father, Joseph, he made his living as a rabbi, a Jewish teacher. In fact, this profession was closer to God the Father's business.

footnote

The image of the lion is used in the Bible to symbolize strength and courage. A similar image, the winged lion described in Ezekiel 1:10, is used to represent the Gospel of Mark. Mark's Gospel account begins with John the Baptist "crying out" in the wilderness that "one mightier" than he is coming. (Mark 1:3,7) It is said that John the Baptist's voice resembled that of a roaring lion like those found in the Judean wilderness, so the symbol of a lion is used for this Gospel.

Take Up Your Cross

JESUS, MODEL OF PRAYER

Though he was the Son of God, Jesus learned to pray according to his human heart. From his mother he learned the formulas of prayer. He learned to pray the words and rhythms of the prayers of his family and neighbors in the synagogue at Nazareth and in the Temple at Jerusalem. As Son of God he has another source of prayer, his intimate relationship with the Father. His life is an example of how to pray as children of the Father. He teaches us to speak with God in the same way that he does.

Jesus also speaks with the Father for us. Jesus, the Word made flesh, shares in his human prayer all that we experience as humans ourselves. His whole life—his words and works—is his prayer made visible for all to see.

We can learn a lot about what being a disciple is like from reading Mark's Gospel. We get to see the disciples discovering, one step at a time, who Jesus is and what following him means for them. In the process, we are invited to reflect on what it means for us to be a disciple of Jesus today. Let's listen to something Jesus told his first disciples.

> He summoned the crowd with his disciples and said to them, "Whoever wishes to come after me must deny himself, take up his cross, and follow me. For whoever wishes to save his life will lose it, but whoever loses his life for my sake and that of the gospel will save it."
>
> **Mark 8:34–35**

Let's spend a few moments in silence to reflect on Jesus' message to his disciples and to us.

In your imagination, join the crowd that gathers around Jesus and his disciples. What are the first things you think of when you hear him talk about denying yourself, taking up your cross, and losing your life for his sake and the sake of the Gospel?

Take a moment and share your thoughts with Jesus.

As you look around, you notice that some people are leaving. Maybe Jesus' words sound too harsh to them. For some reason, you decide to stay. Others do too. Through Jesus' words, you begin to understand a little more that a disciple is someone who follows Jesus to the cross. There are all kinds of crosses. No two are alike. Some crosses arise from the suffering caused by broken relationships. Others take the form of a physical or mental limitation or perhaps come from too much responsibility. What particular crosses are you carrying at this time?

When you are ready, share them with Jesus.

Now Jesus shares how grateful he is to you for the courage you show in carrying your cross and for your willingness to be his disciple. He wants you to know that your actions do not go unnoticed. Jesus reminds you that he's always with you, helping you carry your cross. Spend a moment resting quietly in Jesus' presence. Then thank him for this time together.

Knowing that following Jesus is about making God's kingdom visible on earth, let's close by praying together the Lord's Prayer.

What's WHAT?

■ Main points from this chapter are listed below. Complete each sentence. Refer to the articles and sidebars for help.

• In the Gospel of Mark, Jesus is revealed as

_____

• Jesus is one person who is both

man & Divine (incarnation)

• Mark's Gospel is about

~~*Being a diciple*~~
Being a diciple

• Events surrounding Jesus' birth and the miraculous things he did in his lifetime made some early Christians think

_____

• The Gospel of Mark highlights

being man

• In Mark's Gospel, he devotes all of his attention to

incarnation

Say WHAT?

disciple • Son of God

So WHAT?

■ How does being a disciple of Jesus make a difference in your life?

_____

_____

Now WHAT?

■ Identify how you can express your belief in Jesus Christ to someone this week.

_____

_____

Here's WHAT the Catholic Church Teaches

God has imprinted his own image and likeness on us as human beings and has given us the gift of an incomparable dignity. In the Incarnation God the Son has taken on our humanity by uniting divine nature with human nature in one person—the Word of God. Because of the Incarnation, the guiding principle of Catholic social teaching is the dignity of the human person.

The dignity of the human person is also one of the four "golden threads" of the *Catechism of the Catholic Church* according to the bishops of the United States. The other three are the mystery of the Trinity, the Incarnation, and the Paschal Mystery of Jesus' passion, death, Resurrection, and Ascension.

In their pastoral letter *Economic Justice for All,* the U.S. bishops insisted that every economic decision and institution must be judged in light of whether it protects or destroys the dignity of the human person. "We believe the person is sacred—the clearest reflection of God among us. Human dignity comes from God, not from nationality, race, sex, economic status, or any human accomplishment. We judge any economic system by what it does *for* and *to* people and by how it permits all to *participate* in it. The economy should serve people, not the other way around."

Paired Interview

Your name _____

Your partner's name _____

Title of article read by your partner _____

_____

Q&A

Ask your partner the following questions about the article he or she read and record his or her answers in the space provided.

1. Explain what your article was about in a few sentences.	
2. What is one quote (sentence) from your article that you would put on a poster to inspire the group? Why?	
3. What are some specific things your article helped you to learn or realize about the Catholic faith?	
4. Based on your article, name some specific things we, as Catholics, need to know, do, or believe in order to live as followers of Jesus.	

Happily
EVER AFTER

Have you ever noticed how many stories begin with the words "once upon a time"? Often these stories describe imaginary kingdoms and heroes who face great adventures and overcome incredible odds. The last line of these stories always seems to be "and they all lived happily ever after."

Can you name some stories from fairy tales, books, or movies that describe different kinds of kingdoms?

✓ IT OUT

If you had the opportunity to establish your own imaginative kingdom where everyone would live "happily ever after," what would it be like?

name:

climate:

geography:

national pastime:

types of leaders:

unique characteristic:

A Different Kingdom

There are countries today where royal families—kings, queens, princes, and princesses—are the rulers. In most cases their power to rule is limited by laws that give the real political power to a government elected by the people. King Herod, however, was a ruler who had complete authority to do as he wanted. He was a man whose contempt for life extended to his murder of a wife and of a number of his children. The Gospel of Matthew describes how he ordered the deaths of all the male infants in the area in an attempt to murder the infant Jesus.

Like many of his fellow kings, Herod had no respect for ordinary people. He forced them to work on his building projects for little pay. Then he taxed their earnings without mercy. You had to be rich to live a good life in Herod's kingdom, but even then you could be killed if he lost his temper with you.

King Herod's son, Herod Antipas, controlled the region of Galilee where John the Baptist and Jesus preached. Herod Antipas arrested John the Baptist and eventually had him beheaded. John was executed because he criticized Herod Antipas. It is in this kind of political environment, where rulers had total control over the lives of the people, that Jesus proclaimed the Kingdom of God.

EVERYONE

The kingdom Jesus proclaimed was a kingdom with a difference. Jesus called people to accept a loving God as their ruler and to follow God's direction in their lives. The key to the Kingdom of God is acceptance of Jesus' word. If you believe what Jesus teaches, you are on your way to entering the Kingdom of God.

Jesus invited everyone into the Kingdom of God. He did this by addressing himself first to the people of

> The key to the Kingdom of God is acceptance of Jesus' word.

art • i • fact

Saint John Preaching to Herod, late 15th century, Kunstmuseum, Bern, Switzerland. The Saint John in this painting is John the Baptist.

Feeding God's People

Israel and then to people of all nations. He invited people into the kingdom through signs that showed the nearness of the kingdom. Most importantly, the coming of the kingdom would be accomplished through his suffering, death, and Resurrection.

THE POOR AND LOWLY

The Old Testament shows that throughout the history of God's relationship with his people, he has had a special concern for the poor. The Old Testament prophets constantly reminded the wealthy of their obligation to help the poor. It is no surprise that when Jesus proclaimed the kingdom, he gave special emphasis to God's continuing concern for the poor.

In proclaiming God's special concern for the poor, Jesus is highlighting two points. He is calling all who serve God's kingdom to recognize that they have an obligation to do what they can to see that the needs of the poor are met. He is also calling all people to recognize that no matter how much wealth we may have, we all stand in need before God.

Jesus also made it a point to invite sinners to enter the kingdom. At the time when Jesus was preaching, tax collectors were seen as sinners because they cooperated with the Roman authorities. Because of their involvement with the occupying foreign government, they were shunned by society. Instead of leaving them in social exile, Jesus invited them in. He challenged them to change their lives and promised God's help for them. Jesus compassion for sinners reminds us that God is reaching out to us no matter what we have done in our lives.

PARABLE

Jesus spent plenty of time teaching his disciples about belonging to the kingdom, mostly by telling stories, or parables. He would use ordinary objects and ideas to help people understand what it meant to belong to the kingdom. One common object he used was a mustard seed. (Mark 4:30–32) The point of the parable of the mustard seed was that the Kingdom of God is like that smallest of seeds which, once it is sown in the ground, grows into one of the largest plants whose branches are strong enough to hold birds as they feed. Through this parable Jesus is teaching that the small, kind deeds we do in everyday life are quiet examples that further the Kingdom of God. We don't have to be emperors or lead armies to victory. The kingdom shelters everyone and grows surprisingly beyond its small beginnings.

The image of a shepherd was often used to describe the kings of the Old Testament because the kings were to care for God's people with the same responsibility as a shepherd would care for his flock. God supported the king so that the people would have their needs taken care of.

Jesus is often shown as a shepherd because of his care for God's people. Jesus acts like a concerned shepherd in one story related by Mark. Mark 6:34–44 tells the story of the people who have come to hear Jesus. It is the end of the day, and the crowd must head for home. In these times there were no fast food places to go for dinner, and many people would be quite hungry before they got home. They were like sheep without a shepherd. Jesus had his disciples tell the people to sit down. Then Jesus took loaves of bread, broke them, and gave them to his disciples to distribute. The amount of food Jesus had available did not seem like much. In fact, it was only a few loaves of bread and some fish. But, as the baskets of food were passed around, the food didn't diminish. In time all the people were fed, and there were enough leftovers to fill 12 baskets. Jesus, the Good Shepherd, who proclaims the Kingdom of God, cares for every need.

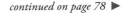

continued on page 78 ▶

► *continued from page 77*

"The kingdom of God is at hand. Repent, and believe in the gospel."
(Mark 1:15)

In another parable, in Luke 15:3–7, Jesus tells the story of a shepherd who had a hundred sheep. One day one of the sheep got away, and the shepherd left behind the other 99 sheep to look for the one that was lost. With this story Jesus made it clear that every single person is important in the kingdom. In earthly kingdoms and countries people are often neglected or forgotten about. That never happens in the Kingdom of God because God treasures each one of us.

Jesus proclaimed a kingdom whose values directly contradicted those of the political kingdoms of his time. The way kings, queens, and presidents rule in the 21st century is different from the way they acted in Jesus' day. What remains the same in every generation is that rulers try to stamp their values upon society. These values and rules may last for years. But the values of the Kingdom of God are timeless. FG

Jesus Calms the Waters

There were stories told in Jesus' time about storm gods who controlled the sea. These gods were the gods of natural powers like thunderstorms and their power was greatly respected. Mark 4:35–51 shows how the legend of these gods met their match in Jesus.

Jesus and the disciples were traveling across the Sea of Galilee. Jesus fell asleep in the boat and while he was asleep a violent storm blew up. Waves broke over the boat, and the disciples were terrified. They woke him up and accused him of not caring that they were going to die. Jesus simply said, "Quiet! Be still!" and the storm died down. Bewildered at the sight, the disciples wondered who Jesus actually was that he was able to calm a storm.

Mark showed that Jesus had God's power to control nature. And just as Jesus calmed the storm at that time, Jesus works today to calm the storms in our hearts and relationships.

Is this Kingdom that Jesus speaks of anything like the Magic Kingdom?

art • i • fact
The Good Shepherd, marble sculpture, Museo Pio Cristiano, Vatican Museums, Vatican State

IT'S LIKE THIS

Did you ever wonder why the image of a shepherd appears so often in the Bible? One reason is that shepherding was the occupation of many people in Palestine during Jesus' time. It is also an apt image for the relationship between Jesus and his people. Sheep are incapable of taking care of themselves; they are dependent on the shepherd to survive. The shepherd checks the purity of their drinking water, scours their grazing fields for sinkholes, and watches for predators. The sheep know their shepherd's voice and respond only to him. How attentive and responsive are you to the words and the call of Jesus, your Shepherd?

A Child Shall Lead Them

The Kingdom of God belongs to people who are like children. That is what Jesus told his disciples in Mark 10:13–16. In this story, the disciples were concerned that the children would disturb Jesus or get in his way. They wanted to keep children away from him. He corrected the disciples and told them to bring the children to him because if the disciples wanted to enter the kingdom, they would have to be like children. In other words, to enter the kingdom, a person has to depend on God the way children depend on their parents.

Children need adults to provide for them and to protect them. They need adults so that they can have love and security as they grow up. Children need adults in order to live and to thrive. Jesus wants us to understand that we too are like children, for we need God so that we can live. To enter the kingdom, we have to recognize that need.

VIRTUE

Just as there is more to a happy childhood than mere survival, there is more to entering the kingdom than recognizing that we need God to care for us like a loving parent. Childhood is all about growing up and growing in maturity. With the help of our parents and our teachers, we make the first steps in the process of becoming more mature. In the same way we need to have a mature relationship with God. Our parents and the other adults in our lives are our examples and our guides in helping us to grow in relationship with God and with others. They direct us on the path of virtue.

> Virtues are the habits and practices that lead us in the direction of doing what is right and good.

continued on page 80 ▶

It Can Be Done

Even at a young age, and even when life gets very hard, it is possible to live in faith, hope, and love. Mattie Stepanek did. He was born with a terrible disease that had already killed three of his brothers and sisters and was now attacking him and his mother. He could not walk and needed a power wheelchair to get around. He was attached to a ventilator to help him breathe, and he received regular blood transfusions. But did Mattie lose his faith in a loving God? Did he give up and lose all hope? Did he stop loving God and everybody else? No, he did not. His faith, hope, and love remained strong. He wrote a letter to God: "Dear God, I've decided to go home. They think I'm going home to die. Please let me go home to live. Whether I live one day or 10 years, please let me spend every minute until I die living and celebrating and spreading my message of hope and peace." He lived two more years, and by then Mattie had inspired many people. At his funeral at St. Catherine Laboure Catholic Church in Wheaton, Maryland, former president Jimmy Carter expressed everyone's admiration for this young man who had lived so beautifully in faith, hope, and love.

▶ *continued from page 79*

Virtues are the practices that lead us in the direction of doing what is right and good. They help us to do our very best in everything. It is through our practice of virtues that the Holy Spirit is calling us to be as much as we can be for God and for others. The three theological virtues in particular are the foundation of our relationship with God.

FAITH

The first one is faith. Faith is a gift of the Holy Spirit that makes it possible for us to believe in God and in all the things that he has revealed to us. We proclaim our faith when we profess the Creed during Sunday Mass and when we celebrate the sacraments. We practice the virtue of faith by trusting God's Word, by listening to his Church, and by living out what we believe. We act out our faith when we live according to the commandments and care for one another. In the act of faith we freely commit ourselves to God. In all our prayers we appeal to God in faith. When we live in faith, we study to understand what it means for our lives. We prepare ourselves to proclaim to others the meaning of who Jesus is and how he leads us to salvation.

HOPE

The Holy Spirit helps us to face the future through the practice of the virtue of hope. Hope helps us in times of discouragement. It sustains us at times when we feel that others have abandoned us. The symbol of hope is the anchor. Hope has been described as the sure and steadfast anchor of the soul in times when discouragement can overwhelm us. It is in times of discouragement that we rely on the Holy Spirit's help rather than our own strength. Hope is the virtue of wanting and looking

WISE GUYS

We need to be.
Just be.
Be for a moment.
Kind and gentle, innocent and trusting,
Like children and lambs,
Never judging or vengeful

—Mattie Stepanek,
Hope Through Heartsongs

Mattie Stepanek
and his mother Jeni

forward to heaven and the happiness of eternal life. We practice the virtue of hope by trusting in the promises Jesus made to us. We recognize Jesus as the one who precedes us on the road to salvation.

LOVE

Saint Paul tells us in his first letter to the Corinthians that we can have as much faith as we want and all the hope in the world, but these virtues do nothing for us if we are not filled with love. Another word for the virtue of love is *charity*, which comes from the Latin word for love, *caritas*. Love is the gift of the Holy Spirit that helps us to love God above all things for his own sake and to love our neighbors as ourselves.

When we practice the virtue of charity, we are imitating the love that Jesus has for us and for others. This means that our love is not to be shared just with the people who are close to us, but it is to include those in need all over the world. We are even called to love those whom we might consider our enemies. When we love as Jesus teaches us to love, we can begin to see and to love others in the same way that Jesus does.

We have seen how Jesus invites us to be like children, to come to him and grow close to him. This is an ongoing invitation for all of us to learn to trust in him, hope in him, and love him. The way we respond to his invitation is through the practice of the virtues of faith, hope, and love. FG

Jesus invites us to be like children. That sounds easy. I'm a kid, I think I can handle that.

The Greatest of Virtues

Charity can be called the first of the virtues. This means that the other virtues find their meaning and effectiveness only when they are practiced in love. Only in love can all of the virtues work together in harmony. Like the instruments in an orchestra the individual virtues make their unique and individual contribution. The virtue of love is the conductor who takes the sounds of each and blends them in a way that the power of the music can move our hearts.

WANT TO KNOW MORE? Visit www.FindingGod.org/teens
to read about living the virtues in everyday life.

Let the Children Come to Me

Jesus told his disciples to bring the children to him. Saint John Bosco took these words to heart. He was ordained a priest in 1841 and sent to Turin, Italy. He inspired young people by the way he taught and by the sincerity of his life of prayer. Soon he was running a boarding house with the help of his mother, Margaret. When more young people came to him, he founded the Society of Saint Francis de Sales. Known as Salesians, these priests and brothers work all over the world helping young men. A related order of religious sisters, the Daughters of Our Lady Help of Christians, works with young women. Inspired by Saint John Bosco, these two groups try to be friends and guides to children who are poor, abandoned, or at risk. They know that by working to give young people a chance to have a full life, they're doing exactly what Jesus wants them to do.

10 childlike qualities adults should possess to seek entry into the Kingdom of God:

1. Dependent
2. Grateful
3. Caring
4. Full of wonder
5. Anxious to please
6. Fun-loving
7. Eager
8. Open to the spiritual
9. Receptive
10. Imaginative

Enter the
Kingdom

UNITING PRAYER AND WORKS

The virtues of faith, hope, and charity draw us to live in relationship with God the Father, Son, and Holy Spirit. They also draw us into prayer. These virtues come from God and draw us to him, making it possible for us to live as his children. Through our faith we believe in God and all that he has revealed to us. Through our hope we desire the Kingdom of God and eternal life as our only true happiness. And through our charity we love God above all things and love our neighbor as ourselves. Charity is the fullness of the Christian life. It unites us with God, who is love, and moves us to make ourselves neighbors to even those far away, loving them as Jesus does. Faith, hope, and charity bind us more closely not only to God but to our neighbors, making prayer and our Christian life inseparable. Uniting prayer to good works we can pray without ceasing.

art • i • fact
La Trinidad
is a 19th century Mexican retablo on heavy gauge tin. The word *retablo* means "behind the alter". It refers to the paintings of various saints hanging behind the alters of many Mexican churches.

All: O God, we freely give ourselves to you. Help us to nurture the gift of faith you have given us by trusting in your Word, by listening to what the Church teaches, and by putting our faith into action.

Leader: If you want to enter the kingdom, you have to be a person of hope.

All: O God, without the gift of hope, our lives would have no meaning. Help us to share our hope with others and always to look forward to the lasting joy and happiness of living with you forever.

Leader: If you want to enter the kingdom, you have to be a person of love.

All: O God, when we look at your Son, Jesus, we learn what it means to love others. Help us to love you above all things, and to show your love to all we meet.

Leader: Let's join together and pray:

All: Loving God, we want to enter your kingdom. We know our need for you and count on your help. The virtues of faith, hope, and love are your gifts to us. May we grow in our relationship with you as we practice them in our daily lives. We ask this in Jesus' name. Amen.

Leader: We often receive messages from society telling us that we should be self-sufficient. These messages can make us think that asking for help is a sign of weakness. Throughout his life Jesus made it clear that in order to enter the kingdom, we have to recognize our need for God. We need God the same way children need parents. Without God's help we could never enter the kingdom. The theological virtues of faith, hope, and love help us to live our daily lives the way God wants us to.

Leader: If you want to enter the kingdom, you have to be a person of faith.

What's WHAT?

■ Look over the main points below. What is one additional important insight you would add to this list? Write it on the lines below.

- The values of the Kingdom of God proclaimed by Jesus contradicted those of the political kingdoms of his times.

- Jesus invited everyone into the Kingdom of God, with special emphasis on the poor and sinners.

- Jesus is often shown as a shepherd because of his care for God's people.

- To enter the kingdom, we need to recognize that we depend on God just as children depend on adults.

- We respond to Jesus' invitation to grow close to him through the practice of the virtues of faith, hope, and love.

- _____

_____

_____

Say WHAT?

Kingdom of God • parable • social justice

So WHAT?

■ Virtues are the habits and practices that lead us in the direction of doing good. *Think about it. Pray about it.*

Now WHAT?

■ What is one thing you will do this week at home to respond to God's invitation to grow closer to him?

_____

_____

_____

_____

_____

Here's WHAT the Catholic Church Teaches

The Church's strong emphasis on **social justice** keeps us faithful to the Kingdom of God. The Kingdom of God announced by Christ not only affirms that the world is good as created by God, but helps us to repair the damage caused by human sin. Through Baptism we are restored in our relationship with God. With the help of God's grace, we are able to continue the work of Jesus.

The Kingdom of God becomes more clear when we work to assure justice for the poor, release the oppressed, console the sorrowful, and actively seek a new social order in which concrete steps are taken so that the needs of people who are poor are addressed.

Making Connections

1. Read the article assigned to your group.

2. Note the main points from your article in the appropriate column below.

3. Join your group with a group who read the other article.

4. Record the main points in the appropriate column below.

5. Work together to complete the "Connect" section to show how the two articles connect.

NOTES FROM ARTICLE 1

A DIFFERENT KINGDOM

Connect

How do these two articles connect?

NOTES FROM ARTICLE 2

A CHILD SHALL LEAD THEM

IT'S aMAZing

One fun type of puzzle is a maze. You work your way from start to finish by winding in and out of dead ends and obstacles. As fall arrives, some farmers plow paths into their corn fields and challenge visitors to find their way through the maze. Why do you think people are so intrigued by mazes?

For Your Eyes Only

Meeting an obstacle is a challenge. What are some obstacles you face in your life these days?

Obstacle Course

It isn't easy to make your way through a maze or an obstacle course, either in real life or in a video game. Things keep getting in the way and you have to work your way around them. It can be a real challenge.

Mark 2:1–12 tells the story of some men who faced an obstacle and had to work around it. The story is about a paralyzed man and his faithful friends. Jesus had come to town and was preaching in someone's house. The house was crowded, and it looked as if the paralyzed man would not be able to see Jesus. His friends, knowing that the packed house was an obstacle for the paralyzed man, decided to do their best to help him. The men knew that like most of the small homes in Palestine, the house had a thatched straw roof. They climbed to the roof and pulled apart the thatching. Then they carried their friend to the roof and lowered him through the hole so that he could see

> ## Our sins turn our lives into obstacle courses.

Jesus. They must have felt happy that they were able to overcome an obstacle for their friend.

FORGIVENESS

Jesus, however, recognized that the paralyzed man faced another obstacle, one that the people in the crowd could not see. He saw the state of the paralyzed man's soul and understood the man's need for forgiveness. He knew that the man's sins were getting in the way of his happiness and well-being. Jesus surprised everyone with the simple words, "Your sins are forgiven." He even went a step further and healed the man physically; he told him to rise, pick up his mat, and go home. This miracle made the surrounding crowd ecstatic. They had never seen anything like it before.

But the forgiveness of sins that Jesus offered the man caused a stir among the crowd. What right did Jesus have to forgive the man's sins? Did he not realize that only God can forgive sins? Jesus knew that this was what the people were thinking, so he used the physical healing as a sign of his power to forgive sins.

THE AUTHORITY TO FORGIVE

The point that Mark wants to make in his story is that the forgiveness of sins is important in order to have a healthy relationship with God and with others. Mark was being faithful to Jesus by making this point because forgiveness of sins was a central part of Jesus' ministry. He taught his followers to forgive others, and he prepared his apostles for their ministry by giving them the authority to forgive sins. That same authority continues to be exercised today in the Sacrament of Penance, in which we receive God's merciful forgiveness for our personal sins. After receiving the sacrament we are reconciled to God, to others, and to all of creation.

REPENTANCE

God does not give up on us when we sin. The Holy Spirit calls us to repentance, to experience real sorrow for what we have done and to decide that we will stay away from sinning in the future. Another word for repentance is *contrition*. When our sorrow is based on love of God above all else, we call it *perfect contrition*. On the other hand, when our sorrow is based more on the fear of punishment that we might receive for our sins, we call it *imperfect contrition*. It is important to recognize our sins for what they are and then make up our minds to turn away from them and turn back to God.

Our sins turn our lives into obstacle courses. The Sacrament of Penance is a gift to the Church from Jesus that helps to remove the obstacles that sin puts in our way. Through celebrating this sacrament, we also receive the grace that we need to help us avoid sin in the future. FG

This Way Out

Sometimes groups intentionally set up an obstacle course so that they can learn to stretch their physical, emotional, or intellectual skills. For example, a group might spend a day on a ropes course, an outdoor structure that challenges people's climbing skills and encourages them to think creatively about overcoming obstacles. Some obstacles are impossible to overcome without the help of the entire group. A person learns how to trust others—and how to be trustworthy—when flying down a zip line 50 feet in the air. The man who was paralyzed knew what it was like to trust his friends. Crowds of people had barred him from seeing Jesus. He trusted his friends to help, even when they hoisted him up onto a roof. He had made good choices about his friendships. How do your friends help you when you face obstacles?

Who Put You in Charge?

In every group of people there always seems to be one person who gives orders to everyone else. You want to say, "Hey, who put you in charge?" That is how the people felt when Jesus forgave the sins of the paralyzed man. Where did Jesus get the authority to do that? Only God has that kind of authority.

Jesus was one step ahead of the crowd. He knew their thoughts, and he showed them that he is more than an ordinary man by curing the paralyzed man. Jesus is God, with the full authority to forgive sins. Later Jesus would pass this authority on to his Church. After his Resurrection he appeared to his disciples and said: "receive the holy Spirit. Whose sins you forgive they are forgiven them, and whose sins you retain, they are retained." (John 20:19–23) Through the power of the Holy Spirit, Jesus shares with the Church the authority to forgive sins. Ordained priests practice the ministry of forgiveness of sins in the Sacrament of Penance.

ABOVE IMAGE: Jesus heals the paralyzed man, painted icon, Pachomian Brotherhood of Monks, Greece

SOUND *Bite*

When the president or another important politician gives a speech, there often is not enough time on the TV news to show the entire speech. The news editors choose a few sentences from the speech that, in their opinion, are the heart of what the speaker was saying. They call these selections sound bites. You might say that Mark was giving us a sound bite of Jesus' teaching when he quoted Jesus at the beginning of his Gospel: "This is the time of fulfillment. The kingdom of God is at hand. Repent, and believe in the gospel." (Mark 1:15)

 IM "I did not come to call the righteous but sinners." (Mark 2:17)

Mark wants us to understand that repentance is at the center of Jesus' teaching. Repentance means sorrow for our sins and a determination not to sin again. When God calls us to repentance through the Sacrament of Penance, he is challenging us to turn our lives around and he is giving us the grace we need to do this.

BLESSED CHARLES DE FOUCAULD

Charles de Foucauld experienced God's call to repentance in his own life. He was born in 1858 in France and was baptized a Catholic. By the time he was an adult, his faith did not mean much to him, and he wondered whether God even existed. Still Charles felt that something was missing in his life, and he asked for a sign to know that God was real. Then one day he met a holy priest named Abbe Huvelin. Charles decided to go to the church where Abbe Huvelin was hearing confessions so that he could discuss a problem with him. Abbe Huvelin had something else in mind. He encouraged Charles to confess his sins. Along with the Sacrament of Penance, Charles also received the Eucharist that day. This was the turning point in his life. His encounter with Abbe Huvelin was the sign from God he had been looking for. He recognized how much God loved him and decided to dedicate his life to prayer and fasting for the sake of the world. From then on Charles was close to God. He became a monk and started a community called the Little Brothers of Jesus.

Charles de Foucauld

Later Charles moved to North Africa to live and serve among the poor. He was killed there during an uprising.

SACRAMENT OF PENANCE

Charles's experience teaches us what the Sacrament of Penance should be in our lives. The Holy Spirit works through this sacrament to turn us away from sin and toward God the Father. It is a powerful sacrament, and it can have the same powerful effect of drawing us closer to God that it had on Charles de Foucauld.

The first step comes from God, who calls us to repentance. We then go to a priest to confess our sins, express sorrow for them, state our intention to avoid these sins in the future, and promise to repair any damage our sins may have done to others. We confess all grave or mortal sins, as well as any venial sins that come to mind. Once the priest has heard our confession, he gives an appropriate penance. Penance consists of prayers or actions that will help repair the damage caused by our sins and will help us to turn

continued on page 90 ▶

IT'S LIKE THIS

The Sacrament of Penance is God's generous gift to us to forgive our sins. When we sin we say, do, or desire something that offends God. Sin is contrary to reason and harms our relationship with God and others. When sin becomes a habit, even venial sins can lead us to commit capital sins. The capital sins are pride, covetousness, envy, anger, gluttony, lust, and sloth.

I decided to forgive the new shark down the block. Last week he took my lunch money—but, at least he didn't take ME for lunch.

Headed in the Right Direction?

One of the first steps we need to take in order to turn our lives around is to recognize that we are lost and headed in the wrong direction. To help us take this step, we make an examination of conscience before celebrating the Sacrament of Penance. A good way to do this is by following the lead of the Ten Commandments.

The first three commandments have to do with our relationship with God. We might ask ourselves the following: Did I turn to God during the day, especially when I was tempted? Did I participate at Mass with attention and devotion on Sundays and holy days? Did I use God's name with love and reverence?

The rest of the commandments concern our relationships with others. We might ask ourselves questions such as: Did I treat others fairly? Was I respectful of my neighbors, my friends, and those in authority? Did I show respect for my body and for the bodies of others? Have I cheated, stolen, or lied? Did I hold grudges and try to hurt people who I think have hurt me? Did I treat God's world with reverence? Did I waste resources that could be used by others?

Making a Good Confession

When we celebrate the Sacrament of Penance, these are the basic steps we follow:

1. The priest greets us, and we pray the Sign of the Cross. The priest invites us to trust in God. He may read a passage from Scripture with us.

2. We confess our sins. The priest may help and counsel us.

3. The priest gives us a penance to perform. Penance is an act of kindness, a prayer to pray, or both.

4. The priest asks us to express our sorrow and repentance, usually by reciting the Act of Contrition.

5. We receive absolution. The priest says, "I absolve you from your sins in the name of the Father, and of the Son, and of the Holy Spirit." We respond, "Amen."

6. The priest dismisses us by saying, "Go in peace." We go forth to perform the act of penance he has given us.

▶ *continued from page 89*

away from our sins and to live closer to God. The priest then speaks the words of absolution.

This kind of individual confession of grave sins followed by absolution from a priest is the ordinary way in which we are reconciled with God and with the Church. The Church encourages us to celebrate the sacrament regularly.

EFFECTS OF PENANCE

We have a lot to gain from the Sacrament of Penance. We are reconciled with God and are filled with his life and love. We are reconciled with the Church and with the people we may have hurt by our sins. If we confessed a mortal sin, we are saved from eternal punishment, and the grace of the sacrament helps us avoid committing that sin in the future. Our conscience is cleared, and we are at peace with ourselves, God, and others. We are strengthened in preparation for future struggles with temptation. FG

✝ Our Roots Are Showing

What's up with the box? You know, that small, dark room in the back of the church or along the side aisle. It's called a confessional. The first confessionals were used in 1564. Over time, our attitude toward the Sacrament of Penance has shifted from a focus on the individual's private confession to a focus on the need for reconciliation with God and the community. Modern church practices reflect this shift. People can now celebrate the Sacrament of Penance either in the confessional or "outside the box" by talking with the priest face to face. In either practice, the dignity of the person is of the greatest importance. The priest is bound to absolute secrecy regarding the sins confessed to him. This secrecy is called the sacramental seal.

Which Is Easier?

ASKING FORGIVENESS

In the Lord's Prayer Jesus teaches us to pray "forgive us our trespasses, as we forgive those who have trespassed against us." The forgiveness that we ask of God is linked to the forgiveness that we grant to other people. It is not always easy to forgive and to make peace with others. But in this prayer Jesus teaches us that the reconciliation we experience with God makes it possible for us to reconcile with others. We become peacemakers. The Holy Spirit can soften hard hearts, and we can experience forgiving and being forgiven in the compassionate love of God.

LEFT: *Prayer Time,*
M.P. Wiggins,
Cincinnati, Ohio

Which Is Easier?

Who doesn't need to be forgiven every now and then? And who knows our need for forgiveness better than Jesus? That was the lesson the paralyzed man learned when he met Jesus. Everyone in that crowded house got more than they bargained for that day. They all expected Jesus to heal the sick. What they didn't expect was that Jesus could see beyond physical illnesses. They witnessed Jesus forgiving the man's sins and healing his soul of its separation from God. They had never seen anything like that before.

Prepare: Begin by focusing your attention on your breath. Be aware of your breath as it flows in and out. Let go of any distracting thoughts. Open yourself to receive the Word of God.

Read: Mark 2:1–12 (The Healing of the Paralyzed Man)

Meditate: In your imagination, place yourself in the crowded house. Look around you and notice the faces of those near you. Listen to Jesus teaching. What do you think when a hole appears in the roof and you see a man being lowered into the middle of the room?

Read a second time: Mark 2:1–12 (The Healing of the Paralyzed Man)

Meditate: Now imagine that you are the person being lowered into the room. Hear Jesus speak these words to you, "Child, your sins are forgiven." Then notice what you feel inside.

Pray: Share your reflections with Jesus in your own words. Ask him if there is anything else in this story he'd like you to notice or anything else he'd like you to understand. Then thank him for this time of prayer.

Contemplate: Spend a few moments in prayerful silence with God.

Close by praying together: Jesus, you forgave the sins of the paralyzed man and healed his broken relationship with God. Help us to know our need of forgiveness and to come to you to be healed. May your healing grace direct our steps ever closer to God. Amen.

What's **WHAT?**

■ Review the main points of this chapter. Choose the one that's most inspiring to you and write your reasons on the lines provided.

• The Sacrament of Penance helps us remove the obstacles that sin puts in our way.

• Ordained priests have the authority to forgive sins through the Sacrament of Penance.

• Mark wants us to understand that repentance is at the center of Jesus' teaching.

• Through the Sacrament of Penance we are reconciled with God, the Church, and those who have been hurt through our sin.

• A good way to examine our conscience is to reflect on how we've obeyed the Ten Commandments.

_____

_____

_____

So **WHAT?**

■ How does celebrating the Sacrament of Penance make a difference in my relationships with God and with others?

_____

_____

_____

_____

Say **WHAT?**

miracle

Now **WHAT?**

■ What will I do at school this week to express forgiveness to someone I've offended?

_____

_____

_____

_____

Here's **WHAT** the Catholic Church Teaches

As the year 2000 approached, many Christians saw a call to engage in the ancient Jewish practice of forgiveness of debts in special years called Jubilee years. In a Jubilee year all debts that the poor owed to the rich were to be forgiven.

A number of early Christian writers thought about the question of debt in an even more radical way. They considered wealth to be a good that comes from God and should be used by as many people as possible. Therefore the goods of the rich belong to the poor as well. According to Saint Gregory the Great, even the goods the rich distribute to the poor really belong to the poor anyway. Giving to those in need, Gregory taught, means paying a debt.

Cornerstones

1. **As the two articles are read, note the cornerstones (main points) from each article in the appropriate column below.**
2. **With your group, share one cornerstone you identified from your group's assigned article. Keep sharing cornerstones until you have no new ones to share. Say "pass" if you have nothing new to add.**

CORNERSTONES — ARTICLE 1	CORNERSTONES — ARTICLE 2
Obstacle Course	**Sound Bite**

A BUMP IN THE Road

Whether in a car, on a skateboard, or on a bike, there are times when we encounter a bump or a pothole in the road. These require that we slow down or swerve to avoid them. In some cases, we may even need to change direction. Do you find such things an annoyance or a challenge? Why?

✓ IT OUT

Some bumps in the road are less serious than others. Sometimes they can even be funny. Which of the following "bumps" have you encountered?

late for school	wore two different socks
missed the bus	lousy lunch
dead cell phone	bad hair day
no permission slip	lost wallet
out of money	grounded again

Acting in His Name

She was the boy's companion on his last journey in life.

A few years ago in Illinois, a commuter train collided with a school bus that had stalled on the tracks. The bus was filled with high-school students on their way to school. Many were injured, and a number of students died. One of the people who assisted the injured was a nurse who had witnessed the accident. She later told the parents of one severely injured boy how she had held his hand, talking to him softly. She told the parents that their son had remained calm and had responded to her voice throughout the experience. She said that the boy died peacefully, knowing that he was not alone. In the midst of this terrible accident, the nurse acted as a sign to the boy of a caring community concerned for his welfare. She also represented the love of his parents, who were not there to care for him themselves. She was the boy's companion on his last journey in life.

This is the quality of care and concern that Jesus had in mind when he sent his disciples on a mission to proclaim the Kingdom of God. (Mark 6:6–13) Jesus told them to travel light, to trust in God to provide for them, and to preach repentance to the people. Mark says that in Jesus' name "[T]hey drove out many demons, and they anointed with oil many who were sick and cured them." (Mark 6:13) They were Jesus' ambassadors with a mission to tell the people that they were not alone, that the healing touch of God was in their midst.

We know from the Letter of James that the mission to anoint and heal the sick that Jesus gave his disciples continued in the early Church. James wrote:

> Is anyone among you sick? He should summon the presbyters of the church, and they should pray over him and anoint [him] with oil in the name of the Lord, and the prayer of faith will save the sick person, and the Lord will raise him up. If he has committed any sins, he will be forgiven.
>
> (James 5:14–15)

God's care and concern for the seriously ill and the elderly is especially shown through the Sacrament of the Anointing of the Sick. We celebrate this sacrament to confer a special grace on a person who is experiencing the difficulties that come from serious illness or old age. Anointing of the Sick is a source of grace, helping the person to grow in faith and to trust in God that he or she is not alone. If God wills, the person may also experience physical healing. Jesus Christ is present, healing the person in a fundamental way and sharing his victory over sin and death.

continued on page 98 ▶

The Apostle James, icon commissioned by St. Elias Antiochian Orthodox Church, Austin, Texas

Can you think of a time when you realized something bad might really be a blessing? I remember a time when a worm on a hook floated past me. It looked scrumptious, but I'm glad I missed it.

A Blessing

The mother looked at her adult daughter lying in bed. In her daughter's arm was a needle connected to a tube carrying the intravenous medications she needed for survival. The daughter had leukemia and had been fighting the disease for a number of years. The mother was upset because her daughter was suffering so much. The daughter asked her mother what was wrong. The mother, a firm believer, said that she was upset because when Jesus came, he only suffered for a short period of time. It did not seem fair that her daughter should suffer so long. The daughter said, "Mom, I know you are upset, but you are wrong. All this time while I have been suffering here, Jesus has been with me!"

The daughter's response to her mother was an act of faith, a declaration of hope, and words of love. We are tempted to think that suffering happens because God has abandoned us. We do not normally see it as a sign of grace. The daughter recognized that while Jesus Christ can no longer suffer, he was her companion at all times as she united her suffering with him. Her response to her mother showed that she knew she was participating in the saving work of Jesus. This is true not only for her, but for everyone who is suffering, of any age, who contributes to the good of the community by uniting personal suffering to the Paschal Mystery—the journey of Jesus Christ through death to Resurrection. When we pray for the well-being of those who suffer, our prayers can also include thanksgiving for the gifts they bring to us.

► *continued from page 97*

Anointing of the Sick was celebrated only with those whose illness or old age place them in danger of death. Before the Second Vatican Council the Sacrament of the Anointing of the Sick was called Extreme Unction. The priest had to wait until the person was about to die before anointing him or her. Today the Church does not ask priests to wait that long, the sacrament can be celebrated any time there is a danger of death.

CELEBRATING THE SACRAMENT

> We celebrate Jesus' concern for those who are seriously ill in the Sacrament of the Anointing of the Sick.

We celebrate Jesus' concern for those who are seriously ill in the Sacrament of the Anointing of the Sick. When the priest approaches the person, who may be conscious or unconscious, he places his hands over the suffering person and prays. With the Sign of the Cross he then anoints the forehead and hands of the person with oil. The ceremony may take place at home, in the hospital, or at church. The sacrament gives the person the grace to be healed spiritually and at times physically. It also provides forgiveness of sins, both venial and mortal, if the person is truly sorry but unable to make a confession.

The sacrament does not have to be a one-time occurrence. If a person is seriously ill and receives the sacrament and then gets well, he or she can receive the sacrament again if the condition gets worse. The Church wants to stay with the person throughout their journey of suffering and death. The anointing of a sick person is an action of the entire Church, and it must be administered by a priest or bishop. The oil used is blessed by the bishop during Holy Week.

The boy who was killed in the accident with the train and the school bus felt the touch of a woman that represented the care and concern of his parents. In helping the boy, she also represented Jesus' care and concern in the same way that every act of kindness is a gift of the Holy Spirit. In the Sacrament of the Anointing of the Sick, Jesus shows his love for those who are suffering and facing death. FG

This Way Out

Sometimes it's hard to know what to say to someone who is sick or dying. We want to be supportive and express our love, but we struggle to find the right words. People who are sick or dying want to be treated the same way everyone does—with respect and consideration. It's important to be patient, to be sensitive to the person's particular needs and respectful of her or his privacy. It's OK to ask the person how he or she feels or what's going on. Talk with the person about the usual things you'd talk about. Take your cues from the person's responses. Offer your assistance by first asking if the person wants help instead of automatically doing what you think is helpful. If you are at a total loss for words, just say so. It's better to be honest than to be hurtful by avoiding the person. Whether the person is fully conscious or not, remember that your physical presence and touch can often express more than words.

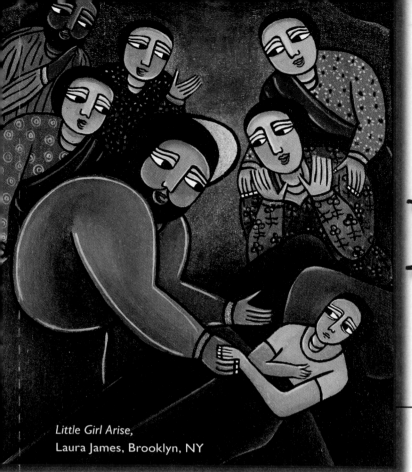

Little Girl Arise,
Laura James, Brooklyn, NY

Jesus' Healing Touch

When Andrew and Simon (who would later be named Peter) began their week of fishing, they probably had no idea of the unexpected way that the week would end. Mark 1:16–39 tells the story of how their lives changed in a way they never could have imagined. As they were casting their nets one day, Jesus came to the shore and told them he would make them fishers of men. They immediately left their nets and followed him. Then they accompanied Jesus to the synagogue where he taught. They watched as he freed a man from an unclean spirit.

After they left the synagogue, Simon and Andrew offered Jesus hospitality and brought him to their home. When they entered the house, they discovered that Simon's mother-in-law was seriously ill. They immediately told Jesus. Jesus went to the woman, grasped her hand, and helped her to get up. Her fever was gone. She then offered hospitality to them all. Simon and Andrew must have been pleased as word about Jesus spread throughout the whole region of Galilee.

HEALING

Most of the first stories we read in the Gospel of Mark are about Jesus as a healer. After he healed Simon's

continued on page 100 ▶

✝ Our Roots Are Showing

An ancient symbol of healing is a staff encircled by a snake. Many medical professionals use this symbol in their logos. A symbol that evolved from this image is the caduceus, a winged staff with two snakes twined around it. The Bible also mentions this ancient symbol. In Numbers 21:8 the Lord told Moses to make a serpent out of bronze and mount it to a pole. When the people who had been bitten by a serpent looked upon it, they were healed. The serpent that had been a source of death would become a source of healing. The Gospel of John picks up on this image as well. In 3:14–15, Jesus says that just as Moses lifted up the serpent, the Son of Man would also be lifted up. Anyone who believes in Jesus would not die but have everlasting life. The cross, a source of death, would become a source of life.

► *continued from page 99*

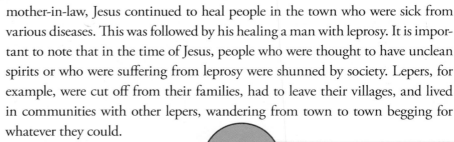

mother-in-law, Jesus continued to heal people in the town who were sick from various diseases. This was followed by his healing a man with leprosy. It is important to note that in the time of Jesus, people who were thought to have unclean spirits or who were suffering from leprosy were shunned by society. Lepers, for example, were cut off from their families, had to leave their villages, and lived in communities with other lepers, wandering from town to town begging for whatever they could.

So when Jesus healed these sick people, he was not only taking care of their physical illness, but he was also making it possible for them to return to

IM "Go your way; your faith has saved you." (Mark 10:52)

the life of their community. When Jesus sent out his disciples to preach, he commanded them to do the same. Jesus knew that along with the physical consequences of illness, people suffered because they were isolated and cut off from their community.

ISOLATION

People continue to suffer today from isolation and loneliness. For whatever reason, they are not included in activities or considered to be part of the "in group." People are stereotyped as unacceptable. In these cases there are two dimensions to the healing process. The first is for society, groups, and individuals to recognize and repent of the attitudes that result in people excluding others. The second is the call to reach out to others, especially to those who have been excluded.

As we have seen, this is what Jesus did. He came not just to heal the person's illness, but to heal the whole person. Whether he was touching a leper or releasing unclean spirits, he was helping people to return as healthy members to their community. This benefited both the person who was healed and the entire community. In a similar way we are called by Jesus not only to reach out to those who are suffering physically, but to bring his healing presence to those who are lonely, isolated, or discriminated against. FG

The mother-in-law of Simon showed an amazing spirit of hospitality and discipleship. After being healed of a high fever, she immediately got out of bed and began to wait on Jesus and the others. Mark reports on her hospitality because he wanted to show the completeness of Jesus' cure. The woman's response to being healed is important to take note of. She does not dwell on the fact that she was sick, rather she gets on with her life by responding to the needs of her guests. This is what discipleship is all about. She experiences the healing touch of Jesus, and her immediate response is to serve others.

A Healing Ministry

At the beginning of the 20th century, Father John LaFarge, S.J., a young priest, spent eight months as a chaplain on Blackwells Island. This was an island in the East River between Manhattan and Queens where poor people were taken when they became sick and helpless. Father LaFarge estimated that during those eight months, he administered the Sacrament of the Anointing of the Sick about three thousand times. One old woman who was mentally ill stood out in his mind. She would yell and scream and flail about so much that she had to be tied to the bed. Nothing seemed to be able to calm her down. "Yet," Father LaFarge recalled, "the moment I merely touched the edge of her eyelid with the holy oils, she relaxed, fell back quietly on the bed, took a deep breath and from that time on until her death was peaceful, tranquil, and rational." Father Lafarge reflected that God had been good to his word. "He was a hundred percent 'there,' in a vigorous, dramatic manner that often took my breath away."

Jesus Healing the Lame,
Corinne Vonaesch

Gather Around

Mark makes it very clear in his Gospel that when the authorities came to arrest Jesus, he had been abandoned by all his disciples. This meant that, as Mark saw it, Jesus had to suffer and die alone, without any friends or relatives to comfort him. The women who followed him could only look on from a distance. That is not what Jesus and his Church wish for those who suffer today. When a member of the Catholic community is suffering from a grave illness, the Church wants us to gather around that person in prayer and consoling help. Catholic parishes offer the sick person the Sacrament of the Anointing of the Sick as well as the prayers of the entire parish community. The healthy members of the parish are united with the parishioners in need through prayers and acts of service. In this way they show their respect for human life as a sacred gift from God.

A Source of Grace

CARE FOR THE SICK

Christ invites us to follow him by taking up our cross as he did. This gives us a new outlook on illness and on people who are sick. Jesus calls us to share in his ministry of compassion and healing. Jesus gives the apostles this commission in Matthew 10:8, "Cure the sick. . . . Without cost you have received; without cost you are to give."

The Church carries out this commission in the Sacrament of the Anointing of the Sick. Yet the sacrament is also a commissioning of all of us to care for the sick and to accompany them in their illness through our prayer and physical care. Jesus' love for the sick has continued through the centuries to draw the special attention of Christians toward those who suffer in body and soul. It is the source of tireless efforts to comfort them.

Sunday is a day that offers special time for reflection, silence, and meditation that can further the growth of our Christian life. This day can also be made holy by performing good works and by being in humble service to the sick, the infirm, and the elderly. Sunday can be a day to devote special time to the care of our family members, relatives, and friends who are ill, which we might find difficult to do the other days of the week.

Have you ever thought of illness as an opportunity for grace? Most people don't. But Jesus saw things differently. He sent his apostles out to anoint and cure the sick. His followers today are called to do the same. It's an opportunity of grace both for the one who is sick and for the one who prays. By surrounding the sick and suffering with the support of our prayers, we serve the Kingdom of God.

Take several deep breaths, and allow yourself to grow still.

Close your eyes, and take a few moments to bring to mind those who are ill. Perhaps they are relatives, friends, or neighbors. Maybe they're people you've never met, but you know about through others or through the media. Call to mind their faces and names.

In your imagination, surround each one with the healing love of God.

Aware of the power of prayer and the promise of Jesus to be in the midst of those who gather in his name, let's join together to pray for the sick. Please feel free to speak aloud the first name of someone you want to pray for.

After each name, we'll respond: Jesus, heal us.

When all are finished praying, conclude with the following prayer:

God of mercy, your Son Jesus walked our earth and shared our humanity. In his name, we ask you to hear our prayer and to comfort all those who are ill in body, mind, or spirit.

Amen.

What's **WHAT?**

■ Review the main points of this chapter. Which one is most important to you? Write your reasons on the lines below.

- God's care and concern for the seriously ill and aged is shown through the Sacrament of the Anointing of the Sick.

- Jesus is our companion in our suffering.

- Jesus heals not only physical sickness, but the whole person.

- We respond to those who are sick or dying by surrounding them with our prayers and acts of service.

_____

_____

Say **WHAT?**

Anointing of the Sick

So **WHAT?**

■ Anointing of the Sick is a sign of God's care, concern, and presence. *Think about it. Pray about it.*

Now **WHAT?**

■ What is one thing I will do this week to bring Christ's healing presence to someone who is sick, lonely, or discriminated against?

_____

_____

Here's **WHAT** the Catholic Church Teaches

The Catholic Church teaches, as we are reminded in the parable of the Good Samaritan in Luke 11:29–37, that our response to suffering is to be active. The parable is told as a response to the question "Who is my neighbor?" In the parable Jesus makes it clear that the neighbor is not necessarily the priest or another person from the same community. The neighbor is the person considered an outcast who stops to care for the person in need. It is essential to stop when confronted with the suffering of our neighbor and do something about it, as the Good Samaritan did. The name *Good Samaritan* fits every individual who is sensitive to the sufferings of others and is moved to help them.

In his encyclical letter *On the Christian Meaning of Human Suffering,* Pope John Paul II wrote, "Suffering is present in the world in order to release love, in order to give birth to works of love towards neighbor, in order to transform the whole of human civilization into a 'civilization of love.'" Jesus' words in the parable of the Last Judgment in Matthew 25:31–46 also help us to understand how we find Jesus in acts of love and in acts of assistance for those in need. Whenever we stop to feed the hungry, care for the sick, or visit the imprisoned, we do it to Jesus. He is present in everyone who suffers. All who suffer become sharers in Christ's suffering.

We Can Change the World

1. Read both articles silently.

2. In your group of four, decide which article each pair will work on.

3. With your partner, complete the "Something to Think About..." section below, listing the important ideas presented in your article.

4. Exchange worksheets with the other pair in your group and complete the "How It Can Change the World" section below.

5. With your partner, select one "Something to Think About...Change the World" idea and explain how and why this idea can make the world a better place.

6. With your partner, think of a role model you feel has changed the world in this way.

ARTICLE NAME _____

SOMETHING TO THINK ABOUT	HOW IT CAN CHANGE THE WORLD

AN Aha! MOMENT

Did you ever answer the phone and the person on the other end began talking as if you knew who it was, yet you really didn't have a clue? Have you ever bumped into someone you know you've seen before, but you can't place where or when? Then, when the other person says or does something, you have an "Aha!" moment. You can place where you know the person from. Share a time when something like this happened to you.

411

In the world of cartoons, an "Aha!" moment is often pictured as a light bulb over the character's head.

In the box at right, create another symbol that could be used as an image for an "Aha!" moment.

The Moment of Truth

Sometimes when watching a movie, we follow the characters through dramatic twists and turns, and since we don't know all the details we can't understand the full story. Then comes the moment of truth when all the pieces fall into place, and we understand what's at the heart of the story. Mark does something like this in his Gospel. From the beginning, people asked who Jesus really was. Near the end of Mark's Gospel comes the moment of truth.

> If you want to know who Jesus is, you have to look at the cross.

MIRACLES

Mark tells several stories in which Jesus performed wonderful miracles. Jesus cast a demon out of a possessed man. He touched people and cured them of leprosy. He restored a man's withered and damaged hand. He walked on water. He calmed a storm at sea. He took a dead child's hand and raised her back to life. He fed over five thousand people with five loaves of bread and two fish. While these miracles are true signs of Jesus' divine nature, Mark also wants us to know there is more to be revealed.

TEACHINGS

Mark also tells us about Jesus' teaching. Much of the teaching comes in the form of parables—stories that Jesus told in order to get across certain points. The parable of the sower is about listening to God's word. The parable of the mustard seed is about the importance of the small things we do in life. Do the parables and other teachings show us who Jesus really is? No, says Mark, the parables don't tell us all that there is to know about Jesus.

TRANSFIGURATION

Another amazing event that Mark tells us about is the Transfiguration. As Jesus was standing on a mountaintop with some of his apostles, his clothes became dazzling white, and Elijah and Moses appeared. The voice of God proclaimed that Jesus was his son. Does this extraordinary event reveal Jesus' true identity? No, says Mark again, the Transfiguration doesn't.

SUFFERING AND DEATH

Where then in Mark's Gospel are the depths of Jesus' love revealed? We only discover the depths of Jesus' love in his death on the cross. (Mark 15:33–39) Crucifixion was a particularly cruel form of execution. It was designed to inflict the greatest possible amount of pain on the person being executed. The Romans never crucified a Roman citizen because they thought that this punishment was too cruel. They saved this form of execution for pirates and other rebels against Roman authority. These were people the Romans had no respect for, and whom they wanted to display as examples for anyone who would dare to question their rule. Jesus' contemporaries thought that crucifixion was such a humiliating and horrible death that it had to be a sign that the person had been abandoned by God.

But for Mark this was the moment of truth. He had described Jesus' healing work, his teaching, and even the transforming experience of the Transfiguration. While all these hinted at Jesus' divinity they did not get to the heart of his identity. Instead Mark shows Jesus alone on the cross, despised by the Romans, ridiculed by his peers and countrymen, and abandoned by his disciples. And as Jesus breathed his last, the Roman soldier proclaimed, "Truly this man was the Son of God!" (Mark 15:39)

Many people had expected a glorious messiah. No, says Mark, the Messiah is a suffering servant. If you want to know who Jesus really is, you have to look at the cross. Once you understand the

continued on page 108 ▶

IT OUT

Imagine that you are in charge of naming a new parish. Because of the community's special love of Mark's Gospel, you decide to look through his Gospel to find a good name. Take some time with Mark's Gospel and find a name for the new parish. Write down the name you've chosen (choose something other than St. Mark's, Our Savior, or Most Holy Redeemer). Make note of the chapter and verse from Mark that refers to the name and the reason why you chose it.

Parish name: _____

Chapter and verse: _____

Reason: _____

Savior and Redeemer

Most Catholic parishes are named after saints, but some are named after Jesus himself. *Our Savior* is a name often used for parishes. It calls attention to Jesus as the one who saved the entire world through his death and Resurrection. Another common name for parishes is *Most Holy Redeemer*. Jesus' entire life brought redemption. He redeemed us through his Incarnation—God becoming man. He redeemed us through the years of his growing up in the home of Mary and Joseph. He redeemed us through his teachings and miracles. He redeemed us through his Resurrection from the dead and his Ascension into heaven. But in Mark's Gospel, it is clear that redemption comes first and foremost through the cross of Jesus—the suffering and dying of our Savior and Redeemer.

I would name a parish after Saint Neot. He's the patron saint of fish. That's right, fish have a protector, too. (And you humans think you're so special.)

Jesus' Journey to Save the Dead

Have you ever wondered what happened to the people who died before Jesus came to save us? What happened to the people who served God so well, the heroes of the Old

Sarah

Testament such as Abraham and Sarah, Moses and his wife Zipporah, King David, and the prophets?

When we pray the Apostles' Creed, we acknowledge that after Jesus died and before he had risen, he went to the realm of the dead to gather all the just who had died before him. What we believe is that there Jesus met them as their Savior, proclaiming the Good News to them. He gathered them and brought them to heaven with him. This shows that Jesus' work of redemption is for the entire human family, of all times and all places.

▶ *continued from page 107*

meaning of the cross, you can go back and make sense of the miracles and the parables. The message of Mark's Gospel is that Jesus' death explains everything. Mark asks us to see the living God most clearly in Jesus' battered and bruised body on the cross.

Jesus' death shows us how much God loves us. It is at the heart of the Paschal Mystery. Through his redeeming death, Resurrection, and Ascension Jesus has saved all of God's creation. Jesus also taught us from the cross the most important lessons we have to learn in order to be his followers. We are to give our lives for others and willingly accept the suffering that comes from doing God's work. Jesus also taught us to love everyone, even our enemies, just as he offered his life for everyone, even those who hated him. In this way we participate in and continue Christ's saving work in the world. FG

art • i • fact

Head of a bishop's crosier depicting the Paschal Lamb, ivory, possibly 12th century (with more recent additions)

✝ Our Roots Are Showing

The Paschal Mystery is at the heart of our life as Catholics. The word *paschal* is associated with the Hebrew word "pesach," or Passover. Passover is celebrated every year and recalls Israel's first Passover in Egypt when the lives of their firstborn children were spared. The Jewish people had to sacrifice a lamb and sprinkle its blood on their doorposts so that the Angel of Death would pass over their homes. The lamb became a symbol of redemption. In the New Testament, Jesus is called the Lamb of God because by his death he takes away the sins of the world and redeems us. We remember Jesus' saving death in a special way in the celebration of the Eucharist.

TO LEARN MORE about how we experience the Paschal Mystery in everyday life, visit www.FindingGod.org/teens.

Where Will I Find Jesus?

The Holy Women at the Sepulchre, Laura James, acrylic on canvas

In Mark 16: 1–7, the very end of the Gospel, Mark tells the story of what happened on the Sunday morning after Jesus died and was buried. Mary Magdalene, Mary the mother of James, and Salome came to the place where Jesus was buried. They wanted to do one more thing for him—anoint his body. They knew there would be one problem, however. A large stone had been placed in front of the tomb, and the women would not be able to move it.

When they got to the tomb, however, they found that the stone had been moved. A young man dressed in white was waiting there to greet them. He told the women that the Jesus they were looking for was not there. He said that Jesus had been raised from the dead. The man told the women that if they wanted to see Jesus, they would have to go to Galilee.

GALILEE

This was a remarkable message. It meant that the women were looking for Jesus in the wrong place. First of all, they were looking for Jesus among the dead, and they had to start looking for him among the living. Moreover, they had to look for Jesus in Galilee, that is, among the people whom Jesus served. The message was a challenge to the women, but it is a challenge to us as well. It raises the question, where are we going to find Jesus?

Some of the places where we will find Jesus are rather obvious. We find Jesus in his Church—the worldwide community of baptized believers who work together to serve the coming of the Kingdom of God under the leadership of the bishops, with the Bishop of Rome at the head. We also find Jesus in church on Sundays and Holy Days of Obligation, where the community gathers to offer the sacrifice of the

> ## We have to look for Jesus in the types of places where he ministered.

Mass. We find Jesus in God's actions in the sacraments, especially in the Sacrament of the Eucharist, where Jesus is present and his Body and Blood are given to us as spiritual food.

continued on page 110 ▶

Finding Jesus in Service to Others

Jean Vanier was a man who achieved much in life. He served in the French navy, earned a doctorate in philosophy, and was a college professor. But he was not satisfied with his life. Something was missing. One day he invited into his home two men, Raphael and Phillippe, who had severe developmental disabilities. They were not able to take care of themselves and depended on others for their care. Jean took them in, and then he took in others like them. Gradually Jean began to reflect on their situation. By living with them, rather than just doing things for them, he began to experience Jesus in them. He found Jesus in people who, some might say, could not do anything productive for society. He found they reflected God's love for us. Other people joined Jean Vanier in his service to these vulnerable people, and they opened other homes named *l'Arche,* the Ark, a symbol of life, hope, and covenant with God. Today there are over a hundred l'Arche communities in 18 countries all over the world, serving people with disabilities.

Jean Vanier

▶ *continued from page 109*

THE POOR

But there are some less obvious places where we have to make an effort to find Jesus. You might say that we too have to travel around Galilee. In other words, we have to look for Jesus in the types of places where he ministered. We know that Jesus spent much of his time among poor people, so we must look for Jesus among the poor. If we can recognize his presence there, our attitude toward the poor will become more Christlike and we will show more concern for their suffering.

THE SUFFERING

Jesus ministered to people who were suffering because of the actions of others. This means that we will find Jesus among the victims of discrimination, people who are mistreated or looked down on because of their race, religion, or sex. It also means that we will find Jesus among the victims of war and among the peacemakers.

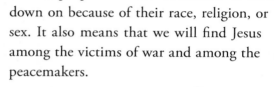

art • i • fact

This mosaic of Mary Magdalene is found in St. Peter in Gallicantu Church in Jerusalem. The church commemorates the place outside of the house of Caiaphas where Peter heard the cock crow after he denied Jesus.

IT'S LIKE THIS

Mary Magdalene, Mary the mother of James, and Salome were just a few of the many women who had significant roles in the life of Jesus and the early Christian community. Unfortunately, many of these women are mentioned only in passing, and many times they are not even named. Luke's Gospel is an exception, as he insists on the important role of women in the Church's life. The role of women is not a major theme in Mark's Gospel so sometimes the same stories are told differently. For example, when Mark writes about the empty tomb, he says that the women ran from the tomb and told no one because they were afraid. By contrast, Luke says that the women did not run away but instead returned and proclaimed the good news to the apostles. Luke presents the women as the first disciples to proclaim the Easter gospel.

Jesus also ministered to people who were suffering because of illness, disease, or accident. He cured lepers. He gave sight to the blind. He cast demons out of people. He made it so that people who were paralyzed could walk and those who were deaf could hear. He even raised the dead back to life. It is among such people that we must learn to find Jesus. A visit to your sick and elderly grandparent is more than just a family visit. When you are helpful to a person with a handicap, you are doing more than just being nice. You are being a follower of Christ, and you are being blessed with an opportunity to find Jesus in that person.

DISCOVERING THE PRESENCE OF GOD

After Jesus was raised from the dead, he ascended to the Father in heaven. From there Jesus and the Father sent the Holy Spirit to teach, guide, and aid us in understanding what Jesus had done in saving us. The Holy Spirit also assists us in helping us to find the presence of God in all things. As we accept and welcome the grace of the Holy Spirit, every day becomes a discovery of the presence of God in places where we least expect it.

The message of Mark's Gospel is clear. Christ is present with us in prayer and worship, in Christian community, in situations of love and respect, and in peacemaking and work for justice. He is among the poor and the vulnerable, the sick and the dying, and anyone who suffers either because of unfortunate situations or at the hands of others. In Mark 8:34 Jesus clearly says that to be a true disciple means to deny ourselves, take up our cross, and follow him. This means that we should accept the sufferings that life brings to us and unite them to the suffering of Jesus. This joins us with all those who are called to serve the needs of others in the Kingdom of God.

IM

"For the Son of Man did not come to be served but to serve and to give his life as a ransom for many."
(Mark 10:45)

Reflecting God's Love

JESUS' JOURNEY TO THE DEAD

The New Testament doesn't describe the Resurrection, and for more than the first 1,000 years of Christianity, Christian art never depicted it. Christians in the West eventually began to produce art depicting the risen Jesus standing before the tomb, often holding a banner. The Orthodox Church, on the other hand, has always depicted the Resurrection through an icon often called "The Resurrection of the Just." In it Jesus is depicted standing on the broken gates of the land of the dead, its shattered lock and key falling into the abyss. The nail prints of his Crucifixion are visible in his hands and feet. Jesus' hand rests gently on Adam's wrist as he raises him and all fallen humanity to new life. Around Jesus are Eve, Abel (the first person to die), King David, Moses, Elijah and other Old Testament prophets, and John the Baptist. The icon remains true to the New Testament, not trying to depict how the Resurrection happened but what it meant for all of us.

Leader: When Jesus died on the cross, he taught us to give our lives for others. His willingness to suffer and die was the result of his deep love of the Father and his deep love for us. The life, death, and Resurrection of Jesus are reflections of God's great love for us. As his followers today, we look for ways to reflect God's love to those we meet each day.

Reader 1: A reading from the Gospel of John

> **This is my commandment: love one another as I love you. No one has greater love than this, to lay down one's life for one's friends.**
> **(John 15:12–13)**

The Gospel of the Lord.

All: Praise to you, Lord Jesus Christ.

Reader 2: Take a moment and think about what Jesus could have meant when he talked about laying down his life for a friend. We probably do it more often than we think. Have you ever gone out of your way to help someone? Or have you ever put your plans aside in order to be with your family? Perhaps you've reached out to someone who needed a word of comfort or encouragement? When we do these things, we are living reflections of God's love.

Reader 3: After each petition, please respond
Lord, hear our prayer.

- That through our prayer and reflection we will grow in our love of God and be true reflections of his love in the world, let us pray to the Lord. ℟

- That we might come to know Jesus more fully though his passion, death, and Resurrection, let us pray to the Lord. ℟

- That we will continue to grow in our ability to reach out to others and to lay down our lives for them, let us pray to the Lord. ℟

Leader: Let us join our prayers together with Christians around the world as we end our prayer with the words that Jesus taught us. Our Father . . .

What's **WHAT?**

■ Review the main points of the chapter. Which point was least familiar to you? Write your new insights on the lines below.

- The message of Mark's Gospel is that Jesus' death reveals who he really is.

- Jesus is our Savior and Redeemer.

- After Jesus died he went to the realm of the dead to gather all of the just who had died before him and to bring them to heaven with him.

- We have to look for Jesus in the types of places where he ministered.

- Jean Vanier is a model of how we can find Jesus in service to others.

_____

_____

_____

_____

So **WHAT?**

■ How does the Paschal Mystery make a difference in how you relate to other people?

_____

_____

_____

_____

Say **WHAT?**

Paschal Mystery

Now **WHAT?**

■ What one thing will you do at school this week to reach out to someone in need of God's love?

_____

_____

_____

_____

Here's **WHAT** the Catholic Church Teaches

Through work we participate in the activity of God himself, our Creator, as well as in the Paschal Mystery of Jesus Christ. The people of Nazareth knew Jesus as a carpenter, a craftsman like his father Joseph, who had an appreciation and respect for human work. Much of his teaching used examples of work.

As Pope John Paul II wrote in his encyclical *On Human Work,* "The Christian finds in human work a small part of the Cross of Christ and accepts it in the same spirit of redemption in which Christ accepted His Cross for us. In work, thanks to the light that penetrates us from the Resurrection of Christ, we always find a glimmer of new life." The wonders produced through human work are signs of God's greatness. Since work contributes to a better human society, it is of vital concern to the Kingdom of God.

If . . . Then . . .

1. **Read the first article.**

2. **Identify the main ideas about our Catholic faith from the article and note them in the "If We Believe . . ." column below.**

3. **In your group, work together to complete the "Then We Are Called to . . ." column.**

4. **Repeat the process for the second article.**

Article 1: The Moment of Truth		**Article 2:** Where Will I Find Jesus?	
IF we believe . . .	THEN we are called to . . .	IF we believe . . .	THEN we are called to . . .

Faith in Action

Faith is alive when we put it into action every day of our lives. It is expressed in the attitudes and values we hold and in the ways we relate to the people and the world around us. Taking action to create a more just world is an essential part of living the Gospel. Jesus preached not only with words but how he lived his life. We are called to do the same.

In this unit we explored what the Gospel of Mark teaches us about Jesus. One of the major images that Mark uses is the Kingdom of God. We are co-creators with God in terms of bringing about his Kingdom. As such, all the work that we do is valuable, no matter how small or seemingly insignificant. Here are some ideas that show how you value workers.

"Pay no attention to that man behind the curtain."

—The Wizard of Oz

Behind the Curtain

Purpose:

Recognize the people in your life who work behind the scenes to help people; show your appreciation for these people and how much you value their work.

Background:

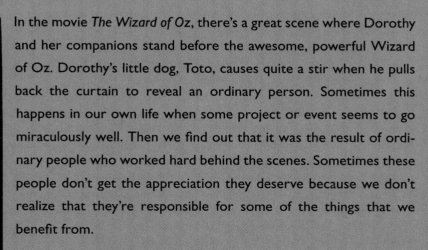

In the movie *The Wizard of Oz*, there's a great scene where Dorothy and her companions stand before the awesome, powerful Wizard of Oz. Dorothy's little dog, Toto, causes quite a stir when he pulls back the curtain to reveal an ordinary person. Sometimes this happens in our own life when some project or event seems to go miraculously well. Then we find out that it was the result of ordinary people who worked hard behind the scenes. Sometimes these people don't get the appreciation they deserve because we don't realize that they're responsible for some of the things that we benefit from.

continued on page 116 ▶

Faith in Action

▶ *continued from page 115*

Steps:

a. Look around your parish, school, or local community. Who are the people who do a lot of the behind-the-scenes work? Who are the people who work hard to help you, but whom we often forget to thank?

b. Think of creative ways that you can show your appreciation for these people.

A Labor of Love

Purpose:

Learn about child labor and the many children who are sold into labor because their families are poor; find out what you can do to raise awareness about child labor and poverty.

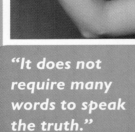

Background:

Although the work that people do is often valued because it is profitable, the people who actually do the work are sometimes not valued. The rights of workers are often ignored and trampled upon. This is a serious injustice and is especially shocking when those workers are children. In 1995, 12-year-old Craig Kielburger decided to do something about it. With 11 school friends, he founded Free the Children to begin fighting child labor. This foundation continues today by helping young people help children throughout the world. Their goal is "to free children from abuse, exploitation, and the idea that they are not old enough or smart enough or capable enough to change the world."

> *"It does not require many words to speak the truth."*
>
> —Chief Joseph, leader of the Nez Percé tribe

Steps:

a. Research child labor and learn about the causes and what can be done.

b. Connect with people in your area or across the world who have the same concerns that you do. Check out the Youth Zone at Free the Children.

c. Take a stand and speak out. Find a way to raise awareness about the issues that you have learned about.

d. Consider ways that you can promote just working conditions in your community.

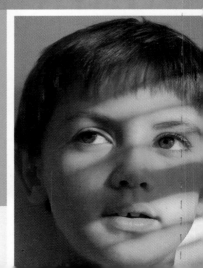

Matthew Presents the New Moses

THE GOSPEL OF MATTHEW

The Gospel of Matthew was written in a Jewish-Christian community in Syria about the year 85. One ancient tradition attributes the Gospel to the disciple and apostle of Jesus named Matthew. It is more likely that the writer was a leader in the local church, possibly a converted rabbi, who was well versed in the Scriptures. As a leader he was faced with a number of issues. Matthew was facing the challenge of Jewish Christians interacting and worshipping with Gentiles, who were also members of the community. When it became clear that the majority of Jews would not become Christian, Matthew encouraged the Jewish Christian community to recognize itself as the true heirs of God's promises to Israel.

For the Gentile members of the community Matthew showed that Jesus came to save the world. Matthew incorporates Gentiles into the very beginning of the story of Jesus. He is the writer who tells the story of the Wise Men from the east who were the first to pay homage to Jesus as the Messiah. (Matthew 2:10–11) The Wise Men were not Jews. They were Gentiles, just like part of the audience of the Gospel. Matthew stresses that Jesus tells the disciples to proclaim the Gospel to the world, baptizing in the name of the Father, the Son, and the Holy Spirit. (Matthew 28:19–20) The message and love of Jesus is not for Jews alone.

Jesus in Matthew's Gospel

Not only does Matthew present Jesus as the new Moses but also as one who is superior to Moses in every way. In his Gospel, Matthew describes how Jesus retraced the steps of Moses' journey. Mary and Joseph took the infant Jesus to Egypt to escape the murderous rage of King Herod. They stayed there until the death of Herod. Like his Hebrew ancestors, Jesus was called out of Egypt, and he retraced their journey to the Holy Land. (Matthew 2:15)

Exodus 19–20 describes how Moses went up on Mt. Sinai to receive the Law from God. Matthew 5–7 recounts how Jesus went up a mountain not to receive the Law, but to deliver the new law. Moses spoke with God's authority, but Jesus spoke with his own authority as the Son of God. As the Son of God, Jesus understands and proclaims the true meaning of the Law. Through faith in Jesus, all Christians will understand the true meaning of the Law as interpreted by Jesus.

The New Law

Matthew had great respect for the Law. He wished to emphasize its continuing validity for the both Jewish and Gentile Christians. Jesus says,

> "Do not think that I have come to abolish the law or the prophets. I have come not to abolish but to fulfill. Amen, I say to you, until heaven and earth pass away, not the smallest letter or the smallest part of a letter will pass from the law, until all things have taken place." (Matthew 5:17–18)

But Jesus is also the one who understands and proclaims the true meaning of the Law. Through faith in Jesus, Christians will follow the true intent of the Law.

Matthew and the Church

Matthew was particularly concerned that the Church was recognized as the group to pass on the real meaning of Jesus' identity. He stresses that Peter, as the head of the disciples, is the leader of the Church. (Matthew 10:2) Since Peter is the leader of the Church, he shares Christ's authority. (Matthew 10:40; 9:8) God is united with his people through the Church that is called to a worldwide mission by Jesus. (Matthew 28:18–20)

Matthew in this Unit

The main theme from Matthew discussed in this unit is Jesus as Emmanuel or "God with us." As the Son of God, Jesus speaks with authority as he teaches us in the Sermon on the Mount. Matthew is also a strong Gospel source for understanding the role of the Church as the group passing on the truth about who Jesus is and what he has accomplished for us. This ministry is continued in the work of popes, bishops, priests, and deacons today and throughout the Church's history. We also examine the Sacraments at the Service of Communion—Holy Orders and Matrimony—and the contributions they make to help us live Christian lives.

ALSO KNOWN AS
A.K.A.

We were all given carefully chosen names at birth. Some of us like to be called by those given names. Others prefer nicknames that have evolved over time. Still others like to be known by their initials, such as D.J. What do you like to be called?

✓ IT OUT

Do you know how you were named? Check those that apply to you.

▭ parent's favorite name	▭ based on a saint's name
▭ sounds good	▭ named after someone
▭ popular name at the time	▭ fits my personality
▭ family member's name	▭ picked at random
▭ based on a song or movie	▭ don't know
▭ reflects cultural heritage	▭ other: ▭▭▭▭▭

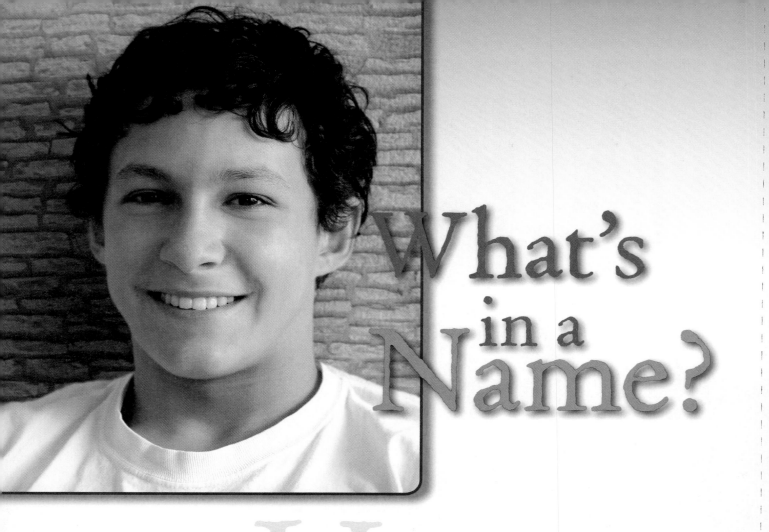

What's in a Name?

Have you ever talked with a friend about the meaning of a name you think is unique or interesting? It may be the name of another friend or the name of a star in pop culture. Back in the days when Matthew wrote his Gospel, people often talked about what names meant. A girl named Elizabeth would grow up knowing that her name meant "God is my oath," and a boy named Isaac would know that his name meant "laughter."

JESUS

The name *Jesus* means something too. It means "God saves" in Aramaic. Why would parents give their child such a loaded name? To answer that question, we have to go back to the time before Mary and Joseph were married.

In Matthew 1:18–25 we learn that when Joseph found out that Mary was pregnant, he was troubled by the news. Not only were they not married yet, but they hadn't had a sexual relationship. Who was the father? Joseph could have told everyone about Mary's pregnancy, and she would have been shamed in front of her family and her village. Joseph, a kind and just man, was unwilling to expose her. Instead he planned to leave her quietly.

Then an angel appeared to Joseph telling him to accept Mary as his wife because she was with child through the power of the Holy Spirit. Mary would have a son. "You are to name him Jesus, because he will save his

> Matthew's Gospel is all about God living and working among us.

people from their sins," the angel said. Joseph would have understood this because he knew that the name *Jesus* meant "God saves." Joseph certainly did not understand how it would happen, but he knew that somehow Jesus would save his people. Jesus' followers came to know that it is only through Jesus that we can have true happiness and live in communion with God. In response to the visit of the angel, Joseph accepted Mary into his household and cared for the child Jesus as his own son.

GOD IS WITH US

After Matthew tells this story in his Gospel, he reflects on the meaning of the angel's visit to Joseph. He says that the birth of Jesus fulfilled an Old Testament prophecy. The prophet Isaiah had said that "the virgin shall be with child and bear a son, and they shall name him Emmanuel." Matthew is not sure that all of his readers know what Emmanuel means, so he tells them—it means "God is with us." But Joseph and Mary would have known. They would have understood that somehow Jesus represented God's presence among us.

The name Emmanuel is a major statement of our faith. God is with us. That is one of the main things that Matthew wants to tell us in his Gospel. He mentions it at the start of his Gospel, telling us that Jesus is Emmanuel—God with us. He mentions it again in the middle of his Gospel, when Jesus tells his followers that wherever two or three are gathered in his name, he is present with them. And he mentions it at the very end of his Gospel, when Jesus says, "I am with you always, even to the end of the age." You might say that Matthew's Gospel is all about God living and working among us.

Another part of the angel's message to Joseph is important for us. It is the part about the Virgin being with child. What takes place in Mary is truly marvelous. It is the completion of a process that had begun many centuries before. After Adam and Eve turned their backs on God in sin, God rescued the human race from total destruction by saving Noah and

continued on page 122 ▶

names describing **God** are given below. **Choose one** that is meaningful to you. **What does this name reveal** about God? **What** does it **call** you to do or be?

The Mighty	The Forgiver
The Protector	The Provider
The Compassionate	The Sublime
The Powerful	The Gatherer
The Responder	The Appreciative

A Friend Is One Who's There

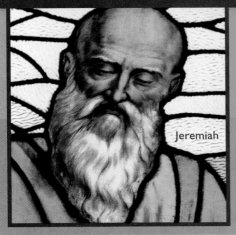

Jeremiah

Ask people what a friend is, and they will usually tell you that a friend is someone who is always there when you need him or her. If that is what a friend is, then God is portrayed as a friend in the Old Testament. God told Abraham not to be afraid because he would be with him. God told Joshua that just as he had been with Moses, so now he would be with Joshua. On several different occasions God told the prophet Jeremiah he would be with him even though he was surrounded by enemies. When the Jewish people were exiled in Babylon for about 50 years, God spoke to them through Ezekiel and told them that he was with them. When they got back to their own land, life was very hard for them. The prophet Haggai assured them that God was still with them.

Jesus fulfilled all these Old Testament experiences of God's presence among his people. God walked among us in the person of Jesus, and after he had ascended into heaven, Jesus and the Father sent the Holy Spirit to the Church so that God will always be with us.

Uncertainty and hardship are inescapable facts of life. Even in the worst of times, however, we have God's word that he will always be there for us when we need him. God is our closest and most reliable friend.

▶ *continued from page 121*

his family during the Flood. God made an everlasting covenant with Noah and with all living beings that never again would a flood destroy the earth.

But God wanted to do more for us. He chose Abraham and made a covenant with him, a covenant which God will never break. God promised Abraham that he and his descendants would be God's special people. God renewed his covenant with Moses on Mount Sinai when he gave Moses the Ten Commandments. God also told King David that he would forever keep his promise to his descendants. The prophets understood that the covenants with Noah, Abraham, Moses, and David were leading up to a "new covenant" that would bring salvation to the whole human race.

MARY

The time had come for God to complete the covenant he had begun many centuries before. The Holy Spirit overshadowed the Virgin Mary and the child she carried was to be named Jesus, the savior of the world. The angel wanted Joseph to understand that Mary's child was the fulfillment of the covenant of old. That is why at the beginning of his message, the angel refers to Joseph as the "Son of David."

IM

"What good must I do to gain eternal life?"
(Matthew 19:16)

As the foster father of Jesus, he passed on this title to Jesus, showing that Jesus fulfills the covenants with Abraham and David.

Jesus himself then represents the "new covenant." The name *Emmanuel* expresses the terms of the covenant. God promises to be with us, and we promise to have faith in Jesus and to follow him. The rest of Matthew's Gospel shows us the things we must do to follow Jesus and the many ways in which God lives and works among us. FG

The Challenge

Matthew 19:16–22 tells the story of a rich young man who came to Jesus and asked what he had to do to be saved. Jesus told him to keep the commandments. The young man said he always did. Then Jesus told him what he had to do if he wanted to strive for more. Jesus told the man that he had to sell all that he owned and follow him. Jesus was teaching something important to young people. If you just want to grow up, all you have to do is what you are told to do. But if you want to grow up to be a mature adult with a full life, then you will have to do more.

Jesus challenges you the way he challenged the rich young man. He wants you to grow up loving him with all your heart. He wants you to love him the way he loves you—completely.

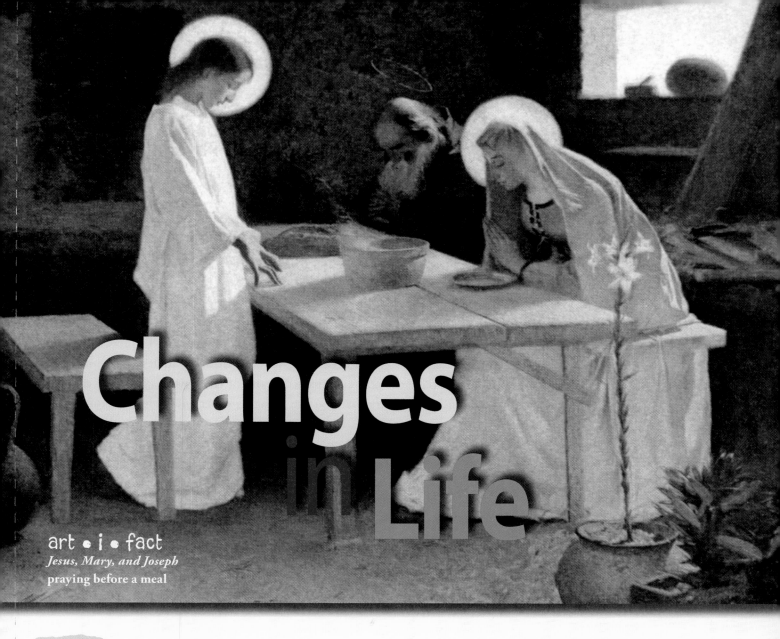

Changes in Life

Parents sometimes get angry with their children and tell them to "grow up." Maybe that has happened to you. Well, now you can tell everybody that you are almost grown up. In a few years you are going to be a high school student. You are entering adolescence. In adolescence you grow up fast, even though sometimes it doesn't seem like it's fast enough.

In adolescence we experience challenges to our faith and the practices that have been passed down to us.

CHANGE

Many things happen to us when we are adolescents. Our bodies grow physically and develop sexually. We think and learn in new ways. We begin to think and feel differently about ourselves. The way we relate to our parents, our friends, and everybody else changes. We want to be more independent, and we want to have lasting relationships.

Another relationship that changes is the one we have with God. Up until our adolescence, we pretty much follow the lead of our parents and relate to God and the Church the way they do. In adolescence we experience challenges to our faith and the practices that have been

continued on page 124 ▶

Testing the Foundation

Jesus was a good teacher. He knew how to get through to his students. One way he did this is shown in Matthew 7:24–27. Jesus used examples from ordinary life as teaching tools. For example, his listeners knew that you should not build a house on top of a sandy beach. The house would simply slide into the water the first time a storm came. On the other hand, if you built your house on top of a hill made of solid rock, your house wouldn't move in a storm. Jesus used this knowledge to help his listeners understand how important it is to base life on a solid foundation. If you try to build your life on the basis of something flimsy, like what people think or what is popular, you will lose control of it. However, if you build your life on a strong foundation, such as accepting Jesus' teaching and acting as he taught us to act, you will be able to overcome life's challenges.

▶ *continued from page 123*

passed down to us. We have free will, and we can choose to cooperate with God and become mature adults, or we can choose to refuse God's help.

ANCHORS

This period of your life into which you are entering may turn out to be difficult for you. If you are fortunate, there are some anchors that will hold you steady and keep you from being lost at sea. One such anchor is a good family—close relatives who love you and are always ready to help you ride out the storms that come your way in life. Another anchor is a good school environment, with teachers who care about you and friends who accompany you in your journey through adolescence.

The anchor that matters most to Christians is the presence of God. When Matthew wrote about Jesus being Emmanuel, God with us, he was thinking about the presence of Jesus to all of humankind. His message has great meaning for teens because Jesus went through adolescence himself. He was a teenager and experienced many of the tensions between childhood and adult years that you are going to experience. How meaningful it is to know that God is with us every moment of our lives. With Jesus at your side, you can learn from your experiences and become the person God wants you to be. Jesus the teenager grew into a man of prayer and service, someone willing to sacrifice himself for the sake of others. He loved everyone, even his enemies, and was especially devoted to the poor, the sick, and those rejected by society. That is the kind of person you can become in your teen years, with the help of Jesus.

God will be with you as you journey through adolescence. You will not have to face all the challenges by yourself. Whenever you face a tough situation, remember Emmanuel, remember that God is with you. FG

I'm not a caviar anymore. Everyday I grow and change.

footnote

We sometimes refer to people as being down to earth. Matthew's Gospel, especially his genealogy of Jesus and the story of Jesus' birth, shows that Jesus is fully human; he is God and man. Matthew refers to Jesus as Emmanuel, meaning "God with us," to show that through Jesus, God became one of us. For this reason, the symbol of Matthew's Gospel has traditionally been a man to represent how "down to earth" God chose to become.

Come, Follow Me

FEELINGS AND PRAYER

Sometimes we are tempted to think that we can pray only when we put our feelings aside and just concentrate on God. But in reality we pray best when we bring our feelings, which connect our senses and our minds, to our prayer. We pray best when not only our will but also our heart is engaged in our prayer.

The Holy Spirit, who makes it possible for us to pray, accomplishes his work in us by mobilizing our whole being, with all of our sorrows, joys, fears, and loves. Jesus learned this by praying the Psalms, which describe the whole range of human emotions. He taught us that our feelings can be part of our prayer when he expressed joy to his Father for revealing the kingdom not only to the educated and to the leaders of the time but to everyone. (Matthew 11:25) Jesus also taught this by example when he expressed the anguish of his agony and Passion. (Matthew 26:38–39)

Come, Follow Me

As we mature in our faith lives, we're always looking for ways to grow closer to Jesus. Sometimes the best way to find out how to grow closer to him is to ask. The rich young man in the Gospel did exactly that and received an answer he wasn't expecting. Sometimes things like material possessions, ideas, or behaviors get in the way of our following Jesus. From time to time it's good to stop and to evaluate our direction and how we can respond more fully to Jesus' call to follow him.

Prepare: Begin by focusing your attention on your breath. Be aware of your breath as it flows in and out. Let go of any distracting thoughts. Open yourself to receive the Word of God.

Read: Matthew 19:16–22 (The Rich Young Man)

Meditate: In your imagination, place yourself at the scene with Jesus and the rich young man. Listen to their conversation and observe their facial expressions. How do you think the young man might have been feeling at the beginning of the conversation? At the end?

Read a second time: Matthew 19:16–22 (The Rich Young Man)

Meditate: Now imagine yourself in the place of the rich young man. Hear yourself ask the same question as the rich young man, "What do I still lack?" and listen to Jesus as he answers you.

Use the space below to write down any words or phrases that you want to remember.

Pray: Share your reflections with God in your own words. Ask him if there is anything else in this story he'd like you to notice. Then thank God for this time of prayer.

Contemplate: Spend a few moments in prayerful silence with God.

Close by praying together: Jesus, you call us to follow you just as you called the rich young man. Help us to be generous in leaving behind what gets in the way of saying yes to your call. We ask this with confidence in your name. Amen.

What's **WHAT?**

■ Main points from this chapter are listed below. Choose one that you could explain further to others. Write what you would say on the lines below.

• Jesus' name in Aramaic means "God saves."

• The word Emmanuel means "God is with us," and expresses the terms of the new covenant between God and his people.

• Jesus himself represents the "new covenant."

• Adolescence is a challenging time when God's presence is needed.

• The Gospel stories of the rich young man and the house built on rock teach us that we will be able to overcome life's challenges with Jesus as our foundation.

_____

_____

_____

Say **WHAT?**

Emmanuel

So **WHAT?**

■ Another name for Jesus is Emmanuel, or God with us. He is available to us anytime, anywhere. *Think about it. Pray about it.*

Now **WHAT?**

■ What is one thing I can do this week to help strengthen the foundation of my faith in Jesus?

_____

_____

_____

Here's **WHAT** the Catholic Church Teaches

Catholic Relief Services was founded in 1943 by the bishops of the United States. Its mission was and still is to assist the poor and disadvantaged, to alleviate the suffering of all people, to promote the development of communities and individuals, and to work for peace and justice throughout the world. The organization focuses on the belief that each person possesses a basic dignity that comes directly from God. It believes that national, cultural, and religious identities are not as important as the fact that we are all part of the global family. Basically, all people in the world, no matter who they are, are our sisters and brothers.

Catholic Relief Services believes that people need help in developing favorable economic, social, political, material, spiritual, and cultural conditions. Providing this help will erase boundaries between people and will help everyone flourish. There is an impact on all of us if anyone is left behind. That is why the organization believes that the poor and forgotten people of the world are in the most dire need for assistance. One way Catholic Relief Services helps is by providing ways for individuals and parishes to participate in the mission to help people in need.

Paired Interview

Your name _____

Your partner's name _____

Title of article read by your partner _____

_____

Q&A

Ask your partner the following questions about the article he or she read and record his or her answers in the space provided.

1. Explain what your article was about in a few sentences.	
2. What is one quote (sentence) from your article that you would put on a poster to inspire the group? Why?	
3. What are some specific things your article helped you to learn or realize about the Catholic faith?	
4. Based on your article, name some specific things we, as Catholics, need to know, do, or believe in order to live as followers of Jesus.	

GOING THE EXTRA

Mile

When you want to achieve a goal, you've got to be willing to stay focused, avoid distractions, and remember the heart of your goal—why you're doing what you're doing. Whether your goal is to perform in the city orchestra, raise money for a neighborhood park, or finish a marathon, the heart of your goal has to be strong enough to make you willing to go the extra mile. What is one thing that you are willing to go the extra mile for?

For Your Eyes Only

What's the goal that is most important to you right now? What are some steps you will take to work toward this goal?

Goal:	Steps:

Living *in a* NEW Way

You can count on it! Every year around Easter, movies about the life or passion of Jesus are rerun on TV. Another film that shows up around the same time is *The Ten Commandments*. Although it is an older movie, it uses what were then state-of-the-art special effects in telling the story of Moses. In one dramatic scene, Moses is on the top of Mount Sinai watching the Ten Commandments being burned into stone tablets. He then reverently picks them up and carries them down the mountain to the people.

If, like Matthew, you had been born and raised a Jew, you would have known Moses' story from your yearly celebrations of Passover. When Matthew wrote his Gospel, he wanted to help his readers understand how Jesus was like Moses and how Jesus was different from Moses. Moses went up the mountain and brought down the Ten Commandments. Jesus went up on a mountain like Moses did. Jesus gave the people instruc-tion, or law, like Moses did. But there was a difference. Moses gave the people the instruction he received from God. Jesus gave them instruction not from someone else but from himself. He spoke with his own authority as the Son of God.

We call Jesus' instruction the Sermon on the Mount. You can find it in chapters 5–7 of Matthew's Gospel. The centerpiece of the Sermon on the Mount is what has become known as the Beatitudes, eight state-ments describing who the "blessed" people are. They are those who meet the challenge to live according to the values of Jesus. Living the Beatitudes will help us enter the Kingdom of Heaven—Matthew's term for the Kingdom of God.

UNDERSTANDING THE BEATITUDES

The Beatitudes are easily misunderstood. One of the beatitudes says that you are blessed when you mourn. Does that mean that Jesus wants you to cry all the time? No, it means that Jesus wants you to be deeply moved to do something when you see people suffering. Another beatitude says that you are blessed when you are meek. Does that mean that you should let people mistreat you or that you should stand by and watch others be mistreated? No, Jesus wants you to stand up for your rights and the rights of others, but in a firm and respectful way.

ACCEPTING THE BEATITUDES

The Beatitudes are not easy to accept. Society encourages you to become wealthy and to live comfortably. The Beatitudes encourage you to be poor in spirit, to detach yourself from craving wealth and comfort so that you can live a life based on Jesus' values. The world encourages you to look out for your own good. The Beatitudes encourage you to be concerned for justice and look out for the good of others. It is easy to see how the teachings of the Beatitudes are the opposite of the way society encourages you to live.

NOT EASY TO LIVE

It takes courage to live the Beatitudes. One of the beatitudes encourages you to be a peacemaker. Sometimes it may seem easier to start wars than to maintain peace. Maybe that is because it takes courage to live out another of the beatitudes, the one that tells us to be merciful. It is hard to be merciful to your enemies. In fact, the Beatitudes challenge us to live in ways that society does not encourage or even understand.

continued on page 132 ▶

ⓕⓞⓞⓣⓝⓞⓣⓔ

The Kingdom of God is spoken about frequently in the Gospels of Matthew, Mark, and Luke. It is interesting to note that in places where Matthew has stories similar to those in Mark and Luke, he uses the phrase "Kingdom of Heaven" instead of "Kingdom of God." Matthew was intentional about changing the phrase. He wrote to a Jewish audience who respected God so much that they would avoid using the word *God* out of respect for his name. Matthew knew this and he also knew that his readers were already familiar with the idea of God's kingdom being in heaven. He may have changed the phrase to make it easier for his readers to connect their Jewish experience of God with the good news of Jesus.

Luke and Matthew

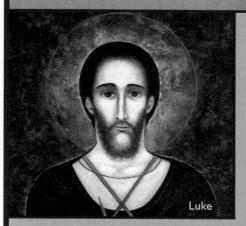

Luke

Matthew and Luke wrote their Gospels at about the same time, but their versions are very different. Matthew writes that Jesus taught from the top of a mountain. He wants to show that Jesus teaches with the authority of God. Luke, on the other hand, writes that Jesus taught on a plain, a flat area, because he wants to place Jesus on our level, as one of us.

In Luke's Gospel the poor are assured that God cares for them and that the Kingdom of God is already theirs. Those who are poor will have the Kingdom of God. Those who are hungry will be satisfied. Those who are weeping will laugh. (Luke 6:20–21) Luke also explicitly warns the rich who ignore their responsibilities to the poor. Those who are rich should know that they have received their consolation now and in this world. If they are filled now, they will be hungry later. If they laugh now, they will weep later. (Luke 6:24–26)

These differences highlight the richness of having four Gospels. Each Gospel writer emphasizes something unique about Jesus and his teaching, so that in reading four different Gospels, we get a more complete picture of Jesus.

THE BEATITUDES

Blessed are the poor in spirit,
for theirs is the kingdom of heaven.

Blessed are they who mourn,
for they will be comforted.

Blessed are the meek,
for they will inherit the land.

Blessed are they who hunger
and thirst for righteousness,
for they will be satisfied.

Blessed are the merciful,
for they will be shown mercy.

Blessed are the clean of heart,
for they will see God.

Blessed are the peacemakers,
for they will be called children
of God.

Blessed are they who are persecuted
for the sake of righteousness,
for theirs is the kingdom of heaven.

(Matthew 5:3–10)

*Blessed are the little fishies,
for they will inherit the ocean
(and hopefully, the big sharkies
will be disinherited).*

▶ *continued from page 131*

KINGDOM OF GOD

The Kingdom of God is the gathering by Jesus of those on earth who will begin to live the divine life the Father calls all of us to live. The more you study the Beatitudes, the more you will understand what the Kingdom of God is like. And the more you live the Beatitudes, the closer you will come to the Kingdom of God. Jesus does not want us to wait until we die to enter into the kingdom. He wants us to be part of God's kingdom now. The way to enter the kingdom is by living the Beatitudes.

> The Beatitudes challenge us to live good lives.

The Beatitudes are at the very center of Jesus' teaching in the Gospel of Matthew. They are gifts from God, teaching us what it means to live with God in eternal happiness. The happiness promised to us in the Beatitudes challenges us to live good lives, lives worthy of the Kingdom of God. We will have to make some difficult moral choices, but the reward will not only be living as God wants us to live. It will be eternal happiness with God. FG

TO LEARN MORE about the Beatitudes,
visit www.FindingGod.org/teens.

Think About What You See

It's unavoidable. If you watch television or play video games, you will undoubtedly see death and killing. The loss of human life is common in pop culture. By seeing so much violence, it's easy to become desensitized to the horror of taking another's life. It happens to all of us. The idea of killing can seem to be an everyday occurrence, like waking up or eating breakfast.

Matthew lived in the Roman empire, where human life was considered expendable. There were deadly gladiatorial games. When a leader wanted to suppress political enemies, he used violence. So Matthew knew something about death and killing. One thing he says that he learned from Jesus is that we should love our enemies, not kill them. In Matthew 5:21–24 Jesus also speaks about the hurt that can be caused by destructive anger, anger that leads to thoughts and acts of revenge or to actually hurting someone. He tells his disciples that those who act in this kind of anger will answer to the judgment of God. Jesus also says that if anyone is holding a grudge against someone, he or she must be reconciled with that person before coming to God in prayer.

IM

"But I say to you, love your enemies, and pray for those who persecute you."
(Matthew 5:44)

In this way Jesus fulfilled the meaning of the Fifth Commandment—"Thou shall not kill."

When Jesus gave us the Beatitudes in the Sermon on the Mount, he was teaching us to live in a healthy relationship with God and with others. Jesus wants us to respect other people and to treat their lives as sacred. That's not the kind of message you receive very often in the movies or on television. It is good to think about our Christian values regarding people and their lives.

Life

Jesus and his Church teach us that every person is created in the image and likeness of God. The life of every single person, therefore, is holy because God created that life and wants it to exist.

continued on page 134 ▶

The Good and the Bad

Let's follow a raindrop as it falls from a cloud. It falls faster and faster until just before it reaches the ground, it realizes that it will fall into the yard belonging to a man who has done a great deal of evil in his life. So the raindrop decides to move over and fall into the yard of the man's next-door neighbor.

Or let's follow a ray from the sun. It takes about eight minutes for the ray to reach the earth, but just as it is about to land, it realizes that it will brighten the day of a woman who has just committed a murder. The ray decides to move over and shine on another person. Sounds crazy, doesn't it? That's because it is crazy.

Raindrops and rays of sunlight do no such thing because the God who made them sends rain and sunshine to everyone, not just the good people. That is the model for us to follow. Our love should go out to everyone—the good and the bad, the just and the unjust. Even though it may not be easy to love those who don't love us or those we might consider our enemies, Jesus made it clear from his life and teaching that we cannot pick and choose when it comes to love. We are called to love everyone, even our enemies.

▶ *continued from page 133*

Many plots in police dramas center on a murder taking place. Killing is depicted so often that it almost becomes an afterthought. Because murder is the deliberate taking of another person's life, it shows great disrespect for life and for the Lord of life. God condemns murder because it goes against the dignity of the person and the holiness of God who made that person. Sometimes, however, someone will kill another person in self defense. That is not murder, and it is not sinful if it is the only way to defend oneself.

ABORTION

Protection of human life includes the life of the unborn. Every child has the right to life from the moment he or she is conceived. You might watch a movie or program in which a woman who is expecting a baby has an abortion. Such an action is gravely wrong, and Catholic mothers who have abortions and those who aid them receive the severe penalty of excommunication. This means that the person is no longer

IT OUT

Sometimes people refer to the Beatitudes as "be-attitudes." It's a catchy way to remember that the Beatitudes show us a set of values and a way of life that can inform our attitudes and help us to truly be persons of God. One reason they are so important is that they help us form healthy attitudes in contrast to the negative values we might pick up from society. The Beatitudes teach us to be steadfast, to be merciful, and to be full of joy and hope. What other be-attitudes can you find in the Beatitudes?

part of the Church community and cannot receive the sacraments or participate in Church activities.

EUTHANASIA

As Catholics we value the dignity of human life from conception until death. Often news reports and discussion programs raise issues about the quality of life that's possible if a person is severely disabled or is dying of old age. The question sometimes is whether it would be more merciful to kill that person. When a sick person is put to death so that he or she will not suffer any more, it is called euthanasia. Euthanasia is always wrong—it is a sin against hope. Instead, in situations of serious illness the person should be treated with care and respect and helped to live as normal a life as possible.

SUICIDE

The act of a person taking his or her own life is suicide. Our life has been entrusted to us by God, and we do not have the authority to take it into our own hands. Neither do we have the authority to kill ourselves in such a way that our action takes the lives of others. Such actions are a denial of justice, hope, and love. These actions also break the bonds of human solidarity because we are called to love one another. When a person privately takes his or her own life, we should remember that it is not our place to pass judgment on this act. Only God knows what causes a person to commit suicide, and we should pray for the salvation of that person.

Human life is the most precious gift that God gives to us. God calls us to respect this gift in the way we value the lives of others and our own lives. FG

IT'S LIKE THIS

Anger is one of those tricky things we call emotions. Like feelings—those natural sensations we all experience—emotions provide important information about ourselves. The more you are aware of what you are feeling or the emotion you are experiencing, the better you know yourself and the better you can relate to the world around you.

Feelings and emotions are neither good nor bad. They just are. The challenge is to channel that energy in healthy, life-giving ways. When Jesus expressed his anger at the money-changers in the Temple at Jerusalem, he was showing his deep respect for the holiness of the Temple and at the same time letting the people know that their actions were disrespectful. (Matthew 21:12)

IMAGE: *Jesus and the Money Changers*, Ed Blackburn, 1988, oil on canvas

Anger

Anger is not necessarily a bad thing. Some things ought to make you angry. If someone is threatening your life or anyone else's life, it should make you angry. If you or people you know and love are being badly and unjustly mistreated, it should make you angry. Anger can be good and necessary. But anger can also be a problem. It can take control of us so that we end up doing things that we shouldn't do. Jesus warned us not to have the kind of anger that will lead us into harmful action. He wants us to make sure that our anger leads us to act positively. He wants us to act to remedy a situation or to right a wrong. Hopefully our anger will always lead us to do things that will help, not hurt either ourselves or others.

20/20 Vision

MATTHEW ON PRAYER

In the Sermon on the Mount, Matthew presents his understanding of Jesus' teaching on prayer. Jesus insists that for true prayer to happen, our hearts must be converted. Reconciliation with others is necessary before we pray. We are to love our enemies and pray for those who persecute us. We are to pray to the Father privately so that others can't see us. In other words, we are not to be showy and make sure that others know we are praying. And we are not to pray by heaping up useless empty phrases. Instead we should pray with purpose, from the depths of our hearts.

Matthew assures us that the Father knows what we need before we ask him. He reminds us that if we seek we will find an answer, if we knock the door will be opened for us. As parents care for their children and provide for their needs, so God the Father will certainly provide for us and give good things to those who ask. It is also in the Sermon on the Mount that Jesus teaches his followers the Lord's Prayer.

Leader: God made us in his own image and likeness. Ever think about what that means? It can be easy to think about ourselves or those we love as made in God's image. But what about other people? Sometimes we have to search for that spark of God. We need 20/20 vision to help us see beyond the surface.

Take several deep breaths and allow yourself to become still. Close your eyes, and with your imagination, see your heart surrounded by light. Rest for just a moment, knowing that this light is from God. It is the same light that shines in every living creature.

All: God of all Creation, each of us has that spark of the divine that makes us holy. There is a reflection of you in each of us that needs to be seen by the world. We want to show others your face and to see you clearly in our sisters and brothers.

Group 1: Jesus, Light of the World, you are always with us and ready to walk with us. Sometimes our vision gets blurred by worldly values that are different from the ones you teach us. We need courage to revere and respect your divine life in all creation. We want to let our light shine.

Group 2: Spirit of Life, you live in us and remind us that we are never alone. When we have difficult choices to make, send your light and truth to guide us. May your wisdom lead us to love others as God loves them. We want others to see your life in us. Help us to see the divine life in others.

Leader: Let us pray the following blessing with and for each other and remember how important it is to support one another in living our life of faith.

All: May God bless you and be with you. May the holiness of God shine forth from you. May God grant you the vision to see his divine life in everyone you meet. Amen.

What's **WHAT?**

■ Review the main points of this chapter. Which one is most important to you? Write your reasons on the lines below.

- Matthew wanted to help his readers understand how Jesus was like Moses and how he was different.
- The centerpiece of Jesus' Sermon on the Mount is the Beatitudes.
- The Beatitudes describe life the way it is lived in the Kingdom of God.
- In the Beatitudes, Jesus teaches us to respect other people and to treat their lives as sacred.
- Jesus taught us to love our enemies and that destructive anger is against the will of God.

_____

_____

_____

Say **WHAT?**

abortion • **Beatitudes** • **euthanasia**
(abortion)

So **WHAT?**

■ How do the Beatitudes challenge you to live your life guided by values different from those of our society?

_____

_____

_____

Now **WHAT?**

■ What is one thing you can do with your friends this week to show your reverence and respect for the gift of life?

_____

_____

_____

_____

Here's **WHAT** the Catholic Church Teaches

The stockpiling of weapons does not ensure peace. Far from making war less likely, accumulating more and more weapons risks causing a war. Spending enormous sums of money to produce and develop new ways to kill fellow humans interferes with efforts to aid those in need around the world.

In 1965, in the *Pastoral Constitution on the Church in the Modern World,* the bishops called the accumulation of weapons "one of the greatest curses on the human race" and said that "the harm it inflicts on the poor is more than can be endured." Building up weapons stockpiles at the cost of helping the poor creates injustice. This injustice leads to excessive economic or social inequalities, envy, and distrust between peoples and nations. It constantly threatens peace and causes wars.

The Church believes that doing everything possible to overcome these injustices contributes to building up peace and avoiding war. Peace is not the mere absence of war. Peace is something that is built up day after day, in the pursuit of the just world God intended.

Making Connections

1. Read the article assigned to your group.
2. Note the main points from your article in the appropriate column below.
3. Join your group with a group who read the other article.
4. Record the main points in the appropriate column below.
5. Work together to complete the "Connect" section to show how the two articles connect.

Connect

How do these two articles connect?

NOTES FROM ARTICLE 1

LIVING IN A NEW WAY

NOTES FROM ARTICLE 2

THINK ABOUT WHAT YOU SEE

Main Points

Connection

Main Points

IT'S NOT *Fair*

How many times have you heard those words? Maybe you've said them yourself when you were loaded down with homework when a championship game was on TV. Maybe it was when "everybody" was going to a party and you couldn't because there was no adult supervision. Name some other times when things just don't seem fair.

First Rate

As you get older you become more and more aware of inequities in society, things on a bigger scale that may not be fair. Rate the following from 1 to 6, number 1 being the area of most concern for you. The left column is how you rate these issues now while the right column is how you might rate them as an adult.

Now		Future
	unemployment	
	taxes	
	distribution of wealth	
	educational opportunities	
	health care	
	welfare system	

Living in a Just Society

art • i • fact

King Herod on His Throne,
**14th century, mosaic,
Hora Church,
Istanbul, Turkey**

There are a lot of things we take for granted in the United States. The Declaration of Independence declares unequivocally that it is self-evident that the government should secure for its people the right to life, liberty, and the pursuit of happiness. The First Amendment of the Bill of Rights ensures that, among other things, there is freedom of speech, religion, press, and assembly.

When Jesus was born, the Jewish people had none of these rights that we enjoy. Their country was ruled by the Romans. To keep control of the population, the Romans imposed a king on the Jewish people. This king, Herod, collected taxes to ensure that roads would be maintained, harbors would be built, and the people would be kept docile, all in service to Rome. Herod was not a just ruler. His taxes hurt the people severely. His government did not exist to help his people. Its only goal was to help the rulers grow more wealthy and powerful.

Out of Egypt

Egypt is an important place in the Old Testament. The Israelites were slaves for four centuries in Egypt. Their escape by the grace of God is the Exodus, the biggest moment in their history. It is recounted in Exodus chapters 12–20. In the New Testament, however, there is only one story about Egypt, and it is found in Matthew's Gospel. In Matthew's congregation there were many Jewish converts, and he wanted them to see in Jesus the fulfillment of the promises made to Moses. Matthew tells how Joseph and Mary took Jesus to Egypt to save him from King Herod. Matthew connects his story to the Exodus, and that is why the way he tells his story is so important. It shows that God was at work in Jesus just as God had been at work in the Exodus. In both the Exodus and in Jesus, God is saving his people. Matthew knew that God used the Passover to help create a people of his own. Now Jesus would create a new people of God.

JUSTICE

The Old Testament model for a king was that of a shepherd—one who cared for the flock as God wanted them to be cared for. Herod didn't fit this ideal. He was like a wolf among the flock. He was ravenous, keeping his people poor and helpless while he used their money to fulfill his plans.

A just leader rules with values that promote virtue among the people. Herod, on the other hand, had no use for the idea of establishing a social order in which he would use his authority for

. . . girls pencil case and tried flushing it down the toilet

the good of the people. He cared only for what he wanted, not for what God desired. When Herod heard that a new king might have been born in the town of Bethlehem, he asked the Magi—the wise men—to tell him where this child, Jesus, was. When the Magi did not assist Herod in locating the child, he sent his soldiers to kill every baby boy living around Bethlehem. Killing innocent babies is a far cry from being a just ruler and promoting virtue among the people.

A Just Ruler

A just ruler's goal is the common good—all those things that make it possible for people to live the best lives they can as human beings. This goal is pursued out of respect for the dignity of all people. A just ruler wants people to have good lives—not only the people within the borders of the country, but people everywhere. A just ruler works with other rulers to help make the world a better place.

But Herod, of course, was not a just ruler. He was not interested in the common good or in people's well-being. He wanted only his own power, and so he created a society in which people lived in fear. In Matthew 2:13–23 we read that Mary and Joseph were afraid of Herod for the sake of Jesus, and they had good reason to be afraid, because Herod wanted to kill Jesus. So they traveled to Egypt and wouldn't come home until they were sure that Herod had died.

Matthew tells us that when Joseph and Mary learned of Herod's death, they took Jesus back to their hometown of Nazareth. But the death of the ruler did not mean that things were perfect. Under continued Roman rule, the Jewish people were treated unjustly. They did not get the kind of support from their government that they deserved as human beings.

Jesus' Way

Matthew makes it clear that Jesus was not born into a society where everyone was treated fairly. But when Jesus grew up and became a teacher, he taught people a different way of living life and building a society. He taught about the dignity of each individual and about God's love for each individual. Jesus taught about justice and love, about respecting other people, and about using political power and authority to help others. In his teachings Jesus emphasized the foundation for human dignity and respect that would eventually help lead to the establishment of governments that worked for the sake of the people and their needs. When you think about the way Herod ran his government, Jesus was a rebel and a revolutionary in his society. FG

Jesus taught about justice and love, about respecting other people, and about using authority to help others.

footnote

The story of Herod introduces us to Jesus' world—Palestine—a region occupied by a foreign power, the Roman empire. Palestine was filled with tense political, economic, social, and ethnic divisions between groupings such as the Pharisees (Jews devoted to the Mosaic Law), the Sadducees (the Jewish priestly aristocracy), the Samaritans (people of mixed ethnicity), the Gentiles (non-Jews), the Herodians (Jews who were Roman sympathizers), and the Zealots (Jews who sought Jewish independence). Matthew's Gospel tells us that Jesus, a Jewish teacher, refused to discriminate according to these divisions and angered many people by interacting with Gentiles, outcasts, and sinners. At the end of Matthew's Gospel, the risen Christ sends his disciples out to cross all boundaries by making disciples of all nations.

When We Are Tempted

Farmers living in Israel back in Jesus' time did not have much to work with. They owned small plots of rocky land. Not all of the land could be used for crops. The house occupied part of the land, and the animals were kept on another part. The rest of the land, every inch of it, had to produce enough grain to feed the people and the animals.

SOWING THE SEED

At the beginning of the growing season, the farmer would walk around his small plot of land and throw seed everywhere. His purpose was to attempt to have seed growing wherever it could grow. Of course, he knew that much of the seed wouldn't make it. Some of the seeds would fall on rocks, and when the rain came, the seeds would open up but they couldn't live because they couldn't spread roots into the solid rock. Other

seeds would fall on the walkways, but people and animals would walk on the seeds and keep them from opening up. Other seeds fell in fertile places, but the birds would come and eat them. Still other seeds would fall underneath bushes, but when they sprouted and grew, the plants became tangled in the bushes and were not able to produce. Fortunately some of the seeds fell on good ground and were not eaten by birds. Where this happened, the seeds were able to take root and the crops flourished.

PARABLE OF THE SOWER

Jesus tells us this parable in Matthew 13:1–13. He was aware that his listeners would know what he was talking about because everybody understood how hard it was to farm the rocky land. In fact, most of his listeners grew their own food in this manner. They all understood about seed falling in the wrong places.

Matthew 13:18–23 goes on to say how Jesus explained the message of the parable. The seed, Jesus taught, is God's Word. Some of it falls in places where it can live and flourish, and some of it falls where it cannot sprout and grow. In other words, there are

IM "But the seed sown on rich soil is the one who hears the word and understands it."
(Matthew 13:23)

Good intentions to avoid temptation can blow away like seeds in the wind if they are not rooted in prayer and perseverance.

people who hear God's message but it does nothing for them. It does not grow within them. But then there are people who hear God's message, and it takes root beautifully in their lives. These people bear much fruit because God is at work in their lives.

TEMPTATIONS

Young people face many temptations—things that can get in the way of being faithful to the Word of God. Bad relationships, drugs, alcohol, violent and sex-filled movies, friends who encourage you to do things you know you shouldn't do—these kinds of temptations can keep the Word of God from bearing fruit in your life. Giving in to temptation makes you like stony ground where seeds can't take root and grow. Good intentions to avoid temptation can blow away like seeds in the wind if they are not rooted in prayer and perseverance.

continued on page 144 ▶

Charles F. Kettering, a great American inventor and engineer, once said, "There is a great difference between knowing and understanding; you can know a lot about something and not really understand it." In other words, there is a difference between merely acquiring information and truly getting its meaning. So it's good to know the details of the story of the temptation of Jesus. However, it's more important to understand that the story encourages us to be faithful in the face of temptations.

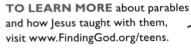

TO LEARN MORE about parables and how Jesus taught with them, visit www.FindingGod.org/teens.

Yes, We Understand

Jesus worked hard to teach his disciples and prepare them to lead his Church. He gave them additional explanations of the parables he used, and he answered their questions. He gave them the example of his own life and tried to help them understand what he was doing. Matthew tells us that at one point in his work with them, Jesus asked his disciples if they understood the meaning of his parables. They answered yes, they did understand. That is important for us to know. If they had not understood Jesus' teachings, they would not have been able to pass them down to us. The correct teaching of Jesus has come to us, safeguarded by apostles who understood Jesus' teaching and by the successors to the apostles—the popes and the bishops. It is because of them that we are able to learn and understand the teachings of Jesus.

When Jesus Was Tempted

Matthew 4:1-11 tells the story of when Jesus was led by the Spirit into the desert to fast and to pray. After 40 days and 40 nights, Satan appears and offers three temptations.

The first temptation tests Jesus' resolve with food, as he has had nothing to eat for 40 days. Jesus rejects the suggestion that he change stones into bread, as the Son of God is fed by God, not by bread alone. Satan then takes Jesus to the top of the Temple and tells him to jump, for surely God would save him. Jesus replies that the Son of God does not put the Father to such foolish tests. Satan then offers Jesus the chance to rule the world if he would only worship Satan. Jesus replies that the Son of God worships God alone.

The temptations recall the Israelites' struggle in the desert, but in this case Jesus succeeds where the Israelites failed to follow God. They also recall the temptations of Adam and Eve in the garden. Jesus, the new Adam, remains faithful where the first Adam gave in. In making his decisions in obedience to his Father, Jesus defeated Satan for us. He truly understands how difficult it is for us when we face temptations. Jesus is like us in every way, but he alone follows God perfectly and without sin.

► *continued from page 143*

Young people are especially challenged with temptations to use the gift of their sexuality in the wrong way. These temptations can't always be avoided, but resisting them gives you the chance to be faithful to God who wants you to live the best life you can. You can successfully resist any temptations when your intentions are rooted in the determination to follow God. In moments of temptation, the many saints who have gone before you can help you in your decisions. Mary also can help you, for she is a shining example of someone who has lived faithfully in God's way.

RESISTING TEMPTATIONS

There are many ways in which you can direct your youthful energy to actions that help yourself and others. You can participate in sports, or you can develop your artistic talents, whether they be in music, dance, writing, or the visual arts. You can also do volunteer work in the community. The more involved you are, the better the chance that your efforts will result in a healthy growth toward adulthood.

Keep in mind the parable of the farmer. Just as he knew that things would get in the way of his seeds growing, so you should know that you are going to have temptations. This means that you should prepare for them ahead of time. Think of the Church as the rich soil that will help the seed of faith grow in you. Think of Jesus as a friend. Turn to him often in prayer. Receive the sacraments, listen to Scripture, and make up your mind that you want to live a good life. By following these practices, you can be faithful to the Word of God. You will be able to bear much fruit in your life. FG

Whistle while you work. Wow, these seeds are growin' like weeds.

This Way Out

It's not easy to live justly or to help bring about justice in society. The temptation we face is to take the easy way out even if it goes against what we believe. Sometimes it's easier to stand by and do nothing than it is to take a stand. It's easy to go to lunch and sit at a table with friends. It's harder to take a stand and sit with the person people make fun of. It's easy to pretend that you didn't see your neighbor struggling to carry the groceries when your friends are waiting for you. It's harder to take a stand and offer a helping hand. A just society is built with seemingly small actions like these. What can you do to take a stand today?

Seeds of New Life

DISCERNMENT OF SPIRITS

How can prayer help you to know how to make decisions about your life? Saint Ignatius of Loyola asked himself this same question. He noticed that some decisions in his life left him feeling good—peaceful, affectionate, charitable—while others left him feeling unsatisfied—anxious, hollow inside, isolated. Ignatius reflected on these different experiences and, over time, developed a way to pray that would help him make good decisions. He called this discernment of spirits.

Ignatius explains that to make a good, prayerful decision, you have to consider the input from all of your senses. How you feel about something is just as important as what you think about it. You also have to consider how you feel and think in the context of what brings you closer to God.

To practice discernment, think about the decision you have to make. Keep your mind free of assumptions or preconceived ideas. Imagine how you would feel if you decided one way. Then, image how you would feel if you decided another way. Pay attention to what you are attracted to and what you resist. Where do you feel the Spirit of God moving you? By praying in this way, you can learn to be more attuned to God's presence in your life and learn how to make good decisions. Good decisions become like seeds of new life, bearing fruit for all the world.

Seeds of New Life

Leader: Just like the farmer in the story we read in Matthew's Gospel, Jesus planted lots of seeds during his life on earth. They weren't the kind of seeds that grow into something edible. They were seeds of justice and love, of respect for others and all of creation. His seeds weren't sown in the ground, but in the human heart. We have them in our hearts too. When carefully tended, these seeds grow and bear fruit that can be seen in the way we live our lives and make the world a better place.

Reader 1: (*Read aloud slowly; pause, then read again.*)

But the seed sown on rich soil is the one who hears the word and understands it, who indeed bears fruit and yields a hundred or sixty or thirty fold.

(Matthew 13:23)

Leader: The seeds that Jesus planted help us remember what it means to be truly human, made in the image and likeness of God. The fruit these seeds yield reminds us to live with values that honor and respect God, ourselves, each other, and all of creation. Let's pray together that the seeds sown in our hearts may bear abundant fruit in our lives for the world.

Reader 2: Our society encourages us to put ourselves and our happiness before the good of others. Open our hearts, O God, to include the needs of others and to be mindful of the ways we can be of service to them. We pray to the Lord.

All: Lord, may we yield a rich harvest.

Reader 3: Sometimes we let things get in the way of hearing God's message and following it. We can make choices that lead us away from God. Open our hearts, O God, to seek to strengthen the seeds you have planted in us through prayer, reading the Scriptures, and receiving the sacraments. We pray to the Lord.

All: Lord, may we yield a rich harvest.

Reader 4: It's easy to forget that the things of this earth are for our use and not to be exploited. Open our hearts, O God, to use wisely the gifts you have given us and to help preserve our natural resources for those who come after us. We pray to the Lord.

All: Lord, may we yield a rich harvest.

Leader: Jesus, sower of the seed, we want to be the good soil that yields a rich harvest of justice, love, and peace in our world. Help us to remember that you are always there to guide us. We ask in this in your name.

All: Amen.

What's **WHAT**?

■ Look over the main points of this chapter. What is one additional important insight you would add to this list? Write it on the lines below.

- A just leader rules with values that promote virtue and protect the common good.
- King Herod was an unjust ruler.
- Jesus taught people how to live with justice and love, respecting the dignity of each individual.
- By connecting the story of the Holy Family's journey to Egypt with the Exodus story, Matthew shows how God is saving his people.
- In the Parable of the Sower Jesus teaches that the seed is the Word of God and whether or not it grows in us depends on how we nurture the seed.
- Both Jesus and the Church will help us to overcome temptations.

- _____

_____

Say **WHAT**?

common good • dignity of the human person Satan

So **WHAT**?

■ How can living as Jesus taught us help make the world a better place?

_____

_____

_____

Now **WHAT**?

■ What is something you will do this week to help nurture the seed of faith planted in you?

_____

_____

Here's **WHAT** the Catholic Church Teaches

There is an obligation for all people to work toward universal respect for human rights and human dignity. This should be the most important goal of the social, economic, and political institutions of the world. No society can live in peace with itself without recognizing the worth and **dignity of the human person**. That is why the center of all Catholic social teaching is the belief in the dignity of the human person.

When any government accepts violence as a means of controlling its citizens, it moves away from this basic belief. And when it accepts violence at home, war in the world at large can be taken for granted.

In a letter written by the United States bishops in 1983 called *The Challenge of Peace*, they stated, "The human person is the clearest reflection of God's presence in the world; all of the Church's work in pursuit of both justice and peace is designed to protect and promote the dignity of every person. For each person not only reflects God, but is the expression of God's creative work and the meaning of Christ's redemptive ministry." In other words, each life is sacred, created so by the Lord of life. Because of this, every government needs to respect the human dignity of its citizens and to treat them with justice.

Cornerstones

1. As the two articles are read, note the cornerstones (main points) from each article in the appropriate column below.
2. With your group, share one cornerstone you identified from your group's assigned article. Keep sharing cornerstones until you have no new ones to share. Say "pass" if you have nothing new to add.

CORNERSTONES — ARTICLE 1	CORNERSTONES — ARTICLE 2
Living in a Just Society	When we are Tempted

MAY I HELP You?

When at a store or restaurant, how often have you heard the question, "May I help you?" People who are in the business of dealing with people are paid to be of service to others. When have you asked to help someone without looking for payment or a favor in return?

For Your Eyes Only

List one way that you can serve without expecting something in return.

at home:	in your parish:	in school:

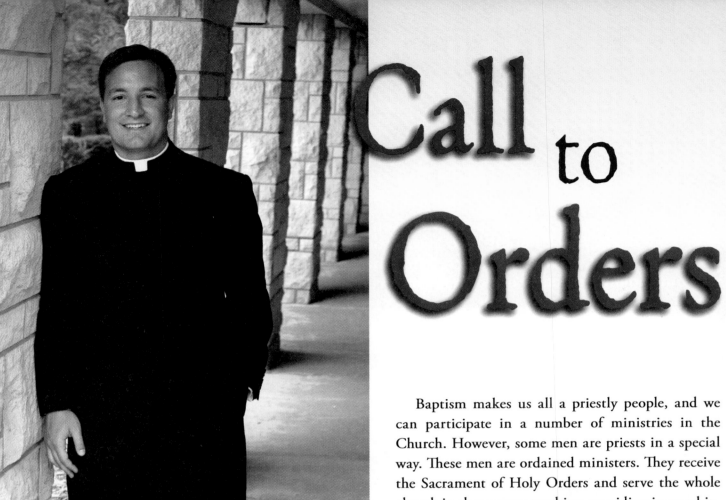

Call to Orders

Baptism makes us all a priestly people, and we can participate in a number of ministries in the Church. However, some men are priests in a special way. These men are ordained ministers. They receive the Sacrament of Holy Orders and serve the whole church in three ways: teaching, presiding in worship, and governing the Church. There are three degrees, or levels, of Holy Orders: deacons, priests, and bishops. All three degrees are essential to the structure of the Church.

DEACONS

Deacons are ordained so that they can serve the Church. Deacons are mentioned in the New Testament, but for many centuries the office of deacon did not play a big role in the Church. Men were ordained deacons as a step on the road to becoming ordained as priests. Then at the Second Vatican Council in the 1960s, the Church decided to give deacons a more prominent role in

When it came time for Jesus to begin his public ministry, he went to the Sea of Galilee. Matthew 4:18–22 tells us how Jesus walked along the banks of the sea and called some men to follow him. They were two pairs of brothers, Simon (Jesus would later name him Peter) and Andrew, and also James and John. They were fishermen who had steady jobs in an active trade, and they led busy lives. After hearing what Jesus had to say, they left everything and everyone behind. Through Baptism Jesus calls us to follow him in the same way.

People who are baptized into the Church are called to be witnesses in the manner of the Old Testament prophets because they speak up for the poor and needy and teach others about God. They are called to be like the Old Testament kings because they serve and protect those who cannot take care of themselves. They are also called to be like the Old Testament priests because they praise and worship God and ask him to help people.

IT'S LIKE THIS

Through our Baptism we participate in the priesthood of Christ. What does that mean? It means we are to make Christ present in the world today through all of our actions. As opportunities present themselves, we can offer a helping hand to someone in need—caring for them as Jesus would if he walked the earth today.

the ministry. Men can now be ordained deacons to serve in parishes without becoming priests. In this expanded role deacons may baptize, preach, and preside at weddings and funerals when there is no Mass. Today many parishes have deacons who assist in leading God's people in service to others and in worship.

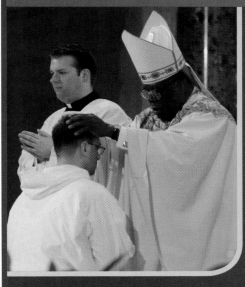

> After hearing what Jesus had to say, they left everything and everyone behind.

PRIESTS

Priests receive the Sacrament of Holy Orders in a higher degree than deacons. In addition to what deacons may do, priests offer the Sacrifice of the Mass and administer the Sacraments of Penance and Anointing of the Sick. They are coworkers with the bishop in teaching and governing the local Church. The bishop usually asks them to be the leader of a particular parish community.

BISHOPS

Bishops receive the fullness of the sacrament of Holy Orders. A bishop is the head of a diocese. He is also a member of the college of bishops and takes part in governing the universal Church under the authority of the Bishop of Rome, the successor of Peter. As bishops are successors of the apostles, they have full authority to teach, to lead the people in worship, and to govern the community. A bishop can administer the Sacrament

continued on page 152 ▶

The Sacrament of Holy Orders gives the Church its leaders in worship, education, and governing. For that reason, the Church takes seriously its obligation to choose the right men for the offices of deacon, priest, and bishop. The sacrament can be conferred only by a bishop acting in the name of the Church. In the Rite of Ordination, the bishop lays his hands on the head of the man being ordained. He then says a prayer of consecration, asking God to give the man the graces he will need to perform his duties as an ordained minister in the Church. The Sacrament of Holy Orders leaves a sacramental character on the man that can never be removed.

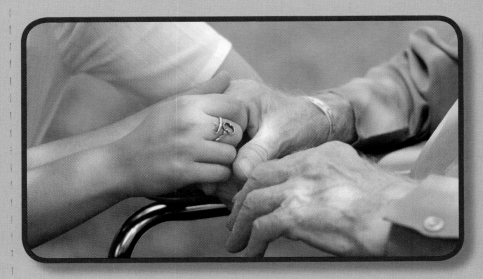

The priest at Holy Mackerel Church is amazing! Last weekend, he held his breath through five underwater Masses, 37 confessions, the annual pancake breakfast, and a lock-in with Young Crustaceans for Christ.

► *continued from page 151*

Of all the people in the Old Testament, why is it Moses and Elijah who appear with Jesus during the Transfiguration? Matthew knew that his Jewish readers would understand the symbolism of the story. Moses is seen as a representative of the law, while Elijah represents the prophets. And so when God says, "This is my beloved Son," Matthew is showing that the law and the prophets support that Jesus is the Son of God. Matthew was also trying to get across the idea that Jesus is hinted at and supported in the Old Testament. At the end of the Transfiguration, Moses and Elijah are gone, which Matthew may have used to signify that they are not as important to the people now that Jesus has been revealed as the Son of God.

of Holy Orders, ordaining deacons, priests, and other bishops. He is also the ordinary minister of the Sacrament of Confirmation.

Bishops, priests, and deacons help us to work together as a community. Each of them has a duty to perform in the Church. With them we all have the duty to work serving the Kingdom of God on earth. FG

art • i • fact
The Transfiguration,
Michael D. O'Brien,
acrylic on masonite

The Transfiguration

Chris wanted to go out on a date with Elaine. Elaine told him that the only day she had free was also the day she planned to visit a child with severe disabilities. She said that Chris could join her if he liked. Chris agreed. When they came to the child's room, Elaine played a tape of the child's favorite music. Then she loosened the necessary braces that kept the child immobile, took him in her arms, and gently held the child as she talked and sang to him. Chris later told Elaine that he had never seen God's love so visible in the world than when he saw the child in her arms. In her actions he saw a glimpse of the divine. Seeing such an act of love and kindness not only amazed him, it inspired him.

In Matthew 17:1–9 Peter, James, and John had a glimpse of the divine when Jesus brought them up on a high mountain. Not only were they followers of Jesus, but they were also his close friends. There they saw a hint of Jesus' glory; his face shone like the sun, and his clothes became white as pure light. Peter, James, and John were stunned. Jesus also appeared to be speaking to Moses and Elijah, two of the most important Old Testament prophets. Peter didn't want to leave—he wanted to linger in the presence of the divine. He wanted to set up three tents, one each for Moses, Elijah, and Jesus.

This was not to happen, though. The three apostles were covered by a cloud and heard the voice of God saying, "'This is my beloved Son, with whom I am well pleased; listen to him.'" (Matthew 17:5) The men were frightened out of their wits but also filled with wonder. They knew their friend, Jesus, was someone special, but this was beyond their wildest dreams. Then the moment passed, and only Jesus remained with the three apostles, telling them not to be afraid. Jesus led them down the mountain. He explained that this was not the time to remain transfixed on the divine. This was the time to continue learning how Jesus wanted them to share the good news of God's love with the world.

LEADERSHIP

in the Church

ABOVE: Pope Benedict XVI talks to a boy in Borreigne, Italy.

One day, after he had been teaching his disciples for some time, Jesus asked them whom they thought he was. Peter spoke up for the rest of them and answered that Jesus was the Messiah, the Son of the Living God. Matthew, Mark, and Luke all tell this story in their Gospels. Matthew, however, adds something the others do not. He says that Jesus then told Peter that he was the "rock" on which he would build his church. Peter would have special authority, and nothing would be able to destroy the church. (Matthew 16:13–20)

COLLEGE OF BISHOPS

Peter was the leader of the group of twelve disciples known as apostles. Jesus called on the apostles to proclaim the faith and serve the Kingdom of God. He sent them out to complete his work and to act in his name. Because the Church was built on the foundation of the apostles, we say that the Church is apostolic. Jesus governs the Church through Peter and the other apostles, who are present today in their successors, the college of bishops.

We use the term *college of bishops* to mean the assembly of the bishops from all over the world. The college of bishops, with the successor of Peter at their head, has full authority over the whole Church. In order to exercise this authority, they must always have the agreement of the successor of Peter.

Who then is the true head of the Church? Only one person has complete authority over the whole Church—Jesus Christ. He is the head of the Church.

But Jesus has ascended into heaven and sits at the right hand of the Father. We need someone here on earth to govern the Church for us. Originally Jesus assigned that task to Peter and his successors. Who carries on this ministry today?

BISHOP OF ROME

The ministry is carried on by the Bishop of Rome, the pope. The apostle Peter died a martyr in Rome, probably during the Emperor Nero's persecution in about 65. From the very beginning, Christians everywhere recognized that the Bishop of Rome was leader of the Church because he was the successor to Peter. He was the rock on which the Church was built.

IM "The harvest is abundant but the laborers are few." (Matthew 9:37)

VICAR OF CHRIST

As the Bishop of Rome, the pope is also the Vicar of Christ. A vicar is someone who acts in the place of another person. Christian authors have pointed out that we all serve as vicars of Christ because through our Baptism and Confirmation we all act as Christ in

continued on page 154 ▶

Instructions

When Matthew wrote his Gospel, he wanted his readers to understand what Jesus expected of them as disciples. In Matthew 10:5–15 he told his readers about Jesus' instructions to the twelve apostles. Jesus told them to go out with the confidence that they could do the same wonderful things Jesus was doing.

They were sent out to cure the sick, raise the dead, cleanse lepers, and drive out demons. If people rejected the apostles' message, they were to shake the dust off their feet and move on. They were not to rely on themselves but on God's grace and the help of others.

Their job was to bring the message and peace of the kingdom. They were not to force others to receive that message and peace. But to those who would listen to them, they were to pass on the good news of the kingdom and to bring peace and healing. Matthew wants us to understand that the instructions given by Jesus to his apostles also teach us what we should do as disciples of Jesus.

IMAGE: This modern icon of St. Matthew was created in the traditional Byzantine style by monks on Greece's Mount Athos.

▶ continued from page 153

the world. But when we use the term "Vicar of Christ" with capital letters, we mean the Bishop of Rome, the pope, the successor of Peter, who acts in the name of Christ in unique way.

We call the pope the Holy Father. As Catholics, we feel personally connected to him. That is where the title *pope* comes from—the Italian word for "papa." So when we say Pope Benedict XVI, we are calling him our father.

PASTOR

The pope is the shepherd of the whole flock that is the Church. The word *pastor* comes from the Latin word for "shepherd." He is our shepherd; that is, he is the one who looks out for our well-being. Each diocese has its own pastor, the bishop, and bishops call priests to be pastors of individual parishes. But the pastor of all Catholics is the successor of Peter, the Bishop of Rome.

Sometimes the pope and bishops exercise their authority in a more universal way. They come together in an ecumenical council, which must be recognized as such by the Holy Father. The last ecumenical council was the Second Vatican Council, held at the Vatican between 1962 and 1965.

THE CATHOLIC CHURCH

The pope, the bishops, the priests, and the laity together make up the Church, which is one, holy, catholic, and apostolic. It is a community where the fullness of God's holiness and truth are found. From this community Catholics are sent into the world to discover the ways in which God's holiness and truth are working and to support those efforts to serve the kingdom. FG

WISE GUYS

"Our priestly life is a life of the Spirit, for the Spirit, in the Spirit of the church."

— Karl Rahner, S.J.

Giving Without Cost

LITURGICAL PRAYER

We call the official prayers of the Church liturgical prayer. Some types of liturgical prayer are the Mass, the Liturgy of the Hours, and the celebration of the sacraments. The original meaning of *liturgy* is "public work," which means service done on behalf of the people. In the liturgy the Church celebrates the Paschal Mystery through which Christ accomplished the work of our salvation. The whole community of the baptized, with Christ at its head, celebrates each liturgy. At Mass different members of the community have different functions. Men ordained as priests lead the Eucharist and most celebrations of the sacraments.

However, lay people are also celebrants of liturgical prayer. Serving as readers, altar servers, and members of the choir are some ways in which the laity can be involved with the liturgy. Even by attending the liturgy the laity is involved in it. Thus the whole assembly celebrates, each according to his or her function and ability, as the Spirit unites and acts in all.

LEFT: *Peaceful Server*, Regina Kubelka, watercolor, Texas

Giving Without Cost

Ever since he called his first disciples, Jesus has been calling people to follow him. Followers of Jesus show their love for God by serving others. Listen again to Jesus' instructions to his first disciples.

> **As you go, make this proclamation: "The kingdom of heaven is at hand." Cure the sick, raise the dead, cleanse lepers, drive out demons. Without cost you have received; without cost you are to give.**
>
> **(Matthew 10:7–8)**

Let's spend a few moments in silence to reflect on Jesus' message to his disciples and to us.

In your imagination, place yourself with Jesus.

What are some things you have received freely from God? It might be a particular talent or special ability, something you are good at or just enjoy doing. Maybe it's a family who loves and supports you, or a friend who cares about you. Share your thoughts with Jesus.

Now Jesus reminds you that these gifts you've received weren't given just for you, but to be shared. We are called to serve others using our particular gifts.

Helping a classmate study for a test, spending time with an elderly relative or neighbor, or befriending a new student in school are all ways to use our gifts. Talk over with Jesus some ways you might use your particular gifts to serve others.

Jesus reminds you that serving others can be challenging and has hidden costs, things like using your free time or your allowance, or being teased by your peers.

You will face challenges in living out your faith in Jesus, just like the first disciples did. But Jesus also reminds you that he is with you to help and encourage you in your service of others. Spend a moment just resting in Jesus' presence. Then thank him for the gifts you've received and for this time of sharing.

Let's close by praying the following prayer aloud together.

> **Lord Jesus, make us aware of the gifts we've freely received from your Father's hands.
> Encourage us to develop our gifts.
> Inspire us to appreciate the gifts we've been given and to be open to the ways you call us to share them with others.
> May our service to others please you and help make the world a better place.
> We ask this with confidence in your name.
> Amen.**

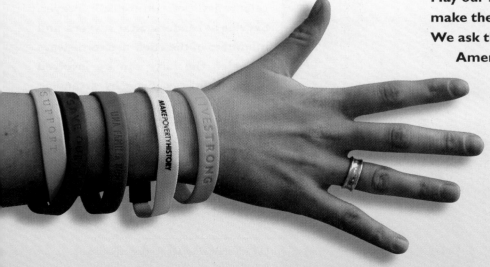

What's WHAT?

■ Main points from this chapter are listed below. Complete each sentence. Refer to the articles and sidebars for help.

• When Jesus called his first disciples, he went to

_____

• The three levels of Holy Orders are

Deacon, Preist, Bishop

• When Jesus called Peter the "rock" he meant that Peter would have

_____

_____

• The pope, bishops, and priests all have the duty to

Pastured the people

• In Matthew's Gospel, Jesus instructs his disciples to

_____

_____

Say WHAT?

**bishop • catholic • liturgy
ministry • pope • priest • subsidiarity**

T

So WHAT?

■ The mission of a disciple is to bring to others the message and peace of God's kingdom. *Think about it. Pray about it.*

Catholic = Universal

Now WHAT?

■ What is one thing you will do this week to grow in your understanding of the work of ordained ministers in the Church?

_____

_____

Here's WHAT the Catholic Church Teaches

The Second Vatican Council described how all the baptized comprise the People of God and how within the People of God the leadership of bishops and priests is called upon to govern, teach, and sanctify. The People of God can be thought of as one body with many parts, each with its own function. Paul describes it this way in 1 Corinthians 12:12–28.

The Church applies this image of how the People of God are organized into a society and calls it the principle of **subsidiarity**. A core principle of Catholic social teaching since the beginning has been that society as a whole is responsible for building up the common good. Issues in social development are best dealt with at the local level by people most directly involved with the issues.

The government's role is to interfere as little as possible at the local level while at the same time encouraging conditions that make rich social activity possible, human rights respected, and justice guaranteed. The United States bishops wrote in 1986 that good government intervention is "that which truly 'helps' other social groups contribute to the common good by directing, urging, restraining, and regulating economic activity." *(Economic Justice for All)*

We Can Change the World

1. **Read both articles silently.**

2. **In your group of 4, decide which article each pair will work on.**

3. **With your partner, complete the "Something to Think About…" section below, listing the important ideas presented in your article.**

4. **Exchange worksheets with the other pair in your group and complete the "How it Can Change the World" section below.**

5. **With your partner, select one "Something to Think About…Change the Word" idea and explain how and why this idea can make the world a better place.**

6. **With your partner, think of a role model you feel has changed the world in this way.**

ARTICLE NAME _____

SOMETHING TO THINK ABOUT	HOW IT CAN CHANGE THE WORLD

FOR WORSE OR
For Better

It's easy to deal with commitments in relationships or responsibilities when they are "for better." It's a bit tougher when they are "for worse." Even though we might be tempted to give up, with a little courage and determination we can stick with our commitments and see them through. When have you put in some extra effort to stick with a commitment?

For Your Eyes Only

Here's a list of some behaviors that are "for worse." What are alternatives that are "for better?"

Worse	Better
bullying	
complaining	
bragging	
rudeness	

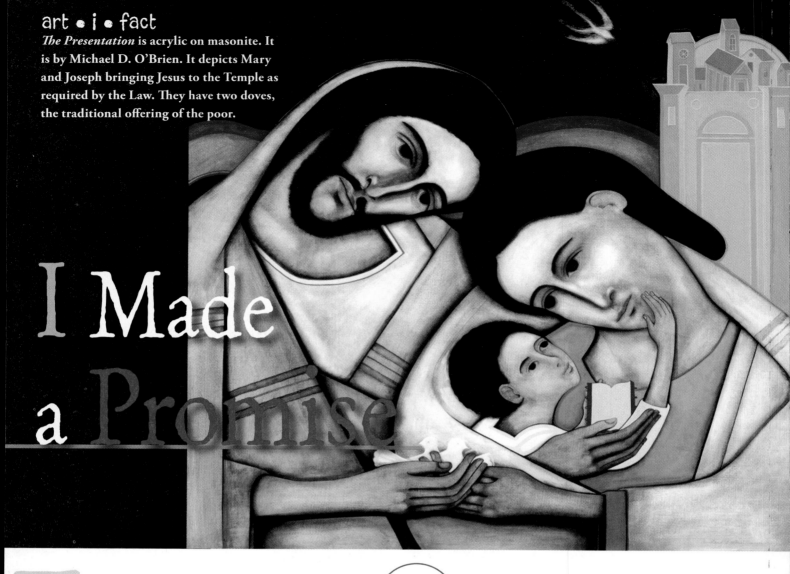

I Made a Promise

In the movie *The Lord of the Rings: The Fellowship of the Ring*, Frodo Baggins, a young hobbit, sets out on a quest to destroy a powerful, magical ring before it falls into the wrong hands. Realizing that his quest is endangering the lives of those in his fellowship, he decides at one point to proceed alone. As he begins to paddle away in his canoe, his best friend, Samwise Gamgee, catches up to him, insisting that he will not let him go alone. After almost drowning in his pursuit of Frodo, Sam fights back tears as he exclaims, "I made a promise, Mr. Frodo. A promise. 'Don't you leave him, Samwise Gamgee.' And I don't mean to. I don't mean to." According to Sam, a promise is a promise.

When Matthew began to write his story of Jesus, he had a promise in mind—a promise that God made to Abraham centuries before Jesus was born. God promised that he would always be with his people. With

IM "So they are no longer two, but one flesh. Therefore, what God has joined together, no human being must separate."

(Matthew 19:6)

this promise, or covenant, in mind, Matthew begins his Gospel with a genealogy. This list of Jesus' ancestors, described in Matthew 1:1–17, traces the covenant from the time of Abraham, our father in faith, through forty-two generations. The most important figure after Abraham is King David, who represents the ideal of a king who rules in justice and mercy.

Matthew's genealogy includes Gentiles and Jews, people who are upright and people who are immoral. Some are the most well known members of the Jewish family and some are completely obscure. Throughout all of these generations, God is faithful to the covenant he has made through Abraham. The genealogy ends with Joseph the husband of Mary. Through all of these generations God has kept his promise, a promise now fulfilled in Jesus.

In their marriage, Mary and Joseph also made a promise—a personal covenant—with God and each other. This was a promise to live together for the rest of their lives in love. This love was expressed in the care they showed for one another and the care they gave to Jesus. Jesus, in turn, learned from their example that marriage was a sacred promise. During his ministry, Jesus raised marriage to the dignity of a sacrament that today we call Matrimony. In this sacrament, a man and a woman freely enter into a covenant, a covenant of faith. Together they experience success and failure and discover God's grace alive in their marriage in the most surprising ways. The promises that a husband and wife make with one another on the day of

During his ministry, Jesus raised marriage to the dignity of a sacrament that today we call Matrimony

continued on page 162 ▶

The Value of Forgiveness

Matthew's community was familiar with the stress of broken relationships and the need for people to forgive one another. In 18:21–35 Matthew tells the story of when Peter asked Jesus how many times you should forgive a person who has done something to anger or hurt you. "As many as seven times?" Peter asked. In the Scriptures seven is the number of completeness. For Peter the number seven meant you were forgiving someone completely. Jesus said that we should forgive 77 times. By using these numbers, Jesus was saying that our willingness to forgive should be infinite.

Jesus then told the story of a worker who owed his master a huge amount of money. When threatened with jail if he did not pay, the man pleaded for forgiveness of the debt, which his master granted. Later on the worker met a colleague who owed him a couple of weeks' worth of wages. When the colleague asked for more time, the man refused to give it to him and had him thrown in prison. When the worker's master heard what he had done, he was furious. He had shown mercy to his worker, but his worker did not extend the same mercy to his fellow man. Because of this the master had his worker thrown into jail until he paid the debt he originally owed.

In this story Jesus was emphasizing how great the forgiveness is that we receive from the Father, and how we are called to forgive others in the same way that the Father forgives us. No marriage can survive without forgiveness. It is in the family—the domestic church—that we learn how to forgive and be forgiven.

Fear of the Unknown

It's not uncommon for young couples who are about to be married to experience a certain amount of fear and anxiety. Fear of the unknown is a natural human reaction. The Gospel of Matthew tells us about the fear that some followers of Jesus experienced on the first Easter morning. At dawn on the day after the Sabbath, Mary Magdalene and another woman named Mary approached the tomb where Jesus was buried. Instead of finding a couple of sleepy guards, they experienced a great earthquake and saw an angel descend from heaven and roll back the stone that was in front of the tomb. As the guards shook with fear, the angel spoke to the women saying, "Do not be afraid!" The women were even more surprised when the angel told them that the crucified Jesus was no longer in the tomb, but had risen from the dead. He was already on his way to Galilee. The women were fearful yet overjoyed. As they made their way to Galilee, they met the risen Jesus on the road and embraced and worshipped him. Their original journey to Jesus' tomb had ended with the unexpected joy of seeing him alive!

Many times, our life journeys twist and turn in directions that we could hardly imagine. A marriage commitment is like being on the road to an unknown future. There are many surprises along the way. Joy can be mingled with fear as the couple faces whatever life brings. Just like with Mary Magdalene and Mary's experience, however, the couple meets Jesus on the road at every turn. In Jesus they can overcome whatever they may fear so that they can live in trust and hope.

their wedding enable them to embark on a journey in faith, leading ultimately to living with Jesus Christ at the end of time. In this way each couple can model the relationship between Christ and the Church. As they teach their children the values of the faith, the family becomes a domestic church, a home that is a community of grace, a school of human virtues and Christian love.

In Jesus' time, divorce was accepted by the religious authorities. People discussed what the grounds for divorce should be. Some thought that even the slightest thing, like burning dinner, was enough to divorce someone. Others thought that the grounds for divorce would have to be for much more serious reasons. What did Jesus think?

Jesus refused to be drawn into the argument between the two sides. Instead he reminded them what God said at the beginning, that God had created men and women. Quoting Genesis 2:24 Jesus said, "'For this reason a man shall leave his father and mother and be joined to his wife, and the two shall become one flesh.' So they are no longer two, but one flesh. Therefore, what God has joined together, no human being must separate." (Matthew 19:5–6)

A promise is a promise. When people keep their promises, trust is sustained. From the beginning of our relationship with God, he has kept his promise. When we witness the public promise made by a husband and wife, we are reminded of the promise that God made to Abraham—a promise that went unbroken and continues to be fulfilled today. FG

Please tell me you didn't leave the house in those get-ups!

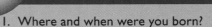

10 questions you can ask **family members** are listed below.
Use them to start a **conversation** about your **family history.**

1. Where and when were you born?
2. What do you remember about growing up?
3. Where did you go to school?
4. What did you want to be when you grew up?
5. Do you know how your parents met?

6. What do you know about your grandparents?
7. What about your great-grandparents?
8. Did anyone in the family come from a different country?
9. What are some of our family traditions?
10. Was there anyone famous in our family?

Giving Light to All

We can't get away from them. Everywhere we go, they seem to be there already. Who are they? Models—those perfect-looking people who adorn the covers of magazines and appear in countless numbers of TV commercials. Models are presented as the ideal. The problem is that the ideal these models represent is superficial. What we need are models we can relate to and truly aspire to imitate. For starters, we need models who represent not simply physical ideals, but spiritual ideals. This is what Jesus had in mind when he told his disciples,

The Sacrament of Matrimony—the lifelong union between husband and wife—is a sign of the union of Christ and the Church.

"You are the light of the world. A city set on a mountain cannot be hidden. Nor do they light a lamp and then put it under a bushel basket; it is set on lampstand, where it gives light to all in the house. Just so, your light must shine before others, that they may see your good deeds and glorify your heavenly Father."

(Matthew 5:14–16)

In Matthew's Gospel, Jesus makes it very clear that his followers, those who make up the Church, are to be a light—a model—for others. Matthew's Gospel is the only Gospel that uses the word *church* to identify those who model their lives after Jesus. (Matthew 18:17) It is clear from Matthew's Gospel that Jesus expects the Church to give witness to his presence in the world.

cotntinued on page 164 ▶

A Shining Light for Over 50 Years

A wedding takes place on one day. A marriage takes place over a lifetime. The longer the marriage, the more powerful is the value of the sign—like a light set on a hill for all to see. One example of this is the marriage of Cy and Mary Jo Wuenschel, who met during their college years in Pittsburgh, fell deeply in love, and were married in 1955. In the following years, they worked hard to create a good life for each other and for their five children. Their lives were filled with joy that was strong enough to live through the sadness of losing their first son at birth. Early in their marriage, Cy and Mary Jo dedicated themselves to serving the Church through professional ministry, helping adults learn the meaning of the Gospel so that they could live their lives more fully. Their journeys took them and their family all over the country, culminating in their most recent years of service in the diocese of Orlando, Florida. In July 2005, they gathered with their 5 children, 16 grandchildren, and 3 great-grandchildren to celebrate 50 years of married life, love, and ministry to the Church.

Those who know Cy and Mary Jo experience the sacrament of Christ's presence in their relationship with each other and in their relationship with the Church. When they spoke their promises to one another on their wedding day, they promised to love through sickness and in health until they departed in death. Throughout their lifelong love for each other, for their family, and for everyone they have met and served, Cy and Mary Jo continue to be a sacrament of Christ's presence in and through his Church—a shining light for all to see.

> ### The selfless love and lifelong commitment between a man and a woman are a sign of the enduring love that God has for us.

▶ *continued from page 163*

By virtue of our Baptism—our entrance into the Church—we are all called to be a light to others by living lives of holiness. However, the Church specifically designates two sacraments—Holy Orders and Matrimony—as Sacraments at the Service of Communion. In other words, through their vocations, priests and married people give special witness to Christ's presence in the world. How do married men and women give witness to Christ's presence in the world?

First, we need to remember that all sacraments are signs—they point to something beyond themselves. All seven sacraments lead us to Jesus and the love that God pours out to us through him. In the Sacrament of Matrimony, the selfless love and lifelong commitment between a man and a woman are a sign of the enduring love that God has for us. The Sacrament of Matrimony—the lifelong union between husband and wife—is a sign of the union of Christ and the Church. Likewise, the fidelity of God to his covenant and that of Christ to his Church are reflected through the fidelity of the spouses. Since marriage is a public statement of the love of the married couple, it is appropriate for the celebration of marriage to be public.

Next, we need to remember that the love the husband and wife share with one another are the sign in the sacrament. Because of the beauty of the sexual union in marriage, the Church believes it is noble and honorable. It brings joy and pleasure to the husband and wife and makes it possible for them to cooperate with God the Creator by having children. That is why the Church stresses that sex belongs in marriage alone.

Finally, Catholic married couples establish a Christian home—a place where their children receive their first proclamation of the faith. In a way, we can say that the parents create a school for their children where they learn virtues, Christian charity, and the practice of prayer. We can call Catholic families the domestic church, meaning that together parents and

I, Darla, take you Pickles, to be my husband, to have and to hold from this day forward, to swim with, to eat with, to splish and splash with.

children create an environment in which faith in Jesus can grow. Each domestic church shines like a light to the world so that others may learn to follow Jesus.

We usually don't see ordinary, everyday people on the covers of magazines or as models on TV commercials. All around us, however, Catholic married couples are serving as models of faith, letting their light shine so that others may see the presence of God in this world. FG

411

Mia read in a magazine that the cost of raising a child is approximately $9,742.94 per year. She was shocked by this fact. Mia asked Jeanette, her mom, if she and her dad would be rich if they had never had her and her five brothers and sisters. Jeanette thought about it and said, "We might have had more money, but we wouldn't be richer."

Our Roots Are Showing

By calling the Sacrament of Matrimony a *Sacrament at the Service of Communion*, the Church is reminding us that the work of God is done not only by priests and religious people.

Every Catholic has God-given gifts and talents that can be used to build the Church and spread the Good News of Jesus Christ. The laity in particular have a special vocation to share this mission in places and circumstances where it is only through them that the Church can be present. Through the *Dogmatic Constitution on the Church*, the bishops encouraged the laity to study theology and Scripture and to become more involved as leaders in the Church through their local parish and diocesan offices.

A Long Line of Sinners and Saints

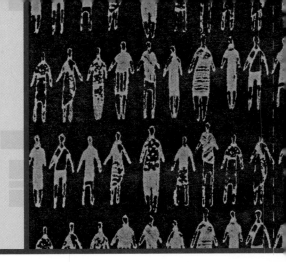

THE FAMILY AND PRAYER

For children, the family is the first place of education about prayer. The family is the "domestic church" where children learn to pray. But learning to pray is much more than simply learning the words of a particular prayer. Jesus promised that wherever two or three were gathered in his name, he would be in the midst of them.

Through living the daily realities of marriage and family life, the Christian family is called to invite Jesus' presence among them and to sanctify the Church and the world. Family prayer is shaped by the circumstances of family life. Pope John Paul II wrote about families: "Joys and sorrows, hopes and disappointments, births and birthday celebrations, wedding anniversaries of the parents, departures, separations and homecomings, important and far-reaching decisions, the death of those who are dear, etc.—all of these mark God's loving intervention in the family's history." (*Role of the Christian Family in the Modern World*) The experiences that every family shares can be seen as moments for thanksgiving, for petition, and for entrusting the family into the hands of God, their common Father. In this way the family becomes more and more the domestic church and a school of prayer.

The genealogy of Jesus reveals not only examples of faith and fidelity, but also examples of people with shaky reputations. The point is clear: God kept his promise for better or for worse, even when some of Jesus' ancestors were undeserving. Each of us is part of a story that began long before we were born and will continue long after we die. Our ancestors, both in our family and in our faith, have given us a heritage of traditions, values, and stories. The stories involve times of faith as well as broken promises. We all come from a long line of saints and sinners. These people influence who we are and how we live our lives today.

Litany of Thanksgiving for Who I Am Today

For our parents and families and the faith we've received . . .

Response: We give you thanks, O Lord.

For our relatives, those we know and those we've never met . . . ℞

For our deceased relatives who live now in the presence of God . . . ℞

For the many ways that faith has been lived and passed down to us through so many generations . . . ℞

For our relatives who struggled through tough times . . . ℞

For the witness of our family members who loved each other through good times and difficult ones . . . ℞

For our ancestors who showed their trust in God when faced with difficulty . . . ℞

For our relatives who reached out in love to those in need . . . ℞

For those whose forgiveness of one another taught us to do the same . . . ℞

Closing Prayer:

God of love, our families are your gift to us. Thank you for their witness of faith and fidelity to you and to one another. May their lives inspire us to look for your presence in times of joy and challenge and to find you in all things. We ask this in the name of Jesus, the Lord. Amen.

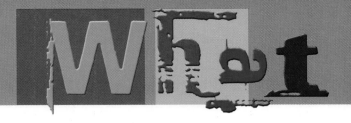

What's **WHAT?**

■ Review the main points of this chapter. Choose one that's most inspiring to you and write your reasons on the lines provided.

- The genealogy of Jesus in Matthew's Gospel is an expression of how God fulfilled his promise to always be with his people.

- In the Sacrament of Matrimony, a man and a woman freely enter into a covenant uniting their families in a covenant of faith.

- Married couples model the relationship between Christ and the Church as they embark on a faith journey which ultimately leads to living with Christ at the end of time.

- We learn how to forgive and be forgiven in our family, the domestic church.

- Because Matrimony is a Sacrament at the Service of Communion, we are reminded that the work of God is done not just by priests and religious people, but by everyone.

_____

_____

So **WHAT?**

■ What does fidelity in the Sacrament of Marriage teach you about your own friendships?

_____

_____

Say **WHAT?**

domestic church • Matrimony

Now **WHAT?**

■ What will you do at home this week to help strengthen your relationship with someone in your family?

_____

_____

_____

_____

Here's **WHAT** the Catholic Church Teaches

People are social beings. Each of us is made to live with others. We are born into a family that is our first example as children of the larger society in which we live. Our nature drives us to have a full family life and to participate in society. This participation is not something extra added to life but is essential to it. We can only grow and become a full person if we have relationships with others.

Pope John Paul II expressed in an encyclical in 1987 that it is vital that people work together to ensure that families and individuals have the ability to participate in the life of society. He wrote: "Today perhaps more than in the past, people are realizing that they are linked together by a common destiny, which is to be constructed together, if catastrophe for all is to be avoided. . . . [T]he idea is slowly emerging," he stressed, "that the good to which we are all called and the happiness to which we aspire cannot be obtained without an effort and commitment on the part of all, nobody excluded." (*On Social Concern*)

If . . . Then . . .

1. Read the first article.

2. Identify the main ideas about our Catholic faith from the article and note them in the "If We Believe . . ." column below.

3. In your group, work together to complete the "Then We Are Called to . . ." column.

4. Repeat the process for the second article.

Article 1: I Made a Promise		Article 2: Giving Light to All	
IF we believe . . .	THEN we are called to . . .	IF we believe . . .	THEN we are called to . . .

Faith in Action

Faith is alive when we put it into action every day of our lives. It is expressed in the attitudes and values we hold and in the ways we relate to the people and the world around us. Taking action to create a more just world is an essential part of living the Gospel. Jesus preached not only with words but how he lived his life. We are called to do the same.

In this unit the Gospel of Matthew presents Jesus as the New Moses, the one who fulfills the Old Testament prophecies and truly saves his people. Our relationship with Jesus makes us new too and calls us to live in justice and peace. One way that we can answer this call is to work for peace in the world. Here are some ideas to help you take a stand against violence and promote peace.

> *"In violence we forget who we are."*
>
> —Mary McCarthy, author and social critic

A Shelter from Violence

Purpose:

Learn about domestic violence and its effects; design a project for your group to raise awareness or to provide assistance to people affected by domestic violence.

Background:

Domestic violence is used to gain or maintain power and control over a partner or family member. It includes anything that would harm someone physically or mentally. It is not just something that happens to adults. Teens are also abused, often by family members or by the people that they are dating.

Steps:

a. Find organizations in your area that serve people who suffer from domestic violence.

continued on page 170 ▶

▶ *continued from page 169*

b. There are many things that you can do to help. Here are just a few:

- ask government officials to continue to support legislation against domestic violence and to provide funding for agencies that deal with domestic violence.

- gather materials for different arts-and-crafts projects that you can teach to children in shelters.

- educate your community by hosting guest speakers, publishing articles on domestic violence, posting information on where to get help.

Toys Against Violence

Purpose:

Become aware of the amount of violence we are exposed to on any given day; take a stand against violence by rediscovering things that surround us with peace, not violence.

Background:

Today we live in a culture in which we are surrounded by violence. Just because some of that violence may be simulated does not mean that it doesn't affect us. What we see, play with, read about, or are exposed to really does shape us. It can make us desensitized to or tolerant of real violence.

Steps:

a. For one week, record every instance of violence that you are exposed to. Examples include toy weapons, violence on TV, and insults. At the end of the week, share your findings with the group. What insights did you gain from this exercise?

b. Brainstorm ways that you can reduce the amount of violence around you.

c. Find ways to bring in new things that are nonviolent yet still fun and engaging.

d. Share your new insights with children. For example, you could teach kids non-violent games and activities. Art supplies, science kits, Frisbees, dominos, and checkers are some ideas to get you started. Be creative and at the same time take a stand against violence.

> *"The main goal of the future is to stop violence. The world is addicted to it."*
>
> —Bill Cosby, comedian and TV star

Luke Celebrates Jesus' Presence

THE GOSPEL OF LUKE AND THE ACTS OF THE APOSTLES

By the year 85 the Christian religion was becoming well established in the cities of the Roman empire. Gentile citizens of the empire were becoming more interested in the Church, but they still had questions. Some Christians expected Christ to return soon, even within their lifetime. But it was becoming apparent that the Christian journey would continue through time. How could they live by their Christian values in a world dominated by Rome? The Gospel of Luke and the Acts of the Apostles, two different works by one author, are in part responses to this question.

THE WRITER OF LUKE

Early Christian tradition attributes the Gospel of Luke and the Acts of the Apostles to Luke, a Syrian from Antioch. He is mentioned in the New Testament in Colossians 4:14, Philippians 1:24, and 2 Timothy 4:11. The writer of Luke identifies himself as a second-generation Christian who uses other sources to help him tell the story. Both the Gospel and the Acts of the Apostles were addressed to Theophilus, which means "friend of God" in Greek. The Gospel of Luke portrays the beginning of the Christian story from the announcement that the Messiah is coming, to the death and Resurrection of Jesus. The Acts of the Apostles starts with the Resurrection and Ascension of Jesus and then continues with events involving the spread of the Church.

CITIZENS OF THE EMPIRE

Luke sets his story in the Roman empire. Although Jesus was condemned by a Roman magistrate, Luke shows the Romans in a positive light. In Luke 7:9, Jesus says of the Roman centurion seeking a cure for his slave, "I tell you, not even in Israel have I found such faith." (Luke 7:9) Later, in Acts of the Apostles, Cornelius, a Roman centurion in Caesarea, is described as a prayerful, God-fearing man who gave generously to the Jewish people. (Acts of the Apostles 10:1–2) Luke wants his readers to understand that Christianity is compatible with the Roman world.

GUIDANCE OF THE HOLY SPIRIT

In both the Gospel of Luke and the Acts of the Apostles, the work of the Holy Spirit is highlighted. Mary is filled with the Spirit to conceive the Messiah. (Luke 1:35) Inspired by the Holy Spirit, Elizabeth recognizes Mary as the mother of the Messiah. (1:41)

The Holy Spirit is active in the life of Jesus. The Spirit leads Jesus into the desert. (Luke 4:1) Jesus returns from the desert in the power of the Spirit. (Luke 4:14) When Jesus returns and reads the Scriptures in the synagogue, he identifies himself as the one on whom the Spirit rests. (Luke 4:18)

The Holy Spirit is especially present in the Acts of the Apostles. The Holy Spirit empowers the disciples to preach the Gospel and sends them as missionaries (Acts of the Apostles 2:1–17;16: 6–7) By telling these stories, Luke is emphasizing that the Holy Spirit is always a part of Christian life. The same Holy Spirit leads and guides the Church today.

PRAYER

Luke stresses the importance of prayer. Salvation is first announced to Zechariah when he is serving in the Temple and the whole assembly is praying. (Luke 3:9–10) Simeon and Anna could recognize the infant Jesus as the Messiah as a result of their years of prayer in the Temple. (Luke 2:25–38) Jesus prays before he chooses the Twelve (Luke 6:12) and before the Transfiguration. (Luke 9:29) Active and enthusiastic prayer is also a characteristic of the early Christian community. (Acts of the Apostles 1:13–14; 2:42; 3:1) By telling these stories, Luke emphasizes the importance of prayer for living the Christian life in the midst of society.

LUKE IN THIS UNIT

If you were asked to tell stories from the Gospels, more than likely the story you would remember would come from the Gospel of Luke. He is a vivid storyteller who highlights Jesus' compassion for those in need. In Luke we find the story of the announcement of the birth of Jesus to the shepherds and the parables of the lost son and the Good Samaritan.

In the Acts of the Apostles we meet a group of people being formed by the Holy Spirit in prayer and action. The early disciples call the people to repentance and to Baptism in Jesus Christ and heal in Jesus' name. We are also called to faith by the Holy Spirit. We are initiated into the life of the Spirit in Baptism, Confirmation, and the Eucharist. Just as the Christians in Luke's time were called to live their values in the difficult Roman world, we, as fully formed members of God's people, recognize the Holy Spirit as the guide who leads us on the way in the world today.

IT'S A Party

When something significant happens in our lives, we don't celebrate alone; we call people together and have a party. What's the most recent event in your life that you've celebrated with others?

IT'S LIKE THIS

Some people have special days that they like to celebrate. It might be a birthday, a civic or religious holiday, or an anniversary. What day do you especially like to celebrate?

Event: _____

People Invited: _____

Decorations: _____

Food: _____

Traditions: _____

The Birth of Jesus

The Nativity, Edward B. Webster, 1956, Smithsonian American Art Museum.

Christmas celebrations follow a familiar pattern every year. Homes and parishes are decorated with lights and trimmed in green and red. Along with the Christmas trees and wreathes, there's a special place for the crèche. The crèche portrays the Nativity, the birth of Jesus in the stable. The crèche has been part of the tradition of celebrating Christmas for so long now that many people have forgotten how it began.

Saint Francis of Assisi (1181–1226) wanted people to share his special devotion to the Christ Child. In 1223 he created a living image of the scene of the birth of Jesus. Francis built a small stable out of wood and gathered together an ox and a donkey. At the midnight mass he placed a small baby boy in a manger and gathered the people around the scene of the Holy Family. Francis spoke of Christmas as a feast of gentleness, generosity, and most important of all, poverty. At one point in his sermon Francis picked up the child from the manger. The baby smiled at Francis, and Francis caressed his cheek. The people in the congregation were moved to tears of joy, hearing Francis' words and watching his tender care for the child.

The scene Francis created was so moving that it has been copied all over the world. Over the centuries, figures of Mary and Joseph, the shepherds and their sheep, and the Wise Men and their camels were added to tell a seamless story of the birth of Jesus. Actually, the images bring together stories from two different Infancy Narratives written in the Gospels of Luke and Matthew. In Matthew 2:1–18 we find the story of the Wise Men, the envy of King Herod, and Herod's order to murder all the infant boys in Bethleham. In Luke 2:1–20 we find the stories of Mary and Joseph's journey to Bethlehem, the birth of Jesus among the animals, the proclamation to the shepherds, and Mary's reflection on all these events in her heart. While the Gospels were written at different times and under different circumstances, they had a single purpose—to proclaim that Jesus is the Messiah, the one who has come to save.

THE STORY IN LUKE

The first thing we notice in Luke's story of Jesus' birth is how he places the story in the context of the Roman empire. (2:1–20) Luke identifies Caesar Augustus as the Roman emperor and Quirinius as the Roman governor of Syria. Luke contrasts Jesus and Caesar Augustus. The Roman emperor was a symbol of Roman power, and Caesar Augustus was praised as a bringer of peace and a savior because he had defeated all his enemies and unified the Roman empire. Luke wants his readers to see Jesus as a bringer of peace as well, but in a completely different way from Caeser Augustus. He wants his audience of Roman citizens to understand that the salvation that Jesus brings is for the entire world, not just for the Roman empire.

Luke doesn't explain how Jesus will bring peace, but he gives some hints. He describes Jesus as being born in humble circumstances. The announcement of Jesus' birth is made not to powerful, important people but to lowly shepherds. Through these hints Luke is saying that the peace proclaimed in Jesus' name is for all those on whom God's favor rests. (2:14)

FIRSTBORN SON

Luke tells us that Mary gave birth to her "firstborn son." (2:7) From the earliest days, the Church has recognized that this does not mean that Mary had other children. It means that Jesus is the firstborn of many brothers and sisters in a spiritual family. He is the first of the always-growing community of people who work together to serve God's kingdom on earth. Mary is the spiritual mother of all Jesus came to save.

continued on page 176 ▶

art • i • fact

Top: *Nativity*, Agustín Cruz Tinoco, 1998, San Juan Oxolotepec, Oaxaca

Bottom: *Andean Nativity*, Feriberto Aylas, ceramic, Peru. The predominance of warm colors underscores the looks of loving tenderness on the faces of Mary and Joseph.

TO LEARN MORE about the nativity scenes, visit www.FindingGod.org/teens.

✝ Our Roots Are Showing

In the past, when homes did not have automatic heating systems, newborn babies were swaddled—wrapped in long narrow bands of cloth—to keep them warm. When Luke reminds us that King Solomon and Jesus were both wrapped in swaddling clothes, he is recalling Wisdom 7:4–6. Here Solomon asserts that all persons, whether a king or a commoner, have the same beginning.

In swaddling clothes and with constant care I was nurtured.

For no king has any different origin or birth,

but one is the entry into life for all; and in one same way they leave it.

Sacramentals

The powerful images in the Gospel of Luke and in the crèche are examples of sacramentals. *Sacramentals* are sacred signs that have been recognized by the Church. They help us grow in a life of prayer so that we can celebrate the sacraments with greater awareness and devotion. Sacramentals help us to recognize as holy all the ordinary events of daily life as well as the special occasions that arise from time to time. The most important sacramentals are those that are used in connection with the liturgy, for example, the palms on Palm Sunday, the ashes on Ash Wednesday, the Paschal candle at Easter, the holy water used to sprinkle the congregation, and the incense used at Mass. The blessing you receive from a priest is also a sacramental, as is the blessing children receive from their parents. Sacramentals are important to us as Catholics because when we use manmade objects like medals, rosaries, paintings, or statues, we are acknowledging and being reminded that all creation is good and can be used to bring us closer to God.

▶ *continued from page 175*

SWADDLING CLOTHES

When Jesus was born, Mary wrapped him in swaddling clothes. The swaddling clothes symbolize two things. First, they show us the poverty and humility of Jesus' birth in a stable among the animals. On the other hand, the swaddling clothes remind Luke's readers of the swaddling clothes that King Solomon was wrapped in as a baby. Luke wants his readers to understand that while Jesus is a king, he is also humble.

MANGER

After Mary wrapped Jesus in swaddling clothes, she placed him in a manger. Mangers are troughs used by shepherds and farmers to feed the animals. Luke wants us to understand from the image of the manger that Jesus is going to be food for the world.

SHEPHERDS

The announcement of Jesus' birth to the shepherds is also significant. Shepherds were usually poor, and they were dismissed by society because they were considered uneducated and unable to keep the Jewish Law. Shepherds lived in pastures with their sheep; they were not the kind of people that society wanted hanging around in towns and villages. Consider then how important it is that the first proclamation of Jesus' birth was made to these poor shepherds, unwelcome in society. Luke is showing that Jesus has come to save everyone, not just a privileged few.

SAVIOR

Luke wants us to understand that Jesus is the Savior. Jesus will not save in the way that the emperor saved Roman citizens, he will save everyone. He will restore us to wholeness, rescue us from sin, and make it possible for us to be reconciled with others and with God.

The story of the birth of Jesus in the Gospel of Luke is so familiar to us that we can miss the details and the deeper meaning. What's important is that it's the whole of his Gospel in miniature. Jesus is proclaimed as the Son of God who came to save the world. In the manner of Jesus' coming, we recognize a powerful critique of the society into which he was born. Those who first recognized him were those who recognized their need and their dependence on God. They were the ones who, like Mary, reflected in their hearts on the true meaning of salvation. Luke's Infancy Narrative speaks to us in the same way today. It is a critique of any society that neglects its obligation to help those in need. It calls us to reflect on how Jesus comes into the world and where he's recognized. We will discover the birth of Jesus in our own hearts whenever we're open to the concerns of others. FG

A nativity scene is big enough for an entire school of fish. It might even be big enough for Shaggy, the family crab.

art • i • fact

Annunciation, Christina Saj,
1999, mixed media on stone
with gold leaf

The Annunciation

IM [F]or nothing will be impossible for God.
(Luke 1:37)

In **Catholic churches** and in many Catholic homes, there is a statue or painting of Mary. These artistic representations often show Mary with her son, Jesus, or with Jesus and her husband, Joseph. Sometimes she is shown at the marriage feast of Cana or at the foot of the cross. One of the most popular representations of Mary is at the moment of the angel Gabriel's announcement to her that God was calling her to be the mother of Jesus. Leonardo da Vinci, Bartolome Murillo, Fra Angelico, Botticelli, and El Greco all have painted the Annunciation. The list of the artists who have depicted this scene goes on and on.

Luke 1:26–38 describes the Annunciation. He tells how the angel Gabriel comes to Mary, who would have been about 15 years old, and tells her that she has found favor with God. She is going to be blessed by God the Almighty. He says that she will have a son through the power of the Holy Spirit and that she is to name her son Jesus, which means "God saves." Understandably, Mary is confused because as she told Gabriel, she has not had sexual relations with any man. Gabriel explains to Mary that through the power of the Holy Spirit, she will remain a virgin in conceiving and giving birth to Jesus. As Catholics, we

continued on page 178 ▶

footnote

Today certain cars are considered status symbols. In Jesus' time wealthy people were identified by the fact that they owned oxen. Oxen were considered precious animals for sacrifice, since the goal of sacrifice was to give back to God your very best. The traditional symbol of Luke's Gospel, which begins with Zechariah offering sacrifice in the Temple, is the ox to represent Jesus' ultimate sacrifice.

Fifty Roses

During the Middle Ages, the farmers who lived and labored near the monasteries would hear the monks singing the psalms. They wanted to join the monks in prayer, but they could not read the psalms. Instead they would recite the Hail Mary, which they had memorized. Since there are 150 psalms, the people would recite 150 Hail Marys. Eventually they divided them up into three groups of 50 Hail Marys each. With each group of prayers, they would reflect on the different aspects of the lives of Jesus and Mary. It became customary to use beads to keep track of the 50 Hail Marys being prayed. This prayer devotion became know as the Rosary, since people thought of the 50 Hail Marys as 50 roses being placed at the feet of Mary. The devotion was especially promoted by Saint Dominic and the Dominican order. In 1572 Saint Pius V instituted the Feast of Our Lady of the Rosary on October 7. Over the centuries the Rosary has been one of the most popular Catholic devotions.

▶ *continued from page 177*

believe that she was a virgin for the remainder of her life. She will always be the "'handmaid of the Lord.'" (Luke 1:38)

Mary was free to say no to this path. After all, she was just about to begin a new life with Joseph. In addition, she already had to deal with the instability of living in a Roman-occupied territory. Mary faced an uncertain future and had no idea what joys or suffering her decision would bring. And yet she chose to say yes to this path. She made the decision out of trust that God would be true to the promises he had made to her. This life-changing act of faith made Mary the mother of Jesus, the Son of God. This is the main reason why we hold Mary in such high regard in our Catholic tradition. Her answer made her the very first person to say yes to Jesus, and so Mary is the first disciple. She was the first one to welcome the Messiah. In this way she is the model for us as we make our daily decisions to trust that God is with us.

In preparation for her call to be the Mother of God, Mary was preserved from original sin from the time of her conception, a truth that we celebrate on the feast of the Immaculate Conception. Mary remained free from personal sin her entire life. Her yes to God was made not just at the moment of Gabriel's announcement but at every moment of her life.

Mary's acceptance of God's will for her brought to completion the preparation for the coming of Jesus to God's people. Jesus was conceived, and Mary became the Mother of God. It is truly appropriate that we honor Mary as the Mother of God since she gave birth to Jesus, who is the Son of God, the Second Person of the Blessed Trinity. FG

art • i • fact
Our Lady of the Rosary,
St. Joseph's Cathedral, LaCross WI

Walking the Talk

In our world today, there are many young people who have a tough time with their families and need healthy ways to deal with their hurt, anger, depression, or fear. In the mid-1990s, Sister Mary Claudina Sanz, O.S.P. (pictured), decided to do something about it. At that time she was the superior general of the Oblate Sisters of Providence, the first Catholic religious community for women of African descent. She and her sisters had lived and worked with the people of Baltimore and knew that there was a great need for a safe, welcoming place for neglected and abused girls. In 1998 the Oblate Sisters opened the Mary Elizabeth Lange Center, named after the foundress of the community, to provide residential care for girls ages 8–15, with the ultimate goal of reuniting them with their families. Since then, the Center has witnessed many family reunions and rejoiced with former residents who have gone on to college so that they could return and help others.

A Reversal of Expectations

At the end of a stage play, the actors take a curtain call. Beginning with the supporting roles, the actors come out to take a bow to the applause of the audience. The cheers grow louder as the more prominent actors appear. Finally, the star of the show comes forward to a standing ovation from the audience.

The Gospel of Luke puts an interesting twist on this technique as it introduces the key players in the story that is about to unfold. In Luke 3:1–2, we are introduced to these impressive-sounding characters: Tiberius Caesar, the emperor of Rome; Pontius Pilate, a governor; Herod, Philip, and Lysanias, tetrarchs;

and Annas and Caiaphas, high priests. A reader might think that the final name will be the most impressive of all in terms of worldly power. Instead, Luke reverses expectations and introduces a man who lives alone in the desert: "the word of God came to John the son of Zechariah in the desert." (Luke 3:2)

Luke is showing the great importance of John the Baptist's supporting role in proclaiming God's Word throughout the region of the Jordan River and preparing the way for Jesus. Luke's point is clear—God uses everyone, even those who are not thought of as great or powerful, to take the lead role in proclaiming his Word.

art • i • fact
Saint John the Baptist,
Laura James

Finding Favor with

God

THE HAIL MARY

Most hymns and prayers to Mary contain two elements. The first element is praising God for the great things he did for her and through her for all human beings. The second element is entrusting our needs to her intercession because she knows the needs of humanity.

These elements are clearly found in the Hail Mary. The angel Gabriel greets her with the words "Hail (or rejoice) Mary." We begin the prayer with the same words God used, through his messenger, to greet Mary. The prayer continues with "full of grace, the Lord is with thee." She is wholly given to God, who has come to dwell in her.

When Mary visits Elizabeth, Mary is greeted with the words, "Blessed art thou among women." Because of her faith, Mary becomes the mother of all believers. All the nations of the earth receive the blessing of God through Mary. Then we pray, "Holy Mary, Mother of God." We entrust all our cares and petitions to her. Like Mary, whose response to God was "Thy will be done," we abandon ourselves to the will of God. We ask her to "Pray for us sinners, now and at the hour of our death." We acknowledge our weakness and ask for her support. We look for her to welcome us into God's presence.

What do you think of when you think of Mary? Maybe a Scripture story comes to mind, or maybe you remember a favorite statue or painting that you've seen. Perhaps your thoughts turn to your favorite Marian hymn or a devotion that is special to you and your family. Whatever it is, it brings you in contact with the qualities of Mary that can help you better understand the place of honor she holds for followers of her Son, Jesus.

Hail, favored one! The Lord is with you.

Imagine yourself in Mary's shoes. What would you think if an angel appeared to you and told you that you had found favor with God? Would you be surprised? Would you be nervous, or even laugh? Would you be so filled with awe at seeing an angel standing before you that you'd be afraid? What would you want to ask the angel?

Now imagine yourself back in your own shoes. Hear the angel say to you the same words he spoke to Mary. "Hail, favored one! The Lord is with you." Letting go of all words, just rest quietly reflecting on the message of the angel. Remember that each of us is favored by God and that he is always with us.

May it be done to me according to your word.

Imagine yourself in Mary's shoes. She was saying yes to the request that to her seemed impossible. What did this request mean? What would she have to do? How would her life change? She didn't have any answers, but she had great faith and trust in God.

Now imagine yourself back in your own shoes. What is it that God is asking you to do at this time in your life? Hear yourself respond with the same words that Mary spoke, "Be it done to me according to your word." Letting go of any thoughts, just rest quietly in the awareness of your acceptance of God's call. Remember that Mary is our mother, too, and she is always ready to help us grow as disciples of her Son.

Let's close this time of prayer by praying aloud the Hail Mary together.

What's **WHAT?**

■ Review the main points of the chapter. Which point was least familiar to you? Write your new insights on the lines below.

- The crèche has its origin in the special devotion of Saint Francis of Assisi for the Christ Child.

- Luke wants us to understand that Jesus is the Savior who came to save everyone, not just a privileged few.

- Sacramentals are sacred signs that are used to bring us closer to God.

- Mary is considered to be the first disciple because she was the first to welcome the Messiah.

- The Rosary began during the Middle Ages as a way for farmers to join in prayer with the monks in nearby monasteries.

_____

_____

Say **WHAT?**

Annunciation • Immaculate Conception
Infancy Narrative • original sin

So **WHAT?**

■ Jesus is Savior, and the manner of his birth gives hope to all who are in need. *Think about it. Pray about it.*

Now **WHAT?**

■ Mary's yes to God made her the first disciple. As a disciple today, what will I do this week to live out my yes to God?

Here's **WHAT** the Catholic Church Teaches

Unlike most people in his culture, Jesus treated women with openness, respect, acceptance, and tenderness. In his 1995 apostolic letter *Letter to Women* Pope John Paul II apologized to women, acknowledging that the Church had been guilty, along with the rest of society, of not following Jesus' lead in his treatment of women.

He also thanked all women who work in every area of life—social, economic, cultural, artistic, and political. They make, he said, an indispensable contribution to the growth of culture and help make economic and political structures more worthy of humanity. The pope went on to say: "I know of course that simply saying thank you is not enough. Unfortunately, we are heirs to a history which has conditioned us to a remarkable extent. In every time and place, this conditioning has been an obstacle to the progress of women. Women's dignity has often been unacknowledged and their prerogatives misrepresented . . . This has prevented women from truly being themselves and it has resulted in a spiritual impoverishment of humanity."

Women have contributed as much to human history as men, and more often than not, they did so in more difficult conditions. It is a matter of justice but also of necessity, the pope said, that social systems be redesigned in a way that favors the processes of humanization that mark the "civilization of love." (*Letter to Women*)

Paired Interview

Your name _____

Your partner's name _____

Title of article read by your partner _____

_____

Ask your partner the following questions about the article he or she read and record his or her answers in the space provided.

1. Explain what your article was about in a few sentences.	
2. What is one quote (sentence) from your article that you would put on a poster to inspire the group? Why?	
3. What are some specific things your article helped you to learn or realize about the Catholic faith?	
4. Based on your article, name some specific things we, as Catholics, need to know, do, or believe in order to live as followers of Jesus.	

FINDING The Way

Most of us have been lost at one time or another. It can be a frightening experience to realize that we have no idea where we are and that we don't know how to find our way. Our pulse races as we try to control the mounting panic and get a grip on the situation. Share with the group a time when you were lost. How did you celebrate being found?

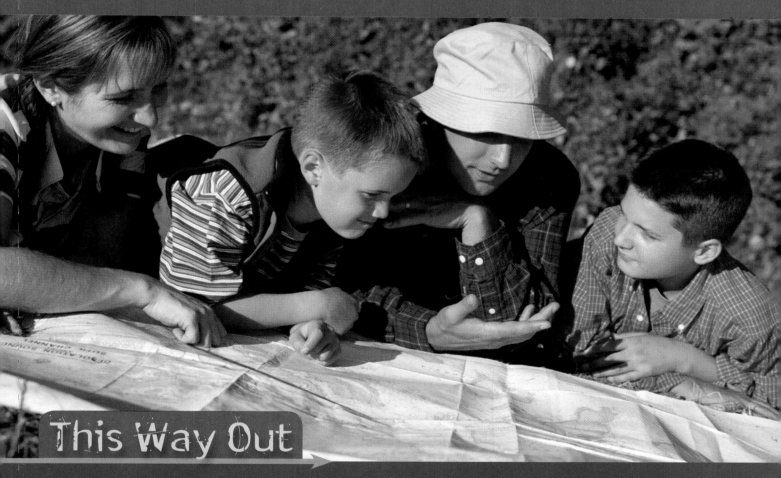

This Way Out

If you were hiking in unfamiliar territory and became separated from your group, what additional steps would you take to insure your survival?

- try to retrace your steps
- check a map or compass
- look for signs or familiar landmarks

- _____
- _____
- _____

Celebration

What do you do when you are getting ready to celebrate an important event? You clean your home (especially your room), decide what to wear, and prepare food. If someone in your family gets married, you may help your family entertain out-of-town guests. You may decorate the house to celebrate Christmas. You may pick out a present for the birthday of a family member or a friend.

Luke has three stories in chapter 15 of his Gospel about people who were celebrating. But wait till you see what they were celebrating!

REJOICE WITH ME

The first story, in Luke 15:1–7, is about a man who has a hundred sheep, and one of them gets lost. The man goes out to find the lost sheep. "And when he does find it, . . . he calls together his friends and neighbors and says to them, 'Rejoice with me because I have found my lost sheep.'" The second story, in Luke 15:8–10, is about a woman who has ten coins, loses one of them, and goes looking for it. "And when she does find it, she calls together her friends and neighbors and says to them, 'Rejoice with me because I have found the coin that I have lost.'"

The most well-known celebration is the third story, in Luke 15:11–32. The story is about a man who has two sons. The older son stays home to help his father, but the younger son asks for his inheritance and leaves

---

The house is filled with the sound of music and dancing.

I'm *always* the main attraction at the dance parties. They don't call me "flamenco fins" for nothing, you know.

with half of his father's money. He travels far away and squanders all the money. After his funds have dried up, he is desperately poor. He decides to return to his father and admit that he made foolish choices. When the young man comes home, his father rushes to embrace him. He tells his servants to bring out his finest robe and place it on his son. Then the father puts a valuable ring on his son's finger and sandals on his feet. Finally he orders his servants to take the fattened calf, kill it, and prepare it so that the whole family can celebrate with a feast. As the evening progresses, the house is filled with the sound of music and dancing. The man is happy because his son had been lost and now was found.

PEOPLE WHO ARE LOST

Luke puts these three stories together in his Gospel because they all tell us the same thing. When we rejoice finding what is lost, God rejoices with us. When a sinner repents, God rejoices like the father whose son has returned home. God cares about the people who are "lost" in society. Who are these "lost" people? In Luke's day, they were people with diseases that could not be cured, such as

continued on page 186 ▶

This Brazilian statue of Saint Lucy features one of her relics (inside the red oval).

✝ Our Roots Are Showing

Since the time of the apostles, Christians have preserved and venerated the mortal remains of saints. These relics are considered sacramentals. While some Christians believed that the actual relics had miraculous powers, the Church holds that relics represent the individual saint. Just as we honor the saints by asking for their intercession, we honor them by respecting their relics. Relics include objects that were used by a saint or that touched the saint's remains. An example of a relic is a piece of Saint Thomas Aquinas' bone or a cloth that has touched Saint Lucy's remains. By venerating relics, we are honoring, not worshipping, saints and celebrating the love of Jesus Christ that was uniquely expressed in their lives.

In the stories about the lost sheep, the lost coin, and the lost son, the common theme is rejoicing and celebrating when what was lost is found. The father of the lost son calls for his son to be dressed in the finest robe, a feast be prepared, and everyone to celebrate. The stories highlight the fact that when we praise God, we use the material things of the world to help us in our prayer.

Catholics have a great sense of *sacramentality*—making use of the material world as a means of relating to God and to one another. Through images and statues of Jesus and the saints, we have the opportunity to express externally what we are experiencing internally. In our celebrations we use candles, incense, and vestments. We anoint with oil and receive the Body and Blood of Christ in the Eucharist. In the liturgical celebration of all of the sacraments, God the Father is blessed and adored as the source of all blessings.

We like to involve our senses in our relationship with God. To express this we say that the Catholic Church is sacramental. We believe that the material things we have are signs of God's love for us, and the ways we use them are signs of our love for God.

Damien the Leper

In the 1800s Father Damien took to heart the values of the Gospel of Luke to care for those who were rejected by society. Father Damien was born and raised in Belgium. He was ordained a priest and was sent to Hawaii as a missionary. He was given a large parish, but he decided to volunteer to minister to the leper colony on the island of Molokai.

People with leprosy had been separated from their families and left to spend the rest of their lives isolated on the island. Father Damien dressed their wounds, shared meals with them, and buried them after their deaths. He built huts, a church, and clinics. He gave the lepers the hope of resurrection and turned their funerals into processions of music and joy.

Father Damien eventually caught the disease, as he knew he would, but he kept on building, planning, begging for supplies, and celebrating Mass for his beloved flock. Before he died, a community of religious sisters and a religious brother came to continue his mission. He died knowing that his work would continue and that his people would not be abandoned.

ABOVE: Father Damien (far left) with patients outside his church on Molokai Island, Hawaii

▶ *continued from page 185*

leprosy, as well as people who were blind or crippled. (In Luke's day many people believed that blindness and other disabilities were punishments from God.) The "lost" people were the tax collectors, Jewish people who worked with the Romans and helped them extort money from their fellow Jews. They were also old people and young people without families.

There are times when we feel lost ourselves. There are days when everything seems to go wrong, or when we know that we have deliberately hurt someone and are sorry for what we have done but don't know how to admit it. Many people feel lost when they have lost all that they have in a natural disaster, or when a parent has lost a job and he or she doesn't know how the family will be able to make ends meet.

IM "There will be rejoicing among the angels of God over one sinner who repents."
(Luke 15:10)

CELEBRATE!

When we reach out to those in need in our society and give them the help they need, God rejoices. God rejoices when we repent and return to him. God rejoices with us when we receive the help we need in times of trouble. Whenever we are working together, helping one another, healing relationships, receiving the help we need, God celebrates with us. FG

IT'S LIKE THIS

Service is about more than what we do or how much we do. Service has to do with the reason we act in the first place—the "why" of our motive. Service done to gain recognition for ourselves is self-serving. When we act out of a loving and compassionate heart, we act like Christ. It's only then that we are truly serving God's kingdom.

Signs of Life

Jesucristo El Lucero Radiante del Alba (Jesus Christ Morning Star), William Hart McNichols, S.J., New Mexico

A lot is happening in Wendy's family this year. Her older sister is getting married in about a month. Her brother is being confirmed this year. Her little sister is making her First Communion. Her aunt's baby is being baptized this Sunday at Mass. Her cousin is soon to be ordained a priest. All of these events are part her family's continuing journey in their relationship with God.

In his Gospel, Luke was also writing about a journey—the journey of Jesus from his birth to his suffering, death, and Resurrection. For Luke the journey continues with the disciples in the Acts of the Apostles where, with the support and guidance of the Holy Spirit, the Christian journey carried on into the future. As with any journey, there are rest areas along the way—places to stop to be refreshed and renewed before facing the next step.

For us Catholics today, the sacraments are important rest areas on our journey of faith. There are seven sacraments in the Catholic Church: Baptism, Confirmation, Eucharist, Penance, Anointing of the Sick, Matrimony, and Holy Orders. What do we know about these sacraments?

> The sacraments are Christ's actions in our lives.

INSTITUTED BY CHRIST

We know that the sacraments were given to us by Jesus Christ. Jesus told his disciples, "Go, therefore, and make disciples of all nations, baptizing them in the name of the Father, and of the Son, and of the holy Spirit." (Matthew 28:19) At the Last Supper Jesus offered his body and blood and then told his disciples, "do this in memory of me." (Luke 22:19) Jesus told his disciples: "Whose sins you forgive are forgiven them, and whose sins you retain are retained." (John 20:23) Each sacra-

ment was given to us by Jesus so that God's life and love could fill our lives.

CHRIST AT WORK

The sacraments are Christ's actions in our lives. When we were baptized, Christ cleansed us of original sin and brought us into his Church. In Confirmation, we are filled with the Holy Spirit. When we confess our sins to a priest, Christ acts through the priest to free us from the guilt and burden of our sinfulness. If we get married at some point in our life, it will be Christ who joins us together—filling us with the love and grace we will need to live together to form a family.

SIGNS

The sacraments are signs, but they are a special kind of sign. What happens when you are riding down the highway and you see a sign that reads "Speed Limit 65"? Because of the road sign, you know how fast the

continued on page 188 ▶

Serving the Community

The three Sacraments of Initiation—Baptism, Confirmation, and Eucharist—bring us into the Church and help us to grow as members. The Sacraments of Healing—Penance and Anointing of the Sick—help us remain healthy in body, mind, and soul. The other two sacraments are Sacraments at the Service of Communion. In the Sacrament of Matrimony, a man and woman give themselves to each other in a lifelong commitment of love. The two of them form a community, and if God blesses them with children, those children will be welcomed into that community. The entire family helps form the basis on which all of society is based. In the Sacrament of Holy Orders, a man commits himself to a life of service to the Church. By serving the Church, the ordained minister places his life at the service of the community.

▶ *continued from page 187*

law allows you to travel, but the speed of your car is not going to change unless you make it happen. In other words, the road sign does not change anything. It simply gives information.

The sacraments are different. Through the power of the Holy Spirit, they make things happen. When the priest consecrates the bread and wine and they become the Body and Blood of Christ, he is giving us a sign of Jesus' death for our salvation. In the Sacrament of the Eucharist, the death of Jesus is made present on that altar and within that church. When the priest baptizes an infant, he pours water on the child. The water is a sign of cleansing and life, and the infant is actually cleansed of original sin and given God's life. That is the way it is with each of the sacraments. They are signs of what God is actually doing in our lives.

The Church also uses the word *sacrament* to refer to other signs of God's love. For example, the Second Vatican Council called the Church itself "the universal sacrament of salvation," meaning that the Church is a sign of God's saving action in the world. The *Catechism of the Catholic Church* says that the humanity of Jesus "appeared as 'sacrament,' that is, the sign and instrument, of his divinity and of the salvation he brings."

The important thing for us to know is that God loves us. He gave us a sign of that love in becoming man. He gave us another sign of that love in giving us the Church as our home. And all through our lives, he gives us the special signs of his love that we call the seven sacraments. FG

Hi! I'm a sign of God's love.

IT OUT

We read signs in order to understand our surroundings. For some people, signs are their primary form of communication. Sign language is a system of communication that is based on signs made by the hands. It is considered the native language for many people who are deaf as well as for some children who can hear but whose parents are deaf. There are many different kinds of sign language, just as there are many kinds of spoken languages. American Sign Language (ASL) is used by more than one million people in Canada and the United States. It is the third-most-common language in the United States, after English and Spanish.

Back on Track

SACRAMENTAL SIGNS

Signs and symbols occupy an important place in our everyday life. Since we are both body and spirit, we use physical signs and symbols to represent things we cannot see, such as friendship. Language and gestures are also signs and symbols that we use to communicate with others. Sign and symbols are also present in our relationship with God.

God speaks to us through creation. In creation we can read traces of the Creator. Light and darkness, wind and fire, water and earth, the tree and its fruit—these all speak of God and symbolize both his greatness and his nearness. Signs and symbols taken from our everyday life, such as washing and anointing, or breaking bread and sharing a cup, can express the sanctifying presence of God.

In the liturgy the Church integrates and sanctifies elements from creation and everyday life, making them signs of grace, of the new creation we have become in Jesus Christ. Since Pentecost, the Holy Spirit has carried on the work of sanctification through the sacramental signs of the Church. The sacraments of the Church keep us on track. They make present the salvation brought by Christ and anticipate the glory of life in God's presence forever.

Back on Track

Ever notice how easy it is to get off track? Sometimes even the smallest distraction is enough to cause us to lose our bearings, whether in a class discussion or on a road trip. We can get off track in our relationships too. We get distracted by things like selfishness, jealousy, or dishonesty. All of a sudden we feel distant from someone we really care about, and we want to find our way back into friendship. The same kinds of things can affect our relationship with God. When we realize that we've been distracted and want to get back on track with God, he's there to celebrate our return.

Prepare: Begin by focusing your attention on your breath. Be aware of your breath as it flows in and out. Let go of any distracting thoughts. Open yourself to receive the Word of God.

Read: Luke 15:11–32 (The Parable of the Lost Son)

Meditate: In your imagination, place yourself in the room with the father and the younger son. Listen to the son demand from his father his share of the inheritance. Is there any advice you'd like to give to the young man? Now notice the father's face. What do you see?

Read a second time: Luke 15:11–32 (The Parable of the Lost Son)

Meditate: Now imagine that you are the son returning home after wasting all the money. What do you want to say to your father when you see him running toward you?

What do you feel when you hear him tell the servant, "Quickly bring the finest robe and put it on him; put a ring on his finger and sandals on his feet . . . because this son of mine was dead, and has come to life again; he was lost, and has been found."

Pray: Share your reflections with Jesus in your own words. Ask him if there is anything else in this story he'd like you to notice or understand better. Ask him for any help you might need. Then thank him for this time of prayer.

Contemplate: Spend a few moments in prayerful silence with God.

Close by praying together: Merciful God, no matter how far away we wander, you are always waiting, ready to welcome us home. Help us to turn to you when we feel lost and to be confident in your great love for us. Amen.

What's **WHAT?**

■ Review the main points of this chapter. Which one is most important to you? Write your reasons on the lines below.

- God cares about the lost and celebrates when they return.

- The common theme in the parables of the lost sheep, lost coin, and lost son is rejoicing and celebrating when what was lost is found.

- Father Damien cared for lepers who were rejected by society.

- The seven sacraments were given to us by Jesus so that God's life and love can fill our lives.

- The three Sacraments of Initiation bring us into the church and help us to grow as members of the Church.

_____

_____

_____

_____

_____

So **WHAT?**

■ What is God trying to show me through the sacraments?

_____

_____

_____

_____

Say **WHAT?**

sacrament

Now **WHAT?**

■ Father Damien lived the Gospel by reaching out to the suffering. What is one thing I can do this week to reach out to someone in need?

_____

_____

_____

_____

_____

Here's **WHAT** the Catholic Church Teaches

The life of Jesus of Nazareth is the best example of the connection between solidarity and conversion. In Jesus we see the immeasurable love of God. He takes on our difficulties, walks with us, saves us, and makes us one in him. In him, life in society, with all its difficulties, becomes an invitation to be more involved in sharing. In the light of faith, solidarity is linked to forgiveness and reconciliation. Like the lost son we have all been forgiven. We are all called to an inner conversion that calls us back to the Father who waits to take us back. The *Catechism of the Catholic Church* reminds us that giving priority to conversion of heart commits us to dedicate ourselves to social change that will assure a society that conforms to the norms of justice and advances the good of all.

Making Connections

1. **Read the article assigned to your group.**

2. **Note the main points from your article in the appropriate column below.**

3. **Join your group with a group who read the other article.**

4. **Record the main points in the appropriate column below.**

5. **Work together to complete the "Connect" section to show how the two articles connect.**

Connect

How do these two articles connect?

NOTES FROM ARTICLE 1

CELEBRATION

NOTES FROM ARTICLE 2

SIGNS OF LIFE

Main Points

Connection

Main Points

THE In Group

It's a fact of life. To be a part of any group there are always changes you will have to make in your life. When you become a member of a team, you have to make time for practices and games. When you join a school club, you have to set aside time for meetings and projects that the club undertakes. When you go to high school, you have to dedicate yourself to studying and involving yourself in extracurricular activities so that your college application will stand out. What group are you a part of and how did membership in this group change your lifestyle?

For Your Eyes Only

List a few groups that you would like to be a part of within the next couple of years, for example, the high school cheerleading squad, the lifeguards at the swimming pool, or the school newspaper staff.

art • i • fact
Pentecost,
M. P. Wiggins

Repent
and Be
Baptized

Sunday morning is prime time for TV preachers. It seems every other channel has someone telling us what we must do to be saved. As Catholics, we have our parents or other adults to thank for looking out for our salvation. Before we even knew to be concerned about our salvation, they were the ones who brought us to the waters of Baptism. Through our Baptism, we received the grace of the Holy Spirit and the amazing gift of new life in Christ, assuring us of our salvation. How do we know this? To answer that question, we have to go back to the early days of the Church.

In the Acts of the Apostles, Luke, who also wrote one of the Gospels, describes the time when the question "What must we do to be saved?" was asked for the first time. Picture the scene that Luke describes in Acts of the Apostles 2:1–41. Jesus is risen from the dead, and the disciples have gathered to pray. They are probably still unsettled by recent events—Jesus, their beloved friend and teacher, had been killed yet three days later he was walking among them! For several weeks he had appeared to them, but then he was gone again, carried up to heaven before their very eyes. You can understand

Both Baptism and the Church are necessary for salvation.

how they must have had mixed feelings on this day of Pentecost. They had no idea what to expect, but all heaven was about to break loose. In 2:2, Luke says that "a noise like a strong driving wind" blew through the entire house, and tongues of fire rested on each person. All of a sudden they knew that the Holy Spirit promised by Jesus had come. Jesus and the Father had sent the Holy Spirit to remain with them forever.

Not only were the disciples filled with the Holy Spirit, but they were so full of joy that they could not hide their excitement. They went out to tell everyone about what had happened to them. We are not exactly sure what they did—perhaps they danced, sang, and shouted. Whatever they did, it made everybody think that they were drunk. They were excited, Peter said, because they had received the Holy Spirit and now knew for certain that Jesus was alive.

Peter explained to the crowd that the mighty deeds and wonders God had promised in the past were now being fulfilled. Their sons and daughters would prophesy, the young would see visions, and the old would dream dreams. He told them that God had raised up Jesus, who now sits exalted at the right hand of the Father. Jesus received the promise of the Holy Spirit from the Father, and now the Spirit is poured forth on the people. Clearly the crowd could see this was happening right in front of them. Jesus is truly Messiah and Lord.

Moved by Peter's words, the crowd asked, "What are we to do?" They weren't asking the apostles what they should do for the rest of the day. They were asking, "What must we do to be saved?"

THREE THOUSAND

Now Peter had an answer, an answer that gave them the key to their participation in God's plan for our salvation. He told them to repent of their sins and to be baptized. Through Baptism, he said, people will receive the forgiveness of their sins in Jesus Christ, and they will receive the gift of the Holy Spirit. Luke tells us at the end of this story that about three thousand people were baptized that day.

The people were called that day to belong to the new People of God. They were washed in the water of Baptism—the first and most

continued on page 196 ▶

IT OUT

Are you wondering who counted the people being baptized by the apostles after the Pentecost event? How did Luke know that "about three thousand persons" were welcomed into the Church that day? (Acts of the Apostles 2:41) Rather than being an accurate count of new converts, the number is meant to impress us with the growth spurt that the early Church experienced after Pentecost due to the preaching of the Gospel. Luke tells us that prior to the coming of the Holy Spirit, the community of followers had numbered only 120. (Acts of the Apostles 1:15) Such is the power of the Holy Spirit and the Gospel of Jesus Christ!

The Ascension

According to Luke, after Jesus rose from the dead, he spent some time with his apostles. He appeared among them for about 40 days before he ascended into heaven. Luke 24:50–53 tells of Jesus leading the disciples out of Jerusalem and blessing them before he departed. Acts of the Apostles 1:9–11 describes how Jesus was lifted up in a cloud, taking him from their sight.

This astounding event, the Ascension, celebrates the entrance of Jesus' humanity into divine glory. Jesus in his risen, glorified humanity is now present at God's right hand. It is from here that Jesus and the Father send the Holy Spirit. It is from here that Jesus will return again to gather all those who will join him and his mother, Mary, in the presence of God.

Jerusalem and Rome

Jerusalem

Jerusalem was the capital of Israel and the center of the Jewish world. Rome was the capital city and center of the Roman empire. When in Acts of the Apostles 1:8 Jesus tells the disciples that they would be his witnesses from Jerusalem to the ends of the earth, he was referring to the extent of the Roman empire.

Luke crafted his writings around two journeys. In the Gospel of Luke, the entire middle section is dedicated to Jesus' journey from Galilee, where he taught and ministered, to Jerusalem, where he was crucified and resurrected. The entire second half of Acts of the Apostles is devoted to the account of Paul's journey to Rome, where he is martyred. Luke wanted to make it clear that through the power of the Holy Spirit in the Church, the work of Jesus did not end with his Ascension into heaven but will continue for all time.

The Vatican, Rome, Italy

▶ *continued from page 195*

important sacrament was the forgiveness of sins. They were united to Christ, who had died for them, risen from the dead, and had given them the Holy Spirit.

BAPTISM

Baptism was for them, as it is for us, the first Sacrament of Initiation. Through Baptism we enter into the Church, and both Baptism and the Church are necessary for our salvation. Baptism gives us birth into a new life in Jesus Christ. We receive forgiveness of original sin and all personal sins, and we become adopted sons and daughters of the Father. Baptism makes us members of Christ and temples of the Holy Spirit. Because we are brought into the Church, which is the Body of Christ, we share in the priesthood of Christ.

The three thousand people who were baptized that day by the apostles and other disciples may not have realized exactly what happened to them. But they knew that something important did happen. A permanent spiritual sign was imprinted on their souls that consecrated them for Christian worship. They went back to their homes, knowing that their life had changed.

We may or may not remember the celebration of our own Baptism. It could have happened during the celebration of Mass, in the quiet of a small ceremony, or before a crowded church celebrating the Easter Vigil. While the dramatic excitement of the wind and tongues of fire that we read about in the Acts of the Apostles did not happen, the Holy Spirit did come to each of us. In our Baptism we receive exactly the same graces given to the first disciples. With the help of these graces, we can live trusting in God and witnessing to our salvation won by Jesus Christ. FG

Excuse me, Mr. Donkey, would you mind telling me how many miles you get per gallon?

footnote

We hear a lot about the travels of Jesus and his apostles, *as well as the travels of Paul. We know they traveled by foot, but how did they manage to go such great distances without cars, trains, or airplanes? They traveled by donkey, or by camel in desert areas. Traveling by horse was reserved for the wealthy and powerful. Knowing that Jesus and his disciples were not wealthy, we begin to appreciate more what they must have endured when traveling great distances to preach the Good News.*

IM All who believed were together and had all things in common. (Acts of the Apostles 2:44)

Coming to the Water

We are all drawn to the water. If we live on the coast, we are drawn to the beach, where we can swim in the ocean. Lakes, rivers, and streams are also likely destinations. If we live in the desert, we look for an oasis or another source of fresh and clean water. Time spent by the water also allows us to stop and reflect—to watch a flowing stream, to wonder about the depths of the ocean.

What brought people to the waters of Baptism in the earliest years of the Church? A careful reading of the Acts of the Apostles shows people being drawn to Baptism in different ways. At Pentecost, the first day of the Church's life, the apostles preached a compelling, Spirit-filled message to the crowd just after they themselves had been filled with the Holy Spirit. Their enthusiasm and the hopeful message of God's forgiveness made a powerful impression on people, and three thousand were baptized.

COMMUNITY

That event took place in Jerusalem, and very soon the Christians there developed a lively community. Luke describes that community as one that stayed together, cared for its needy members, shared with one another, prayed and worshiped God, and learned from the apostles. After describing this community, Luke says that "every day the Lord added to their number those who were being saved." (Acts of the Apostles 2:47) In other words, the beauty of the community was so inspiring that others wanted to join. They came to the waters of Baptism because of the values they saw in the Christian community.

THE WORD

Luke also makes it clear that people came to the waters of Baptism because of the Good News that was being preached by the apostles and other disciples. He writes that "once they began to believe Philip as he preached the good news about the kingdom of God and

All of life is dependent upon water. Yet for an estimated 1.1 billion people on our planet, access to affordable, clean water is a daily challenge and its absence, a threat of death.

the name of Jesus Christ, men and women alike were baptized." (Acts of the Apostles 8:12) The message of the Gospel brought the people to the waters of Baptism because they saw in that message the love of God and the hope of salvation.

PAUL

One of the most powerful stories of conversion, found in Acts of the Apostles 9:1–19, is the story of Paul's experience. Paul, then known as Saul, had assisted in helping those who killed Stephen, the first Christian martyr. Saul was traveling to Damascus, carrying with him letters authorizing him to persecute the city's Christians. Suddenly he was blinded by a bright light and was thrown to the ground. A voice asked him, "'Saul, Saul, why are you persecuting me?'" Saul asked who was speaking. The voice answered, "'I am Jesus, whom you are persecuting. Now get up and go into the city and you will be told what you must do.'" (Acts of the Apostles 9:4–6) Paul got up but he was unable to see. He was taken to Damascus to wait for what Jesus wanted him to do next. Jesus then appeared to a Christian in Damascus named Ananias and told him to baptize Paul. Ananias was hesitant because he knew Paul's reputation for persecuting Christians. Jesus told Ananias that he was calling Paul to be a great missionary. As Ananias ministered to Paul, things like scales fell from his eyes, and he could again see.

> The beauty of the community was so inspiring that others wanted to join.

Paul was not looking to be baptized, but God called him to belong to the new People of God. Paul responded. His Baptism confirmed the change God had brought about in his life. He then began a worldwide ministry of bringing others to the waters of Baptism. This story in Luke makes it clear that God's call to faith is at the center of Baptism.

All of the newly baptized had their lives changed by their Baptism. They would not go back to living the way they lived before. Paul, of course, is the greatest example of this change. He spent every moment of the rest of his life spreading the Good News of Jesus Christ. He is not the only one who experienced such a change. All of the early Christians were so changed by their Baptism that their movement spread throughout the Roman world and even to Rome itself. The Church we have today owes its life and strength in good part to those early, enthusiastic Christians who came to the waters of Baptism and began to live changed lives. FG

Anna and Simeon, Laura James, Brooklyn, NY

The Presentation

In the Jewish faith, Mosaic Law required that firstborn sons be consecrated to God. Luke 2:22–38 tells the story of how Mary and Joseph obeyed this law by bringing Jesus to the Temple. He had already been circumcised, and now he would be consecrated and presented to God. By telling us about Jesus' circumcision and presentation to God, Luke makes it clear that Mary and Joseph were devout Jews and faithful observers of God's law. They were bringing their child into the family of God's people. They were doing the same thing that parents do today when they bring their infants to church to be baptized.

In Luke's story, Jesus was welcomed at the entrance of the Temple by two people. The first person was a man named Simeon, who was inspired by the Holy Spirit to recognize Jesus as the Messiah. The second person was a prophetess named Anna, who gave thanks to God for Jesus and proclaimed him as the Messiah to all who were waiting for the redemption of the people. In the same way, infants who are baptized today are welcomed by the community into the Church. As we look to what the future will hold for them we can imagine the good that they will do for God and others with the help of the Holy Spirit.

Accepting the
Challenge

CONVERSION

Jesus calls us to conversion. It is an essential part of the proclamation of the Kingdom of God. "'This is the time of fulfillment,'" Jesus says in Mark 1:15, "'The kingdom of God is at hand. Repent, and believe in the gospel.'"

Baptism is the event of our conversion. In the preaching of the apostles at Pentecost and throughout history, the Church's call is addressed first to those who do not yet know Christ and his Gospel. It is by faith in the Gospel and through Baptism that we renounce evil and gain salvation, the forgiveness of our sins, and the gift of new life. Jesus' call to ongoing conversion is addressed to us throughout our lives. It is a central part of the Lord's Prayer, where we recognize God as our loving Father and our need to be forgiven by him. This conversion is an uninterrupted task for the entire Church, which is at once holy and always in need of purification. It is also a task for each Christian, who is saved and yet always in need of repentance. This task of conversion is not just a human one. It is the movement of a contrite heart. In prayer we are drawn and moved by grace to respond to the merciful love of God, who loved us first.

The story of Paul's conversion from a persecutor of Christians to a great missionary is mind-boggling. Who but God would choose a man with Paul's background to go out and preach about Jesus? Because Paul accepted God's challenge to change his life, other people experienced conversion in their lives. It was like watching the ripples go out when you throw a rock into water. Christians who knew Paul before his conversion had to change their attitudes and learn to trust him. Those who heard Paul preach and were baptized experienced conversion to new life in Christ. God challenges each of us to ongoing conversion in our lives too.

Take several deep breaths and allow yourself to become still.

Close your eyes, and with your imagination, picture the flame from a candle. It is the candle used at your Baptism, signifying the light of Christ and your Christian commitment.

Rest for just a moment, allowing that light to fill you.

Group 1: You do amazing things, O God. Your ways and your thoughts are far beyond what we can imagine. You call people like Paul and like us to be followers of your Son, Jesus. Help us to be true to our baptismal commitment to be the light of Christ in our world. Strengthen our desire to be open to your call and to be willing to accept your challenge to change our lives in order to stay close to you.

Group 2: We ask you also for the grace to allow other people to change and not to hold their pasts against them. Help us to remember that as we grow closer to you, the change in our lives will have the same ripple effect in the lives of others that Paul's conversion did. May the grace we received at our Baptism be the strength we need to accept your challenge to conversion throughout our lives.

All: Amen.

What's **WHAT?**

■ Main points from this chapter are listed below. Choose the one that you could explain the best to others. Write what you would say on the lines below.

- Through Baptism we enter the Church and receive new life in Jesus Christ.
- The Ascension celebrates the entrance of Jesus into heaven.
- Jerusalem and Rome are important in Luke's Gospel and the Acts of the Apostles because of the journeys of Jesus and Paul.
- In the earliest days of the Church, people were drawn to Baptism because of the values they saw in the Christian community.
- The story of the Presentation of Jesus describes how Mary and Joseph brought him to the temple to be consecrated to God.

_____

_____

_____

Say **WHAT?** Jesus → heaven

Acts of the Apostles • *Ascension*

So **WHAT?**

■ In what ways have I noticed my commitment to God growing as I grow older?

_____

_____

_____

Michael Vinci

Now **WHAT?**

■ What is one thing I can do this week to remember and make real my baptismal commitment?

_____

_____

_____

_____

Here's **WHAT** the Catholic Church Teaches

Like the first Christians, we need to be concerned about the common good of the entire community. People have the right to develop their talents and skills and become the best individuals they can be. All the conditions of social, economic, political, and cultural life, ought to enable everyone to do this.

The common good is not the good for the greatest number of people. That would leave some people out. Catholic Social Teaching insists that each and every person participates in the common good, not just the smartest, the most powerful, or the luckiest. "At the national level promoting community and the common good requires creating employment for all, caring for the less privileged, and providing for the future. At the global level, it increasingly requires analogous intervention on behalf of the whole human family." (*On the Hundredth Anniversary of Rerum Novarum*)

Cornerstones

1. As the two articles are read, note the cornerstones (main points) from each article in the appropriate column below.
2. With your group, share one cornerstone you identified from your group's assigned article. Keep sharing cornerstones until you have no new ones to share. Say "pass" if you have nothing new to add.

CORNERSTONES — ARTICLE 1	CORNERSTONES — ARTICLE 2
Repent and Be Baptized	**Coming to the Water**

A Dream COME TRUE

When we dream at night, some of our dreams frighten us, some we can't completely recall, and some occur over and over again. But there are dreams we can control; we call them daydreams. What kinds of things do you daydream about?

For Your Eyes Only

To make a dream come true, you need a plan. Imagine how you'd like your life to be 10 years from now. What steps would you have to take to realize that dream?

STEP 1:

STEP 2:

STEP 3:

Obedience and Respect

The Finding in the Temple, Michael D. O'Brien

"What do you want to be when you grow up?" You've probably heard this question often enough. You may already know for certain, or perhaps you haven't a clue. Either way it helps to talk it over with people you look up to and to take opportunities to develop your skills and interests. These are great ways to test the waters and imagine your future.

THE PASSOVER

Luke 2:41–52 tells the story of when Jesus was young and faced a similar situation. Mary and Joseph took him to Jerusalem to celebrate the great Jewish festival of Passover. Jerusalem, the capital city of Israel, was the spiritual home of the Jewish people. People in the caravan knew that this would be Jesus' first celebration of Passover, marking his coming-of-age in the Jewish faith. Since he was moving toward adulthood, he probably even heard the question, "What do you want to be when you grow up, Jesus?" more times than he wanted to. Maybe people encouraged him to become a carpenter like Joseph. Or maybe his friends urged him to think about becoming a fisherman like the other young men in his neighborhood. We don't know what Jesus was thinking at the time. But we do know that after the celebration in Jerusalem, something major happened.

> Jesus realized that his Father had a special calling for him.

When it was time to return home to Nazareth the caravan left. Jesus did not leave with the caravan. He stayed behind in Jerusalem. Luke tells us that at first Mary and Joseph didn't notice Jesus was missing because they figured that he was somewhere else in the huge caravan. When they finally realized that Jesus wasn't with them, they hurried back to Jerusalem. You can imagine how worried they were. Their 12-year-old boy was lost in the big city.

JESUS IN THE TEMPLE

After searching for three days, Mary and Joseph finally found Jesus calmly sitting in the Temple, and they were astonished at the scene. He was listening intently to the Jewish teachers and asking them questions. His ability to understand and speak about the Jewish faith seemed so natural that it impressed the teachers who had studied the faith and law their entire life. Luke says that "all who heard him were astounded at his understanding and his answers." (Luke 2:47)

Like any mother would, Mary asked Jesus why he had disappeared without telling anyone. In response, Jesus said, "'Why were you looking for me? Did you not know that I must be in my Father's house?'" (Luke 2:49)

Jesus realized that his Father had a special calling for him. He had a sense of what he would be doing when he grew up, though as a 12-year-old boy, he could not have understood everything about that mission.

At the time that they found Jesus in the Temple, we can well imagine that Mary and Joseph were probably thinking less about Jesus' future occupation and more about how happy they were that he was safe and sound. Luke points out that Mary and Joseph still didn't exactly understand what his reply meant. Yet having seen Jesus so clearly in his element, they must have known that he had found his calling. Mary remembered Jesus' words in her heart. She would think about them later on, knowing that her son loved and respected her but that he had to follow his call from God, his Father.

Even though this was an extraordinary moment, Luke tells us that Jesus didn't stay in the Temple in Jerusalem. He returned with his parents to Nazareth and was obedient to them. He had learned the commandments and was familiar with the Fourth Commandment; he knew that he was to respect and obey his parents. So far from this being a story about a son disobeying his parents, it is a story about a boy growing up and beginning to understand how God his Father is calling him to a special mission. Jesus was in the Temple because in some way he was preparing to follow this mission. We begin to appreciate Jesus' special relationship with God, his Father. It's also a story about parents dealing with the growing independence of a maturing son. Mary and Joseph knew that the Fourth Commandment didn't apply only to children. It applied to parents as well, calling them to prepare their children for the work that God wants them to do.

Like Jesus, you, too, have a special calling from God. You have been given unique talents and abilities and the support and encouragement of your parents or guardians. What calling from God is growing in your heart? FG

Wisdom, Age, and Favor

In Luke 2:51–52 we learn that while Jesus was living with his parents in Nazareth, he advanced in wisdom, age, and favor before God and others. He did so by practicing the virtues that lead a person to live in relationship with God and others. He learned to be prudent, choosing the right course of action. He learned to be just, giving God and his neighbors what is due them. He learned to be strong, determined to do what is right in the face of obstacles. He learned to be moderate, both in seeking pleasure and in using his possessions. These four virtues—prudence, justice, fortitude, and temperance—are called the cardinal virtues because they are essential to living close to God and others.

IT OUT

We're all familiar with the Fourth Commandment: Honor your father and mother. We respect our parents and are grateful for all the things they do for us. But did you know that this commandment isn't addressed only to children? It applies to parents as well. The Fourth Commandment calls parents to respect their children and to do everything they can to help them live a full, healthy life. They are called to provide for their children and to educate them properly to prepare them for the work that God wants them to do. Parents also have a sacred duty to teach their children about prayer and to lead them in growing in their faith.

Dreaming Dreams

Suppose one of the athletic teams at your school started out the season with no idea of how well they wanted to do this year and with no plan for winning games. Or suppose you joined a club and found out that nothing ever happened because nobody understood why the club existed and what it was supposed to do. There is a good chance that the team would end the season without winning a game and that you would quit the club. Teams and clubs need to have a vision and a plan if they are to succeed.

Acts of the Apostles 2:14–19 tells the story of when the apostles and other disciples were filled with the Holy Spirit on Pentecost. They were overjoyed. When a gathering crowd wondered what was going on, Peter spoke for all the disciples. He explained that the excitement the disciples were showing came from the fact that they were Spirit-filled. They were doing what the prophet Joel said would happen when people are filled with the Spirit—they were seeing visions and dreaming dreams. In other words, they were looking toward a bright future, dreaming of the world that God wants for them. Luke was describing the effects of the outpouring of the Holy Spirit on the entire community. The same Holy Spirit comes to us in Baptism and strengthens us in the Sacrament of Confirmation.

CONFIRMATION

Confirmation ties us more closely to the Body of Christ. It makes our link to the Church stronger and involves us more closely in the Church's mission. Confirmation helps us be witnesses to the Christian faith in the things we say and do.

I dream pretty much all day long. And you can really see that when you look at my report card.

Confirmation is a sacrament, placing a spiritual mark on us that cannot be taken away. Confirmation can be received only one time. In order to receive the Sacrament of Confirmation, we must be in the state of grace, we must want to receive the sacrament, we must profess our belief in the Catholic faith, and we must be ready to join with Jesus Christ in proclaiming the kingdom. As part of the Rite of Confirmation, oil is placed on the forehead of the baptized person, and the bishop places his hands over him or her. Then these words are spoken by the bishop: "Be sealed with the Gift of the Holy Spirit."

"But you, go and proclaim the kingdom of God." (Luke 9:60)

IM

With the Sacrament of Confirmation, we are filled with the Holy Spirit and are charged with helping the Church carry out its mission. This is where the dreams and visions come in. Remember the example of a team that doesn't have a clear idea of its direction? We said that it

continued on page 208 ▶

Ark sculpture, bronze, Joseph and Georgia Pozycinski

IT'S LIKE THIS

Noah dreamed of saving his family and God's creatures from a flood. He built an ark even though his neighbors mocked and laughed at him. But Noah, his family, and the animals were saved. Jesus proclaimed the Kingdom of God here on earth. He preached a message of love and worked miracles, but he was made fun of, rejected by the people of his hometown, and eventually killed. Yet he won salvation for all. When you dream of living a holy life in a peaceful and just world, you too may meet with criticism and pressure to conform to society's norms. But you have the power of the Holy Spirit on your side. The Holy Spirit will help you work to realize your dream.

Jesuit Volunteer Corps

When young people go to college, it is often because they have a dream, an idea of what they want for their lives. Sometimes as young people go through college, they develop another dream, an idea of what they want for others. College-aged young people have the opportunity to join the Jesuit Volunteer Corps. This group is made up of young people who live out the Sacrament of Confirmation by working with people in need. They work with the homeless, the unemployed, refugees, people living with AIDS, the elderly, women and children who have been abused, and people with mental illnesses. Jesuit Volunteers live simple lives in a small communities but work for social justice and peace in the world. After serving for a year or two as Jesuit Volunteers, they begin their next calling. Their time as Jesuit Volunteers teaches them about God and his world in a way they could never learn in a classroom.

Our Roots Are Showing

In the early days of the Church, Jesus' followers did not have a specific name. As evidenced in the Acts of the Apostles, they were known as "all who believed" (2:44), "the disciples of the Lord" (9:1), "men [and] women who belonged to the Way" (9:2), "the holy ones" (9:32), and "the sect of the Nazoreans" (24:5). The name *Christian*, by which they were recognized in Antioch, was sometimes used as an insult, reflecting the suspicion and hostility met by the first followers of Christ. However, it is the name that stuck.

► *continued from page 207*

would probably have a bad season. Through the power of the Holy Spirit, we can move forward as witnesses to Jesus Christ. We gain the vision of the kind of world God wants us to have. The Holy Spirit inspires us to dream God's dream.

THE KINGDOM

Jesus proclaimed the Kingdom of God and he gave us a glimpse of that world. By curing the sick, he showed us that the kingdom will be a place of health and wholeness. By raising the dead to life, he showed us that it will be a place in which all life is respected and killing does not take place. By caring for the poor, Jesus showed us that in the kingdom, everyone will have what they need, and everyone will be respected.

Guided by the Holy Spirit, we will dream about a better world, and we will work to bring about that dream. Confirmation gives us the ability to dream that dream and to serve God's kingdom. FG

WANT TO KNOW MORE? visit www.FindingGod.org/teens for more on Confirmation.

What's in a Name?

We learn about the church at Antioch in Acts of the Apostles 11:19–26. It was an interesting city. It was located in the area north of Israel known as Syria. Antioch was not as old as Jerusalem, but it had grown fast, many Jews and non-Jews (Gentiles) lived there. Many Jewish Christians who had fled the persecution in Jerusalem settled in Antioch and helped proclaim the Gospel to many Greek-speaking Gentiles.

The Jewish Christians reported to the church in Jerusalem about their success proclaiming the Good News. The church in Jerusalem sent Barnabas (pictured) to take charge of the church in Antioch, and he asked Paul to see what was happening. It was from Antioch that Paul made his first two missionary journeys into the Mediterranean world to spread the Gospel.

Barnabas and Paul found the grace of the Holy Spirit alive and well in the community. It was in Antioch that people first referred to the followers of Jesus as Christians—those who belonged to Christ. *Christ* was the Greek translation of the word "Messiah." In Confirmation we receive the same outpouring of the Holy Spirit that helped to create the vibrant Christian community in Antioch. We still call ourselves Christians because the center of our faith, the person whom we look up to and follow as our Savior, our Redeemer, our teacher, and our Lord, is Christ, the Son of God made man.

Stretching Our Wings

OBEDIENCE AND PRAYER

The Bible, especially in the Ten Commandments and in the Beatitudes, teaches us how to obey God. Although the word *obey* is sometimes understood as being submissive or compliant, its original meaning comes from a Latin word that means "to hear" or "to listen to." Obedience, then, is linked to prayer because prayer includes listening to what God has to say.

Through prayer the Holy Spirit helps us to stretch our wings, giving us the strength and grace to follow God's call to us. In fact prayer is an indispensable condition for being able to obey God's commandments. Through obedience, we develop a sensitivity to God's call, and we develop an attitude of openness to go beyond just what we want or need to wanting what is best for everyone.

The First Commandment shows how obedience and prayer are inseparable. It calls us to have no other gods before God the Father. Adoring God, offering him the worship that belongs to him, and fulfilling the promises made to him are all expressions of obedience to the First Commandment. Prayer and obedience to God's commandments help us to remain faithful to our baptismal promises and to resist temptation.

Jesus is the perfect model of someone who combined prayer and obedience to God the Father's call. That's why in teaching his disciples and us how to pray, Jesus included the words "thy will be done."

Stretching Our Wings

Moving into adolescence involves taking on greater responsibility. To do that well, we take the positive values we've learned from our parents, teachers, and others in authority and begin to think for ourselves. We begin to stretch our wings, trying on new behaviors and dreaming new dreams of how life can be. We need to ask for the Holy Spirit's help to know God's will for us and to do it generously.

Leader: Let us pray for the Holy Spirit's help to know God's will for us and to do it generously.

All: Come, Holy Spirit, fill our hearts and kindle in us the fire of your love.

Group 1: Come, Holy Spirit, open our minds and hearts to hear God's voice and to know God's will for us.

Group 2: Come, Holy Spirit, help us to know God's plan for the world and to do our part to make it happen.

Group 1: Come, Holy Spirit, make us generous in using our gifts and talents to serve God's kingdom here on earth.

Group 2: Come, Holy Spirit, help us to treat others with dignity and to respect others as we begin to stretch our wings.

All: With faith and trust in the Holy Spirit, we ask God to hear and grant our prayers, which we make in Jesus' name. Amen.

Mosaic, Basilica of St. Thérèse, Lisieux, France

What's **WHAT?**

■ Review the main points of this chapter. Which one is most important to you? Write your reasons on the lines below.

- The Fourth Commandment directs that children and parents should respect each other.

- While living with his parents in Nazareth, Jesus practiced the virtues that lead him to be a person living in relationship with God and others.

- Confirmation helps us to be witnesses to the Christian faith in the things we say and do.

- Jesuit Volunteers live simple lives in a small community but work for social justice and peace in the world.

- Paul made his first two missionary journeys from Antioch to spread the Gospel.

_____

_____

_____

_____

_____

Say **WHAT?**

Pentecost • rite

So **WHAT?**

■ Jesus' example shows us how to balance our growing independence with obedience to our parents. *Think about it. Pray about it.*

Now **WHAT?**

■ As I reflect on God's will for the world, what is one thing I can do this week to help make it come true?

_____

_____

_____

_____

Here's **WHAT** the Catholic Church Teaches

The Church has coexisted with many types of government. But whether the form of government is a monarchy or a democracy, the Church teaches that all political authority comes from the people who are governed. The democratic system best ensures the participation of its citizens in making political choices. Pope John Paul II wrote in *In the Hundredth Anniversary of Rerum Novarum* that the democratic system of government "guarantees to the governed the possibility both of electing and holding accountable those who govern them and of replacing them through peaceful means when appropriate."

Democracy is the best guarantee that narrow political groups with rigid religious or scientific ideologies will not replace the authority of the citizens. Christianity is not an ideology. The Christian faith does not restrict the changing realities of everyday life to rigid ways of thinking. It knows that change happens. The priorities are respect for freedom and respect for the dignity of the person.

We Can Change the World

1. **Read both articles silently.**

2. **In your group of four, decide which article each pair will work on.**

3. **With your partner, complete the "Something to Think About..." section below, listing the important ideas presented in your article.**

4. **Exchange worksheets with the other pair in your group and complete the "How it Can Change the World" section below.**

5. **With your partner, select one "Something to Think About...Change the World" idea and explain how and why this idea can make the world a better place.**

6. **With your partner, think of a role model you feel has changed the world in this way.**

ARTICLE NAME _____

SOMETHING TO THINK ABOUT	HOW IT CAN CHANGE THE WORLD

FOOD FOR Thought

Just as we eat in order to satisfy our hunger and provide nutrition for our bodies, we need to satisfy other cravings such as our hunger for knowledge, our curiosity about the world, and our desire to connect with other people. What are some other cravings that people have?

IT'S LIKE THIS

When we talk about our desire for food, we often use the word *appetite*. What satisfies your appetite for the following?

sweets: _____

entertainment: _____

comfort food: _____

recreation: _____

This Is My Body

When we look around our homes we cannot help but notice the keepsakes that help us remember the special people and events in our lives. We may keep a diary or a scrapbook filled with photos of vacations, holidays, family, and friends. Looking at these, we remember the good times we had. There are even times when these memories help us make it through a tough day.

When we use the word *memory*, we usually mean recalling past events. But what is past is past. When the Bible uses the word *memory*, especially in regard to celebrating the great festivals of faith, it means more than recalling something from the past. Remembering what God has done in the past is the means by which we acknowledge God's action in our lives today.

THE LAST SUPPER

Jesus wanted his disciples to remember his last meal with them. He was sitting down to eat supper with his closest friends. It was the feast of Passover, the celebration of God leading the Hebrew people out of slavery to freedom, and one of the holiest days of the year. What made this meal different for Jesus was that he knew something his friends did not know. He knew that right after supper he was going to be arrested, tortured, and eventually killed.

Luke 22:7–20 tells how Jesus took advantage of this moment to give his friends, the disciples, something special. The Passover meal followed a ritual outlined in the Scripture, and it included a ceremony in which the family would share unleavened bread and a cup of wine.

art • i • fact
Jesus Breaking Bread,
Fr. John Giuliani

In the Eucharist, Jesus shows us how to be his followers.

Initiation and Renewal

The process of initiation into the Catholic Church has three steps. The first step is Baptism, in which original sin is taken away, and we receive new life in the Holy Spirit. We become adopted sons and daughters of God. The second step is Confirmation, in which we are strengthened with the Holy Spirit and dedicated to the serving of the Kingdom of God on earth. The final step is receiving the Eucharist, in which our bodies and souls are nourished with the Body and Blood of Jesus Christ. The first two steps don't have to be repeated because they leave a permanent spiritual mark on us. We celebrate the Eucharist over and over again because we constantly need nourishment as we go through life. Celebrating the Eucharist regularly is our way of renewing the commitments we made in Baptism and Confirmation to belong to God's People and to serve God's kingdom.

God separating light from darkness, Michelangelo, 1475-1564, Sistine Chapel, Vatican Palace, Vatican State

This sharing of bread and wine called to mind the actual Passover, when the people of Israel hurriedly ate unleavened bread before leaving behind the slavery of Egypt. As Jesus and his disciples shared the bread and wine, Jesus gave the traditional items a completely different meaning.

BODY AND BLOOD

Luke tells us that as Jesus broke the bread and gave it to his disciples, he said a blessing, "'This is my body, which will be given for you; do this in memory of me.'" (Luke 22:19) Jesus was giving himself to his disciples—he himself was the sacrifice. Jesus then made it clear how he would give himself for his disciples and for us. He gave the disciples the wine and said, "'This cup is the new covenant in my blood, which will be shed for you.'" (Luke 22:20) Jesus was going to shed his blood, and his sacrifice would establish a new covenant with God. Then Jesus said, "Do this in memory of me."

In the Eucharist, we remember what Jesus gave the disciples and the entire Church at the Last Supper. When we celebrate this sacrament, the bread and wine become the Body and Blood of Jesus Christ. As the celebration of Jesus' supreme sacrifice, the Eucharist is the heart and the high point of the life of the Church.

SACRIFICE

In the Eucharist we celebrate the memorial of Christ's Passover, his journey through life, death, and Resurrection that brought about our salvation. When we say that the Eucharist is a memorial, we mean that it is more than a simple memory of past events. It is a proclamation of how God is working in our lives today. In celebrating this memorial, what Jesus did for us through his suffering and death becomes present to us in our lives. When we celebrate the Eucharist, the work toward our salvation in Jesus Christ is made present today. The Eucharist is a sacrifice offered by Christ himself, the high priest of the New Covenant, acting through the priest presiding at the Mass of every single Catholic community throughout the world.

If Sunday is the Lord's Day, then why do we sometimes celebrate on Saturday night? We have to go all the way back to the beginning for our answer. In the first story of Creation we read that "God called the light 'day,' and the darkness he called 'night.' Thus evening came, and morning followed—the first day." (Genesis 1:5) So the first day of creation began with night and ended with day. Since our Christian roots are in the Jewish tradition, we inherited this understanding of a day. Therefore, when we celebrate Mass on Saturday evening, it is considered Sunday Mass because for us Sunday has already begun.

SUNDAY AND BEYOND

The principal day for celebrating the Eucharist is Sunday, the Lord's Day, the day of the Resurrection. This is the day of the Christian family, the day on which we rest from work and come together as God's people.

In the Eucharist, Jesus shows us how to be his followers. Just as he gave himself as a sacrifice for others and continues to give himself to us in the Eucharist, we are to give ourselves to others. When you receive Holy Communion with the words "The Body of Christ" or "The Blood of Christ," it is as if Jesus is saying, "Here I am, ready to help you in any way I can." That's what Jesus wants us to do when we leave the church after Mass—go out into the world and offer ourselves to others. "Here we are," Jesus wants us to say to our friends and relatives and even to strangers in need of aid, "ready to help you in any way we can." With the help of the grace of the Sacrament of Eucharist, we serve others in Jesus' name.

Our memories are powerful. They help us to recall times, events, and family celebrations that have shaped who we are. They are powerful images that also shape the way we see the world and our future. In celebrating the Eucharist, we remember all that Jesus has done for us in his sacrifice on the cross. In celebrating this memorial, we are also recognizing the presence of Jesus Christ in our life today. He is shaping who we are and the direction of our lives in the future.

Who Is This Stranger?

It's hard to watch one of our friends get in trouble for something we know he or she didn't do. We might want to speak up to defend our friend, but we're scared. We don't want to draw attention to ourselves and be unjustly accused as well. Even though we didn't do anything wrong, we're not willing to take the chance of getting in trouble. What do we do? We keep a low profile, and, if at all possible, remove ourselves completely from the situation, just in case. Better to be safe than sorry.

Luke 24:13–35 tells the story of two disciples who were scared after Jesus had been arrested and crucified. They were running away from danger in Jerusalem. Who knew what might happen? Maybe the Roman soldiers or the Temple guards would start looking for all of Jesus' disciples! So they were getting out of town. They were headed towards the village of Emmaus, and as they walked along talking about what had happened over the weekend, they met a man who walked along with them. It was Jesus, but they did not recognize him.

They saw the bread being blessed, broken, and shared, and they knew it was Jesus.

He was made known to them in the breaking of the bread.

(Luke 24:35)

They told the stranger about how Jesus, whom they called "a prophet mighty in deed and word before God and all the people," was arrested and crucified. (Luke 24:19) The disciples were upset because they had hoped that Jesus was the one who had come to redeem Israel. But then, they told the stranger, something very confusing had happened that morning. Some women went to the tomb where Jesus was buried and found it empty. They had a vision of angels who said that Jesus was alive. The two disciples weren't sure what to think.

THE WORD

Jesus began to explain to them what happened and why it had happened. He showed them how the prophets said that the Messiah would have to suffer. He also showed them that Moses and all the other prophets pointed to the coming of Jesus. The two disciples listened to Jesus talking about the Scriptures, and they were deeply moved. So when they arrived at Emmaus, they invited Jesus to stay with them because it was nearly evening. Their act of hospitality set the stage for everything that followed.

When it came time to eat dinner, Luke tells us that Jesus took bread, blessed and broke it, and gave it to them. At that very moment, the disciples realized that he was Jesus, and as soon as they recognized him, he disappeared. They now knew for sure that he had risen from the dead.

continued on page 218 ▶

This Way Out

We live in a society where it seems that everything has to be done fast. Sometimes we don't even have time to breeze through a fast-food restaurant. Instead we eat on the run. We grab a cup of soup-in-the-can or a protein bar, and we're off. These quick fixes are often called meal replacements because they are supposed to contain all the nutrition you would get from a balanced meal. But you can't put in a package the time for rest or companionship that are necessary to nourish our bodies and spirits. The Eucharistic celebration is a great example of how a meal can meet all our needs for nourishment—spiritual food, companionship with God and with others, and spiritual renewal. This is the meal that gives us energy for life with and in God.

Blessed Are the Hungry

Luke makes it clear in his Gospel that Jesus wanted people to have food. In his Sermon on the Plain, Jesus says that the hungry are blessed and will be satisfied. Luke 9:11–17 tells us that after Jesus had preached to a large crowd, he realized that they would not be able to get food so late in the day. So he blessed the tiny bit of food that was available and had his disciples pass the food around. Everyone had plenty to eat, and there were several baskets of leftovers.

But Luke went a step further. He also wants us to know that Jesus himself is food for others. For example, in the story about the birth of Jesus, Luke says that Mary laid the baby Jesus in a manger, a trough used to feed animals. Luke uses this image to symbolize that Jesus has come to be food for the world. In his description of the Last Supper, Luke tells how Jesus gave his disciples bread and said, "This is my Body," and then he gave them wine and said, "This is my Blood." The Eucharist is Jesus feeding his people with the food that is himself. In receiving the Eucharist, the hungry are indeed blessed and satisfied with the greatest food imaginable, the Body and Blood of Jesus Christ, the Son of God.

Food for the Journey

The images of the way and the journey are at the heart of Luke's writing. In his Gospel Luke tells us that Jesus "guide[s] our feet into the path of peace." (Luke 1:79) Jesus' Resurrection makes known the "paths of life." (Acts of the Apostles 2:28) The central image in Luke's Gospel is Jesus' journey to Jerusalem. In the Acts of the Apostles the focus is on the spread of Christianity to Rome. Rome was seen as the political and cultural center of the world, through which one would go to the ends of the earth.

The early Christian community identified itself as the Way. The two disciples walking to Emmaus are on a journey, and Jesus comes to them in the Eucharist and gives them the strength to complete their journey. That is what the Eucharist is. It is the food we need in order to make our way through life. In the Eucharist Jesus feeds us and gives us the nourishment we must have so that we can complete our own journey on the Way.

▶ *continued from page 217*

BREAKING THE BREAD

Luke points out at the very end of the Emmaus story that the disciples recognized Jesus "in the breaking of the bread." (Luke 24:35) They saw the bread being blessed, broken, and shared, and they knew it was Jesus. That is why the Eucharist is so close to the hearts of Catholics—we know it is Jesus. We eat what looks like bread and we drink what tastes like wine, but we know this is not bread and wine. It is Jesus Christ. It is the Body and the Blood of the Messiah given for our salvation.

It is interesting how Luke tells the story. First the disciples listened to Jesus, the Word of God, explaining the Scriptures to them. Then they gathered around the table and received the bread from Jesus. Does that sound familiar? At Mass, the first thing we do is listen to the Scriptures as they are read and explained to us. Then we gather around the altar and receive the consecrated bread and wine. Luke's story shows us that this is what Christians have been doing since the time of Jesus—worshipping God by listening to the Word of God and receiving the Eucharist.

> Their encounter with Jesus had changed them, and they were no longer running away.

STRENGTH

What did the two disciples do after they recognized Jesus? They went back to Jerusalem. Their encounter with Jesus had changed them, and they were no longer running away. They would face the dangers of life in Jerusalem, strengthened by their meeting with Jesus in the Eucharist. Luke wants us to understand that the Eucharist calls us to act in the same way. The Eucharist strengthens us in our struggles in life. With the Eucharist, we do not have to run away from the challenges we meet in life. We can face them with courage, because Jesus is with us. *FG*

Transutasiation? Transylvanian? No, Transistor? Wait, transwulstation… TRANSUBSTANTIATION, I GOT IT!

Here's a big word for you to digest—*transubstantiation*. It refers to what happens at the words of consecration when the bread and wine are transformed into the **Body and Blood of Jesus Christ** while their appearance and taste remain the same.

Refreshing Our Memory

LUKE ON PRAYER AND SHARING MEALS

Of all the Gospel writers, Luke gives the most attention to Jesus' prayer life. Luke shows Jesus retreating to quiet places to pray and to be alone with God the Father. We also see Jesus praying during significant moments in his ministry. For example, Luke tells us that after Jesus is baptized, he prays and the Holy Spirit descends upon him. (3:21–22) Jesus prays before he calls the disciples. (6:12–13) He prays before he asks Peter who he thinks Jesus is. (9:20) He also prays in Gethsemane (22:40–42), on the cross (23:34,46), and at the table with the disciples at Emmaus. (24:30)

Along with the importance of prayer, Luke also shows the importance Jesus placed on sharing a meal with others and the memories this creates. Meal scenes fill Luke's Gospel. Jesus eats with sinners and tax collectors, with Pharisees, with crowds of people, and with the disciples. Jesus teaches through parables that center on meals shared in friendship. In one parable, we see the poor and the outcasts being invited to a fancy banquet instead of the rich. (14:11) In another, we see a rich man condemned for excluding the beggar Lazarus from his table. (16:19–31) These parables give a deeper meaning to the Eucharist at the Last Supper (22:14–23), the most important meal Jesus shared with his disciples, and to the Emmaus story in which the disciples recognize Jesus in the breaking of the bread.

In the Acts of the Apostles, Luke shows us how prayer and meals come together in the life of the young Christian community after Pentecost. "They devoted themselves to the teaching of the apostles and to the communal life, to the breaking of the bread and to the prayers." (Acts of the Apostles 2:42)

Refreshing Our Memory

All: In the name of the Father, and of the Son, and of the Holy Spirit. Amen.

Leader: In the story of the two disciples on their way to Emmaus, we learn the value of memory for our spiritual life. Those disciples had studied the Scripture since their childhood. And they had been with Jesus at the table before his Crucifixion. On this day, their cares and burdens kept them from recognizing him. Jesus needed to refresh their memories and to remind them of what they already knew but had temporarily forgotten.

Reader: A reading from the Gospel of Luke 24: 25–32.
>   The Gospel of the Lord.

All: Praise to you, Lord Jesus Christ.

Leader: Have you ever forgotten something important because you were distracted by worry or fear, as the disciples were when they met Jesus on the road? Perhaps you forgot your manners and misbehaved. Or maybe you forgot a promise you'd made and disappointed someone you really cared about. Think of a time you needed to be reminded of something you already knew. *(pause)*

How did you feel when your memory was refreshed, and your thoughts or actions were resolved? *(pause)*

The two disciples described feeling like their hearts were burning. What image would you use? *(pause)*

Let's gather our thoughts and pray together in gratitude for the gift of memory. Our response to each petition will be **We praise you, Lord, and give you thanks.**

Reader 2: Jesus, thank you for the gift of our memory, and for all that we know of you from our study of Scripture, we pray to the Lord. ℟

Reader 3: Jesus, thank you for the gift of yourself that we receive in the celebration of the Eucharist, we pray to the Lord. ℟

Reader 4: Jesus, thank you for the people and events in our lives that help us to remember that we are your disciples and that we share your life, we pray to the Lord. ℟

Leader: Let's pause for a moment to add our own intentions. *(pause)*

Now let's pray together in the words that Jesus taught us. **Our Father . . .**

All: Lord Jesus, in the Eucharist we are refreshed with the Scriptures and with your own Body and Blood. Teach us to use the strength we receive to go out into the world and help others to remember your message. When we face challenges living out the Gospel, remind us of what we already know—that you are always with us as we make our way through life. Amen.

Jesus Christ appears to the Apostles on the road to Emmaus, 6th Century, mosaic, Saint Apollinare Nuovo, Ravenna, Italy

What's **WHAT?**

■ Review the main points of this chapter. Choose one that's most inspiring to you and write your reasons on the lines provided.

• In the Eucharist we celebrate the memorial of Christ's life, death, and Resurrection which brought about our salvation.

• Initiation into the Catholic Church takes place in three steps: Baptism, Confirmation, and Eucharist.

• When we listen to the Word of God and receive the Eucharist, we are doing what Luke describes the two disciples did on the road to Emmaus.

• Luke wants us to know that Jesus himself is food for others.

• The image of the way and of journey are at the heart of Luke's writing.

_____

_____

_____

Say **WHAT?**

Last Supper • Resurrection

So **WHAT?**

■ What are some things I need to remember each time I participate in the celebration of the Eucharist?

_____

_____

_____

Now **WHAT?**

■ When we celebrate Eucharist, we recognize that Jesus Christ is present in our lives today. What is one thing I will do this week to share Christ's presence with others?

_____

_____

_____

Here's **WHAT** the Catholic Church Teaches

When we gather for Mass, we gather around a table much as the disciples did with Jesus at Emmaus. We too come to know the Lord Jesus in the breaking of the bread. But often the social implications of the Eucharist are ignored or neglected in our daily lives. Many people have no food to put on their table or even a table to gather around.

To receive the Body and Blood of Christ in truth, we need to see Christ in our poorest neighbors. We cannot gather at Eucharist if Jesus' concern for those in need is not consistently reflected in our liturgical celebrations. The poor and the vulnerable should never be forgotten in our worship. Pope John Paul II wrote in preparation for the year of the Eucharist in 2004: "By our mutual love and, in particular, by our concern for those in need we will be recognized as true followers of Christ. This will be the criterion by which the authenticity of our Eucharistic celebrations is judged." (*Remain with Us, Lord*)

If ... Then ...

1. Read the first article.

2. Identify the main ideas about our Catholic faith from the article and note them in the "If We Believe ..." column below.

3. In your group, work together to complete the "Then We Are Called to ..." column.

4. Repeat the process for the second article.

Article 1: This Is My Body		Article 2: Who Is This Stranger?	
IF we believe ...	**THEN we are called to ...**	**IF we believe ...**	**THEN we are called to ...**

Faith in Action

Faith is alive when we put it into action every day of our lives. It is expressed in the attitudes and values we hold and in the ways we relate to the people and the world around us. Taking action to create a more just world is an essential part of living the Gospel. Jesus preached not only with words but how he lived his life. We are called to do the same.

In this unit we explored the writings of Luke and celebrated the many ways Jesus is present to us. Though the sacraments, and especially the celebration of the Eucharist, we are strengthened in our faith and inspired to respond to the needs of our world. Here are some ideas to help you engage your faith with social and political issues.

Faithful Citizenship

> *"There is plenty to do, for each one of us, working on our own hearts, changing our own attitudes, in our own neighbor-hoods."*
>
> –Dorothy Day, social activist and founder of the Catholic Worker movement

Purpose:

Explore what it means to be a faithful citizen by learning about significant witnesses of the Catholic social movement.

Background:

In 2003, the United States bishops issued a statement on how our faith calls us to be active citizens in our nation and in our world. This statement served as a reminder that each person is responsible for witnessing to the Church's commitment to human life and dignity. Young people too are called to this mission. "We must ensure that our nation's young people—especially the poor, those with disabilities, and the most vulnerable—are properly prepared to be good citizens, to lead productive lives, and to be socially and morally responsible in the complicated and technologically challenging world of the twenty-first century." (*Faithful Citizenship: A Catholic Call to Political Responsibility*)

Steps:

a. Choose from among a list of significant witnesses of the Catholic social movement in the last century, such as Dorothy Day, César Chávez, Archbishop

continued on page 224 ▶

Faith in Action

► *continued from page 223*

Oscar Romero, Blessed Teresa of Calcutta, or Sister Helen Prejean. Research their lives and the stands they took in response to contemporary political thought of their time in light of the call to social justice.

b. Share your findings with one another and discuss ways that you can share the insights of people who have worked for justice in our world. Here are some ideas to get your creativity going.

- Make trading cards featuring the many people who have worked for justice. Include a picture, vital statistics, contributions to justice, and a compelling quotation. Distribute to the children in your parish.

- Invite a well-known local justice leader to talk with your parish, school, or community about what it means to be a faithful citizen.

Engaging in the Public Forum

Purpose:

Design a project that engages your faith in the public forum.

Background:

Sometimes we might be reluctant to get involved in politics. However, we have a duty as citizens and as Catholics to engage with politics. "Many political issues have important moral dimensions that must be considered. . . 'Pursing Social Justice' requires working for a more just economic life with decent jobs and just wages, providing adequate assistance to poor families, overcoming a culture of violence, combating discrimination, and defending the right to quality health care, housing, and food." (USCCB, *The Challenge of Faithful Citizenship*)

Steps:

a. Learn about the major public policy issues in your community or state.

b. Choose one of the issues and research the topic. What are the different positions? What is the moral dimension of the issue? How does Catholic Social Teaching address this issue?

c. Design a project that puts your faith into action. For example, your group can write letters to political leaders to present your position. You might design posters and pamphlets to raise awareness about the moral dimensions of the issue in your local community.

> *"...ask not what your country can do for you; ask what you can do for your country."*
>
> —John F. Kennedy, U.S. president

Paul Proclaims Jesus to the World

Paul
Paul

PAUL THE APOSTLE

Paul the Apostle was the greatest of the early Christian missionaries. He was a Pharisee and an early opponent of the Christian Church. Paul believed in the strict observance of God's Law, both for himself and for all Jews. While journeying to Damascus, Paul had an encounter with the risen Christ. (Acts of the Apostles 9:1–19) Paul became convinced that fellowship with the risen Jesus Christ, not the observance of the Law, was all that was needed to receive God's promise for salvation. (Galatians 1:11–12; 3:1–5)

PAUL'S WRITINGS

All together, there are 13 epistles that bear Paul's name as the author. However, scholars do not believe that he wrote them all. Paul himself was the author of first and second Thessalonians, Galatians, Philippians, first and second Corinthians, Romans, and Philemon. The epistles to the Ephesians, Colossians, Titus, and first and second Timothy bear Paul's name, but it is believed that they were written after his death. The writers of these letters were disciples of Paul who wanted to continue his teaching. Whoever the authors of these epistles were, these writings have been accepted as inspired by the Holy Spirit and are part of the New Testament.

CENTRALITY OF JESUS CHRIST

The most profound and moving day in Paul's life was when he met the risen Jesus Christ. Paul was a person who was well respected by the Jewish community and his peers. But he gave it all up for Christ. "More than that, I even consider everything as a loss because of the supreme good of knowing Jesus Christ my Lord." (Philippians 3:8) Jesus Christ, Paul realized, was sent by the Father to bring salvation for all. Paul taught that we are united with Christ in faith and Baptism; "We were indeed buried with him through baptism into death, so that, just as Christ was raised from the dead by the glory of the Father, we too might live in newness of life." (Romans 6:4)

On the personal level, individual Christians recognize that when they are united with and justified by Christ, they are given the grace needed to overcome sin and to live moral lives. (Galatians 5:16–26)

JUSTIFICATION

Paul thought that the justice of God was saving justice at its best. God is faithful, fulfilling the promises made in the covenant with his people. God has taken the initiative to call the human family back to him through Christ. This process of reuniting the human family with God is called justification. (Romans 3:21–31) We cannot justify ourselves; we can only be justified by being united in faith with Jesus Christ and by accepting the grace won by Christ. (Romans 5:1–2) People can only be made right with God and set free from a life of immorality by accepting God's reconciling grace.

LIFE IN THE SPIRIT

Paul teaches that it is through the Holy Spirit that the love of God has been poured out to us. (Romans 5:5) The Holy Spirit is the source of all love, and he creates a bond between ourselves and God like children bound to a father. (Romans 8:14–16) The Holy Spirit not only establishes our relationship with the Father. Even though we are weak, the Holy Spirit helps us to live faithfully within that relationship. (Romans 8:26–27) It is through the Holy Spirit that we can live in love with all people. (1 Corinthians 13:3–7)

PAUL IN THIS UNIT

This unit discusses many issues concerning living a Christian moral life. Paul was raised following the strict moral code of the

Law. So he experienced the issues raised by the Law as serious choices he had to make so that he could work his own way to salvation. After his experience with Jesus Christ, he realized that he was not alone in facing these issues. Jesus Christ has already accomplished salvation for us. In faith and Baptism we receive the grace of the Holy Spirit, who is our constant guide and helps us to live in relationship with God and others. As pastor for his widely spread-out communities, Paul was concerned that we understand that living in Jesus means making choices that reflect our faith. Our moral choices reflect our commitment to Jesus and to one another. In making these choices we are not alone, Paul tells us. Jesus Christ is our constant companion.

yoU turn

On the median strip of a busy street or a multi-lane highway, there's often a No U-turn sign telling drivers that they can't turn around and change direction. Drivers must obey this sign; otherwise, an accident is bound to happen. Fortunately life doesn't have No U-turn signs. When we get on the wrong road, we always have the chance to make a U-turn. Describe a U-turn you've made recently.

IT OUT

The following are examples of other road signs that can be applied to life. Can you match the sign with its application?

Yield	When one door closes, another one opens.
Don't Litter	Stay alert because life is about to get more interesting.
No Parking	Let other people have their way.
Detour	Respect your neighborhood and the earth.
Winding Road	It's time to get off the couch and take some action.

Moving *On*

Have you ever noticed how you get into certain patterns of behavior, like doing the same workout before every soccer game? Sometimes you develop these habits because it's the easiest way to do something or because that's the way it's always been done. You might not even remember how you developed the habit.

But then something happens that changes everything, and you learn that your one way isn't the only way. You might get a new coach for the soccer team, or you might transfer to a new school. But if you're open to trying something new, you might be surprised at how well it works. The new coach might introduce a different kind of workout that really energizes you for the game. It doesn't mean that the old way was wrong; it means it got you where you needed to be and now you can go further.

SAUL, A FAITHFUL JEW

This was the situation faced by Saul, a young Jewish man who lived during the time of Jesus. Saul was a brilliant student who memorized a great deal of the Old Testament. He wanted to be a Jewish teacher. As a devout and faithful Jew, Saul studied the first

I'm moving on and getting my own room. It's hard to *sleep* when my 537 brothers and sisters are snoring.

five books of the Bible—Genesis, Exodus, Leviticus, Numbers, and Deuteronomy. Collectively, these books are called the *Torah,* or "the Law," by Jews. They tell the fundamental story of God's revelation to his people and are considered the most revered books in the Jewish faith. These books tell the story of Creation, of Abraham's faith, and of the liberation of the Hebrew people from slavery. They also give the fundamental rules and regulations of how to live as a person wanting to do God's will.

As a Jewish Pharisee, Saul believed in strict observance of the Law, both for himself and for all Jews. He was extremely upset when he saw a community of Jews who believed that Jesus was the long-awaited Messiah. The Jewish leaders at the time did not believe that Jesus was the Messiah foretold by the prophets. In order to defend his religion, Saul led a persecution of the Jewish followers of Jesus in Jerusalem. He later describes this experience in a letter to the Galatians:

> For you heard of my former way of life in Judaism, how I persecuted the church of God beyond measure and tried to destroy it, and progressed in Judaism beyond many of my contemporaries among my race, since I was even more a zealot for my ancestral traditions. (Galatians 1:13–14)

SAUL ENCOUNTERS THE RISEN JESUS

Saul continued his persecution of Jewish Christians throughout the land. As he was traveling to Damascus, however, he had an unexpected stop. Saul encountered the risen Jesus Christ who said, "Saul, Saul why are you persecuting me?" (Acts of the Apostles 9:4) Saul was shocked and blinded and had to be led by the hand to Damascus where he fasted and prayed. This shattering experience led to Saul's conversion. He moved from his practice of strictly following and enforcing the laws of his ancestors, to proclaiming that salvation had been won through the saving life, death, and Resurrection of

Jesus Christ. Saul became Paul the Apostle, the greatest missionary in the early Church.

From his experience of the risen Lord, Paul realized that he would have to see the rules he had learned as a youth in a new light. He now recognized that the whole human race was mired in the consequences of the sin of Adam and Eve that we call original sin. It is as if we are all stuck in a tar pit and try as hard as we can, we cannot free ourselves.

HELPLESS TO HELP OURSELVES

If we get stuck in a real tar pit, there are a couple of ways we can respond. One is to panic and thrash around wildly until we are so exhausted that we give up. The second is to try to figure out a way to escape. Our mind goes through dozens of survival rules, searching for something that will help. It would help if we had a lever so that we could pry ourselves out of the pit. But all our knowledge and wishful thinking are useless because we are so deeply mired in the tar that we cannot move, let alone act on any survival rules. Any way we respond, we are still helpless to help ourselves.

Paul knew that we are all stuck in the tar pit of original sin, but that we have a choice. We can thrash about in the pit by creating false gods and living lawlessly. Or we can search for a way out by following God's

continued on page 230 ▶

God Justifies Us

When we accept responsibility for hurting a friend or family member, we would do almost anything to make the situation right. We may ask the person what we can do to heal the relationship—what we can do to make it right.

Paul says that the same thing happens in our relationship with God. Because of original sin that we inherited, we can't make things right with God by ourselves. The good news is that God has reached out to us to repair the relationship and reconcile us to himself. Paul calls this saving action of God *justification.*

Justification is the action of the Holy Spirit that cleanses us from sin in Baptism and that continually gives us the grace to walk in right relationship with God. Through justification we are healed, and our relationship with God is made right .

10 interesting facts about Paul

1. **Paul was from the Roman city of Tarsus, located in what is today southern Turkey.** (Acts of the Apostles 21:39)
2. **Paul was not physically impressive, nor was he a very good speaker.** (1 Corinthians 2:1 and 2 Corinthians 10:10; 11:6)
3. **Paul had a sister and a nephew.** (Acts of the Apostles 23:16)
4. **Paul was educated in Jerusalem under the famous Jewish teacher Gamaliel.** (Acts of the Apostles 22:3)
5. **Paul was a Pharisee** (Acts of the Apostles 26:5) **and a tentmaker.** (Acts of the Apostles 18:3)
6. **Paul was a Roman citizen from a wealthy family.** (Acts of the Apostles 22:25–28)
7. **Paul participated in the stoning of Stephen, the first Christian martyr.** (Acts of the Apostles 7:58)
8. **Paul was the most prominent apostle in the early Church because he was so effective at forming Christian communities.**
9. **Although Paul wrote the most books of the New Testament, Luke, who only wrote two books, still gets the prize for writing over half of the New Testament.**
10. **Paul's conversion is among the most well-known.**

We Are Made Righteous Through Faith

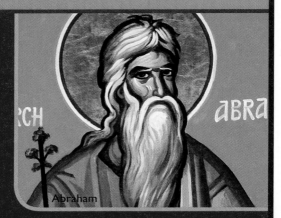

Abraham

As Paul traced our relationship with God, he realized that before all the Old Testament laws were written, Abraham made a fundamental decision to believe in God. Abraham's belief in God was regarded as righteousness. Because of this, Paul sees Abraham as the father of faith. He writes about Abraham's righteousness in a letter to the Romans:

> He did not doubt God's promise in unbelief; rather, he was empowered by faith and gave glory to God and was fully convinced that what he had promised he was also able to do. That is why "it was credited to him as righteousness."
>
> (Romans 4:20–22)

Reflecting on Abraham's faith, Paul emphasizes that for Christians, faith will also be counted toward righteousness. Two lines later in his letter to the Romans, he writes:

> It was also for us, to whom it will be credited, who believe in the one who raised Jesus our Lord from the dead, who was handed over for our transgressions and was raised for our justification.
>
> (Romans 4:24–25)

Justification is the act of God that gives us righteousness.

► *continued from page 229*

Law. The Jewish people had received God's Law in the Torah, especially the Ten Commandments, and they had developed hundreds of rules and regulations to help them keep the Law. But they were still stuck. The law just helped them to know what they were stuck in. Paul wrote to the Romans about this:

> Now we know that what the law says is addressed to those under the law, so that every mouth may be silenced and the whole world stand accountable to God, since no human being will be justified in his sight by observing the law; for through the law comes consciousness of sin. (Romans 3:19–20)

The Jewish people, like the rest of the human family, longed for a way out of the pit of original sin. They wanted to be more than just conscious of sin. They wanted to be freed.

SALVATION THROUGH JESUS CHRIST

What astounded Paul about his encounter with Jesus was his realization that God too longs for the human family to be freed. God has freely given us salvation through Jesus Christ by reaching out to us and reconciling us to himself. In Jesus, God provided us with the lever to pull ourselves out of the tar pit of sin. What we couldn't do for ourselves, God did for us. Through faith and Baptism we receive the grace that we need to take away original sin and to live a new life in Jesus Christ. We also receive the daily graces we need to live as God wants. FG

✝ Our Roots Are Showing

You say to-may-to, I say to-mah-to. Which one is it? We can ask the same thing about the great apostle and missionary of the New Testament. You say Saul, I say Paul. Which one is it? Well both, really. Luke first introduces us to Saul, a young man who witnessed Stephen's brutal execution. (Acts of the Apostles 7:58) Luke then tells us about his conversion and early missions. Then there is a curious shift: Luke makes reference to "Saul, also known as Paul" (Acts of the Apostles 13:9) and from then on refers to him as Paul. What gives? A slip of the pen? An alter ego? A nickname? Actually, the use of a double name was quite common at that time. Saul was the Hebrew name, and Paul was the Roman name. In his letters Paul refers to himself as Paul, not Saul. Maybe he decided that the Roman name would be more acceptable among the Gentiles. Maybe he wanted to show that he was a new man after his conversion. For whatever reason, the Roman name stuck.

Taking Time for God

We know a great deal about Paul because of the letters he wrote. He wrote these letters to a variety of communities, but they were written for us as well. Imagine what it would have been like to be a member of the church in Philippi and to receive these words from Paul:

> I give thanks to my God at every remembrance of you, praying always with joy in my every prayer for all of you, because of your partnership for the gospel from the first day until now. . . . And this is my prayer: that your love may increase ever more and more in knowledge and every kind of perception, to discern what is of value, so that you may be pure and blameless for the day of Christ, filled with the fruit of righteousness that comes through Jesus Christ for the glory and praise of God. (Philippians 1:3–5,9–11)

In the midst of his praise for our faith, Paul asks us to "discern what is of value." Things often happen in our lives that lead us to question what is of value. It's not uncommon to turn on the TV and see news stories about survivors of major catastrophes like hurricanes, floods, earthquakes, and tornadoes. Standing in front of the rubble that used to be their homes, the survivors are usually devastated and grieving. They often say, however, that they are grateful that they and their friends and family are alive. Although it's painful to lose all of one's possessions, many people also come to realize that those possessions were of limited value. As they rebuild their lives, they have a new sense of what is truly important.

continued on page 232 ▶

IM

Therefore, since we have been justified by faith, we have peace with God through our Lord Jesus Christ.

(Romans 5:1)

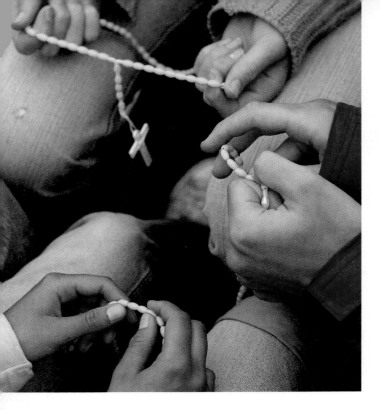

▶ *continued from page 231*

THINGS THAT GET IN THE WAY

The ways we spend our money and time are strong indicators of the values in our lives. The spending by teens in the United States averaged $104 for a week, a total of $169 billion in 2004. Thirty-three percent of that money was spent on clothes. Teens also watched 3 hours of music videos a day, played video games 90 minutes a day, and watched television for an average of 6¹/₂ hours a day. These distractions have not only drained cash, they have also shaped values.

The values of Roman society were reflected in the images of the gods the people believed in. Images of these gods surrounded Paul. When the Hebrew people were slaves in Egypt, they, too, were surrounded by images of gods. One Egyptian god was in the shape of a falcon while another resembled a human with a ram's head. The Egyptians believed that they were justified in enslaving others because they had the support of the gods.

Commenting on the pagan use of images, Paul wrote, "While claiming to be wise, they became fools and exchanged the glory of the immortal God for the likeness of an image of mortal man or of birds or of four-legged animals or of snakes." (Romans 1:22–23) Paul recognized that the result was that the people were distracted from true love of God. "They exchanged the truth of God for a lie and revered and worshiped the creature rather than the creator, who is blessed forever. Amen." (Romans 1:25)

FROM SLAVERY TO FREEDOM

Paul's comments help us recognize the importance of the First Commandment: "I am the Lord your God: you shall not have strange gods before me." Having lib-

f o o t n o t e

Talk about getting stuck in a tar pit. Paul himself was in a bit of a pit when he was in Damascus. He had been preaching about Jesus, and he made enemies of some of the local leaders. They were so outraged with Paul that the governor of Damascus decided to detain him. The governor had the guards at the city gates keep watch for Paul.

Paul found out about the plot to capture and kill him and made a daring escape from the city. He says, "I was lowered in a basket through a window in the wall and escaped his hands." (2 Corinthians 11:33) Pretty crafty, that Paul. He tells us this story in order to show that he got into some pretty sticky situations through his own folly, sin, or weakness. However, despite the deepest tar pit, God delivered Paul from harm. What can you do or say to remind yourself to rely on God the next time you get stuck in a pit?

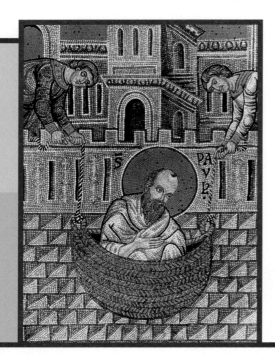

erated the Hebrew people from slavery, God emphasized that in order for the people to be free they could not place their faith in things of limited value. They were not to place anything as a god before him.

There is only one God, whose goal today is to help us to live in relationship with him and one another. Worshipping the one true God, whose nature no image can capture, means that we have a God whose holiness is expressed as gracious and loving, forgiving and merciful. His holiness is not expressed in images.

The First Commandment continues to call us to believe in God, to hope in him, and to love him above all else. God is greater than anything or anyone we can imagine. Paul understood this, and he wrote: "Oh, the depth of the riches and wisdom and knowledge of God! How inscrutable are his judgments and how unsearchable his ways!" (Romans 11:33)

God is greater than anything or anyone we can imagine.

CENTERING ON GOD TODAY

Paul saw that the worship of idols in any form was based on an attempt to manipulate God through superstition and magic. While we may not worship actual idols or images of gods today, our time, attention, and money are spent in pursuit of things of limited value. Our possessions, obsessions, jobs, and even money itself can become like gods to us.

Compare the time we spend on any personal pursuit with the time we spend in conversation with God or caring for others. While we might believe in God wholeheartedly, we sometimes behave as if God were of no consequence.

All this energy spent on limited pursuits can leave us with a sense of emptiness. How can we refocus our lives? When we approach this question, we should take a step back and think of the First Commandment. We should make choices based on what is of value to us. Worshipping God gives us the chance to detach ourselves from the fast pace of our lives and recognize that God does not want us to use all our energy pursuing false gods. The path to freedom and to God is through true worship of God. Then we can live, as Paul wrote, "filled with the righteousness that comes through Jesus Christ for the glory and the praise of God." (Philippians 1:11) FG

The Name of the Lord

Back in the time of Jesus, people's names were an expression of who they were. The Second Commandment says "You shall not take the name of the Lord in vain." This means that we are obliged to use God's name with respect, not in a way that dishonors him.

In Philippians 2:1–11 Paul teaches us that Jesus' name is above every other name. Jesus humbled himself by becoming one of us and was obedient even to his death on the cross. Because of his obedience, God exalted him, giving him a name above every name:

that at the name of Jesus
every knee should bend,
of those in heaven and on earth and
    under the earth,
    and every tongue confess that
Jesus Christ is Lord,
to the glory of God the Father.
(Philippians 2:10–11)

We are also careful not to dishonor the name of Jesus Christ, the name of his mother, Mary, or the names of the saints. We also do not lie to others by using God's name to convince them that we are telling the truth. It is considered blasphemy to misuse God's name in any way. God's name is sacred, and not to be abused.

What Do I Value?

PRAYER AND CONVERSION

When God created human beings, he created within us a desire for himself. Just like a stomach hungers to be satisfied with food, our whole being hungers to be satisfied with God. God's deepest desire is for us to turn to him, for just as we hunger for him, he hungers for us. Everyone is created with this hunger for God.

Sometimes we try to satisfy our hunger for God with other things that end up leading us away from him. Still God doesn't abandon us. Instead he tirelessly calls each person to himself. He calls us to a change of heart, a conversion back toward him. God's very desire and love for us gives us the grace to turn to him. When we do, even if it's just a glance in God's direction at first, we are acknowledging our built-in desire for God. This is a profound moment of prayer, for it is the encounter of God's hunger with our own. This prayer unfolds throughout our whole lives as God continually calls us to himself.

Sometimes events in our lives call us to think about what we truly value. That's what Saint Paul prayed in the letter to the Philippians—that they might discern what is of value both for themselves and for their community. Followers of Jesus strive to match their values with those of the kingdom, and to serve the kingdom by living out those values.

Imagine yourself in a quiet place with Jesus. As you sit together, hear him ask you about what you value. You might need to think about it for a moment. Are they things? Relationships? Your faith? Personal characteristics or attitudes? He asks you to name three things you value. What do you say?

If you'd like, write your three values on the lines provided.

_____

_____

_____

You hear Jesus ask you one more question: If someone observed you for 24 hours, would they be able to tell what is most valuable to you? Jesus' question may inspire some questions of your own. How does the way I live my life reveal my values? The choices I make, the friends I spend time with, the things I buy—do they reflect what I say I value? *(pause)*

Share your thoughts with Jesus, and listen to whatever he wants to share with you. *(pause)*

You may want to ask Jesus for help to sort through your values and to make them visible in your life.

When all are ready, continue with the following prayer.

All: Jesus, we want to be your disciples. Grant us the strength and courage to let our lives be signs of your kingdom by the choices we make. We ask this in your name. Amen.

What's **WHAT?**

■ Main points from the chapter are listed below. Choose one that you could explain further to others. Write what you would say on the lines below.

- Through faith and Baptism we receive the grace we need to take away original sin and live a new life in Christ.

- Justification is the action of the Holy Spirit to cleanse us from sin in Baptism and give us the grace to walk in right relationship with God.

- Abraham's fundamental decision to believe in God was reckoned as righteousness.

- The First Commandment calls us to believe in God and not place our faith in things of limited value.

- Paul teaches us that Jesus' name is above every other name.

_____

_____

_____

So **WHAT?**

■ What kind of support do I need to live my faith? What kind of support can I offer others?

_____

_____

_____

_____

Say **WHAT?**

blasphemy • conversion • righteousness

Now **WHAT?**

■ The way we spend our time and money can point to what we value. What choice will I make this week to use my time and money to reflect my values as a follower of Jesus?

_____

_____

_____

_____

_____

Here's **WHAT** the Catholic Church Teaches

The belief in one loving God leads us to understand our own dignity as human beings. Men and women who are made new through the experience of coming to faith in a loving God are able to transform social structures. They become people able to bring peace where there is conflict, build loving relationships where there is hatred, and seek justice where there is exploitation. Personal conversion can lead to social conversion. And only love is capable of radically transforming people's relationships. Faith allows every person of good will to see the broad horizons of justice and the human development people are capable of in truth and goodness.

Paired Interview

Your name _____

Your partner's name _____

Title of article read by your partner _____

_____

Q&A

Ask your partner the following questions about the article he or she read and record his or her answers in the space provided.	
1. Explain what your article was about in a few sentences.	
2. What is one quote (sentence) from your article that you would put on a poster to inspire the group? Why?	
3. What are some specific things your article helped you to learn or realize about the Catholic faith?	
4. Based on your article, name some specific things we, as Catholics, need to know, do, or believe in order to live as followers of Jesus.	

Rights and RESPONSIBILITIES

When you are a member of a club or team, you have certain rights. For example, if you belong to a gym, you have the right to use the exercise equipment. There are also responsibilities that come with being a member. You have to abide by the rules that you agreed to when you signed up. The rules are there to protect everybody's rights, not to make life more difficult. Name a club or team to which you belong. What are your rights and responsibilities?

First Rate

Although laws are a serious matter, sometimes they can be really funny when they are out-dated or taken out of context. Which of these do you think is the silliest?

- It is against the law for monsters to enter the corporate limits (Urbana, Illinois).
- No one is allowed to lend a vacuum cleaner to their next-door neighbor (Denver, Colorado).
- It's illegal to eat peanuts and walk backwards on sidewalks during a concert (Greene, New York).
- You are not allowed to carry an ice cream cone in your pocket (Lexington, Kentucky).
- Horses are forbidden to eat fire hydrants (Marshalltown, Iowa).
- It is against the law to sing in the bathtub (Pennsylvania).

Celebrating
the Lord's Supper

One of the first cities where Paul had success in establishing a Christian church was Corinth. Corinth was a seaport where goods were loaded and unloaded from all over the Mediterranean. It was a city where travelers were looking for a good time, resulting in the city having a reputation for trouble and vice. Among these challenges Paul discovered that many people were ready to hear about salvation in Jesus Christ. After spending time building the foundation of the church in Corinth, Paul moved on to continue to proclaim the Gospel. He kept in contact with the church in Corinth through his epistles. In his epistles we discover that this church gave him many reasons for heartache. They often needed to be reminded about what he had taught them about the essentials of being a Christian.

When the Christians in Corinth gathered to celebrate the Eucharist, they used it as a social occasion. Some members were rich, and others were less well off. Those who could afford it would bring food for themselves and their friends, and they would eat it in front of those who were poor. They were selfish and didn't share. Apparently, some of the celebrations also got quite rowdy, and wine flowed freely. People embarrassed themselves by drinking too much.

WHAT WE CELEBRATE WITH THE EUCHARIST

Paul could not overlook this behavior. It was causing scandal in the Church and showed that the revelers did not have a true appreciation of what they were celebrating. Paul reminded the Corinthians of the real meaning of the Last Supper in his letter to them:

> For I received from the Lord what I also handed on to you, that the Lord Jesus, on the night he was handed over, took bread, and after he had given thanks, broke it and said, "This is my body that is for you. Do this in remembrance of me." In the same way also the cup, after supper, saying, "This cup is the new covenant in my blood. Do this, as often as you drink it, in remembrance of me." For as often as you eat this bread and drink the cup, you proclaim the death of the Lord until he comes.
>
> Therefore whoever eats the bread or drinks the cup of the Lord unworthily will have to answer for the body and blood of the Lord.
> (1 Corinthians 11:23–27)

> "This is my body that is for you. Do this in remembrance of me."

Paul teaches that those who behave in a way that dishonors the Eucharist will have to answer to God for their behavior.

WORSHIPPING GOD

Paul's lesson to the Corinthians reminds us of what God had called his people to do in the Third Commandment: "Remember to keep holy the Lord's day." For the Jewish people, the Lord's Day was the Sabbath, celebrated on Saturday, the day the Lord rested after creation. They understood this to mean that their rest from work should include worship of God.

SUNDAY, THE LORD'S DAY

After Jesus' death and Resurrection, Christians began to celebrate Sunday as the Lord's Day because it was on Sunday that Jesus rose from the dead. Paul reminded the Corinthians that "if Christ has not been raised, then empty is our preaching; empty, too, your faith." (1 Corinthians 15:14) The early Christians understood the importance of the Resurrection, so they celebrated the Lord's Day on Sunday rather than Saturday.

continued on page 240 ▶

God wants us to remember every day what he has done for us, so we may be of service to others.

The Cost of Discipleship

Paul founded the church in Corinth around the year 51. He spent about a year with them, instructing them and praying with them. He then continued his missionary journeys. But Paul remained in communication with the Corinthians. While he was proud of the people there, he was also disturbed by some of their attitudes he heard about. He was especially upset when he heard that there were Christians in Corinth attacking his credibility. So in his second letter to them, Paul describes the difficulties he has faced proclaiming the Gospel of Jesus Christ:

> Are they ministers of Christ? (I am talking like an insane person.) I am still more, with far greater labors, far more imprisonments, far worse beatings, and numerous brushes with death. Five times at the hands of the Jews I received forty lashes minus one. Three times I was beaten with rods, once I was stoned, three times I was shipwrecked, I passed a night and a day on the deep; on frequent journeys, in dangers from rivers, dangers from robbers, dangers from my own race, dangers from Gentiles, dangers in the city, dangers in the wilderness, dangers at sea, dangers among false brothers; in toil and hardship, through many sleepless nights, through hunger and thirst, through frequent fastings, through cold and exposure. And apart from these things, there is the daily pressure upon me of my anxiety for all the churches. (2 Corinthians 11: 23–28)

Paul was able to survive this difficult life because he was in constant dialogue with God through prayer. He understood the importance of his work in proclaiming salvation in Jesus Christ throughout the world.

▶ *continued from page 239*

The Lord's Day in the New Testament celebrates the new creation brought about by the Resurrection of Christ. It is a day of rest and worship when we as Catholics participate at Sunday Mass. We are also obliged to participate at Mass on holy days like Christmas and All Saints Day. These are opportunities to grow in our faith and come closer to God.

DAY OF REST

Along with these responsibilities, it is our duty to rest from work on the Lord's Day. This obligation has to be defined by each of us according to the circumstances of our lives. The purpose of resting on the Lord's Day is to allow us time to give worship to God. We need a certain amount of rest so that we can spend time with our families and friends, take part in social events, and develop our spiritual lives. Besides getting the rest we need, we also allow others to get the rest that they need. The connection between the duty to worship God and the duty to rest is an important one. As long as we keep ourselves busy with a million things to do, we will never have the time to worship God as we should.

These were the values that Paul wanted the Corinthians to think about when they celebrated the Eucharist. It is not simply coming together and going through the motions. Rather, it is about reminding ourselves of what God is all about so that in our thoughts and actions, we may honor him all week long. When we celebrate, we include the whole community. When we are sent forth, it is to recognize that God wants us to remember every day what he has done for us, so we may be of service to others. FG

IM

If I speak in human and angelic tongues but do not have love, I am a resounding gong or a clashing cymbal.

(1 Corinthians 13:1)

Ah yes, the Lord's Day, day of rest. Good thing I have my sleeping cap.

Our Roots Are Showing

Ready for a time warp? Sunday, the day of the Lord's Resurrection, is considered both the first *and* the eighth day of the week. How is this possible when a week has only seven days? It's a challenge to wrap your mind around this idea. However, it carries a very important message. First, how did we get an eighth day? Although technically a week has only seven days, the early Church began to see Sunday as the eighth day because it followed Saturday, the seventh day. As the first day of the week, the Lord's Day recalls the first day of creation. As the last day, it symbolizes the age to come brought about by Christ's Resurrection. Having an eighth day in a seven-day week showed just how extraordinary the Lord's Day is. On that one day, we celebrate both the beginning and the end of time. We are connected to all of creation throughout all of history, and we celebrate our common goal of life everlasting with God.

Respecting Authority

Paul made it clear that Christians are obliged to obey legitimate authority. He wrote in his letter to the Romans: "Let every person be subordinate to the higher authorities, for there is no authority except from God, and those that exist have been established by God. Therefore; whoever resists authority opposes what God has appointed." (Romans 13:1–2)

This idea is tied to the Fourth Commandment. The Fourth Commandment sounds simple: "Honor your father and your mother." But this commandment has broader implications. There are four aspects of the commandment to reflect on: (1) Respect and obey your parents, (2) Respect the family you belong to and help it function properly, (3) Respect and obey all those who have authority in your school, city, state, country, world, and Church, (4) Respect the communities you live in—your school, city, state, country, world, and Church—and help them function properly.

Paul taught us that we have a moral obligation to obey laws. For example, we are obliged to obey the traffic laws in order to prevent accidents. By following traffic laws, we make our world safer. We are obeying the Fourth Commandment when we pay taxes, for as Paul told the Romans, "Pay to all their dues, taxes to whom taxes are due, toll to whom toll is due, respect to whom respect is due, honor to whom honor is due." (Romans 13:7)

continued on page 242 ▶

> We can set an example by living our lives in the light of the Gospel.

Did you know that the first words attributed to God in the Bible are "'Let there be light'"? (Genesis 1:3) Light must be important if it was the first thing God created. Writers like Paul are also interested in light. He tells us to shine like lights.

What does this mean? Shine like a soft white bulb, a desk lamp, a flashlight, florescent overhead lighting, or a 3000-watt halogen spotlight so intense and bright that it can cause a person to see spots if they stare at it? These are probably not what Paul had in mind. There was no electricity in Paul's time; he was more familiar with the light of oil lamps. He knew that the light of a single oil lamp could illuminate an entire house. So to "shine like lights" means to illuminate the entire area around us with the light of God's presence. What kind of light are you?

▶ *continued from page 241*

TRUTH AND JUSTICE

Perhaps the hardest aspect of the Fourth Commandment to follow is respecting the communities in which we live. This commandment obligates us to work with those in authority to make our society a place of truth, justice, solidarity, and freedom. How do we do that?

We can honor the authority in our schools, making them a place of truth by not cheating on tests or on homework. We can make our schools a place of justice by stopping rumors that hurt classmates. On a larger level, we can make society a place of solidarity by caring about everyone—the young and the old, the healthy and the sick, the wealthy and the poor.

BASIC RIGHTS

Another important aspect of the Fourth Commandment is respecting the basic rights of all individuals. Every person has a right to life and to basic necessities that help him or her survive such as food and clothing. Every person also has the right to a good reputation. We can help defend people's

art • i • fact
St. Paul, **early Christian mosaic, St. Peter's Basilica, Vatican State**

Shine Like Lights

Paul told the Philippians to "shine like lights in the world." (2:15) He told the Romans not to follow what everybody else says and does. (12:2) It was clear that Paul wanted the followers of Jesus to be in the world so that they could have a positive influence on it. He did not want them, however, to go along with every trend they found in the world. They were to work in the world, but they were to belong to God. That was Paul's vision—the same vision presented in the Fourth Commandment. The commandment tells us to obey authority, but not when the laws are immoral. Good citizenship calls us to help society pass laws that are moral and truthful while at the same time respectful of the rights of everyone.

rights to the means of survival by taking part in clothing and food drives. We can protect our classmates' good reputations by defending them when others begin to spread rumors.

People in positions of authority also have an obligation under the Fourth Commandment to make sure that everyone's rights are respected. They must make rules and pass laws that help people live good, healthy lives. We can set an example by living our lives in the light of the Gospel. Sometimes this might mean disobeying laws that are immoral. For example, when Adolf Hitler, the ruler of Nazi Germany, ordered German citizens to kill Jews, some Christians refused to obey those orders. These Christians were not breaking the Fourth Commandment because the purpose of the commandment is to build up society, not to tear it apart.

RESPECT AND OBEDIENCE

The Fourth Commandment is about respect and obedience. The first object of our respect and obedience is God. When we respect God, we are also respecting other people and their rights. When we obey God and his laws, we are also obeying those in authority wherever we are—at home, in school, and in society. FG

WANT TO KNOW MORE? Visit www.FindingGod.org/teens to read about leaders in promoting social justice.

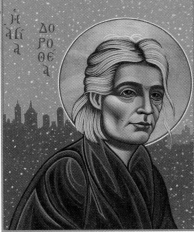

We have a duty to respect authority. But when civil laws go against the higher law of God, the Catholic Church says that acts of civil disobedience are acceptable. Civil disobedience is the refusal to obey a law in an effort to change unjust laws or policies. This refusal is expressed in a variety of nonviolent ways such as forming a peaceful blockade or engaging in a sit-in.

Martin Luther King, Jr. and Mahatma Gandhi are two well-known people who inspired modern civil disobedience. Some well-known Catholics who engaged in civil disobedience to protest unjust laws are Dorothy Day, who founded the Catholic Worker movement with Peter Maurin; Father Daniel Berrigan, S.J., a renowned peace activist; Dom Helder Camara, a Brazilian archbishop; and César Chávez, who worked for labor rights for migrant workers.

In Roman society the father had complete authority over the other members of his family. His children were legally bound to obey him. In the Letter to the Ephesians we read, "Children, obey your parents [in the Lord], for this is right" and "Fathers, do not provoke your children to anger, but bring them up with the training and instruction of the Lord." (Ephesians 6:1,4) Note here that Paul directs fathers to train their children in instruction of the Lord. We can find these values in Psalm 78:2–4

I will open my mouth in story,
    drawing lessons from of old.
We have heard them, we know them;
    our ancestors have recited them to us.
We do not keep them from our children;
    we recite them to the next generation,
The praiseworthy and mighty deeds of the LORD,
    the wonders that he performed.

Parents are to tell their children the great things God has done and continues to do in Jesus Christ. Children are to be nurtured in the Lord. Fathers are not to dominate their children in ways that lead to discouragement. (Colossians 3:21)

Honoring the Holy

SUNDAY WORSHIP

We celebrate Sunday as part of our observance of the Third Commandment. Sunday worship fulfills the commandment to build into our lives a weekly rhythm to celebrate God who has created us and saved us through his Son, Jesus. God rested on the seventh day from all the work he had undertaken.

Human life also has a rhythm of work and rest. For Christians, the Saturday Sabbath, which celebrated the completion of the first creation, has been replaced by Sunday, which recalls the new creation begun in the Resurrection of Christ. It is also the principal day for the celebration of the Eucharist because it is the day of the Resurrection.

Sunday is the most important day to gather with our fellow Catholics for liturgical prayer. It is the day of the Christian family and the day of joy and rest from work. The Lord's Day gives us the time for rest and leisure to help our family, cultural, social, and religious lives grow. Sunday is the foundation of the entire liturgical year.

Reflecting on the Third Commandment invites us to expand our ideas about how to keep the Lord's Day holy. Participation in the Eucharist is the center of the Lord's Day. Adequate rest and service to others influence the quality of our worship, which extends beyond the hour that we spend at Mass.

Paul's letter to the Corinthians is a reminder to them and to us of the attitudes with which we honor God.

Prepare: Begin by focusing your attention on your breath. Be aware of your breath as it flows in and out. Let go of any distracting thoughts. Open yourself to receive the Word of God.

Read: 1 Corinthians 11:23–27 (Paul's Retelling of the Last Supper)

Meditate: In your imagination, place yourself at a celebration of the Eucharist with the Christian community in Corinth during the time of Saint Paul. Look around and notice what people are doing. What happens when Paul's letter is read?

Read a Second Time: 1 Corinthians 11:23–27 (Paul's Retelling of the Last Supper)

Meditate: Now imagine yourself in your parish church on Sunday. As you prepare to receive Holy Communion, begin to think about ways you can carry Christ's presence with you as you leave Mass today. Whom will you share it with? How might you be able to honor the holy in yourself and others by your actions this day? How can celebrating the Eucharist help you?

Pray: Share your reflections with Jesus. Then ask him if there is anything else in this story he'd like you to notice or to understand better. When you are ready, thank him for this time of prayer.

Contemplate: Spend a few moments in prayerful silence with God.

Close by praying together: God of life, thank you for giving us Sunday as a day of rest to honor and praise you. Help us to remember that everything we do is a reflection of your life in us. Amen.

What's **WHAT?**

■ Look over the main points of the chapter. What is one additional important insight you would add to this list? Write it on the lines below.

- Christians began to celebrate Sunday as the Lord's Day because it was the day that Jesus rose from the dead.
- Paul endured many hardships in order to proclaim the Gospel of Jesus Christ.
- Obeying the Fourth Commandment implies respecting the basic rights of all individuals and the communities in which we live.
- The Fourth Commandment tells us to obey authority, but not when the laws are immoral.
- In the letter to the Ephesians, parents are reminded of their responsibilities toward their children.
- _____
  _____

Say **WHAT?**

epistle

So **WHAT?**

■ When we respect God, we will also have respect for other people and their rights. *Think about it. Pray about it.*

Now **WHAT?**

■ When our lives get too busy, there's no time for God. How can I include worship of God?

_____

_____

Here's **WHAT** the Catholic Church Teaches

When Paul wrote to the Christians of Rome, he recognized that honoring authority, as the Fourth Commandment demands, includes obedience to the state. He explained, "Let every person be subordinate to the higher authorities, for there is no authority except from God, and those that exist have been established by God." (Romans 13:1) But he also recognized that authorities must be worthy of that respect, "respect to whom respect is due, honor to whom honor is due." (Romans 13:7)

The Church teaches that government authority carries serious responsibilities. The chief concern of civil authorities must be to ensure that the rights of individual citizens are acknowledged, respected, defended, and promoted. In this way each person may more easily carry out his or her duties. Governments that do not respect human rights and do not assure justice for all members of society lack true authority.

Blessed Pope John XXIII wrote in his encyclical *Peace on Earth*: "For to safeguard the inviolable rights of the human person, and to facilitate the fulfillment of his duties, should be the chief duty of every public authority. This means that, if any government does not acknowledge the rights of man or violates them, it not only fails in its duty, but its orders completely lack juridical force."

Making Connections

1. Read the article assigned to your group.

2. Note the main points from your article in the appropriate column below.

3. Join your group with a group who read the other article.

4. Record the main points in the appropriate column below.

5. Work together to complete the "Connect" section to show how the two articles connect.

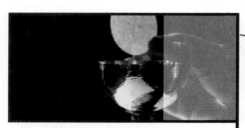

NOTES FROM ARTICLE 1

Celebrating the Lord's Supper

How do these two articles connect?

NOTES FROM ARTICLE 2

Respecting Authority

DAYS OF OUR Lives

Every day has only 24 hours, which is just 1,440 minutes, a mere 86,400 seconds. While some of this time is planned with things like school or sleep, the rest is ours to do with as we please. How do you choose to spend your free time?

HOMEWORK   FRIENDS   GUITAR

IT'S LIKE THIS

Our weekdays and sometimes even our weekends have packed schedules. If you had a completely free weekend with no responsibilities, what would you choose to do? Imagine that money is no object, so live it up!

Saturday A.M.	Sunday A.M.
Saturday P.M.	Sunday P.M.

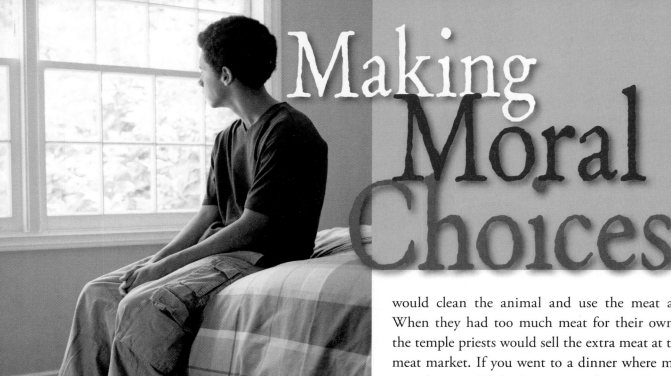

Making Moral Choices

Perhaps you visit a fast-food restaurant a couple of times a week. You could be hanging out with your friends, or you might be having a meal with your family. As you face the clerk to order your meal, you look at the menu on the wall above to see the variety of meals you have to choose from. You usually order the same thing every time, but if you are in the mood for something else, there are plenty of options. It's easy to take all these choices for granted.

People who lived in New Testament times did not have these options. They had no refrigeration, so food spoiled quickly. When early Christians prayed for their daily bread, at times they did not even know if any food was available in the city. Since it spoiled so fast, meat was scarce. One of the best sources for meat was at one of the local temples.

Corinth was a city with many temples dedicated to a variety of pagan gods. Each temple had a staff of priests for that particular cult. When a person wanted to offer a sacrifice to a particular god, he or she would bring an animal for the priests to kill. After the sacrifice, the slaughtered animal would remain at the temple as partial payment for the offering. The priests would clean the animal and use the meat as food. When they had too much meat for their own needs, the temple priests would sell the extra meat at the local meat market. If you went to a dinner where meat was served, it was likely that it came from an animal that had been offered in sacrifice earlier that day.

This raised an issue that Paul needed to address with the church in Corinth. Some church members were upset that other members were eating meat that had been offered to pagan gods. Paul addressed this issue in 1 Corinthians 8.

EATING THE MEAT OF IDOLS

The Christians in Corinth who realized that there is one God and that Jesus was the Son of God and Lord were not troubled by eating the meat that had once been offered to idols. Some Christians would even have meals in the temples with the temple priests. Meat was meat, and those gods did not exist.

There were other members of the church, however, whose understanding of Christian teaching was not clear. They were unsure of the relationship between pagan gods and the one God. These Christians were uncomfortable

WISE GALS

"Whoever wishes to do much good for the honour of God and the salvation of her neighbour must place the common profit before her own."

— Mary Ward, founder, Institute of the Blessed Virgin Mary

RIGHT: 17th century painting of Mary Ward with early companions

being served meat that had been used in temple sacrifices. They were criticized by the Christians who ate the meat from the temples. The Christians who ate the meat thought that they had greater insight into the freedom won by Jesus Christ because they were not worried about pagan gods.

Paul was critical of those Christians who thought they had greater insight than their fellow Christians. He agreed with them in principle that meat was meat, and so they were technically correct in eating it. However their actions in acting superior and shaming their fellow Christians were morally wrong. They were building themselves up at the expense of others.

> ## Corinth was a city with many temples dedicated to pagan gods.

KNOWING HOW TO CHOOSE

We can look at the situation Paul was addressing in terms of the process of making a moral decision. Moral decisions are made by people who are free and take responsibility for their actions. The morality of any act has three dimensions—the act chosen, the intention behind the act, and the circumstances that surround the act.

In this case the act chosen is the good of feeding oneself and others. We need to eat to live, and offering hospitality to others is a Christian obligation. So those Corinthians who served the meat or who were dining with friends in the temple were acting in a morally good way. The meat helped fulfill their need for food.

The second issue is the intention behind their act. Here things get a little more complicated. If their intention was to serve themselves and their guests a good meal, this was a morally good thing to do. But

continued on page 250 ▶

How Much Is Enough?

When we choose to eat a meal, we do not think in terms of making a moral choice based on whether the meat had been offered in sacrifice to pagan gods. What we choose to eat does have moral implications, however.

People in the United States eat a lot of beef. We are less than 5 percent of the world's population, but we eat 25 percent of the world's beef. The demand for beef from fast-food restaurants in the United States has led to vast areas of the rain forest in Central and South America being cleared to raise cattle. Since the soil of the rain forests does not contain many nutrients, it soon becomes worthless even for growing grass to feed the cattle. So more forests are cut down. Cutting down on visits to fast-food restaurants and eating less beef can help slow the destruction of the rain forests and the harm done to the people and animals that live in them.

On average we eat 1.5 times the food we need to survive. This is in a world where 800 million people do not have enough to eat. Each day 40,000 people die from poverty-related issues like starvation. Over one billion people throughout the world, four times the population of the United States, are living on less than one dollar a day. One way that you can help is by sacrificing one visit a week to a fast-food restaurant and donating that money to organizations that work to alleviate poverty and hunger around the world.

Hi, Mary. Do you and your friends want to go go swimming with me later? I see you ladies brought your inner tubes.

An Informed Conscience

In Corinth, Paul ministered to help people have a more fully formed conscience. Why does the Church place so much emphasis on the formation of conscience? The Church understands that we must always obey the certain judgment of our own consciences. We are called to develop a fully formed conscience. We begin to do this when we learn from our mistakes and those of others. We also pray for guidance, read and listen to Scripture, and learn about the teachings of the Church. We learn to consider the effects of our actions on others. Without a fully formed conscience, we are left to follow a useless guide. The consequence of a poorly formed conscience is that it may lead to a life of self-destruction.

This Way Out

The Christians in Corinth argued about what kind of meat was acceptable to eat. Paul was upset with them because they couldn't seem to come to a peaceful solution. Paul had to step in and tell them to "encourage one another, agree with one another, live in peace, and the God of love and peace will be with you." (2 Corinthians 13:11) If Paul were writing a letter to people today, he would say something like this: *Learn to discuss things with people instead of getting into arguments with them. Listen to people instead of writing them off. Never get into a fight, and do what you can to keep others from fighting.* If people would do those things, Paul's response would be, "the God of love and peace will be with you."

▶ *continued from page 249*

suppose they knew that serving meat that had been part of a pagan sacrifice would make their guests uncomfortable and they served it anyway because they wanted to watch their guests squirm or they wanted to show off their superior understanding of Christian teaching. In either case, the act would be morally wrong because they did not have good intentions.

The third issue is the circumstances surrounding the act. As we have seen, in ancient times food was scarce and people had to eat what they received or what they could find. The food supply for the next day was uncertain. A Christian might serve meat from a pagan temple to his or her guests because that was the only food available to serve. There might not have been fruits, vegetables, or fish in the market that day. If meat from a pagan temple was all there was to eat, it would lessen the moral issue of whether the host was offending the conscience of his guest. In the same way today, a person's responsibility is lessened if he or she is forced or tricked into committing an immoral act. It is important to recognize that it is never a good moral choice to do an immoral act for the sake of some imagined positive result.

IM Some, by rejecting conscience, have made a shipwreck of their faith.
(1 Timothy 1:19)

Paul wants Christians to support one another, not present one another with situations in which some people build themselves up at the expense of others. He explains this in his letter to the Corinthians:

> Thus through your knowledge, the weak person is brought to destruction, the brother for whom Christ died. When you sin in this way against your brothers and wound their consciences, weak as they are, you are sinning against Christ.
> (1 Corinthians 8:11–12) FG

Paul

TEMPLES
of the
Holy
Spirit

For the Jewish people in Jesus' time, the Temple in Jerusalem was considered the holiest place in the world. All religious, political, and economic life revolved around the Temple. This was the place where heaven and earth met. Communities would send delegations from all over the world to offer worship. In the Old Testament the Temple is described as the "center of nations" and "the navel of the earth."

MAN AND WOMAN

These images were on Paul's mind when he emphasized with the early Christians how they were to respect themselves. Through Baptism they received the Holy Spirit and became united with the risen Jesus Christ. They were individual members of the Church and part of a community, a new temple of God. When he heard that men and women were dishonoring their bodies by committing acts of adultery, he reminded them what it had cost for them to become free in Christ. Paul wrote to the Corinthians:

> Do you not know that your body is a temple of the holy Spirit within you, whom you have from God, and that you are not your own? For you have been purchased at a price. Therefore glorify God in your body.
>
> (1 Corinthians 6:19–20)

In this teaching Paul was discussing the meaning of the Sixth Commandment: "You shall not commit adultery." The Sixth Commandment is not concerned only with adultery; it also teaches against divorce, polygamy, and living together outside of marriage. The basic meaning of the Sixth Commandment is that our sexuality is a gift from God. God gave each of us the personal dignity of being a man or a woman, and we must show respect for that dignity just as we would show respect for a place of worship.

CHASTITY

The Sixth Commandment calls us to lead chaste lives. Chastity is the essential virtue that helps us live out

continued on page 252 ▶

Some people say the Church is against sex. Quite the opposite! The Church recognizes sex and sexual activity as God-given gifts. What the Church objects to is the use of sex as an advertising gimmick to sell things like clothes, perfumes, soft drinks, cars, movies, and TV programs. This type of use turns sex into a marketing tool, a far cry from its real purpose.

Chastity is practiced differently by people according to their circumstances. For single people, chastity means learning to express their sexuality in ways other than physical intimacy. For married couples, chastity means doing all those things that will help both husband and wife remain faithful to each other. It also means not practicing morally unacceptable means of birth control.

NEW LIFE IN CHRIST

Paul wanted people to remember that in Christ and the Holy Spirit, new life is possible. What God had commanded, he would make possible through grace. After Paul listed the misery of the peoples' sinful lives before they had received Jesus, he explained that they were now a new people:

> That is what some of you used to be; but now you have had yourselves washed, you were sanctified, you were justified in the name of the Lord Jesus Christ and in the Spirit of our God.
>
> (1 Corinthians 6:11)

In reminding us of the price of our salvation, Paul was reminding us of the dignity we have as children of God and temples of the Holy Spirit. FG

▶ continued from page 251

our sexuality in a proper manner. A chaste person is someone who is in control of his or her emotions and keeps them directed toward what is good for him or her. Our Baptism challenges us to follow Christ, the model of chastity, and live chaste lives.

The Church Is the Body of Christ

Abraham Lincoln loved the Bible. He read it and quoted it often, and he was a firm believer in Jesus. But he had little use for the church. Many people today have the same attitude. This is not the attitude we see reflected in Paul and in other early Christian writers. Early Christians could not think about Jesus except in terms of their relationship with the Church.

The word *church* means "the convocation of all those who are gathered together in assembly to form the People of God." Paul describes the Church by calling it the Body of Christ. "As a body is one though it has many parts, and all the parts of the body, though many, are one body, so also Christ." (I Corinthians 12:12) Through faith and Baptism we belong to the People of God, becoming "'a chosen race, a royal priesthood, a holy nation, a people of his own, so that you may announce the praises' of him who called you out of darkness into his wonderful light." (I Peter 2:9)

Jesus Christ is the head of the Church. "He is before all things, and in him all things hold together. He is the head of the body, the church." (Colossians 1:17–18)

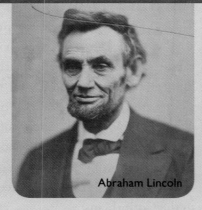
Abraham Lincoln

In the letter to the Ephesians, the Church is vividly described as the bride of Christ who "loved the church and handed himself over for her to sanctify her, cleansing her by the bath of water with the word, that he might present himself to the church in splendor, without spot or wrinkle or any such thing, that she might be holy and without blemish." (Ephesians 5:25–28)

Taking
Responsibility

PAUL AND PRAYER

We can see from Paul's letters that prayer was an important part of his life. He prayed because God was the center of his universe. "For from him and through him and for him are all things. To him be glory forever. Amen." (Romans 11:36) "Pray without ceasing," he told the Thessalonians, "In all circumstances give thanks, for this is the will of God for you in Christ Jesus." (1 Thessalonians 5:17–18)

Paul addresses his prayer to God the Father, in the name of Jesus, and by the power of the Holy Spirit: "In the same way, the Spirit too comes to the aid of our weakness; for we do not know how to pray as we ought, but the Spirit itself intercedes with inexpressible groanings." (Romans 8:26) Paul rarely prays for worldly things like health, prosperity, or healing. These things don't last. He says that "we look not to what is seen but to what is unseen; for what is seen is transitory, but what is unseen is eternal." (2 Corinthians 4:18)

Ephesians offers a good summary of Pauline prayer when he prays, "that Christ may dwell in your hearts through faith; that you, rooted and grounded in love, may have strength to comprehend with all the holy ones what is the breadth and length and height and depth, and to know the love of Christ that surpasses knowledge, so that you may be filled with all the fullness of God." (Ephesians 3:17–19)

Illustration by Elizabeth Wang, "Through Him, With Him," © Radiant Light 2006, www.radiantlight.org.uk

Leader: Paul devoted much of his time to help the early Christians take responsibility for putting their faith into action. We also are called to take responsibility for living our faith and making good choices.

Let us begin this time of prayer together by praying the Sign of the Cross.

In the name of the Father, and of the Son, and of the Holy Spirit. Amen.

All: Loving God, we come before you with gratitude for all you have given us. We ask for your help as we pause and take responsibility for our lives and the choices we make. We ask this through Christ, your Son and our Lord. Amen.

Reader: A reading from the First Letter of Paul to the Corinthians.

Thus through your knowledge, the weak person is brought to destruction, the brother for whom Christ died. When you sin in this way against your brothers and wound their consciences, weak as they are, you are sinning against Christ.

(1 Corinthians 8:11–12)

The Word of the Lord.

All: Thanks be to God.

Leader: In light of the Word of God we've just heard, let's spend a few minutes in silence to reflect on how we take responsibility for living our faith. Read the questions below silently. Choose two or three to answer for yourself. When our reflection time is over, we'll pray together the Lord's Prayer.

- Do I make myself look good at the expense of others?
- Do I sometimes choose to do the right thing for the wrong reason?
- Do I learn from my own mistakes as well as those of others?
- Do I consider what effect my actions may have on others?
- Do I show respect for my body and the bodies of others?

Leader: Let us pray.

All: Our Father . . .

Leader: The LORD bless you and keep you!
The LORD let his face shine upon you, and be gracious to you!
The LORD look upon you kindly and give you peace!

(Numbers 6:24–26)

All: Amen.

What's **WHAT?**

■ Review the main points of the chapter. Which point was least familiar to you? Write your new insights on the lines below.

- The morality of human acts has three dimensions—the act chosen, the intention of the act, and the circumstances that surround the act.

- What we choose to eat has moral implications.

- We are responsible for developing a fully formed conscience through learning from mistakes, prayer, Scripture, and Church teachings.

- The basic meaning of the Sixth Commandment is that we should accept our sexuality as a gift from God.

- Some of the images that Peter and Paul used to describe the Church are the Body of Christ, the People of God, and the bride of Christ.

_____

_____

_____

Say **WHAT?**

chastity • conscience

So **WHAT?**

■ How can regular reflection on my actions help me make good choices in my life?

_____

_____

_____

Now **WHAT?**

■ Forming our conscience is an ongoing responsibility. What step will I take this week that will help me inform my conscience?

_____

_____

Here's **WHAT** the Catholic Church Teaches

The Catholic Church recognizes that because a well-formed conscience is necessary for making moral decisions, we cannot turn over to anyone, including the government, the responsibility for our moral decisions. All members of the armed forces, for example, are morally obliged to resist orders that call for committing crimes against the moral law. Every soldier remains morally responsible for the acts he or she commits that violate the rights of individuals and groups of people. These acts cannot be justified by claiming obedience to the orders of superiors.

Conscientious objectors are people who refuse military service out of principle because their conscience rejects any kind of recourse to the use of force. The Church recognizes their right to refuse to go to war. In any war, civilians, soldiers, and political leaders are obliged to ensure that military or political demands never outweigh the value of the human person.

Pope John Paul II told a general audience in August 1999: "Today we are aware of the need to find a new consensus on humanitarian principles and to reinforce their foundation to prevent the recurrence of atrocities and abuse."

Cornerstones

1. As the two articles are read, note the cornerstones (main points) from each article in the appropriate column below.
2. With your group, share one cornerstone you identified from your group's assigned article. Keep sharing cornerstones until you have no new ones to share. Say "pass" if you have nothing new to add.

CORNERSTONES — ARTICLE 1	CORNERSTONES — ARTICLE 2
Making Moral Choices	**Temples of the Holy Spirit**

MAKE IT Work

" Use it up, wear it out, make it do, or do without.**"** This Appalachian folk saying offers us some good advice the next time we are tempted to throw something away. What is something you're ready to toss that could be reused?

10 things that you might be tempted to toss

Choose an alternative: (U) use it up, (F) fix it up, or (R) recycle it

- rusty bicycle frame
- sticky pop can
- tattered notebook
- jeans with hole in the knee
- grandma's collection of doilies

- the last bit of toothpaste
- packaging from a microwave dinner
- empty refrigerator cardboard box
- chocolate bar wedged between couch cushions
- dad's dusty old CB radio

Respect for Creation

When we look at the statistics on the environment, it can be unsettling. In the year 2003 the United States generated 236 million tons of trash. That amounted to 4.5 pounds of trash per person per day. Tropical rain forests once covered 14 percent of the earth's surface. Today the rain forests have dwindled to 6 percent of the earth's surface, and estimates have been made that the rain forests will be completely gone in 40 years. Every second 1½ acres of rain forest are lost to development and industry. An estimated 50,000 species of plants and animals become extinct every year due to deforestation. The rain forests also play a major role in recycling the earth's oxygen.

When we see that the earth is under stress from the way we are treating it, we can appreciate what Paul wrote in his letter to the Romans. While Paul was not addressing the specifics of ecology as we know it today, he was concerned about the depth of suffering that is the direct outcome of human sinfulness and greed.

For creation awaits with eager expectation the revelation of the children of God; for creation was made subject to futility, not of its own accord but because of the one who subjected it, in hope that creation itself would be set free from slavery to corruption and share in the glorious freedom of the children of God. We know that all creation is groaning in labor pains even until now; and not only that, but we ourselves, who have the first fruits of the Spirit, we also groan within ourselves as we wait for adoption, the redemption of our bodies.

(Romans 8:19–23)

Paul's point is that those who are redeemed in Christ can make positive decisions for themselves and for the world. They recognize that the goods of God's creation belong to everyone.

Whenever we destroy any part of the environment, we are damaging what belongs to everyone. When we

WISE GUYS

God has cared for these trees, saved them from drought, disease, avalanches, and a thousand tempests and floods. But he cannot save them from fools.

— John Muir (1838–1914) naturalist and founder of the Sierra Club

act irresponsibly in this way, we are stealing from our grandchildren and their grandchildren.

RESPECT

The Seventh Commandment tells us that we must be respectful of the earth just as we are respectful of each other. All of creation reflects the image of God and deserves our respect. And just as we must respect what others create through their work, so we should respect what the earth produces for the good of us all. This is why the Church has always encouraged us to love and to care for the poor. The whole human family has the right in justice to receive what is needed to live a productive and healthy life.

THINGS WE CAN DO

The Seventh Commandment tells us not to steal. Any time we steal, no matter how we go about it, we are breaking the commandment. We must return the stolen goods to the owner and make up for the injustice we have done.

> All of creation reflects the image of God and deserves our respect.

As members of the human family, we have stolen much from future generations. Over the course of history, individuals have made sinful choices that make it easier for us to sin. Not addressing these sins as a community leads to the creation of social sin. For example, people have cut down forests and forced many species of animals and plants into extinction. We cannot return the natural resources we have stolen to people today or to the people who will come in the future.

All is not bleak, however. There are things that we can do to address this social sin of not acting to preserve the environment. We can stop using so much of the earth's resources. This is why it is important to recycle. We can restore some things to the earth. This is why we plant trees. We can also study the environment and learn about the problems we face as a community. Then we can learn how to solve or prevent future problems.

The Seventh Commandment imposes an obligation on us to respect what belongs to others, including the earth itself. Pope John Paul II addressed this issue in his message for the World Day of Peace on January 1, 1990. He said that "The commitment of believers to a healthy environment for everyone stems directly from their belief in God the Creator, from their recognition of the effects of original and personal sin, and from the certainty of having been redeemed by Christ. Respect for life and for the dignity of the human person extends also to the rest of creation, which is called to join man in praising God." It is our obligation to protect the environment and all that is in it, including all people who live in it. FG

It Is Not Yours

The temptation to cheat on tests and homework can be pretty powerful at times. Students want to succeed in school. They want their parents and teachers to think well of them. They might be feeling a lot of pressure to get good grades. Their friends might be getting good grades, and they want to keep up with them.

But cheating is stealing—taking knowledge and information that belongs to someone else. When we are tempted to cheat, perhaps we should recall the words of one of Paul's students: "The thief must no longer steal, but rather labor, doing honest work with his [own] hands." (Ephesians 4:28)

Co-workers with God

Communal Work, Gerard Valcin, Haitian, 20th century

Paul lived in a culture in which people made offerings to different pagan gods with a variety of powers. They believed that if they could satisfy the gods, they would receive a favor from them. The portrayal of many of the pagan gods was not very flattering. The Greek gods were portrayed as temperamental and unreliable. They couldn't be bothered to do anything for their worshipers unless they received gifts. They seemed to do little except loaf around in the heavens and quarrel with each other. Sometimes for entertainment, they would provoke the mortals on earth.

Contrast this image of the pagan gods with the portrait of God in Genesis 2:4–24. God works ceaselessly for the benefit of the human family. He creates and maintains a world for us and proclaims that it is very good. Genesis 2:15 tells us how God created a garden for the first man to work in: "The Lord God then took the man and settled him in the garden of Eden, to cultivate and care for it." God's work of creation is the model for human work. It helps us to understand that human work in the world is something good.

Jesus understood the dignity of work. He was raised as a carpenter, and much of his life was spent as a teacher. Most of the images in his parables concern issues of work. He tells of a farmer going out to sow his fields and the workers in the vineyard. His story of the shepherd caring for his sheep, especially the one that is lost, is one of his most important images. In his stories Jesus shows how God's action in our lives involves the ordinary tasks in life.

> **We are God's co-workers.**
> **(I Corinthians 3:9)**
>
> **IM**

Throughout his ministry, Paul supported himself financially as a tent-maker. He did not want himself or his followers to be a burden to others:

> For you know how one must imitate us. For we did not act in a disorderly way among you, nor did we eat food received free from anyone. On the contrary, in toil and drudgery, night and day we worked, so as not to burden any of you. (2 Thessalonians 3:7–8)

There are times when we think that it would be wonderful if no one had to work. Hanging out like those Greek gods can sound attractive. But without work our lives would have no meaning.

The work you are doing at school is preparing you for the future. The work you do at home serves the well-being of your family—whether you take out the garbage, clean your room, or take care of a younger sibling. Some of your outside work, such as babysitting or mowing people's lawns, might earn you some cash. These types of jobs also help you learn the skill of accepting a task and completing it.

Co-workers

God is a tireless worker and in Jesus' time on earth he valued work and supported those who needed to get their jobs done. (Luke 5:1–11) Just as

continued on page 262 ▶

art • i • fact

God the Father Measuring the Universe, Bible Moralisé, mid-13th century, perhaps from Reims, France

ⓕⓞⓞⓣⓝⓞⓣⓔ

Genesis 1:26 says that God created human beings in his image and likeness. The early Greeks, however, made the gods and goddesses in their own image, giving them human faults and weaknesses. Aphrodite, for example, was the grand diva of the heavens, exuding beauty and love but also vanity and moodiness. Ares, the god of war, was often depicted as a barbarian, violent and quick to anger—not someone you'd want to fall out of favor with.

Though the Greek gods and goddesses always made for great drama, they were totally unpredictable and often careless with human life. Don't you think that we've got it good with God?

Generosity

In his letter to the Romans, Paul writes about a trip he is making to Jerusalem to bring "the poor among the holy ones in Jerusalem" money that has been collected for them in Greece. (15:25–28) The Christians in Greece recognized that they were responsible to help other Christians throughout the world. In his letter to the Corinthians, Paul explains why such generosity is an important part of being a Christian.

> Moreover, God is able to make every grace abundant for you, so that in all things, always having all you need, you may have an abundance for every good work. As it is written:
>
>> "He scatters abroad,
>> he gives to the poor;
>> his righteousness endures
>> forever." (2 Corinthians 9:8–9)

God's generous grace allows us to give freely to others who are in need so that their needs will be filled and so they'll know how much God cares for them. Paul says that we'll also be enriched for participating in God's generosity: "[F]or the administration of this public service is not only supplying the needs of the holy ones but is also overflowing in many acts of thanksgiving to God." (2 Corinthians 9:11–12)

When we give to those in need and gain a better understanding of their situation, Paul says that we glorify God because we are truly living the gospel of Jesus Christ.

▶ *continued from page 261*

Jesus redeems us through his life, death, and Resurrection, he redeems our work through the power of the Holy Spirit. In Jesus Christ we are a new creation, and as stewards of God we help to redeem the world through our work.

THE DIGNITY OF WORK

The work that people do is an important part of society. It not only enables people to earn the money they need in order to live decent lives, but it helps them to be active participants in society. Work gives people a sense of dignity and accomplishment. It makes it possible for them to be independent and self-reliant. This is why the Church is so concerned about work issues. This is also why the Church opposes slavery in any of its forms. Does everyone have the opportunity to work? Are people paid enough for their work so that they can live decently? Are the places where people work safe and healthy? Are people given enough time to rest from work? These are issues that touch all of our lives and have a direct connection to our spiritual well-being. This is the source of the Church's concern.

IT'S A MATTER OF JUSTICE

Since we are guardians of God's creation, we recognize that everything we have and everything we work for is on loan to us from God. When we have worked to fulfill our basic needs and those of our family, God calls us to be generous with what we have to help those in need. This is more than helping out; it is a matter of justice.

Each of us is called by God to be co-creators with him. The work we do is an answer to God's call because it helps make society function properly. This vocation must always be taken seriously because it is through our work that we express to God and to others who we are and what we want in our lives. The dignity of the work we do is modeled on the action of God who works ceaselessly for our good, continuously creating a future for us. When we work toward our own future, we are cooperating with God in his work in order to benefit ourselves and the world. FG

For Your Eyes Only

Our talents indicate the kind of work that we would be good at and that we'd find meaningful. Some people love to write, and so they'd enjoy working for a book or magazine publisher. Other people love to figure out how to make things work, so they'd make great engineers. How do your dreams for your future match up with your talents?

Equal Before God

Most of Paul's epistles were dictated to a secretary who was responsible for accurately communicating Paul's thinking. However, Paul wrote the epistle to Philemon in his own hand so that he could make a personal plea on behalf of Onesimus. Paul found himself in jail with Onesimus, a slave who had run away from his owner Philemon. Paul helped Onesimus become a Christian. When Onesimus was released from prison, Paul gave him a letter to take to Philemon. In the letter Paul explains that he has baptized Onesimus, and he asks his owner to take him back, not as a slave, but as his brother. As Paul had baptized Philemon, he felt he had the right to make this request. In asking Philemon to accept Onesimus as his brother, Paul established the foundation for understanding that there can be no slaves in Christ. We are all equal before him.

Handle with Care

THE PSALMS AND CREATION

The ongoing life of prayer, which is our conversation with God and his response, has unfolded throughout all of human history. In the creation of the world, God gave us the first statement of who he is and of his plan of loving goodness for us.

The Book of Psalms contains some beautiful prayers of the people of Israel that express the desire for God as he is found in all creation. Psalms 8, 19, 33, 65, and 104 are especially beautiful prayers of blessing and adoration of God as creator. "The heavens declare the glory of God," and the complex beauty of the universe shows its builder's craft. (Psalm 19:2)

How can we not respond with praise? God has made us little less than a god, crowned us with glory and honor. (Psalm 8:6) How can we not respond with humble thanks? And God's work as creator continues today:

You visit the earth and water it,
make it abundantly fertile.

God's stream is filled with water;
with it you supply the world with grain.

(Psalm 65:10)

God's work of creation is for us a continual source of praise.

Handle with Care

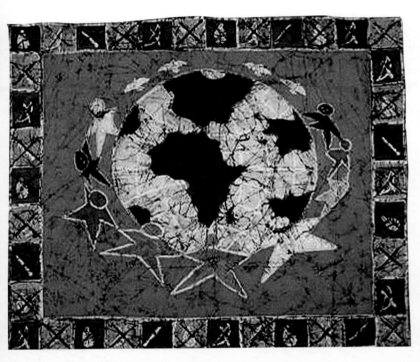

art • i • fact
Teamwork, Alexander Nyankson,
batik wall hanging

Leader: Everything we have is on loan to us from God. The Seventh Commandment, "You shall not steal," is about respect. When someone loans us something, we take care of it and return it in good condition.

God, the Creator, has given us everything we need for life, and we are called to care for these gifts with respect and reverence. Psalm 104 calls us to remember all that God has loaned to us and to return praise to him for his great gifts.

Let us pray this psalm together, aware of God's abundant generosity and his timeless graciousness. Our response will be
℟ May the glory of the Lord endure forever.

Group 1:
Bless the LORD, my soul!
    LORD, my God, you are great indeed!
You are clothed with majesty and glory,
    robed in light as with a cloak. ℟

Group 2:
You fixed the earth on its foundation,
    never to be moved.
The ocean covered it like a garment;
    above the mountains stood the waters. ℟

Group 1:
You water the mountains from your palace;
    by your labor the earth abounds.
You raise grass for the cattle
    and plants for our beasts of burden. ℟

Group 2:
You made the moon to mark the seasons,
    the sun that knows the hour of its setting.
You bring darkness and night falls,
    then all the beasts of the forest roam abroad. ℟

Group 1:
How varied are your works, LORD!
    In wisdom you have wrought them all;
    the earth is full of your creatures. ℟

All: May the glory of the LORD endure forever,
    May the LORD be glad in these works!
I will sing to the LORD all my life;
    I will sing praise to my God while I live.

What's **WHAT**?

■ Review the main points of the chapter. Choose the one that's most inspiring to you and write your reasons on the lines provided.

- The Seventh Commandment calls us to respect what belongs to others, including the earth and all that is in it.

- Cheating is a form of stealing.

- The work we do contributes to society and expresses our vocation to be co-creators with God.

- Paul encourages generosity as a way of sharing all that we have received from God.

- In his letter to Philemon, Paul established the foundation for understanding that all are equal before God.

_____

_____

_____

Say **WHAT**?

dignity of work • social sin

So **WHAT**?

■ God calls us to respect what belongs to others, including the earth and all that is in it.
Think about it. Pray about it.

Now **WHAT**?

■ Daily life offers many opportunities to be generous with what we have. What is something I will do this week to show that I value people more than things?

_____

_____

Here's **WHAT** the Catholic Church Teaches

In June 2001 the Catholic bishops of the United States issued a statement called *Global Climate Change: A Plea for Dialogue, Prudence, and the Common Good.* In it they said: "Because of the blessings God has bestowed on our nation and the power it possesses, the United States bears a special responsibility in its stewardship of God's creation to shape responses that serve the entire human family." In this statement they remind us that true stewardship requires changes in human actions, in moral behavior, and in technological advancement.

Our faith has always urged moderation in the use of material goods. We must not allow our desire for more material things to overtake our concern for the basic needs of people and the environment.

Sacrifice should not be an unpopular concept. A life focused less on material gain may remind us that we are more than what we own. When we realize this, we will have more time for family and friends, and for our responsibilities to society. A renewed sense of sacrifice and restraint on our part can make an essential contribution to addressing global climate change.

We Can Change the World

1. **Read both articles silently.**

2. **In your group of four, decide which article each pair will work on.**

3. **With your partner, complete the "Something to Think About..." section below, listing the important ideas presented in your article.**

4. **Exchange worksheets with the other pair in your group and complete the "How It Can Change the World" section below.**

5. **With your partner, select one "Something to Think About...Change the World" idea and explain how and why this idea can make the world a better place.**

6. **With your partner, think of a role model you feel has changed the world in this way.**

ARTICLE NAME _____

SOMETHING TO THINK ABOUT	HOW IT CAN CHANGE THE WORLD

THE GRASS IS Greener

Most of us have heard the expression "The grass is always greener on the other side of the fence." How would you explain the meaning of this expression to someone who's never heard it before?

For Your Eyes Only

What is one thing that you got that you thought would make you happy, but then it didn't? Why did you think it would make you happy?

JOURNEY *in* Truth

From *The Spiritual Journey of St. Ignatius Loyola*, Dora Nikolova Bittau

Ignatius of Loyola was a young Spanish nobleman who thought that living an honest, good life meant winning fame on the battlefield, getting a high-profile job in the court, and being seen as a hero by beautiful women. So he became a soldier. He led the defense of the city of Pamplona against overwhelming odds until a cannonball shattered his leg. Pamplona fell, and the injured Ignatius was taken prisoner. However, because his enemies were impressed with his bravery, they cared for his wounds and carried him back to his family's castle to recover.

Ignatius thought that he had done his duty. He had achieved his goal of military fame, and now he waited impatiently to return to life at the court. He became bored as he waited for his wounds to heal, so he asked if there were any books of adventure stories in his family's castle. He wanted to read the stories so that he could continue to dream about the life he wanted to live. But the only books in the castle were a book on the life of Christ and a collection on the lives of the saints. So Ignatius read them to pass the time.

> Ignatius made the decision to live in the truth of Christ.

Ignatius was impressed with what Jesus had done for the world in saving us from sin. He was impressed with the heroic efforts of saints like Francis of Assisi and Dominic Guzman to live holy lives proclaiming the Good News of Christ in the midst of the world. Then Ignatius noticed something else. When he returned to his dreams of being a knight, he would come away with an empty feeling. He realized that these dreams led him away from living a truthful, honest life with integrity.

When he thought about being a holy person like Francis and Dominic, however, he came away feeling refreshed, encouraged, and excited. The positive reaction that Ignatius experienced when he dreamed of doing heroic deeds for God changed his life. Following the road to sanctity was the only way he could live in truth with himself and with God. Ignatius decided to do penance for his sins. He gave away his fancy clothes in exchange for a simple robe, and he dedicated himself to doing heroic deeds on behalf of God. Ignatius eventually gathered a group of like-minded men, and together they founded the Society of Jesus.

Ignatius discovered what it means to live in truth. This is the type of truth that is described in the letter to the Ephesians 4:20–24. After describing how not living in truth leads to futility and lack of understanding, the letter continues as follows:

This is not how you learned Christ, assuming that you have heard of him and were taught in him, as truth is in Jesus, that you should put away the old self of your former way of life, corrupted through deceitful desires, and be renewed in the spirit of your minds, and put on a new self, created in God's way in righteousness and holiness of truth. (Ephesians 4:20–24)

A TRUTHFUL PERSON

What does it mean to live as a truthful person? This is the main issue when we think about the Eighth Commandment, "You shall not bear false witness against your neighbor." The Eighth Commandment is about more than not saying things that hurt others. It is about being a truthful person. The commandment challenges us to exercise the virtue of truthfulness. We should be true in the things we do and say and in the way we live. This is what Ignatius discovered in his reflections on the two ways he could live his life.

It's a sin against truth to lie about another person or to spread false stories that harm someone's reputation. It's also a sin against truth to share information about a person that they asked you not to share. These sins are forbidden by the Eighth Commandment. They are actions that leave us feeling hollow and unsatisfied. The damage we deliberately do to others

continued on page 270 ▶

Walkin' the Talk

After Ignatius's conversion, he decided he would go to Jerusalem so he could follow in the steps of Jesus. On his way he stopped at Manresa, a town along the river Cardoner. He had planned to stay just long enough to rest, but he ended up staying for 10 months. There on the banks of the Cardoner, he had a profound experience of God. It changed his entire life and the way he understood and related to God and the world. Ignatius doesn't describe exactly what happened, but after the experience, he was able to recognize God in all things.

True to Her Vocation

A Jewish mother with her son, who was being sheltered from the Nazis at a Belgian convent

During World War II many convents and monasteries sheltered Jewish men, women, and children from Nazi persecution. The La Providence orphanage in Verviers, Belgium, played a major part in sheltering and caring for hundreds of children whose parents had been shipped to concentration camps or were in hiding themselves. The orphanage was operated by the Sisters of Charity of Saint Vincent de Paul. Sister Marie (birth name Mathilde Leruth) was in charge and made sure that the Jewish children didn't give away their identities during the many unexpected visits by the Nazis. She did not tell the Nazis who the children were, knowing that they had no right to that information. Once, when a major Nazi raid was expected, Sister Marie put the children on a bus and took them on an impromptu outing to a nearby village for the afternoon. Sylvain Brachfeld, who was one of the children at the orphanage, described Sister Marie years later as "a marvel of love under circumstances which obliged her to risk her life and liberty every day." Sister Marie was honored by Yad Vashem, the Holocaust Memorial in Israel, and was named to the "Righteous Among the Nations," an honor granted to non-Jews who risked their lives to save Jews during the Holocaust.

Boast in the Lord

► *continued from page 269*

Apparently, Paul was not the most impressive public speaker. This made for quite a challenge for him in his preaching since the people of his time were strongly persuaded by public speakers, known as rhetoricians, who were strong in voice, eloquent in speech, and impressive in appearance.

How then did Paul win over so many people for Jesus Christ? Paul taught people not to be easily swayed by appearances or by people who boast of their own accomplishments and skills but who, in reality, have little to offer. Paul was one of the first Christians to use the medium of letter-writing to persuade people. He wrote in such a powerful and truthful manner that the lives of countless people were changed and the message of Jesus spread throughout the world. Paul used his own weakness to draw attention to the power of God. He taught the people of Corinth, and he teaches us, not to place too much faith in people who boast about themselves because the truth can be easily lost. Rather, he teaches, "Whoever boasts, should boast in the Lord." (I Corinthians I:31)

impacts our own sense of worth. We are called by the Holy Spirit to make amends for any damage we have caused to others through our words.

LIVING IN TRUTH

When we say that Ignatius made the decision to live in the truth of Christ, we mean that he chose to live with sincerity and integrity. He chose not to follow the false trails in building up himself, but chose to live in relationship with God and others. This decision transformed his life. He became a hero for God, leaving behind the self-centered dreams of his past. Ignatius discovered the Fruits of the Holy Spirit in his life. Paul discussed the Fruits of the Holy Spirit in his letter to the Galatians:

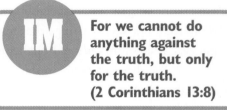

For we cannot do anything against the truth, but only for the truth. (2 Corinthians 13:8)

> In contrast, the fruit of the Spirit is love, joy, peace, patience, kindness, generosity, faithfulness, gentleness, self-control. Against such there is no law. (Galatians 5:22–23)

Like Ignatius, we are called to live in truth and in integrity with God and with others. Jesus Christ has saved us from false ways of living and recreates us through the grace we receive from the Holy Spirit. In faith we can let the old things pass away, and the new things come to be. In this way we can also live in love, joy, peace, and patience. 🔲

TO LEARN MORE about Saint Ignatius of Loyola, visit www.FindingGod.org/teens.

IT'S LIKE THIS

Your mother probably taught you not to boast. But Paul gives us permission to boast, so long as we boast in the Lord. What did he mean exactly? That we should go around saying, "My God can beat up your god"? Of course not. Boasting in the Lord means that we acknowledge that God is at the center of our lives and that all the good that we do comes from him. In a way, we're saying, "See how little I have to offer but how much God has to offer." Our boasting is not really about ourselves but about how awesome God is.

do not Covet

At times it's easy to be envious of others when we think they are getting ahead of us. They have more things, get better grades, or live in a bigger house. They seem to have everything that we want. Although we know that the Ninth and Tenth Commandments warn us against coveting the things we do not have, it's difficult to keep our feelings from getting in the way. Paul felt this frustration when tempted by sin. In his letter to the Romans he describes how it feels to be a slave to temptation and to be unable to shake the urge to sin:

> That I do, I do not understand. For I do not do what I want, but I do what I hate. . . . For I do not do the good I want, but I do the evil I do not want. Now if [I] do what I do not want, it is no longer I who do it, but sin that dwells in me. (Romans 7:15, 19–20)

Paul teaches that we are helpless to lift ourselves out of our sinful condition and that we make the situation worse when we give in to temptation. Our only solution is to let ourselves be open to the grace won for us by Jesus Christ:

> Miserable one that I am! Who will deliver me from this mortal body? Thanks be to God through Jesus Christ our Lord. (Romans 7:24–25)

We need the grace of the Holy Spirit in order to keep the Tenth Commandment, "You shall not covet your neighbor's goods." This commandment calls us not to be envious of what others have because that could lead us to act in ways that would harm ourselves and others.

Our attitudes determine what our actions will be.

It is not wrong to want something. It is wrong, however, to be unhappy with the good fortune of others and to want for ourselves what they have. Our attitudes determine what our actions will be. The Tenth Commandment is about having the right attitude toward others, an attitude based on love. Paul explained this in his first letter to the Corinthians:

> Love is patient, love is kind. It is not jealous, [love] is not pompous, it is not inflated, it is not rude, it does not seek its own interests, it is not quick-tempered, it does not brood over injury, it does not rejoice over wrong-doing but rejoices with the truth. It bears all things, believes all things, hopes all things, endures all things. (1 Corinthians 13:4–7)

continued on page 272 ▶

Use of Wealth

The issue of the gap between the rich and the poor was prevalent in the early Church. People who spent their lives accumulating as much wealth and as many material goods as they could found themselves consumed by greed. Paul called them to find their way out of their greed and their envy of others who were even wealthier than they. He challenged them to practice humility and good will, and to trust in the care of God. The letter to Timothy addresses this issue directly:

> Tell the rich in the present age not to be proud and not to rely on so uncertain a thing as wealth but rather on God, who richly provides us with all things for our enjoyment. Tell them to do good, to be rich in good works, to be generous, ready to share, thus accumulating as treasure a good foundation for the future, so as to win the life that is true life.
>
> (1 Timothy 6:17–19)

▶ *continued from page 271*

If our attitude is one of love, we'll want good things for others and we'll be happy when they get them.

The Tenth Commandment also helps us keep the proper attitude toward things. The proper attitude is one of gratefulness to God for what he has given us. This means living with a sense of detachment—recognizing that things are good in themselves, but they should not dominate our lives. As Catholics called to serve the Kingdom of God, we do our best to let go of things and to grow in our ability to value people more than things.

10 ideas for creative giving

Make a donation to a person's favorite cause.

Collect favorite family recipes and make a recipe book.

Create coupons offering free babysitting or help around the house.

Make cards from your own photographs or drawings.

Write a poem, short story, or song and creatively present it.

Buy gifts that support artisans from poorer countries.

Pass on a book you love to someone.

Make a calendar with your own pictures and familiar sayings.

Volunteer time at a local soup kitchen or shelter.

Take someone on a mystery adventure.

 Once, I found a pearl on the ocean floor and gave it to my sister. But, she said she wouldn't be caught dead disrespecting oysters.

In Our Own Way

PRAYER AND DETACHMENT

Prayer can help us remain detached from the desire for things we don't need and from envy of others who have what we want. Prayer can also help us to experience God's constant care for us more deeply and to turn ourselves over to the Father who frees us from anxiety about tomorrow.

Prayer leads us away from envy—sadness at the sight of what another person has and the desire to have those things for ourselves.

Saint Gregory of Nyssa said, "Whoever sees God has obtained all the goods of which he can conceive." In prayer, God himself can become the goal of all our desires.

In Our Own Way

Before their conversions, both Ignatius and Paul led lives of privilege. After their encounters with Christ, they felt called to leave behind their former way of life. They moved from a life based on false ideas to one based on truth. Each in his own way became a hero for God. That's what we are called to be as well.

In your imagination, go to a quiet place where you can be alone. Make yourself comfortable and then be still. Notice that Jesus comes to join you.

He asks you what caught your attention in the lives of Ignatius and Paul. You think about it for a moment. Was it the way that God intervened in their lives? Or maybe it was the heroic things they did for God after their conversions. Share with Jesus whatever strikes you about their lives.

Then Jesus reminds you that we all are called to live in truth and to put our faith into action. Living in truth means living with integrity. Paul and Ignatius did this each in his own way. And you will do it in the way God calls *you*. Jesus mentions that he already seen the ways you live with integrity—stopping gossip by not repeating it to others, having a positive attitude toward yourself and others, and valuing relationships over possessions. Listen as Jesus shares all that he's noticed in you.

Jesus thanks you and calls you a hero for God. You might be surprised at first. Maybe you feel proud. Let Jesus know how you feel. Then thank him for this time together.

End your reflection by praying the Glory Be to the Father.

art • i • fact
Saint Ignatius of Loyola,
oil on canvas, French School,
17th Century

What's WHAT?

■ Review the main points of the chapter. Which one is most important to you? Write your reasons on the lines below.

- The Eighth Commandment calls us to live with integrity as a truthful person in all that we say and do.

- Sister Marie rescued many Jewish children whose parents were sent to Nazi concentration camps.

- Paul wrote letters to spread the Good News about Jesus Christ.

- The Ninth and Tenth Commandments call us to have a loving attitude toward people and things and to be grateful to God.

- Paul challenged those consumed by greed to trust in God's care and practice humility and good will.

_____

_____

_____

_____

So WHAT?

■ What difference do I notice in my behavior when I choose to live in truth with God, myself, and others?

_____

_____

_____

_____

Say WHAT?

envy

Now WHAT?

■ Think of one object you wish you could have. List three reasons why you can be happy without it.

_____

_____

_____

Here's WHAT the Catholic Church Teaches

Everyone has the right to use the earth's goods for himself or herself and his or her family. The Tenth Commandment teaches us not to want more than we need or what belongs to our neighbors. From the earliest times the Church has taught that God wanted everything on and in the earth to be used by all people.

The *Pastoral Constitution on the Church in the Modern World* of the Second Vatican Council taught that we should regard what we have as also meant for the benefit of others. The bishops at the Council taught that people "are obliged to come to the relief of the poor and to do so not merely out of their superfluous goods."

In an audience with seven new ambassadors to the Holy See on June 16, 2005, Pope Benedict XVI reaffirmed that everyone has a right to the earth's goods: "The earth, in fact, can produce enough to nourish all its inhabitants, on the condition that the rich countries do not keep for themselves what belongs to all."

If . . . Then . . .

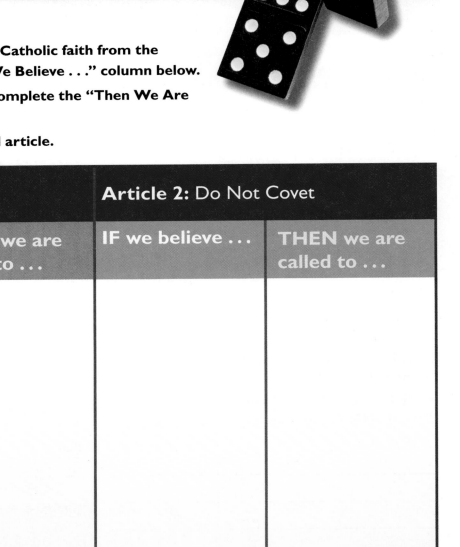

1. **Read the first article.**

2. **Identify the main ideas about our Catholic faith from the article and note them in the "If We Believe . . ." column below.**

3. **In your group, work together to complete the "Then We Are Called to . . ." column.**

4. **Repeat the process for the second article.**

Article 1: Journey in Truth		**Article 2:** Do Not Covet	
IF we believe . . .	**THEN we are called to . . .**	**IF we believe . . .**	**THEN we are called to . . .**

Faith in Action

Faith is alive when we put it into action every day of our lives. It is expressed in the attitudes and values we hold and in the ways we relate to the people and the world around us. Taking action to create a more just world is an essential part of living the Gospel. Jesus preached not only with words but with the way he lived his life. We are called to do the same.

In this unit we explored the writings of Paul and his proclamation of Jesus to the world. In his life and teaching, Jesus showed his care for human beings and for all creation. He often used images from nature and from the world around him to teach people about God. Here are some ideas to get you involved in nature and to proclaim Jesus to the world.

"Judge each day not by the harvest you reap but by the seeds you plant."

—Robert Louis Stevenson, novelist, poet, and travel writer

Plant Seeds

Purpose:

Learn about the process of a seed taking root; plant seeds of flowers or herbs that can be given to others as gifts.

Background:

Paul teaches us that we must be generous in sowing the seeds of God's message in our world. (2 Corinthians 9:6) One way we can sow seeds of God's message is to literally sow seeds. Planting seeds of flowers, fruits, grains, vegetables, and trees are ways to show our care for the earth. They can also become seeds of God's message because of the beauty, shade, nourishment, habitat, or joy that they provide.

Steps:

a. Read the parable of the mustard seed in the Gospel of Mark 4:30–32. Reflect on the power of one little seed to do so much good. Share your reflections with one another.

continued on page 278 ▶

▶ *continued from page 277*

b. Research the nature of a seed. What is inside? What makes it start growing? What are the conditions that help it take root and grow strong?

c. Choose flowers or herbs that you can grow from seeds. Research how to plant these particular seeds.

d. Collect the particular supplies you'll need for those seeds. Yogurt cups and egg cartons make good pots for the initial planting of seeds.

e. Decide what you are going to do with the plants. How can you use them in ways that sow God's message for someone else?

Recycle Bin Bonanza

WE RECYCLE

Purpose:

Establish or enhance recycling systems in your school or parish; raise awareness about the importance of recycling.

Background:

Almost everything that we use can be recycled and made into something new. When we throw things away, we add to landfills and other environmental hazards, and we take more of the earth's resources to make things that could have been made with recycled material.

"Gather the fragments left over, so that nothing will be wasted."

—Jesus, John 6:12

Steps:

a. Find out what recycling systems are already in place in your school or parish. If there are none, talk with school or parish leaders about how you can help.

b. Create recycling bins by reusing discarded containers and decorating them with fun colors, pictures, and words that remind people to recycle. Consult a local recycling facility to see how materials should be grouped. For example, you might have recycling bins for each of the following: mixed paper, glass, metal cans, batteries, printer cartridges, newspaper, and corrugated cardboard.

c. Place bins in high-trash zones.

d. Keep track of how much is recycled and educate others by posting a chart each month that shows the impact of your recycling efforts.

Liturgical Year

281

ADVENT marks the beginning of the Church year. It is a time of anticipation that begins four Sundays before Christmas.

285

The Christmas Season includes **CHRISTMAS,** the celebration of Jesus' birth, and Epiphany, the celebration of his manifestation to the world.

285
Christmas

289

LENT is a season of conversion that begins on Ash Wednesday. It is a time of turning toward God in preparation for Easter.

293

During **HOLY WEEK** we recall the events leading to the suffering and death of Jesus. Holy Week begins with Palm Sunday and ends on Holy Saturday.

293
Holy Week

297

EASTER celebrates Jesus' being raised from the dead. The Resurrection is the central mystery of the Christian faith. The Ascension celebrates Jesus' return to the Father in heaven.

301

The coming of the Holy Spirit is celebrated on **PENTECOST.** With this feast, the Easter Season ends.

305

ALL SAINTS DAY celebrates the victory of all of the holy persons in heaven. On All Souls Day, we pray for those who have died but are still in purgatory.

The time set aside for celebrating our call to follow Jesus day by day as his disciples is Ordinary Time.

297
Easter

The Year in Our Church

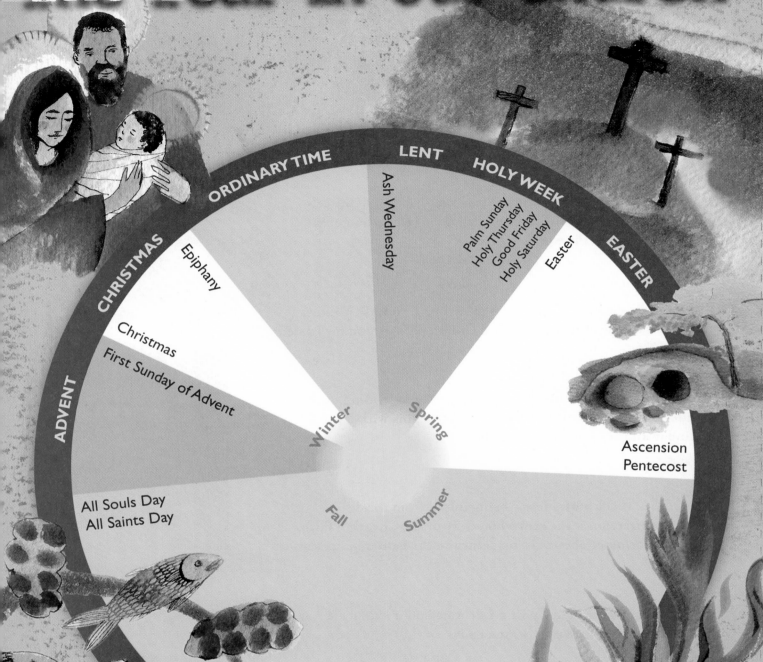

ORDINARY TIME

LENT

HOLY WEEK

EASTER

Ash Wednesday

Palm Sunday
Holy Thursday
Good Friday
Holy Saturday

Easter

CHRISTMAS

Epiphany

Christmas

First Sunday of Advent

ADVENT

Ascension
Pentecost

All Souls Day
All Saints Day

Winter

Spring

Fall

Summer

ORDINARY TIME

Liturgical Calendar

The liturgical calendar highlights the feast days and seasons
of the Church year. Various colors symbolize the different seasons.

Advent

Advent begins on the fourth Sunday before Christmas and marks the beginning of the Church's liturgical year. During Advent, we remember how the people of Israel awaited the Messiah. We also prepare ourselves to celebrate the birth of Jesus. Advent is a time of joyful anticipation for the day when Christ will return in glory.

art • i • fact
The Angel's Message,
George Hillyard Swinstead,
(1860–1926), England

Mary Accepts God's Promise

The Gospel of Luke tells us how Mary was chosen by God to be the mother of Jesus and how she responded in faith. This story, found in Luke 1:26–38, is called the Annunciation.

Mary was from a small town in Galilee called Nazareth. She was engaged to marry a man named Joseph. An angel of God visited Mary and announced that she had been chosen by God to bear a son, who was to be named Jesus. The angel told her that this child would be the Son of God.

Mary wondered aloud how this could be, since she was a virgin. The angel told her that she would conceive this son by the power of the Holy Spirit. The angel also gave Mary a sign that she would bear a child: Mary's relative, Elizabeth, who was believed to be unable to have children, also was pregnant. Mary accepted the message of the angel with the words, "Behold, I am the handmaid of the Lord. May it be done to me according to your word." (Luke 1:38) Then the angel left her.

Mary is a model of discipleship for us. She responded to God's messenger with a resounding "yes." Her words to the angel are sometimes called Mary's *fiat,* a Latin word that means "let it be done." During Advent, we reflect on Mary's acceptance of God's call to be the mother of Jesus. We pray that we'll be as open to God's call as Mary was and that we'll respond with our own *fiat.*

After the visit from the angel, Mary traveled to see her relative Elizabeth

During Advent, we pray that we'll be as open to God's call as Mary was.

and found her with a child, just as the angel had said. We call this special event in Mary's life the Visitation.

Elizabeth and Mary greeted each other joyfully, because they recognized the wonderful things that God was doing for them. We're reminded to spend time during Advent remembering the great things God has done throughout history and in our own lives.

ADVENT PRAYER: THE ADVENT WREATH

The Church provides us with special prayers and devotions during Advent. One of these devotions is the Advent wreath. The Advent wreath is used to decorate the church during Advent. It also can be used at home. For example, some people place an Advent wreath on their dinner table.

An Advent wreath consists of a circle of evergreens. It has four candles that represent each of the four Sundays of Advent. The greenery in the wreath reminds us of the new life that Jesus will bring to us. The circle of the wreath represents God's unending love. The candles on the wreath are usually purple, the liturgical color for Advent, or white. A pink candle ordinarily is used for the third Sunday of Advent. This reminds us to rejoice because the Lord is near. The light from the candles represents the light that came into the world at Jesus' birth. A new candle is lit each week. FG

During Advent we celebrate the Feast of the Immaculate Conception on December 8. On this day, a Holy Day of Obligation, we remember that Mary was born without original sin. Even before she was born, Mary was chosen by God to be the mother of Jesus. Several important celebrations occur during Advent. Many celebrations reflect ethnic and cultural traditions and recall saints of our Catholic tradition. For example, the Feast of Our Lady of Guadalupe is an important Mexican celebration of Mary's appearance to Juan Diego. It's celebrated on December 12 in the United States. *Los Posadas* is a Mexican celebration of the novena—a nine-day prayer—before Christmas. December 13 is the Feast of Saint Lucia, whose name means light. It's celebrated during the time of the longest nights of winter. What Advent celebrations are part of your family's preparation for Christmas?

Hail Mary and Magnificat

Read Luke 1:26–45, the story of the Annunciation and the beginning of the story of the Visitation. In these passages are the origins of the words to the first part of the prayer we call the Hail Mary. Find the words and reflect on what they mean. Now read Mary's response to Elizabeth's greeting in Luke 1:46–56. Mary responded to Elizabeth by giving praise to God for the wonders he had done throughout the history of Israel. We call this prayer the Magnificat. It's prayed during Evening Prayer, which is part of the Liturgy of the Hours.

God Is Great

Leader: Praise be to God, who has done great things for us.

All: Praise be to God.

Leader: In this Advent season, we remember Mary's "yes" to God. Like Mary, we recognize that God has done marvelous deeds throughout history and in our own lives.

Leader: Let us pray together Mary's Magnificat and praise God for all of his wondrous deeds.

All: My soul proclaims the greatness of the Lord,
My spirit rejoices in God my Savior;
for he has looked with favor on his lowly servant.

Group 1:   From this day all generations will call me blessed: the Almighty has done great things for me, and holy is his Name.

Group 2:   He has mercy on those who fear him in every generation. He has shown the strength of his arm, he has scattered the proud in their conceit.

Group 1:   He has cast down the mighty from their thrones, and has lifted up the lowly.

Group 2:   He has filled the hungry with good things, and the rich he has sent away empty.

All: He has come to the help of his servant Israel
for he has remembered his promise of mercy,
the promise he made to our fathers,
to Abraham and his children for ever.

Leader: Now let us offer our own prayers of thanksgiving. After each prayer, we will respond together, "God has done great things for us!"

[Members of the group take turns offering prayers of thanksgiving aloud.]

All: God has done great things for us!

Leader: Lord our God, you fill us with good things. Continue to bless us as we prepare to celebrate the coming of your Son, Jesus Christ, who reigns with you and the Holy Spirit, now and forever.

All: Amen.

Christmas

At Christmas, we celebrate the fulfillment of God's promise to send to the world a savior. We know this Savior to be Jesus, God's own Son. Jesus' birth in Bethlehem brings to the world God's promise of peace and salvation.

art • i • fact
Let All That Hath Breath Praise the Lord, Lillian Delevoryas, 1997, watercolor on paper

The Birth of Jesus

art • i • fact
Painting of Mary and Jesus
in the Beitang
(North Church),
Beijing, China

Most of us can easily tell the story of Jesus' birth from heart. We've all heard the story told and retold every year. But if we were asked to find the sources for the story, we might have more difficulty.

There are four Gospels in the New Testament, but only two of them, Matthew and Luke, include the stories of Jesus' birth. While both Gospels have some details in common, they both also note unique aspects of his birth. You might be surprised to learn that only Matthew's Gospel records the visit of the Magi, sometimes called wise men or kings. Meanwhile, the angels' announcement to the shepherds that the Messiah was born is found only in Luke's Gospel. Because each Gospel highlights different details from Jesus' birth, let's focus only on Luke's Gospel as we consider the mystery we celebrate at Christmas.

The Gospel of Luke sets the scene for Jesus' birth by telling the story of the announcement and birth of John the Baptist. Luke also reports the Annunciation, the angel's announcement of Jesus' birth to Mary, and the Visitation, Mary's visit to her relative Elizabeth. Immediately after reporting the details of the birth of John the Baptist, Luke tells the story of Jesus' birth. As we'll read, Luke makes a connection between the lives of John the Baptist and Jesus.

Luke also tells us about the world into which Jesus was born. He tells us that Caesar Augustus was the Roman emperor, which is a little like telling who the president was when you were born. Luke also notes that a census has been announced, which brings Mary and Joseph to Bethlehem, where Jesus is born. Luke wants us to understand that Jesus' birth is an event of importance for the world. This is one of the themes emphasized throughout Luke's Gospel.

The Gospel of Luke also notes in detail that there was no room for Mary and Joseph at the inn. When Jesus was born he was laid in a manger, the feeding trough for animals. This signals for us another important theme of Luke's Gospel. Jesus comes to the world as someone who is poor and lowly. Beginning with his birth, Jesus is known as one who associates with those who are considered outcasts of society.

Continuing with this theme, Luke's Gospel next reports that angels appeared to shepherds tending their flock. These angels announce to the shepherds the good news of Jesus' birth and sing praises to God. The shepherds journey to Bethlehem and find Mary, Joseph, and Jesus just as the angels had announced.

Shepherds were not considered wealthy or prominent people in Jesus' time. They worked in the fields and struggled to get by. They spent their time with animals and were considered unclean and unkempt. These lowly ones were the first to receive and acknowledge the appearance of the Savior. They return from Bethlehem singing praise and glory to God. Throughout Luke's Gospel, those who respond most faithfully to Jesus' teaching are those least thought to be chosen by God: the poor, the sinner, the leper, the outcast, the foreigner.

Luke's Gospel also highlights Mary's role and response to Jesus' birth. After the visit from the shepherds, Mary spent time reflecting on these things in her heart. Among other things, she's a model of how we should

We are called to respond to the miracle of Christmas.

pray and reflect on what God is asking of us. We are called to respond in prayer to the miracle and mystery of Christmas. The Christmas season includes a Holy Day of Obligation, on January 1, devoted to remembering Mary's role as mother of Jesus: the Solemnity of Mary.

In Luke's story of Jesus' birth, we find good news to celebrate. Jesus' birth is good news because he brings salvation to the whole world. In particular, Jesus brings good news to those who are poor and lowly. During the Christmas season, we, like Mary, are called to pray and reflect on this good news of salvation. FG

Names for Jesus

Jesus' name was given to him by the angel who announced his birth to Mary. However, Luke's Gospel doesn't use the name *Jesus* again until it discusses Jesus' circumcision and naming, eight days after his birth. In noting these details, we learn about Jesus' devout Jewish upbringing. Instead of using the name *Jesus*, Luke refers to him as Mary's "first born son," Mary and Joseph's "child," and "the infant." The angels use other titles for Jesus in their message to the shepherds: Savior, Messiah, and Lord.

What Are Angels?

Angels figure prominently in the accounts of Jesus' birth. In Luke's Gospel, angels appear to Zechariah, Mary, and the shepherds. Angels also appear as God's messengers in Matthew's Gospel, usually in dreams. For example, Joseph had a dream in which an angel announced to him Jesus' birth, and another in which an angel warned him to flee Egypt. Angels are spiritual creatures who worship God in heaven and serve as God's messengers. They tell us about God's plans for our salvation.

Welcome Jesus!

Leader: Let us prayerfully reflect on the good news of Jesus' birth. Like Mary, let us ponder this mystery in our hearts.

Reader: A reading from the Gospel of Luke.
[Luke 2:1–16]
The Gospel of the Lord.

Leader: Glory to God in the highest.

All: Glory to God in the highest.

Group 1: Sing to the LORD a new song;
sing to the LORD, all the earth.
Sing to the LORD, bless his name;
announce his salvation day after day.

Group 2: Give to the LORD, you families of nations,
give to the LORD glory and might;
give to the LORD the glory due his name!
Bring gifts and enter his courts;
bow down to the LORD, splendid in holiness.

Group 1: Let the heavens be glad and the earth rejoice;
let the sea and what fills it resound;
let the plains be joyful and all that is in them.

Group 2: Then let all the trees of the forest rejoice
before the LORD who comes,
who comes to govern the earth,
To govern the world with justice
and the peoples with faithfulness.

All: Glory to God in the highest.
(Psalm 96:1–2; 7-8; 11–13)

All: Praise to you, Lord Jesus Christ.

[Time for silent reflection]

Leader: Let us pray. God sent to us a savior, Jesus, our Messiah and Lord. He was born as one of us. May we, like the shepherds, give glory to God for the great gift of salvation. We pray this in Jesus' name.

All: Amen.

Lent

The liturgical season of Lent begins on Ash Wednesday. Lent is a time when the whole community is led by the Holy Spirit to pray and to prepare to celebrate Easter. Lent is a season of repentance and renewal. We turn away from our sinfulness and recommit ourselves to following Jesus. Just as Jesus fasted and prayed in the desert for 40 days before beginning his ministry, we spend these 40 days fasting and praying. During this time, we prepare ourselves to celebrate—at Easter—Christ's Resurrection.

art • i • fact
Wall painting, Crosier
Monastery, Belgium

A Retreat in the Desert

After Jesus was baptized in the Jordan River by John the Baptist, Scripture tells us that the Holy Spirit led him into the desert. There, Jesus prayed to God and fasted for 40 days. He prepared himself for the preaching and ministry that God wanted him to do. During this time, Scripture also tells us that Jesus was tempted by Satan. Jesus resisted temptation and was attended to by the angels. (based on Mark 1:12–13)

It's important to our spiritual life to think about what Jesus did. His baptism by John was a crucial event in his life. Jesus needed time afterward to pray about what had happened to him and its meaning for his life. At his baptism, a voice from heaven proclaimed to Jesus, "'You are my beloved Son; with you I am well pleased.'" (Mark 1:11) We, too, need to take time in our lives to pray about the events of our lives and to learn what God intends for us. When something happens—good or bad—it's helpful for us to take time alone to think about what God is telling us.

Lent begins on Ash Wednesday, when we receive ashes on our foreheads as a sign of our dependence on God. The priest or minister traces a Sign of the Cross on our foreheads with the blessed ashes. As this is done, one of two prayers is prayed: "Turn away from sin and be faithful to the Gospel" or "Remember, man, you are dust and to dust you will return." During Lent, we focus on three things as we prepare ourselves for Easter: prayer, fasting, and almsgiving.

THE LENTEN PRACTICE OF PRAYER

Of course, we should pray daily. But during the season of Lent, we're asked to take some time to consider our life of prayer. We're asked to renew our commitment to this central action of our spiritual life. We might choose to read Scripture daily, to pray the Rosary, or to pray the Stations of the Cross. In addition to our daily prayer, the Church encourages us to celebrate the Sacrament of Penance during Lent.

THE LENTEN PRACTICE OF FASTING

Fasting is another important spiritual practice that we observe during Lent. To fast means to limit the amount of food we eat for a period of time. When we fast, we do so to express sorrow for our sins and to become more aware of our dependence upon God. Another part of the practice of fasting is to choose not to eat particular foods for a period of time. When we do this, we say that we abstain from a kind of food.

There are two days on which the Church asks us to fast and to abstain from eating meat: Ash Wednesday and Good Friday. Also on Fridays during Lent, we're asked to abstain from eating meat. In addition to these practices that the Church asks of all of us, we might also choose our own personal fast or abstinence during Lent. For example, some people choose not to eat candy or other sweets during Lent. Others choose to give up a favorite food, such as pizza. When we give up these things, we remind ourselves that God comes first in our lives and that we are dependent on God for everything.

THE LENTEN PRACTICE OF ALMSGIVING

We're asked to consider one more practice during Lent: almsgiving. To give alms is to offer our money, possessions, time, or talent to those in need. We remember those in need when we give these things. Some people combine this practice with their fasting. For example, they might give up one meal each week and donate to those in need the money that would have been spent on this food. During Lent, we also might look at ways to simplify our lives by leaving behind the things we really don't need.

In these ways, we can make Lent our own retreat to the desert. Then when it's time for Holy Week and Easter, we'll find ourselves ready to rejoice in the good news of Jesus' Resurrection. FG

A Sign of Repentance

In the Old Testament, people put on a sackcloth and ashes as a sign of repentance and to acknowledge their sinfulness. In the early Christian Church, those seeking forgiveness put on a sackcloth and ashes and begged members of the community to pray for them. The ashes we use on Ash Wednesday are made by burning the palms that were blessed on Palm Sunday the previous year.

Another Way to Fast

There's another way that people choose to fast during Lent. Some "fast" from certain habits as a sign of their repentance from sin. For example, they might choose not to watch TV during Lent or during particular days of Lent. Others try to "fast" from behaviors they wish to change, such as gossiping. When we fast in these ways, we do something positive to develop more Christ-like habits and to become better disciples of Jesus.

Operation Rice Bowl, a Lenten program of Catholic Relief Services, includes praying, fasting, and giving. Money raised through the program benefits people in 40 countries around the world.

Renew Our Hearts

Leader: The grace of our Lord Jesus Christ be with us now and forever.

All: Amen.

Leader: During Lent, we follow the model of Jesus in the desert. In our prayer and fasting, we remind ourselves of our need for God in our lives. In our almsgiving, we show our commitment to the poor. As we begin this Lent, let us ask God to renew our hearts and help us to return to his ways.

Reader: A reading from the book of Joel.
[Joel 2:12–18]
The Word of the Lord.

All: Thanks be to God.

Leader: Let us take time in silent prayer to consider how we will renew our lives this Lent through prayer, fasting, and almsgiving. Silently reflect on these questions.

- What can I do to renew my prayer life?

- What can I fast from that will help me to hear what God is asking of me?

- What can I do to help those in need this Lent?

Tell God what you will do this Lent as you turn away from sin and grow more faithful to the Gospel.

[Time for quiet reflection]

Leader: We pray that God will accept our Lenten sacrifices and give us the strength to persevere in our promises. We ask this through Christ our Lord.

All: Amen.

Holy Week

Holy Week, the week that precedes Easter, begins with Palm Sunday. We remember Jesus' triumphant entry into Jerusalem on Palm Sunday. On Holy Thursday we celebrate the gift that Jesus gave us in the Eucharist as we remember Jesus' Last Supper. On Good Friday we venerate the cross and remember Jesus' Passion and death. During the Easter Vigil, we wait to celebrate Christ's Resurrection, and we welcome new members into the Church in the Sacrament of Baptism. So beginning with the Mass of the Lord's Supper on Holy Thursday and ending with Evening Prayer on Easter Sunday the Church celebrates the Triduum.

The Holiest Week of the Year

art • i • fact
Christ Carrying the Cross,
Gian Francesco de Maineri,
early 16th century, Italy

Our final preparations for Easter are made during Holy Week. We remember and commemorate the events that led to Jesus' acceptance of death on the cross for our sins. We remember these events with great hope, because we know that death and evil do not triumph. Jesus will rise on Easter!

On Palm Sunday we remember that Jesus' journey to the cross began with his glorious entry into Jerusalem. The crowds received him as their king. They laid out palm branches and shouted,

> **"Blessed is the king who comes
> in the name of the Lord.
> Peace in heaven
> and glory in the highest."**
> **(Luke 19:38)**

Some Pharisees told Jesus to rebuke the crowd for calling him a king, but Jesus did not. Jesus then went to the Temple, where he drove out the merchants and taught the people. After this, the religious leaders began to make plans to arrest Jesus. (based on Luke 19:28–48)

On Holy Thursday we recall how Jesus celebrated his Last Supper with his disciples. This was a Passover meal, the Jewish feast that celebrates God's deliverance of Israel from its slavery in Egypt. As Jesus celebrated Passover, he gave it a new meaning for his disciples. Jesus said that his death would begin the new covenant. He would give his life for the forgiveness of everyone's sins.

Jesus and his disciples left their Passover meal and went to the Mount of Olives to pray. There Judas, one of Jesus' disciples, found them and betrayed Jesus to those who arrested him. The events that we remember on Good Friday begin with Jesus' arrest.

A lot happened between Jesus' arrest and his crucifixion. Jesus first was taken to the house of the high priest and tried by the Sanhedrin—the council of Jewish elders, chief priests, and scribes. Peter followed Jesus to the courtyard of the high priest's house. Peter was recognized by some of those present, and three times he denied knowing Jesus. Meanwhile, the Sanhedrin determined that Jesus was guilty of inciting the people by claiming to be the Messiah and king. The Sanhedrin sent him to the Roman governor, Pontius Pilate. Only Pilate had the authority to sentence Jesus to death.

At first, Pilate didn't find Jesus guilty of anything. But he sent Jesus to Herod, the Jewish ruler of Galilee, to appease Jesus' accusers. Herod and his court questioned and mistreated Jesus and sent him back to Pilate. Pilate again found Jesus not guilty of the crimes of which he was accused. He wanted to have Jesus flogged and released. But Jesus' accusers persisted and called for his crucifixion. In Jesus' place they asked for the release of another prisoner, Barabbas. Pilate protested a third time, saying he didn't find Jesus guilty of anything. But Pilate finally gave in to the demands of the people. He released Barabbas and sentenced Jesus to death on the cross.

Jesus was led away and forced to carry the cross to the place of execution, as was the custom. On the way a bystander named Simon of Cyrene carried Jesus' cross for him. Then Jesus met some women who were his followers and friends. He stopped to warn them of bad times to come. Finally, with two other criminals, Jesus was nailed to the cross.

As Jesus hung on the cross, his garments were divided among the soldiers. Jesus was taunted by the crowd. An inscription was placed above his head that read, "This is the King of the Jews." (Luke 23:38) One of the two criminals crucified with Jesus taunted him as well. But the other man asked Jesus to remember him when he entered his kingdom. Jesus promised this second criminal that he would join Jesus in paradise. Finally, Jesus cried out, "Father, into your hands I commend my spirit," and died. (based on Luke 23:46)

In his Passion and death for our sins, Jesus showed the full depth of his love for us. We remember these events as we hope that one day we, too, will be with Jesus in paradise. FG

Stations of the Cross

The Stations of the Cross are an important prayer through which we remember Jesus' death for our salvation. They can be prayed any time of the year, but they are prayed more frequently during Lent and Holy Week. The Stations of the Cross originated from the early Christian tradition of making a pilgrimage through Jerusalem to visit and pray along the path of Jesus' journey to the cross. Along this pilgrimage were 14 stations—places to stop and recall important moments of Jesus' journey. These became our Stations of the Cross. When we pray the Stations—most churches have depictions of them—we walk from station to station. At these stations, we remember the event depicted, and we pray a prayer. Sometimes a 15th station, the Resurrection of Jesus, is added to the Stations of the Cross.

Passover

When Jesus gathered with his disciples for the Last Supper, they celebrated the Jewish feast of Passover. Passover is celebrated with a special meal and prayers that recall how God freed the people of Israel from slavery in Egypt. When celebrated, the events remembered at Passover are understood to be taking place in the lives of those at the meal. Special foods eaten during Passover remind those who celebrate about the bitterness of slavery and about how the people were saved. Unleavened bread is shared, bitter herbs are eaten, wine is poured, and a special Passover lamb is the main course. Our Jewish sisters and brothers continue to celebrate Passover in this way today.

We Thank Jesus

Leader: Praise be to God, who fills our lives with love and joy.

All: Praise be to God.

Leader: Jesus died so that our sins might be forgiven. Let us pray that we will one day be received by Jesus in paradise.

Reader: A reading from the Gospel of Luke.
[Luke 23:33–46]
The Gospel of the Lord.

All: Praise to you, Lord Jesus Christ.

[Time for quiet reflection]

Leader: Remembering all that Jesus has done for us, we offer our petitions to God.

That we follow the example of your only Son, who, even as he died on the cross, forgave those who crucified him, we pray to the Lord.

All: Lord, hear our prayer.

Leader: That we forgive those who do us harm so that we will not be filled with anger but with your love, we pray to the Lord.

All: Lord, hear our prayer.

Leader: Father, we pray to you with a spirit of forgiveness so that we can be open to the love you are offering us. Hear these prayers and the prayers of our heart. We pray through Jesus, your Son, and with the Holy Spirit.

All: Amen.

Easter

"He is not here, but he has been raised..."

Luke 24:6

At Easter we celebrate God's most amazing surprise: Jesus was raised from the dead and appeared to his disciples! Each of the four Gospels tells how the disciples found Jesus' tomb empty after his death on the cross. Using the Gospel of Luke, let's reflect on this story and discover another amazing surprise that we can experience still today.

art • i • fact

He Is Risen, He Qi, China. He Qi has blended together traditional Chinese painting techniques and styles with European painting styles of the Middle and Modern Ages.

Jesus Is Risen

Jesus was put to death on the cross. Imagine what it must have been like to be Jesus' friend, his disciple, on the day of his death. Jesus was tried as a criminal, found guilty, and put to death in a most horrible way.

The disciples probably gathered together after his death. All of Jesus' friends were sad. Many were also scared. Some might even have been angry. They probably tried to comfort one another as Jesus' body was placed in the tomb.

The day after Jesus' death was the Jewish Sabbath day; it was a Sabbath day for Jesus' friends. The Sabbath laws restricted activities on this day, and no one could go to visit Jesus' tomb.

art • i • fact

Russian mosaic of the Resurrection depicting Jesus breaking the doors of death and freeing Adam and Eve and other men and women of the Old Testament.

AMAZING NEWS: JESUS' TOMB IS EMPTY!

The Gospel of Luke 24:1–35 states that on the day after the Sabbath, some women who were friends of Jesus went to Jesus' tomb with spices to embalm his body. This was part of their Jewish custom. However, they returned from the tomb with an amazing report. The stone had been moved from the entrance to the tomb. Jesus' body was not there. *And* they had seen a vision of two men in white who told them that Jesus had been raised from the dead.

The women reported this to all of Jesus' disciples. They probably thought, "Those crazy women." In first-century Jewish society, women couldn't serve as public witnesses. Luke's Gospel tells us, "Their story seemed like nonsense and they did not believe them." (Luke 24:11) Imagine what it must have been like to be one of these women.

But Luke's Gospel tells us that Peter went to Jesus' tomb and found the burial cloths but not Jesus' body. And he left amazed.

Every Sunday we celebrate Jesus' Resurrection from the dead.

BUT WHAT HAPPENED?

At first Jesus' disciples seemed to believe that Jesus' body had been stolen. That seemed possible, perhaps even logical. But why were the burial cloths found in the tomb? Even grave robbers would keep a dead body wrapped. It seemed to take the disciples some time to understand fully that Jesus had been raised from the dead.

What led the disciples to believe that Jesus had been raised from the dead? The angels at the tomb said to them, "'Why do you seek the living one among the dead? He is not here, but he has been raised.'" (Luke 24:5–6) The angels also reminded the women that Jesus had predicted that he would be put to death by sinners and would rise again on the third day.

Then Jesus himself began to appear to his disciples. First, Luke tells us about Jesus' appearance to two disciples on the road to Emmaus, a village seven miles from Jerusalem. These two disciples talked with someone whom they believed to be a stranger. In the course of their conversation, the stranger explained and interpreted for the disciples all that Scripture predicted about Jesus. Finally, while breaking bread together at a meal, the disciples recognized that the stranger was Jesus.

Amazed, these two disciples returned to Jerusalem to share the news with the other disciples. However, they arrived in Jerusalem to hear the reports from the disciples there: "The Lord has truly been raised and has appeared to Simon!" (Luke 24:34) The most amazing, most surprising news, was indeed true!

OUR ENCOUNTER WITH JESUS

The most amazing, most surprising news didn't end there. We share in this experience too. As the disciples on the road to Emmaus encountered Jesus in the breaking of the bread, we too encounter Jesus every time we celebrate the Eucharist. In the Eucharist we experience Jesus' Real Presence with us in his Body and Blood, which we receive in Holy Communion. Every Sunday we celebrate Jesus' Resurrection from the dead. Like the women who found the empty tomb and the disciples who encountered Jesus risen from the dead, we can't help but share this amazing good news with others. FG

Alleluia!

Alleluia is a Hebrew word used to offer praise to God. During the season of Lent, the word *Alleluia* is not said during Mass (for instance, the Alleluia before the Gospel is replaced with an alternate acclamation). When we pray Alleluia again during the Easter liturgies, we pray and sing it with extra joy.

Symbols of the Resurrection

Many signs of spring have become for us symbols of the new life promised to us in the Resurrection. An egg has new life growing in it, and the chick eventually breaks out of it. Spring flowers rise out of the dead earth of winter as a promise of new life. In spring, animals give birth to their young. For example, rabbits with their large litters are a sign of new life.

Alleluia! Jesus is Risen

All: Alleluia! Jesus is truly risen!

Leader: As the first disciples came to have faith in Jesus' Resurrection from the dead, so too may we have faith in the power of God, who has conquered death.

All: Alleluia! Jesus is truly risen!

Leader: As the hearts of the disciples on the road to Emmaus were enlivened when Jesus talked with them about the Scriptures, so too may we be enlivened when we encounter Jesus through the words of Scripture.

All: Alleluia! Jesus is truly risen!

Leader: The grace of the risen Jesus Christ be with us all, now and forever.

All: Amen.

Reader: A reading from the Gospel of Luke.
[Luke 24:1–6]
The Gospel of the Lord.

All: Praise to you, Lord Jesus Christ.

Leader: Let us pray together in praise and thanksgiving. Jesus has been raised from the dead! Alleluia! Alleluia!

Leader: As the disciples on the road to Emmaus recognized Jesus in the breaking of the bread, so too may we recognize Jesus present to us in the Eucharist.

All: Alleluia! Jesus is truly risen!

Leader: As the disciples proclaimed the good news of Jesus' Resurrection to others, so too may we be witnesses to the world of Christ's Resurrection.

All: Alleluia! Jesus is truly risen!

Leader: Lord, hear our prayers and continue to deepen our faith in the power of Christ's Resurrection. We ask this through your Son, who lives and reigns with you and the Holy Spirit for ever and ever.

All: Amen.

Pentecost

They were all filled with the holy Spirit...

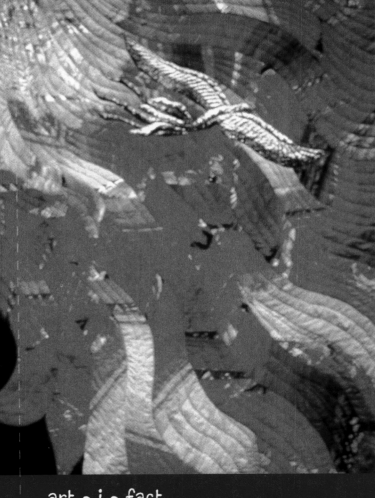

After he rose from the dead, Jesus appeared to his disciples many times. Then, as the disciples watched, Jesus was taken into heaven. However, Jesus had promised that he would not leave them alone. He had promised to send them a helper. After Jesus ascended into heaven, the disciples returned to Jerusalem to wait for the promise to come true.

art • i • fact
Pentecost, Linda Schmidt,
textile quilt

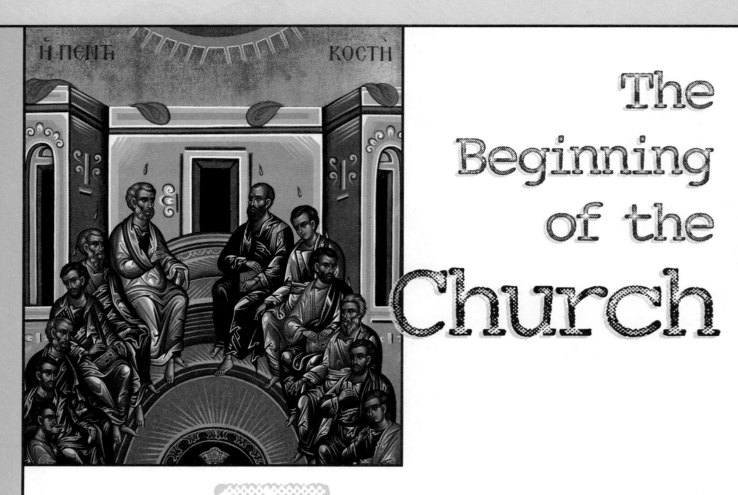

ἩΠΕΝΤ ΚΟCΤΗ

The Beginning of the Church

art • i • fact
In this typical Orthodox Greek icon of Pentecost, disciples of Jesus are depicted with flames above their heads.

The Ascension of Jesus into heaven appeared to be the end of the disciples' encounters with Jesus. But they would soon find out that they were to participate in a new and wonderful beginning. The story of the beginning of the Church is found in the book of the New Testament called the Acts of the Apostles.

The Acts of the Apostles was written by the same person who recorded the Gospel of Luke. The Gospel of Luke tells the story of the life, death, and Resurrection of Jesus. The Acts of the Apostles continues the story by telling how the Holy Spirit led the apostles to preach the message of Jesus throughout the Roman Empire.

THE GIFT OF THE HOLY SPIRIT
The Acts of the Apostles 2:1–12 says that after Jesus was taken to heaven, the disciples returned to Jerusalem and gathered in the house where they had been staying. These disciples included the twelve apostles (Matthias had been chosen to replace Judas, who betrayed Jesus), as well as women disciples and Mary, the mother of Jesus. As this group of Jesus' closest friends was together on the Jewish feast of Pentecost, an extraordinary thing happened. The Acts of the Apostles tells us that a loud noise, like wind, filled the house.

Jesus had to leave his disciples, but he did not abandon them.

And then it looked as if tongues of fire touched each of them. They felt themselves filled with the Holy Spirit, and they began to speak.

As the disciples spoke, a crowd began to gather outside the house. The crowd took interest not only because the voices were so loud but also because they heard the disciples speaking in a variety of languages. In fact, it's noted that the crowd represented many different nations. And yet each heard the disciples speaking in their own language of "the mighty acts of God." (Acts of the Apostles 2:11)

Those in the crowd offered differing opinions about this experience. Some were said to have been amazed but were unsure about what it meant. Others dismissed what they heard by saying that these people "have had too much new wine." (Acts of the Apostles 2:13)

"What Does This Mean?"

This is the question we are left with: What does this Pentecost experience mean? It means that Jesus fulfilled his promise and sent his Holy Spirit to the disciples. The disciples immediately began doing the work of the Church: proclaiming the life, death, and Resurrection of

Jesus and calling the whole world to faith in him. In the passage that follows the story of Pentecost, Peter boldly proclaims to the crowd that Jesus, who was crucified, is Messiah and Lord. The remainder of the Acts of the Apostles tells how the Holy Spirit led the first Christian community and how the good news of Jesus was spread throughout the Roman Empire.

The Holy Spirit transformed the early Christian community and strengthened it for the task of witnessing to Jesus the Lord. This same Holy Spirit continues to strengthen the Church today. This means that all of us who are baptized have been given the strength of the Holy Spirit, which empowers us to be Christ's witnesses in the world today. At Pentecost we celebrate the Spirit's presence in us. FG

Festival of Weeks

The Acts of the Apostles tells us that the disciples received the Holy Spirit on Pentecost. Pentecost is the Greek name for *Shavuot*, the Jewish Festival of Weeks, which celebrates God's gift of the Five Books of Moses—the Pentateuch. In the Jewish tradition, *Shavuot* is celebrated 50 days after Passover. Christians celebrate the Feast of Pentecost 50 days after Easter Sunday. Pentecost is the last day of the Easter Season.

Gifts of the Holy Spirit

We received the Holy Spirit at our Baptism. In the Sacrament of Confirmation, the grace of Baptism is strengthened through the seven Gifts of the Holy Spirit. These seven gifts help us to live as Christians. Six of the Gifts of the Holy Spirit are identified in the Book of Isaiah.

"The spirit of the LORD shall rest upon him:

a spirit of wisdom and
   of understanding,

A spirit of counsel and
   of strength,

a spirit of knowledge and of fear of the LORD."

(Isaiah 11:2)

Church tradition has added the gift of piety to make a total of seven Gifts.

Lord, Send Down Your Spirit

Leader: Let us praise the God of wisdom and grace. Blessed be God forever.

All: Blessed be God forever.

Leader: Just as the Holy Spirit strengthened Jesus' first disciples and enabled them to witness to the Lord, so too may we be strengthened by the Gifts of the Holy Spirit.

Reader 1: May we receive the gift of wisdom that we may recognize God's action in our lives. We pray,

All: Lord, help us to be open to your Spirit.

Reader 2: May we receive the gift of fortitude that we may persevere in our love of God. We pray,

All: Lord, help us to be open to your Spirit.

Reader 3: May we receive the gift of understanding that our hearts may be open to the message of God's great love. We pray,

All: Lord, help us to be open to your Spirit.

Reader 4: May we receive the gift of knowledge that we will always seek to know more about God. We pray,

All: Lord, help us to be open to your Spirit.

Reader 5: May we receive the gift of counsel that we may always show right judgment in the decisions we make. We pray,

All: Lord, help us to be open to your Spirit.

Reader 6: May we receive the gift of piety that others may see in us a life of faithfulness. We pray,

All: Lord, help us to be open to your Spirit.

Reader 7: May we receive the gift of fear of the Lord that we may always be in wonder and awe of God's kindness to us. We pray,

All: Lord, help us to be open to your Spirit.

Leader: May the Spirit's gifts make us faithful witnesses to Christ and strengthen the Church's mission today. We pray this in Jesus' name.

All: Amen.

All Saints Day

November 1 is All Saints Day. On this day we celebrate the relationship we share with all the holy women and men who have gone before us in the faith and who live now with God in heaven. November 2 is All Souls Day. On this day we pray for those who have died and are in purgatory, being prepared for heaven.

art • i • fact
Saint Clare of Assisi, Saint Martin de Porres, and *Saint Helen* by Steve Erspamer, O.S.B.

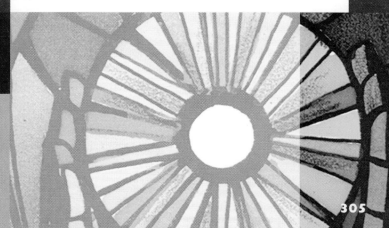

Our Fan Club in Heaven

Prayer for one another is an integral part of our Catholic Tradition. We believe it's beneficial to ourselves and to the entire Christian community to pray for one another's needs. The Communion of Saints shows us that prayer for one another doesn't end with death. The saints in heaven continue to pray for us and to intercede on our behalf before God. At a performance or a sporting event, the participants sometimes perform better because the crowd or audience is cheering for them. This is a little like the Communion of Saints. The holy men and women who have died continue to cheer us on in our life of faith and to support us through their intercession.

Another aspect of the Communion of Saints is our prayer for those who have died. We, the living, pray for those who have died and are being prepared to see the face of God. The living and the dead are one family before God.

WHO IS A SAINT?

The Church raises up certain individuals whose lives exemplify for us what it means to love God. The saints are not said to be perfect; no one is perfect. But through God's grace, the saints have received what we all hope to receive one day: God's promised salvation. A saint is a person who the Church believes now lives with God in heaven. By declaring a person a saint, the Church acknowledges that the evidence of God's grace at work in this person's life is an authentic witness to Christ. Because of the abundance of God's grace in their lives, the saints can intercede before God on behalf of the living.

A CALENDAR FULL OF SAINTS

Our Church calendar is filled with the names of people whose lives are worth celebrating and who we believe live now with God in heaven. Many of us know the feast days for some popular saints: March 17 is Saint Patrick's Day, February 14 is Saint Valentine's Day, March 19 is Saint Joseph's Day, and December 12 is the Feast of Our Lady of Guadalupe.

We too are called to be saints.

By popular devotion, some saints are considered patrons for particular needs or causes, which are usually related to an aspect of their life. Saint Francis of Assisi is the patron saint of ecology because of his reverence for God's creation. Saint Frances Xavier Cabrini is the patron saint of immigrants because of all the work she did to help immigrants. Sometimes individuals, organizations, churches, and even countries are placed under the patronage of a particular saint.

On November 1, we remember all of these holy men and women recognized by the Church as saints. However, there are many individuals who live now with God in heaven who haven't been officially declared saints by the Church. Many of us remember the life and witness of family members and friends whom we believe to be unofficial saints. On All Saints Day we also celebrate these undeclared saints. These people also pray for us before God, and their prayers benefit us as well.

ALL SAINTS DAY IS ALSO OUR FEAST DAY

When Saint Paul wrote to the early Christian communities, he sometimes addressed the living Christian community as "saints." He was acknowledging their holy lives and their destiny—salvation through Christ. We too are called to be saints. We dedicate our lives to God and pray that, through God's grace, we may join the saints in heaven and live forever in his presence. FG

Our Catholic Tradition distinguishes the prayer and worship we offer to God from the veneration and honor given to Mary and the saints. Prayer is only properly directed toward God. When we honor the saints, we ask their intercession on our behalf with God. The effects of our devotion to the saints come from God's grace alone. Of all the saints, Mary is given a place of honor, and we offer special devotion to her.

Litany of the Saints

A litany is a form of prayer in which a number of petitions are offered and the congregation responds. A special form of litany is the Litany of the Saints. In this prayer we ask the saints to pray for us by naming individual saints. This prayer is often prayed as part of the Easter Vigil and at ordinations. However, we might choose to pray this form of prayer anytime we wish to call upon the witness and prayers of those who've gone before us in the faith.

A Litany of the Saints

gone before us in the Communion of Saints. We long for the day when we will see you face to face.

Reader: A reading from the First Letter of John.
[1 John 3:1–3]
The Word of the Lord.

All: Thanks be to God.

Leader: Let us pray a Litany of the Saints, asking the holy men and women who are with God in heaven to pray for us.

Leader: Saint Mary Magdalene

All: Pray for us.

Leader: Saint Basil

All: Pray for us.

Leader: Saint Elizabeth

All: Pray for us.

Leader: Saint Anthony

All: Pray for us.

Leader: [Invite all who would like to continue naming saints to invoke the names of their favorite saints. Invite the group to respond "Pray for us" after each saint is named.]

May the example of the lives of the saints and their prayers for us lead us to join them one day in the presence of God. We ask this through Christ our Lord.

All: Amen.

All: In the name of the Father and of the Son and of the Holy Spirit. Amen.

Leader: God, you have called us to be your children and have given us the grace to become holy. We thank you for uniting us with the holy men and women who have

art • i • fact
Young people at World Youth Day in Paris (1997) raise a banner depicting Saint Thérèse of Lisieux as a teenager.

PRAYERS AND PRACTICES OF OUR Faith

PRAYERS AND PRACTICES OF OUR FAITH

CELEBRATING AND LIVING OUR FAITH

UNDERSTANDING THE WORDS OF OUR FAITH

The Bible is the story of God's promise . . .

God speaks to us in many ways. One way God speaks to us is through the Bible. The Bible is the most important book in Christian life because it is God's message, or revelation. The Bible is the story of God's promise to care for us, especially through his Son, Jesus. At Mass we hear stories from the Bible. We can also read the Bible on our own.

The Bible is not just one book; it is a collection of many books. The writings in the Bible were inspired by the Holy Spirit and written by many different authors using different styles.

The Bible is made up of two parts: The Old Testament and the New Testament. The Old Testament contains 46 books that tell stories about the Jewish people and their faith in God before Jesus was born.

The first five books of the Old Testament—Genesis, Exodus, Leviticus, Numbers, and Deuteronomy—are referred to as the Torah, meaning "instruction" or "law." The central story in the Torah is the Exodus, the liberation of the Hebrew slaves as Moses led them out of Egypt and to the Promised Land. During the journey God gave the Ten Commandments to Moses and the people.

A beautiful part of the Old Testament is the Book of Psalms. A psalm is a prayer in the form of a poem. Each psalm expresses an aspect, or feature, of the depth of human emotion. Over several centuries 150 psalms were gathered to form the Book of Psalms. They were once sung at the Temple in Jerusalem, and they have been used in the public worship of the Church since its beginning. Catholics also pray the Psalms as part of their private prayer and reflection.

The prophets were called by God to speak for him and urge the Jewish people to be faithful to the Covenant. A large part—18 books—of the Old Testament presents the messages and actions of the prophets.

continued on page 312 ▶

▶ *continued from page 311*

The New Testament contains 27 books that tell the story of Jesus' life, death, and Resurrection and the experience of the early Christians. For Christians the most important books of the New Testament are the four Gospels—Matthew, Mark, Luke, and John. Many of the 27 books are letters written by leaders such as Paul.

How can you find a passage in the Bible? Bible passages are identified by book, chapter, and verse, for example, Exodus 3:1–4. The name of the book comes first. Sometimes it is in abbreviated form. Your Bible's table of contents will help you determine what the abbreviation means. For example, Ex stands for Exodus. After the name of the book, there are two numbers. The first one identifies the chapter, which in our example is chapter three; it is followed by a colon. The second number identifies the verse or verses, which in our example are verses one to four.

Book: *Genesis*   Chapter: *1*   Verse: *27–28*

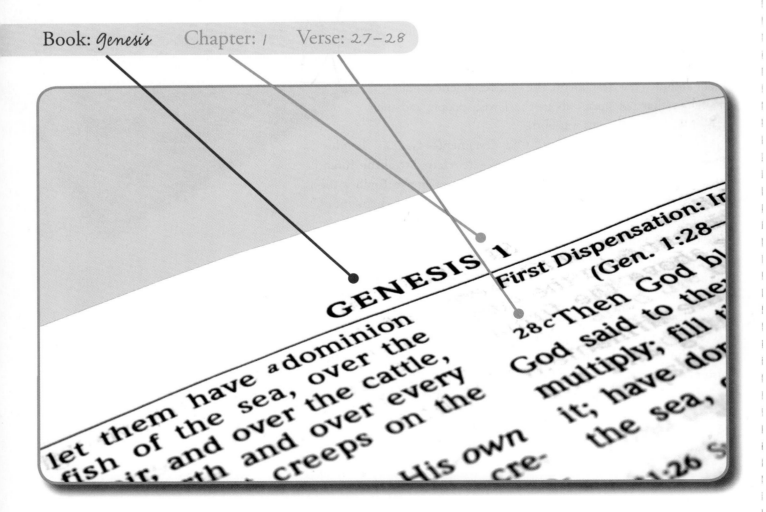

How the Old Testament and the New Testament Were Put Together

The Old and New Testaments developed in oral cultures and much of the material in them was passed on by word of mouth before ever being written down. Probably the first part of the Old Testament to be written down were stories from the pre-history of Israel. These can be found in parts of the 2nd through 11th chapters of Genesis. They would have been written by the court historian of King David around 1000 B.C. This writer always referred to God as Yahweh and spoke of God in very human terms. It was this writer who wrote the story of God walking in the Garden with Adam and Eve. Other stories developed in the Northern Kingdom of Israel and favor the religious sites of that region, such as Bethel.

The Old Testament as we know it today did not begin to take shape until the Babylonian Exile (587–537 B.C.). It was in Babylon that members of the priestly class took many of the oral and written accounts of God's saving work and put them together in what we know as the Torah, the first five books of the bible—Genesis, Exodus, Leviticus, Numbers, and Deuteronomy.

The central story in the Torah is the Exodus, the liberation of the Hebrew slaves as Moses led them out of Egypt and to the Promised Land. During the journey, God gave the Ten Commandments to Moses and the people. The writers in Babylon also wrote the opening chapter of Genesis that tells of God's orderly creation of the world in six days and his rest on the seventh.

The historical books were put together from the court accounts of various kings of Israel and Judah. The Psalms were gathered from collections of prayers and new psalms were written for the temple that was rebuilt after 537 B.C. Other Wisdom literature was also gathered. Finally the writings of the prophets were collected by their followers and gathered together. They included prophets who preached and wrote from 150 years before the exile, such as the first Isaiah

Moses and the Ten Commandments

> The central story in the Torah is the Exodus, the liberation of the Hebrew slaves as Moses led them out of Egypt

continued on page 314 ▶

▶ *continued from page 313*

and Amos, to the second part of the book of Zechariah which was probably written after 330 B.C. In the mid third century BC these books were translated from Hebrew into Greek in Alexandria, Egypt. In time a number of other books, such as 1 and 2 Maccabees, were added to the bible in Greek. By the end of the 1st century A.D. religious leaders in Israel decided on which books would be in the bible. They included only those Old Testament books written in Hebrew.

About the year 50, Paul wrote his first letter to the Thessalonians, followed by a second one later that year. This was more than 20 years after the death and Resurrection of Jesus. Over the next 13 years he wrote letters to other Christian communities as well as to the Christians of Rome, a city he hoped to visit. Meanwhile Christians were passing on stories about Jesus, his message, his miracles, and others things he did. Probably the first stories to come together centered on his final days, his passion, death, and Resurrection. This is why all four Gospels tell very similar stories of Jesus' last days.

The first Gospel to be written was the Gospel of Mark. It was written in Rome during and after Nero's persecution in the second half of the 60s. In the 80s the authors of the gospels of Matthew and Luke, using Mark's Gospel as a starting point, wrote their own Gospels for their specific Christian communities. Matthew, Mark, and Luke, though writing about Jesus in different ways, tell stories that are similar enough to be read side-by-side. Because of this we call them *synoptic*. They also made use of a collection of Jesus' sayings. The Gospel of John was written in the mid to late 90s. It is very different in tone and theology. The last book of the New Testament to be written was 2 Peter, shortly after the year 100.

Saint Paul

All four Gospels tell very similar stories of Jesus' last days.

Discovering Jesus in the Scriptures

The Four Gospels and the Acts of the Apostles

Mark

The Gospel of Mark was written for Jewish and Gentile Christians living through Nero's persecution in Rome The author was the first to develop the type of literature we call *gospel*. The central message of Mark's gospel is that the only way to be a true follower of Jesus is to take up the cross as he did and follow him. Almost immediately after Peter's profession of faith—"You are the Messiah"—the disciples begin to misunderstand the true identity of Jesus. Finally, at the Crucifixion, Jesus is all alone. None of the disciples could follow him to the end. The Roman centurion at the foot of the cross says "Truly this man was the son of God." This echoes the beginning of the gospel, "The gospel of Jesus Christ the Son of God." Mark writes his gospel to reassure his community that the persecutions they are enduring are not a sign that God has abandoned them. Rather it is only through suffering that they can really know Jesus as the Son of God.

Mark

Matthew

The Gospel of Matthew was written for a mainly Jewish Christian community, probably in the city of Antioch. It was a community that wanted to continue to assert its Jewish identity while at the same time profess Jesus as the awaited Messiah. Because of their belief of Jesus as the Messiah, the community was in conflict with Jews who did not accept Jesus. To support his community's belief, Matthew often quotes the Jewish scriptures to show how Jesus was the long awaited Messiah. He begins his gospel with two chapters about the birth of Jesus which emphasize that Jesus was predicted in the Old Testament. This created a comparison between Jesus and Moses. Herod, like Pharaoh, kills the male children. Jesus escapes to Egypt so that like Moses

Matthew

continued on page 316 ▶

▶ continued from page 315

he can one day leave Egypt. Matthew divides his gospel into five sections, like the five books of Moses. As Moses received the Ten Commandments on a mountain, Jesus delivers the new law in the Sermon on the Mount. In Matthew, Jesus is the new Moses.

Luke and the Acts of the Apostles

The Gospel of Luke was written for a Gentile Christian community. It presents Jesus as the savior of all humanity. It does not want to present what might seem like a brand new religion so it grounds Jesus in Judaism. Like Matthew, Luke's first two chapters describe Jesus' infancy and childhood. These two chapters read like the Hebrew scriptures but unlike Matthew, they never quote them. Luke seldom quotes from the Old Testament because his readers were not familiar with it. The gospel opens in the Temple, with Zechariah being told he will be the father of John the Baptist. It ends in the Temple with the followers of Jesus praising God. The gospel itself tells the story of Jesus' ministry as a journey from northern Palestine to Jerusalem. Luke's second volume, the Acts of the Apostles, tells of the spread of Christianity from Jerusalem to Rome and beyond.

Luke's gospel shows a special concern for simple people and is harsh towards the rich. Some of the most favorite parables of Jesus, such as the Prodigal Son and the Good Samaritan, are found in Luke.

John

The Gospel of John is very different from the three synoptic gospels. Most of the miracles and sayings of those gospels are not found in John. In John, Jesus speaks in long, symbolic speeches. Instead of the story of Jesus' infancy, John's gospel begins, "In the beginning was the Word, and the Word was with God, and the Word was God." In John, Jesus only performs seven miracles, which are called signs. Their purpose is to strengthen the disciples faith in Jesus. Jesus goes to great length to explain the significance of these signs. His ministry takes place over the period of three years. Every year a trip to Jerusalem at Passover plays a central role. John was written for a Jewish Christian community that resented being rejected by the main Jewish community. The last chapter is a later addition. It shows the attempt of the community of John to be reconciled with the more mainstream Church centered around Peter.

John

Luke

"In the beginning was the Word, and the Word was with God, and the Word was God."

Paul and His Letters

About the year 50, Paul wrote a letter to the first Christian community he had founded, the Thessalonians. This was the first of his many famous letters. Some time later that year, according to many scholars, he wrote a second letter to correct some misunderstandings that had arisen. Over the next ten or so years her wrote to other communities he had founded in response to their questions or improper behavior. The letter to the Romans is the only letter he wrote to a community he had not founded. He was planning to visit Rome and wanted to convince them that he was an orthodox Christian with a true teaching of the message of Jesus. His letter to Philemon is a personal letter on behalf of a Christian slave being returned to his master. The remaining books of Paul's letters are Timothy and Titus.

Other Epistles and the Book of Revelation

The remaining letters include the letters of Peter, reflecting the concerns of the Church in Rome, the letter to the Hebrews, a homily on early Christian themes, the letter of Jude, the letters of John, and the Revelation of John. Revelation is an example of writing popular in Judaism at the time. It pretends to present a vision of the end of the world in which the good and just triumph. These visions actually address a crisis facing the writer and the community. In the case of John, the crisis is the persecution of Christians by Domitian. Revelation is John's way of offering words of encouragement to the people.

Revelation is John's way of offering words of encouragement to the people.

Timeline of the New Testament

New Testament Books

IMAGE: Byzantine Mosaic, Church of the Multiplication of the Loaves and Fishes

c. 50	1 Thessalonians, 2 Thessalonians
54	Galatians
c. 56	Philippians
57	1 Corinthians, 2 Corinthians
58	Romans
c. 62–63	Philemon, Colossians
64	James (?)
68–70	Gospel of Mark
Late 70s	Gospel of Matthew
Early 80s	Gospel of Luke, Acts of the Apostles
Late 80s	Hebrews
Early 90s	Ephesians
Mid to Late 90s	Gospel of John, 1 John, Revelation, 2 John, 3 John, Jude, Titus, 1 Timothy, 2 Timothy, 1 Peter
After 100	2 Peter

History

c. 4 B.C.	Birth of Jesus in Bethlehem
14	Death of Caesar Augustus (at right); Tiberius becomes Roman emperor
c. 28	Death and Resurrection of Jesus; Pentecost; birth of the Church
c. 34	Martyrdom of Saint Stephen
c. 34–36	Conversion of Paul
45	Paul begins missionary travels
49	Council of Jerusalem
c. 62–63	Paul arrives in Rome
64	Nero begins a persecution of Christians in Rome
67–68	Deaths of Peter and Paul in Rome
70	The Temple is destroyed by the Romans
Late 90s	Decision made on which books are part of the Hebrew scriptures
96	Death of Emperor Domitian (Book of Revelation was written in reaction to him)
122–135	Final Jewish uprising under Bar Kochba; Jerusalem completely destroyed

Timeline markers: 5, 15, 25, 35, 45, 55, 65, 75, 85, 95, 105

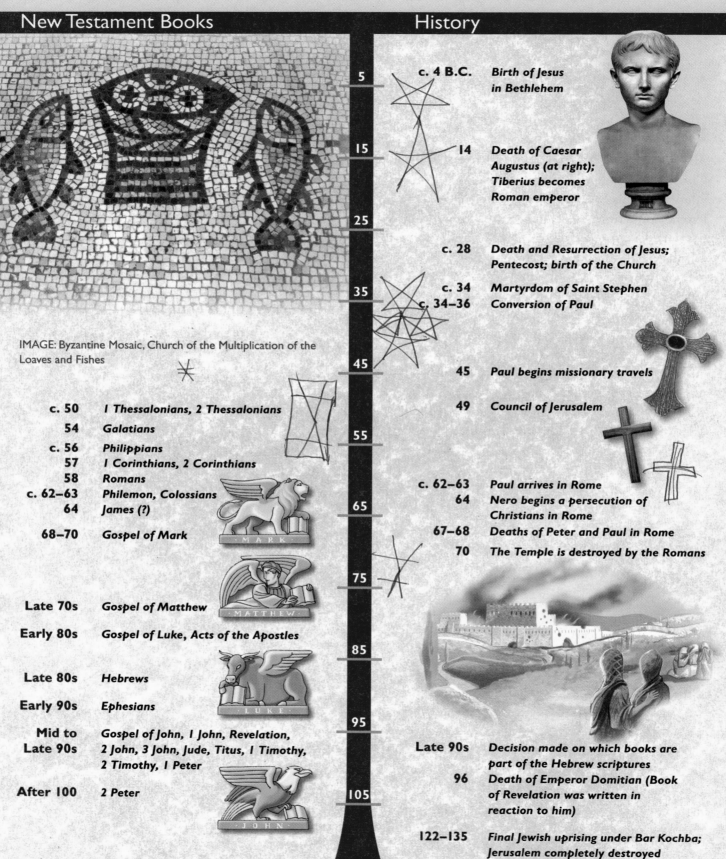

Map of the Mediterranean with Paul's Journeys

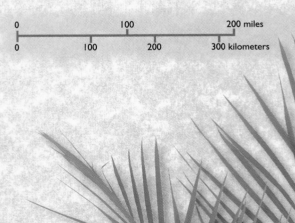

First Missionary Journey
(47– 49 A.D.)

Second Missionary Journey
(49–52 A.D.)

Third Missionary Journey
(53–58 A.D.)

Journey to Rome
(60–61 A.D.)

| 0 | 100 | 200 miles |
| 0 | 100 | 200 | 300 kilometers |

"Love one another. As I have loved you, so you also should love one another."

— (John 13:34)

The following formulas present the basic teachings of the Catholic Church. Pope Benedict XVI has emphasized that they are core teachings that every Catholic should know.

The Great Commandment

The Ten Commandments are fulfilled in Jesus' Great Commandment: "You shall love the Lord your God with all your heart, with all your soul, with all your mind, and with all your strength. . . . You shall love your neighbor as yourself." (adapted from Mark 12:30–31)

The New Commandment

Before his death on the cross, Jesus gave his disciples a new commandment: "Love one another. As I have loved you, so you also should love one another." (John 13:34)

The Golden Rule

"Do to others whatever you would have them do to you." (Matthew 7:12)

The Beatitudes

The Beatitudes are the teachings of Jesus in the Sermon on the Mount. They can be found in Matthew 5:1–10. Jesus teaches us that if we live according to the Beatitudes, we will live a happy Christian life. The Beatitudes fulfill God's promises made to Abraham and his descendants and describe the rewards that will be ours as loyal followers of Christ.

Blessed are the poor in spirit,
for theirs is the kingdom of heaven.
Blessed are they who mourn,
for they will be comforted.
Blessed are the meek,
for they will inherit the land.
Blessed are they who hunger and
thirst for righteousness,
for they will be satisfied.
Blessed are the merciful,
for they will be shown mercy.
Blessed are the clean in heart,
for they will see God.
Blessed are the peacemakers,
for they will be called children
of God.
Blessed are they who are
persecuted for the sake
of righteousness,
for theirs is the kingdom of heaven.

Sermon on the Mount, 6th Century, mosaic, Saint Apollinare Nuovo, Ravenna, Italy

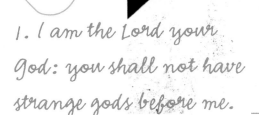

1. I am the Lord your God: you shall not have strange gods before me.

The Ten Commandments

As believers in Jesus Christ, we are called to a new life and are asked to make moral choices that keep us united with God. With the help and grace of the Holy Spirit, we can choose ways to act to keep us close to God, to help other people, and to be witnesses to Jesus.

The Ten Commandments guide us in making choices that help us to live as God wants us to live. The first three commandments tell us how to love God; the other seven tell us how to love our neighbor.

1. I am the Lord your God: you shall not have strange gods before me.

2. You shall not take the name of the Lord your God in vain.

3. Remember to keep holy the Lord's Day.

4. Honor your father and your mother.

5. You shall not kill.

6. You shall not commit adultery.

7. You shall not steal.

8. You shall not bear false witness against your neighbor.

9. You shall not covet your neighbor's wife.

10. You shall not covet your neighbor's goods.

Precepts of the Church

The Precepts of the Church describe the minimum effort we must make in prayer and in living a moral life. All Catholics are called to move beyond the minimum by growing in love of God and love of neighbor. The Precepts are as follows:

1. attendance at Mass on Sundays and Holy Days of Obligation

2. confession of serious sin at least once a year

3. reception of Holy Communion at least once a year during the Easter season

4. observance of the days of fast and abstinence

5. providing for the needs of the Church

The Four Last Things

There are four things that describe the end of all human life.

death judgment heaven hell

First is the death of the individual. Then immediately after death is the judgement by Christ. The result of this judgement is either heaven, perhaps with a stay in purgatory, or hell.

Virtues

Virtues are gifts from God that lead us to live in a close relationship with him. Virtues are like habits. They need to be practiced; they can be lost if they are neglected.

Theological Virtues

The three most important virtues are called *theological* virtues because they come from God and lead to God.

faith   hope   charity

Cardinal Virtues

The *cardinal* virtues are human virtues, acquired by education and good actions. *Cardinal* comes from *cardo,* the Latin word for "hinge," meaning "that on which other things depend."

prudence   justice   fortitude   temperance

Gifts and Fruits of the Holy Spirit

The Holy Spirit makes it possible for us to do what God asks of us by giving us these many gifts.

wisdom   understanding   counsel   piety

fortitude   knowledge   fear of the Lord

The Fruits of the Holy Spirit are signs of the Holy Spirit's action in our lives.

love   joy   peace

patience   kindness   generosity

faithfulness gentleness   self-control

Church tradition also includes goodness, modesty, and chastity as Fruits of the Holy Spirit.

Works of Mercy

The Corporal and Spiritual Works of Mercy are actions we can perform that extend God's compassion and mercy to those in need.

Corporal Works of Mercy

The Corporal Works of Mercy are these kind acts by which we help our neighbors with their material and physical needs:

- *feed the hungry*
- *shelter the homeless*
- *clothe the naked*
- *visit the sick and imprisoned*
- *bury the dead*
- *give alms to the poor*

Spiritual Works of Mercy

The Spiritual Works of Mercy are acts of compassion by which we help our neighbors with their emotional and spiritual needs:

- *instruct*
- *advise*
- *console*
- *comfort*
- *forgive*
- *bear wrongs patiently*

Prayer and Forms of Prayer

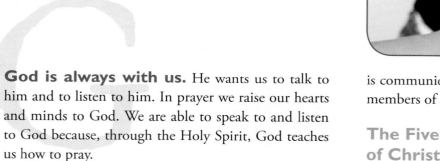

God is always with us. He wants us to talk to him and to listen to him. In prayer we raise our hearts and minds to God. We are able to speak to and listen to God because, through the Holy Spirit, God teaches us how to pray.

What is Prayer?

Being a Christian requires that we believe all that God has revealed to us, that we celebrate it in the liturgy and sacraments, and that we live what we believe. All of this depends on a vital and personal relationship with the living and true God. This relationship is found in prayer. Prayer is first of all a gift from God. We can pray because God first seeks us out and calls us to meet him. We become aware of our thirst for God because God thirsts for us. Prayer arises from our heart, beyond the grasp of reason. Only the Spirit of God can understand the human heart and know it fully. Prayer is the habit of being with God—Father, Son and Holy Spirit. This communion with God is always possible because through our Baptism we are united with Christ. By being united with Christ we are united with others. Christian prayer

is communion with Christ that branches out to all the members of his body the Church.

The Five Basic Forms of Christian Prayer

The Holy Spirit, who teaches us to pray, leads us to pray in a number of ways. This conversation with God can take the form of blessing, petition, intercession, thanksgiving, or praise.

Blessing

To bless someone is to acknowledge the goodness of that person. The prayer of blessing or adoration is our response to God's goodness because of all the gifts he has given us. In the prayer of blessing, God's gifts and our acceptance of them come together. Because God blesses the human heart, the human heart can in return bless him who is the source of every blessing.

Petition

Petition is much more than asking God for things we want or need. By prayer of petition we express our

relationship with God as our creator. We depend on him and we ask him for something for ourselves. Sometimes we sin and turn away from him. So the first step in the prayer of petition is turning back toward him and asking for forgiveness. We can then ask God for what we need, confident that he knows what we need before we ask.

Intercession

In prayers of intercession we ask something on behalf of another. As a prayer form, intercession is a prayer of petition which leads us to pray as Jesus did. Throughout his life on earth, Jesus interceded with the Father on behalf of all people. To pray in this way means that our hearts are turned outward, focused on the needs around us.

Thanksgiving

Thanksgiving is a characteristic of Christian prayer, especially in the Eucharist. *Eucharist* means "thanksgiving." Through his death and Resurrection Christ has reconciled us to God. His sacrifice is made present in every Eucharist. Every joy we experience as well as our every need can become an offering of thanksgiving in the Eucharist. In celebrating the Eucharist the Church reveals and becomes more fully what she is, a people of thanksgiving.

Thanksgiving is a characteristic of Christian prayer, especially in the Eucharist. Eucharist means "thanksgiving."

Praise

Praise is the form of prayer that recognizes that God is God and gives him glory. Praise goes beyond thanking God for what he has done for us and gives him glory simply because he is. Praise embraces the other forms of prayer and carries them to God who is the source of all that is.

We Meditate and Contemplate

One way to pray is to meditate. To meditate is to think about God. We try to keep our attention and focus on God. In meditation we may use Scripture, prayer books, or icons, which are religious images, to help us concentrate and to spark our imagination.

Another way to pray is to contemplate. This means that we rest quietly in God's presence.

We Get Ready to Pray

We live in a very busy, noisy, and fast-paced world. Sometimes, because of this, we have difficulty concentrating. In order to meditate or reflect, we need to prepare ourselves.

We can get ready for meditation by resting our bodies in a comfortable position. Sitting with our backs straight and both feet on the floor is one comfortable position. We can close our eyes, fold our hands comfortably in front of us, and silently take a deep breath and then let it out slowly. We can establish a rhythm by slowly counting to three while breathing in and slowly counting to three while breathing out. Concentrating on our breathing helps us to quiet our thoughts.

We Avoid Distractions

If we become distracted by thinking about something, such as the day at school or a sports event, we can just go back to thinking about our breathing.

After a little practice we will be able to avoid distractions, pray with our imagination, and spend time with God or Jesus in our hearts.

Prayers to Take to Heart

We can pray with any words that come to mind. Sometimes, when we find that choosing our own words is difficult, we can use traditional prayers. Likewise, when we pray aloud with others, we rely on traditional prayers to unite our minds, hearts, and voices. Memorizing traditional prayers such as the following can be very helpful. When we memorize prayers, we take them to heart, meaning that we not only learn the words but also try to understand and live them.

Pope Benedict XVI has identified four prayers that are shared by the universal Church. If they are learned in Latin they could be prayed as a sign of the universal nature of the Church. All Catholics throughout the world would be praying in the same language. The Latin for these five prayers is included across from each of them.

Lord's Prayer

Our Father,
who art in heaven,
hallowed be thy name;
thy kingdom come;
thy will be done
on earth as it is in heaven.
Give us this day our daily bread;
and forgive us our trespasses
as we forgive those who trespass against us;
and lead us not into temptation,
but deliver us from evil.
Amen.

Pater Noster

Pater noster,
qui es in caelis,
sanctificetur nomen tuum.
Adveniat regnum tuum.
Fiat voluntas tua,
sicut in caelo et in terra.
Panem nostrum quotidianum da nobis hodie,
et dimitte nobis debita nostra
sicut et nos dimittimus debitoribus nostris.
Et ne nos inducas in tentationem,
sed libera nos a malo.
Amen.

Hail Mary

Hail Mary, full of grace,
the Lord is with you.
Blessed are you among women,
and blessed is the fruit of your womb, Jesus.
Holy Mary, Mother of God,
pray for us sinners,
now and at the hour of our death.
Amen.

Ave Maria

Ave Maria, gratia plena,
Dominus tecum.
Benedicta tu in mulieribus,
et benedictus fructus ventris tui, Iesus.
Sancta Maria, Mater Dei,
ora pro nobis peccatoribus,
nunc, et in hora mortis nostrae.
Amen.

The Sign of the Cross

In the name of the Father, and of the Son,
and of the Holy Spirit.
Amen.

Signum Crucis

In nomine Patris, et Filii,
et Spiritus Sancti.
Amen.

Glory Be to the Father (Doxology)

Glory be to the Father, and to the Son, and to the Holy Spirit. As it was in the beginning, is now, and ever shall be, world without end.
Amen.

Morning Offering

My God, I offer you my prayers,
works, joys and sufferings of this day
in union with the holy sacrifice of the Mass throughout the world.
I offer them for all the intentions of your Son's Sacred Heart,
for the salvation of souls, reparation for sin,
and the reunion of Christians.
Amen.

Prayer Before Meals

Bless us, O Lord, and these your gifts
which we are about to receive from your goodness.
Through Christ our Lord.
Amen.

Prayer After Meals

We give you thanks
for all your gifts,
almighty God,
living and reigning
now and for ever.
Amen.

Gloria Patri

Gloria Patri, et Filio, et Spiritui Sancto.
Sicut erat in principio, et nunc, et semper,
et in saecula saeculorum.
Amen.

Act of Contrition

My God,
I am sorry for my sins with all my heart.
In choosing to do wrong
and failing to do good,
I have sinned against you
whom I should love above all things.
I firmly intend, with your help,
to do penance,
to sin no more,
and to avoid whatever leads me to sin.
Our Savior Jesus Christ
suffered and died for us.
In his name, my God, have mercy.

Prayer to the Holy Spirit

Come, Holy Spirit, fill the hearts of your faithful.
And kindle in them the fire of your love.
Send forth your Spirit and they shall be created.
And you will renew the face of the earth.
Lord, by the light of the Holy Spirit
you have taught the hearts of your faithful.
In the same Spirit
help us to relish what is right
and always rejoice in your consolation.
We ask this through Christ our Lord.
Amen.

Apostles' Creed

I believe in God, the Father almighty,
    creator of heaven and earth.
I believe in Jesus Christ, his only Son, our Lord.
    He was conceived by the power of the Holy Spirit
        and born of the Virgin Mary.
    He suffered under Pontius Pilate,
        was crucified, died, and was buried.
    He descended into hell.
    On the third day he rose again.
    He ascended into heaven,
        and is seated at the right hand of the Father.
    He will come again to judge the living and the dead.
I believe in the Holy Spirit,
    the holy catholic Church,
    the communion of saints,
    the forgiveness of sins,
    the resurrection of the body,
    and the life everlasting.
    Amen.

Nicene Creed

We believe in one God,
    the Father, the Almighty,
    maker of heaven and earth,
    of all that is seen and unseen.
We believe in one Lord, Jesus Christ,
    the only Son of God,
    eternally begotten of the Father,
    God from God, Light from Light,
    true God from true God,
    begotten, not made, one in Being with the Father.
    Through him all things were made.
    For us men and for our salvation
        he came down from heaven:
by the power of the Holy Spirit
    he was born of the Virgin Mary, and became man.

For our sake he was crucified under Pontius Pilate;
    he suffered, died, and was buried.
    On the third day he rose again
        in fulfillment of the Scriptures;
    he ascended into heaven
        and is seated at the right hand of the Father.
He will come again in glory to judge the living and the dead,
    and his kingdom will have no end.
We believe in the Holy Spirit, the Lord, the giver of life,
    who proceeds from the Father and the Son.
    With the Father and the Son he is worshiped and glorified.
    He has spoken through the Prophets.
    We believe in one holy catholic and apostolic Church.
    We acknowledge one baptism for the forgiveness of sins.
    We look for the resurrection of the dead,
        and the life of the world to come.
    Amen.

Act of Faith

O my God, I firmly believe that you are one God in three divine Persons, Father, Son, and Holy Spirit. I believe that your divine Son became man and died for our sins, and that he will come to judge the living and the dead. I believe these and all the truths which the holy Catholic Church teaches, because you have revealed them, who can neither deceive nor be deceived.
Amen.

Act of Hope

O my God, relying on your infinite mercy and promises, I hope to obtain pardon of my sins, the help of your grace, and life everlasting, through the merits of Jesus Christ, my Lord and Redeemer.
Amen.

Act of Love

O my God, I love you above all things with my whole heart and soul, because you are all good and worthy of all my love. I love my neighbor as myself for the love of you. I forgive all who have injured me and I ask pardon of those whom I have injured.
Amen.

Prayer for Vocations

God, in Baptism you called me by name
and made me a member of your people,
    the Church.
Help all your people to know their vocation
    in life,
and to respond by living a life of holiness.

For your greater glory and for the service
    of your people,
raise up dedicated and generous leaders
who will serve as sisters, priests,
brothers, deacons, and lay ministers.
Send your Spirit to guide and strengthen me
that I may serve your people
following the example of your Son, Jesus Christ,
in whose name I offer this prayer.
Amen.

The Daily Examen

St. Ignatius of Loyola gave the Church a great gift in his Spiritual Exercises, a plan for spending thirty days to discover God's plan for a person's life and the ability to carry it out. In the Spiritual Exercises he suggests a simple daily way to examine your conscience. He called it the Daily Examen and suggests it could be done a number of times during the day, especially before going to bed.

Begin by being aware of all the blessings you received from God through the events of that day and the people you spent time with. Then ask to know where you might have turned away from God's presence during the day. Review your thoughts, words, and actions since your day began and consider what has brought you closer to God and what has led you away from him. Ask God's pardon for any time you failed to love. And finally, resolve to respond more completely to the generous love of God. Conclude with the Lord's Prayer. This Examen can help you become more aware of God's action in your life and help you find God in all things.

"Ask God's pardon for any time you failed to love."
—St. Ignatius of Loyola

Hail, Holy Queen

Hail, holy Queen, Mother of mercy,
hail, our life, our sweetness, and
   our hope.
To you we cry, the children of Eve;
to you we send up our sighs,
mourning and weeping in this land
   of exile.
Turn, then, most gracious advocate,
your eyes of mercy toward us;
lead us home at last
and show us the blessed fruit of
   your womb, Jesus:
O clement, O loving, O sweet
   Virgin Mary.

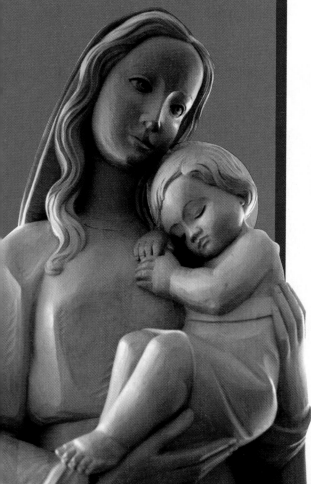

The Rosary

The Rosary helps us to pray to Jesus through Mary.
When we pray the Rosary, we think about the special events, or mysteries, in the lives of Jesus and Mary.

The Rosary is made up of a string of beads and a crucifix. We hold the crucifix in our hands as we pray the Sign of the Cross. Then we pray the Apostles' Creed.

Next to the crucifix, there is a single bead, followed by a set of three beads and another single bead. We pray the Lord's Prayer as we hold the first single bead and a Hail Mary at each bead in the set of three that follows. Then we pray the Glory Be to the Father. On the next single bead we think about the first mystery and pray the Lord's Prayer.

There are five sets of ten beads; each set is called a decade. We pray a Hail Mary on each bead of a decade as we reflect on a particular mystery in the lives of Jesus and Mary. The Glory Be to the Father is prayed at the end of each set. Between sets is a single bead on which we think about one of the mysteries and pray the Lord's Prayer.

In his Apostolic Letter *Rosary of the Virgin Mary* Pope John Paul II wrote that the rosary could take on a variety of legitimate forms adapted to different spiritual traditions and different Christian communities. "What is really important," he said, "is that the Rosary should always be seen and experienced as a path of contemplation." So it is traditional in some places to pray the Hail Holy Queen after the last decade.

We end by holding the crucifix in our hands as we pray the Sign of the Cross.

"What is really important," he said, "is that the Rosary should always be seen and experienced as a path of contemplation."
—Pope John Paul II

Praying the Rosary

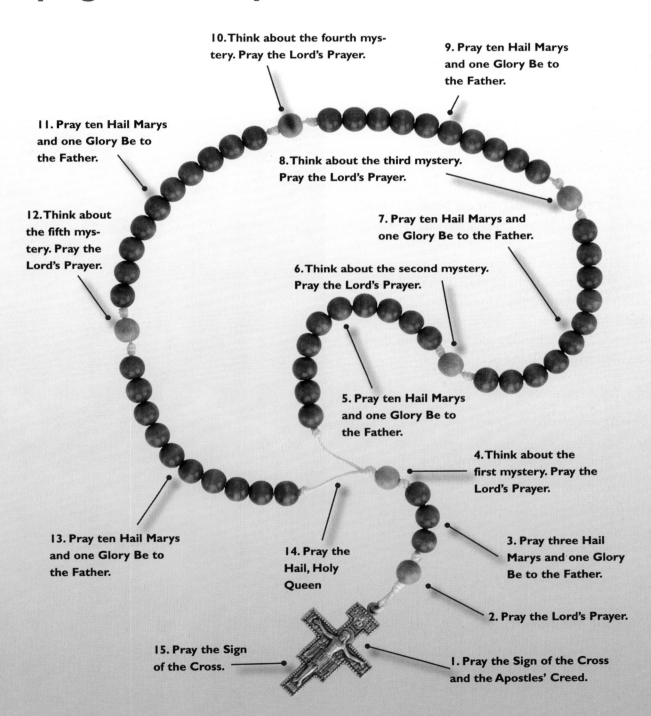

10. Think about the fourth mystery. Pray the Lord's Prayer.

9. Pray ten Hail Marys and one Glory Be to the Father.

11. Pray ten Hail Marys and one Glory Be to the Father.

8. Think about the third mystery. Pray the Lord's Prayer.

12. Think about the fifth mystery. Pray the Lord's Prayer.

7. Pray ten Hail Marys and one Glory Be to the Father.

6. Think about the second mystery. Pray the Lord's Prayer.

5. Pray ten Hail Marys and one Glory Be to the Father.

4. Think about the first mystery. Pray the Lord's Prayer.

13. Pray ten Hail Marys and one Glory Be to the Father.

14. Pray the Hail, Holy Queen

3. Pray three Hail Marys and one Glory Be to the Father.

2. Pray the Lord's Prayer.

15. Pray the Sign of the Cross.

1. Pray the Sign of the Cross and the Apostles' Creed.

Mysteries of the Rosary

The Church has used three sets of mysteries for many centuries. In 2002 Pope John Paul II proposed a fourth set of mysteries—the Luminous Mysteries, or the Mysteries of Light. According to his suggestion, the four sets of mysteries might be prayed on the following days: the Joyful Mysteries on Monday and Saturday, the Sorrowful Mysteries on Tuesday and Friday, the Glorious Mysteries on Wednesday and Sunday, and the Luminous Mysteries on Thursday.

The Joyful Mysteries

1. **The Annunciation**

   Mary learns that she has been chosen to be the mother of Jesus.

2. **The Visitation**

   Mary visits Elizabeth, who tells her that she will always be remembered.

3. **The Nativity**

   Jesus is born in a stable in Bethlehem.

4. **The Presentation**

   Mary and Joseph take the infant Jesus to the Temple to present him to God.

5. **The Finding of Jesus in the Temple**

   Jesus is found in the Temple discussing his faith with the teachers.

Annunciation, Guido Reni, 1575-1642, S. Pietro in Valle, Fano, Italy

The Luminous Mysteries

1. **The Baptism of Jesus in the River Jordan**

   God proclaims that Jesus is his beloved Son.

2. **The Wedding Feast at Cana**

   At Mary's request, Jesus performs his first miracle.

3. **The Proclamation of the Kingdom of God**

   Jesus calls all to conversion and service to the Kingdom.

4. **The Transfiguration of Jesus**

   Jesus is revealed in glory to Peter, James, and John.

5. **The Institution of the Eucharist**

   Jesus offers his Body and Blood at the Last Supper.

The Sorrowful Mysteries

1. **The Agony in the Garden**

   Jesus prays in the Garden of Gethsemane on the night before he dies.

2. **The Scourging at the Pillar**

   Jesus is lashed with whips.

3. **The Crowning With Thorns**

   Jesus is mocked and crowned with thorns.

4. **The Carrying of the Cross**

   Jesus carries the cross that will be used to crucify him.

5. **The Crucifixion**

   Jesus is nailed to the cross and dies.

In 2002 Pope John Paul II proposed a fourth set of mysteries— the Luminous Mysteries, or the Mysteries of Light.

Pope John Paul II, 1980, Vatican City

The Glorious Mysteries

1. **The Resurrection**

   God the Father raises Jesus from the dead.

2. **The Ascension**

   Jesus returns to his Father in heaven.

3. **The Coming of the Holy Spirit**

   The Holy Spirit comes to bring new life to the disciples.

4. **The Assumption of Mary**

   At the end of her life on earth, Mary is taken body and soul into heaven.

5. **The Coronation of Mary**

   Mary is crowned as Queen of Heaven and Earth.

Stations of the Cross

The 14 Stations of the Cross represent events from Jesus' passion and death. Even before the gospels were written down, the followers of Jesus told the story of his passion, death, and Resurrection. When people went on pilgrimage to Jerusalem, they were anxious to see the sites where Jesus lived and died. Eventually, following in the footsteps of the Lord on the way to his death became an important part of the pilgrimage.

The stations, as we know them today, came about when it was no longer easy or even possible to visit the holy sites in Palestine. In the 1500s, villages all over Europe started creating replicas of the way of the cross, with small shrines commemorating the places along the route in Jerusalem. Eventually, these shrines became the set of 14 stations we now know.

The first thing to remember about the stations is that they are a prayer. They are not an exercise in remembering events from the past. They are an invitation to make present the final hours of Jesus' life and experience who Jesus is. It becomes prayer when we open our hearts to be touched, and it leads us to express our response in prayer. Jesus wants to use any means available to move our hearts to know his love for us.

At each station we use our senses and our imagination to reflect prayerfully upon Jesus' suffering, death, and Resurrection. The stations can allow us to imaginatively visualize the meaning of his passion and death and lead us to gratitude. They can also lead us into a sense of solidarity with all our brothers and sisters, especially those who suffer, who are unjustly accused or victimized, who sit on death row, who carry difficult burdens, or who face terminal illnesses.

1. Jesus Is Condemned to Death.
Pontius Pilate condemns Jesus to death.

2. Jesus Takes Up His Cross.
Jesus willingly accepts and patiently bears his cross.

3. Jesus Falls the First Time.
Weakened by torments and by loss of blood, Jesus falls beneath his cross.

4. Jesus Meets His Sorrowful Mother.
Jesus meets his mother, Mary, who is filled with grief.

5. Simon of Cyrene Helps Jesus Carry the Cross.
Soldiers force Simon of Cyrene to carry the cross.

6. Veronica Wipes the Face of Jesus.
Veronica steps through the crowd to wipe the face of Jesus.

7. Jesus Falls a Second Time.
Jesus falls beneath the weight of the cross a second time.

8. Jesus Meets the Women of Jerusalem.
Jesus tells the women to weep not for him but for themselves and for their children.

9. Jesus Falls the Third Time.
Weakened almost to the point of death, Jesus falls a third time.

10. Jesus Is Stripped of His Garments.
The soldiers strip Jesus of his garments, treating him as a common criminal.

11. Jesus Is Nailed to the Cross.
Jesus' hands and feet are nailed to the cross.

12. Jesus Dies on the Cross.
After suffering greatly on the cross, Jesus bows his head and dies.

13. Jesus Is Taken Down From the Cross.
The lifeless body of Jesus is tenderly placed in the arms of Mary, his mother.

14. Jesus Is Laid in the Tomb.
Jesus' disciples place his body in the tomb.

The closing prayer—sometimes included as a 15th station—reflects on the Resurrection of Jesus.

The Mystery of Faith Made Present

The Church was revealed to the world with the coming of the Spirit on Pentecost. This gift of the Spirit ushered in a new era in the history of salvation. This era is the age of the Church in which Christ makes present and communicates his work of salvation through the liturgy of his Church. The Church, as Christ's Body, is the first sacrament, the sign and instrument through which the Holy Spirit dispenses the mystery of salvation. In this age of the Church Christ lives and acts through the sacraments.

The Seven Sacraments

Jesus touches our lives through the sacraments. In the sacraments physical objects—water, bread and wine, oil, and others—are the signs of Jesus' presence.

Sacraments of Initiation

These sacraments lay the foundation of every Christian life.

Baptism

In Baptism we are born into new life in Christ. Baptism takes away original sin and makes us members of the Church. Its sign is the pouring of water.

Confirmation

Confirmation seals our life of faith in Jesus. Its signs are the laying on of hands on a person's head, most often by a bishop, and the anointing with oil. Like Baptism, it is received only once.

Eucharist

The Eucharist nourishes our life of faith. We receive the Body and Blood of Christ under the appearance of bread and wine.

> *Jesus touches our lives through the sacraments.*

Sacraments of Healing

These sacraments celebrate the healing power of Jesus.

Penance

Through Penance we receive God's forgiveness. Forgiveness requires being sorry for our sins. In Penance we receive Jesus' healing grace through absolution by the priest. The signs of this sacrament are our confession of sins, our repentance and satisfaction, and the words of absolution.

Anointing of the Sick

This sacrament unites a sick person's sufferings with those of Jesus. Oil, a symbol of strength, is the sign of this sacrament. A person is anointed with oil and receives the laying on of hands from a priest.

Sacraments at the Service of Communion

These sacraments help members serve the community.

Matrimony

In Matrimony, a baptized man and woman are united with each other as a sign of the unity between Jesus and his Church. Matrimony requires the consent of the couple, as expressed in the marriage promises. The couple are the sign of this sacrament.

Holy Orders

In Holy Orders, men are ordained priests to be leaders of the community or deacons to be reminders of our baptismal call to serve others. The signs of this sacrament are the laying on of hands and the prayer asking God for the outpouring of the Holy Spirit by the bishop.

Holy Days of Obligation

The Holy Days of Obligation are the days other than Sundays on which we celebrate the great things God has done for us through Jesus and the saints. On Holy Days of Obligation, Catholics attend Mass.

Six Holy Days of Obligation are celebrated in the United States.

January 1—*Mary, Mother of God*

Fortieth day after Easter (or the 7th Sunday of the Easter season)—*Ascension*

August 15—*Assumption of the Blessed Virgin Mary*

November 1—*All Saints*

December 8—*Immaculate Conception*

December 25—*Nativity of Our Lord Jesus Christ*

Celebrating the Lord's Day

The Sabbath, the day on which God rested after creating the world, represents the completion of creation. Saturday has been replaced by Sunday for Christians because it recalls the beginning of the new creation through the Resurrection of Christ. The Sunday celebration of the Lord's Day is at the heart of the Church's life. That is why on Sundays and other holy days of obligation we are required to participate in the Mass. We also rest from work, take time to enjoy our families and to enrich our cultural and social lives, and perform works of mercy. On Sunday people from all over the world gather at God's Eucharistic table.

Order of the Mass

The Mass is the high point of Christian life, and it always follows a set order.

Introductory Rite
We prepare to celebrate the Eucharist.

Entrance Procession and Song
We gather as a community praising God in song.

Sign of the Cross and Greeting
We pray the Sign of the Cross, recognizing the presence of Christ in the community.

Penitential Rite
We remember our sins and ask God for mercy.

Gloria
We praise God in song.

Opening Prayer
Focuses the attention of all gathered.

> The Mass is a high point of Christian life.

The Liturgy of the Word

We hear the story of God's plan for salvation.

First Reading

We listen to God's Word, usually from the Old Testament.

Responsorial Psalm

We respond to God's Word in song.

Second Reading

We listen to God's Word from the New Testament.

Alleluia or Gospel Acclamation

We sing "Alleluia!" to praise God for the Good News. During Lent we sing "Praise to you, Lord Jesus Christ."

Gospel

We stand to acclaim Christ present in the Gospel.

Homily

The priest or deacon explains God's Word.

Profession of Faith

We proclaim our faith through the Creed.

General Intercessions

We pray for our needs and the needs of others.

The Liturgy of the Eucharist

We celebrate the meal that Jesus instituted at the Last Supper and remember the sacrifice he made for us.

The Preparation of the Gifts

We bring gifts of bread and wine to the altar.

Prayer over the Gifts

The priest prays that God will accept our sacrifice.

Eucharistic Prayer

This prayer of thanksgiving is the center and high point of the entire celebration.

- Preface—We give thanks and praise to God.
- Holy, Holy, Holy—We sing an acclamation of praise.
- Consecration—The bread and wine become the Body and Blood of Jesus Christ.
- Memorial Acclamation—We proclaim the mystery of faith.
- Great Amen—We affirm the words and actions of the Eucharistic prayer.

Communion Rite

We prepare to receive the Body and Blood of Jesus.

- Lord's Prayer—We pray the Our Father.
- Sign of Peace—We offer one another Christ's peace.
- Breaking of the Bread and the Lamb of God—We pray for forgiveness, mercy, and peace.
- Communion—We receive the Body and Blood of Jesus Christ.
- Prayer After Communion—We pray that the Eucharist will strengthen us to live as Jesus did.

Concluding Rite

We go forth to serve the Lord and one another.

Blessing

We receive God's blessing.

Dismissal

We go in peace to love and serve the Lord and one another.

making Good choices

Our conscience is the inner voice that helps us to know the law God has placed in our hearts. Our conscience helps us to judge the moral qualities of our own actions. It guides us to do good and avoid evil.

The Holy Spirit can help us to form a good conscience. We form our conscience by studying the teachings of the Church and following the guidance of our parents and pastoral leaders.

God has given every human being freedom of choice. This does not mean that we have the right to do whatever we please. We can live in true freedom if we cooperate with the Holy Spirit, who gives us the virtue of prudence. This virtue helps us to recognize what is good in every situation and to make correct choices. The Holy Spirit gives us the gifts of wisdom and understanding to help us make the right choices in life in relationship to God and others. The gift of counsel helps us to reflect on making correct choices in life.

The Ten Commandments help us to make moral choices that are pleasing to God. We have the grace of the sacraments, the teachings of the Church, and the good example of saints and fellow Christians to help us make good choices.

Making moral choices involves the following steps:

1. Ask the Holy Spirit for help.

2. Think about God's law and the teachings of the Church.

The Holy Spirit can help us form a good conscience.

3. Think about what will happen as a result of your choice. Ask yourself, will the consequences be pleasing to God? Will my choice hurt someone else?

4. Seek advice from someone you respect and remember that Jesus is with you.

5. Ask yourself how your choice will affect your relationships with God and others.

Making moral choices takes into consideration the object of the choice, our intention in making the choice, and the circumstances in which the choice is made. It is never right to make an evil choice in the hope of gaining something good.

Human Sinfulness

Original Sin

Tempted by the devil in the Garden, Adam and Eve let their trust in their Creator die in their hearts and abused their freedom by choosing to disobey God. They choose themselves over God. They believed the devil and choose to "be like God." All subsequent sin would be disobedience toward God and lack of trust in his goodness. Adam and Eve committed a personal sin, but this sin affected the human nature that they would then transmit to humanity. Human nature would now be deprived of the original holiness and justice that God had intended. Original sin is not a sin we commit but a state we are born into. Baptism, by giving us the life of Christ's grace, erases original sin and turns a us back towards God. But the consequences of our nature, weakened and inclined to evil, remain in us.

Mortal Sin

Mortal sin destroys the love of God in our heart. A conversion of heart, through the Sacrament of Penance, is necessary to experience God's mercy again. For a sin to be mortal, three conditions must be met. The matter of the sin must be serious. The Ten Commandments offer examples of serious matter such as lying, not honoring parents, stealing, murder, and so on. Secondly, mortal sin also requires full knowledge of the seriousness of the act. Finally, there must be complete consent. In other words, the sin is really a personal choice.

Venial Sin

Venial sin allows the love of God to remain in our heart, but it offends and wounds it. One commits a venial sin when the offense is of a less serious matter

IMAGE: Adam and Eve Expelled from Paradise, Detail from *Annunciation*, Fra Angelico

or, if the matter is serious, it is chosen without full knowledge or complete consent. Venial sin weakens love in us. It interferes with our practice of the virtues, makes it harder to do good, and can lead us to mortal sin. Venial sin is forgiven through the Sacrament of Penance, the practice of good works, and reception of the Eucharist.

Capital Sins

Saint John Cassian and Saint Gregory the Great distinguished seven sins they called capital because they produce other sins and other vices.

pride	*covetousness*	*envy*	*anger*
lust	*gluttony*	*sloth*	

The Morality of Human Acts

Human beings are able to act morally only because we are free. If we were not free to decide what to do our acts could not be good or evil. Human acts that are freely chosen after a judgment of conscience can be morally evaluated. They are either good or evil.

The morality of human acts depends on:

- the object chosen;
- the end in view or the intention;
- the circumstances of the action.

For an act to be good what you choose to do must be good in itself. If the choice is not good the intention or the circumstances cannot make it good. You cannot steal a digital camera because it is your father's birthday and it would make him very happy to have one. But a good act done with a bad intention is not necessarily good as well. Participating in a Hunger Walk not out of concern for the poor but to impress a teacher from whom you want a good grade is not necessarily a good act. Circumstances can affect the morality of an act. They can increase or lessen the goodness of an act. Acting out of fear of harm lessens a person's responsibility for an act.

> For an act to be good, what you choose to do must be good in itself.

An Examination of Conscience

An examination of conscience is the act of looking prayerfully into our hearts to ask how we have hurt our relationships with God and other people through our thoughts, words, and actions. We reflect on the Ten Commandments and the teachings of the Church.

The questions below help us in our examination of conscience.

My Relationship With God

What steps am I taking to help me grow closer to God and to others? Do I turn to God often during the day, especially when I am tempted?

Do I participate at Mass with attention and devotion on Sundays and holy days? Do I pray often and read the Bible?

Do I use God's name and the names of Jesus, Mary, and the saints with love and reverence?

My Relationships With Family, Friends, and Neighbors

Have I set a bad example through my words or actions? Do I treat others fairly? Do I spread stories that hurt other people?

Am I loving of those in my family? Am I respectful of my neighbors, my friends, and those in authority?

Do I value human life? Do I do what I can to promote peace and end violence? Do I avoid talking about others in ways that could harm them?

Do I show respect for my body and for the bodies of others? Do I keep away from forms of entertainment that do not respect God's gift of sexuality?

Have I taken or damaged anything that did not belong to me? Do I show concern for the poor and offer assistance to them in the ways I am able? Do I show concern for the environment and care for it as God has asked me to?

Have I cheated or copied homework? Have I told the truth even when it was difficult?

Do I quarrel with others just so I can get my own way? Do I insult others to try to make them think they are less than I am? Do I hold grudges and try to hurt people who I think have hurt me?

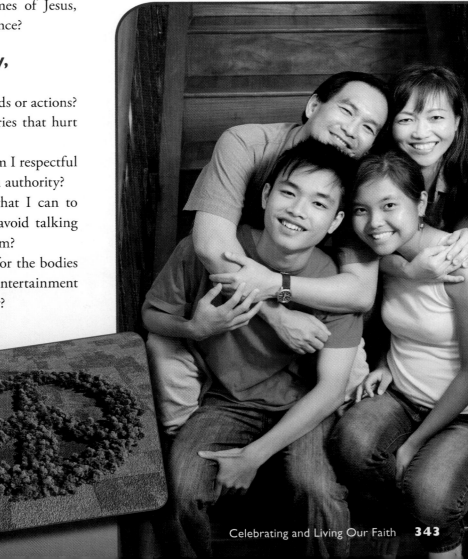

How to Make a Good Confession

An examination of conscience is an important part of preparing for the Sacrament of Penance. The Sacrament of Penance includes the following steps:

1. The priest greets us, and we pray the Sign of the Cross. He invites us to trust in God. He may read God's Word with us.

2. We confess our sins. The priest may help and counsel us.

3. The priest gives us a penance to perform. Penance is an act of kindness or prayers to pray, or both.

4. The priest asks us to express our sorrow, usually by reciting the Act of Contrition.

5. We receive absolution. The priest says, "I absolve you from your sins in the name of the Father, and of the Son, and of the Holy Spirit." We respond, "Amen."

6. The priest dismisses us by saying, "Go in peace." We go forth to perform the act of penance he has given us.

BELOW:
Purple screens create privacy for outdoor confessions during World Youth Day.

Showing Our Love for the World

The Catholic Church has a developed a large body of teaching on social justice issues because action on behalf of justice and work to create a more just world are essential parts of preaching the Gospel. In the story of the Good Samaritan (Luke 10:29–37), Jesus makes clear our responsibility to care for those in need.

The major development of the social doctrine of the Church began in the 19th century when the Gospel encountered modern industrial society. There were new structures for the production of consumer goods, new concepts of society, new types of states and authorities, and new forms of labor and ownership.

Since that time the Church has been making judgments about economic and social matters that relate to the basic rights of individuals and communities. The Church's social teaching is a rich treasure of wisdom about how to build a just society and live holy lives amid the challenges of the modern world. The Catholic Church teaches this responsibility in the following themes of Catholic Social Teaching.

Life and Dignity of the Human Person

All human life is sacred, and all people must be respected and valued over material goods. We are called to ask whether our actions as a society respect or threaten the life and dignity of the human person.

continued on page 346 ▶

▶ *continued from page 345*

Call to Family, Community, and Participation

Participation in family and community is central to our faith and to a healthy society. Families must be supported so that people can participate in society, build a community spirit, and promote the well-being of all, especially the poor and vulnerable.

Rights and Responsibilities

Every person has a right to life as well as a right to those things required for human decency. As Catholics, we have a responsibility to protect these basic human rights in order to achieve a healthy society.

Option for the Poor and Vulnerable

In our world many people are very rich while at the same time many are extremely poor. As Catholics, we are called to pay special attention to the needs of the poor by defending and promoting their dignity and by meeting their immediate material needs.

The Dignity of Work and the Rights of Workers

The basic rights of workers must be respected: the right to productive work, fair wages, and private property; and the right to organize, join unions, and pursue economic opportunity. Catholics believe that the economy is meant to serve people and that work is not merely a way to make a living but an important way in which we participate in God's creation.

Solidarity

Because God is our Father, we are all brothers and sisters with the responsibility to care for one another. Solidarity is the attitude that leads Christians to share spiritual and material goods. Solidarity unites rich and poor, weak and strong, and helps to create a society that recognizes that we all depend upon one another.

Care for God's Creation

God is the creator of all people and all things, and he wants us to enjoy his creation. The responsibility to care for all God has made is a requirement of our faith.

Glossary

A

Abba an informal word for *father* in Aramaic, the language Jesus spoke. It is like "dad" in English. When Jesus spoke to God the Father, he called him "Abba." [Abba]

abortion the deliberate ending of a pregnancy that results in the death of the unborn child. The Church teaches that since life begins at conception, abortion is a serious crime against life and is gravely against the moral law. [aborto]

Abraham the model of faith in God in the Old Testament. Because of his faith he left his home and traveled to Canaan, where God made a covenant with him that promised him land and many descendants. He became the father of the Chosen People. [Abraham]

absolution the forgiveness we receive from God through the priest in the Sacrament of Penance [absolución]

Acts of the Apostles the second volume of Luke's two-volume work. Written for a Greek Christian audience, it continues the story of Jesus' Resurrection and Ascension and reports the beginnings of the Church at Pentecost. It then tells how the Church spread from Jerusalem to the ends of the earth. [Hechos de los Apóstoles]

actual grace the gift of God, freely given to all of us, that unites us with the life of the Trinity. Actual grace is given to help us make the choices that help us conform our lives to God's will. (*See* grace and sanctifying grace.) [gracia actual]

adultery an injury to the marriage bond covenant. It occurs when two people have sexual relations while one of them is married to another person. The Sixth Commandment forbids adultery because it undermines the institution of marriage and is harmful to children, who need the stability of their parents' marriage commitment. [adulterio]

Advent the four weeks before Christmas. It is a time of joyful preparation for the celebration of the Incarnation, Jesus' birth as our savior, and a time for anticipating the coming of Jesus Christ at the end of time. [Adviento]

Advocate Jesus' name for the Holy Spirit. The Holy Spirit comforts us, speaks for us in difficult times, and makes Jesus present to us. [consolador]

All Saints Day November 1, the day on which the Church honors all who have died and now live with God as saints in heaven. This group includes those who are officially recognized as saints as well as many unknown people who after a good life have died and now live in God's presence. The feast celebrates our union with those who have gone before us and points to our ultimate goal of union with God. [Día de Todos los Santos]

All Souls Day November 2, the day on which the Church prays that all friends of God who have died may rest in peace. Those who have died may need purification in purgatory before living fully in God's presence. Our prayers and good works can help them in this process. Along with All Saints Day, this feast reminds us that all who love God, living and dead, are united in living communion with Jesus Christ and with one another. [Día de los Muertos]

altar the table in the church on which the priest celebrates Mass, where the sacrifice of Christ on the cross is made present in the Sacrament of the Eucharist. The altar represents two aspects of the mystery of the Eucharist. It is the place where Jesus Christ offers himself for our sins and where he gives us himself as our food for eternal life. [altar]

ambo

ambo a raised stand from which a person reads the Word of God during Mass [ambón]

Amen the Hebrew word used to conclude Jewish and Christian prayers. It means "This is true," "So be it," or "Let it be so." We end prayers with "Amen" to show that we mean what we have just said. [Amén]

angel a spiritual creature who worships God in heaven. Angels serve God as messengers. They tell us of his plans for our salvation. [ángel]

annulment a finding by a Church tribunal that at least one essential element for a real marriage was not present on the day of the wedding. The Church can declare that the Sacrament of Marriage did not take place if at least one of the parties was not freely choosing to marry, had been married before and that marriage was not annulled, or was not open to having children. An annulment cannot be considered until after a person is divorced. Catholics who receive an annulment are free to marry in the Church and can receive Communion. [anulación]

Annunciation the announcement to Mary by the angel Gabriel that God had chosen her to be the mother of Jesus. When Mary agreed, the Son of God became human in her. The feast of the Annunciation is celebrated on March 25, nine months before Christmas. [Anunciación]

Anointing of the Sick one of the seven sacraments. In this sacrament a sick person has holy oil applied and receives the strength, peace, and courage to overcome the difficulties associated with illness. Through this sacrament, Jesus brings the sick person spiritual healing and forgiveness of sins. If it is God's will, healing of the body is given as well. [unción de los enfermos]

apostle one of twelve special men who accompanied Jesus in his ministry and were witnesses to the Resurrection. Apostle means "one sent." These were the people sent to preach the gospel to the whole world. [apóstol]

Apostles' Creed a statement of Christian belief that developed out of a creed used in Baptism in Rome. The Apostles' Creed lists simple statements of belief in God the Father, Jesus Christ the Son, and the Holy Spirit. The profession of faith used in Baptism today is based on it. [Credo de los Apóstoles]

apostolic one of the four Marks of the Church. The Church is apostolic because it continues to hand on the teaching of the apostles through their successors, the bishops, in union with the successor of Saint Peter, the pope. [apostólico]

Ark of the Covenant a portable box in which were placed the tablets of the Ten Commandments. The Ark was the most important item in the shrine that was carried through the desert and then placed in the holiest part of the Temple in Jerusalem. Two angels are depicted on the cover of the Ark of the Covenant. The wings of the angels curve upward, representing the place where God came close to Israel and revealed his will. [Arca de la Alianza]

Ascension the entry of Jesus into God's presence in heaven. In the Acts of the Apostles, it is written that Jesus, after his Resurrection, spent 40 days on earth, instructing his followers. He then returned to his Father in heaven. [Ascensión]

Ash Wednesday the first day of Lent, on which we receive ashes on our foreheads. The ashes remind us to prepare for Easter by repenting and showing sorrow for the choices we make that offend God and hurt our relationships with others. [Miércoles de Ceniza]

assembly the people of God when they are gathered together to worship him [asamblea]

Ark of the Covenant

Assumption Mary's being taken, body and soul, into heaven. Mary had a special relationship with her Son, Jesus, from the very beginning, when she conceived him. Because of this relationship, she enjoys a special participation in Jesus' Resurrection and has been taken into heaven where she now lives with him. We celebrate this event in the feast of the Assumption on August 15. [Asunción]

Assumption

B

Baptism the first of the seven sacraments. Baptism frees us from original sin and is necessary for salvation. Baptism gives us new life in Jesus Christ through the Holy Spirit. The celebration of Baptism consists of immersing a person in water while declaring that the person is baptized in the name of the Father, the Son, and the Holy Spirit. [bautismo]

Beatitudes the teachings of Jesus in the Sermon on the Mount in Matthew's Gospel. The Beatitudes are eight ways of living the Christian life. They are the fulfillment of the commandments given to Moses. These teachings present the way to true happiness. [Bienaventuranzas]

Bible the collection of books containing the truths of God's revelation to us. These writings were inspired by the Holy Spirit and written by human beings. The Bible is made up of the 46 books in the Old Testament and 27 books in the New Testament. [Biblia]

bishop a man who has received the fullness of Holy Orders. As a successor to the original apostles, he takes care of the Church and is a principal teacher in it. [Obispo]

blasphemy any word, thought, or action done in hatred or defiance against God. It extends to using language that disrespects the Church, the saints, or holy things. It is also blasphemy to use God's name as an excuse to enslave people, to torture them, or to put them to death. Using God's name to do these things can cause others to reject religion. [blasfemia]

Blessed Sacrament the bread that has been consecrated by the priest at Mass. It is kept in the tabernacle to adore and to be taken to the sick. [Santísimo Sacramento]

blessing a prayer that calls for God's power and care upon some person, place, thing, or special activity [bendición]

Body and Blood of Christ the bread and wine that has been consecrated by the priest at Mass. In the Sacrament of the Eucharist, all of the risen Lord Jesus Christ—body, blood, soul, and divinity—is present under the appearances of bread and wine. [Cuerpo y Sangre de Cristo]

Buddhism Buddhism is a religion that is based on the teaching of Siddhartha Gautama, who was known as the Buddha, which means "Enlightened One." The Buddha was born to a royal family in northern India about five and a half centuries before Jesus. At age 29 he became disillusioned with life and left his comfortable home to find an answer to the question of why humans suffer. [Budismo]

C

calumny (slander) a false statement about the reputation of someone that makes other people think bad of that person. Calumny, also called slander, is a sin against the Eighth Commandment. [calumnia]

canonize to declare that a Christian who has died is already in heaven and may be looked to as a model of Christian life who may intercede for us as a saint [canonizar]

capital sins those sins that can lead us to more serious sin. They are pride, covetousness, envy, anger, gluttony, lust, and sloth. [pecados capitales]

catechumen a person being formed in the Christian life through instruction and by the example of the parish community. Through conversion and maturity of faith, a catechumen is preparing to be welcomed into the Church at Easter through the Sacraments of Baptism, Confirmation, and Eucharist. [catecúmeno]

catholic one of the four Marks of the Church. The Church is catholic because Jesus is fully present in it, because it proclaims the fullness of faith, and because Jesus has given the Church to the whole world. The Church is universal. [católica]

Catholic Social Teaching the body of teaching on social justice issues, action on behalf of justice, and work to create a more just world. The Church makes judgments about economic and social matters that relate to the basic rights of individuals and communities. The Church's social teaching is a rich treasure of wisdom about how to build a just society. [doctrina social católica]

character a permanent spiritual mark. Character shows that a person has a new relationship with Jesus and a special standing in the Church. Baptism, Confirmation, and Holy Orders each have a specific permanent character and therefore may be received only once. [carácter]

charity a virtue given to us by God that helps us love God above all things and our neighbor as ourselves [caridad]

chastity the integration of our physical sexuality with our spiritual nature. Chastity helps us to be completely human, able to give to others our whole life and love. All people, married and single, are called to practice chastity. [castidad]

Chosen People the people set apart by God to have a special relationship with him. God first formed a Chosen People when he made a covenant, or solemn agreement, with Abraham. He reaffirmed the covenant through Moses at Mount Sinai. The covenant is fulfilled in Jesus and his Church. [Pueblo Elegido]

chrism a perfumed oil, consecrated by a bishop, that is used in the Sacraments of Baptism, Confirmation, and Holy Orders. Anointing with chrism signifies the call of the baptized to the threefold ministry of priest, prophet, and king. [crisma]

Christ a title that means "anointed one." It is from a Greek word that means the same thing as the Hebrew word *Messiah,* or "anointed." It is the name given to Jesus as priest, prophet, and king. [Cristo]

Christian the name given to all those who have been anointed through the gift of the Holy Spirit in Baptism and have become followers of Jesus Christ [cristiano]

Christmas the feast of the birth of Jesus (December 25) [Navidad]

Church the people of God throughout the whole world, or diocese (the local Church), or the assembly of those called together to worship God. The Church is one, holy, catholic, and apostolic. [Iglesia]

clergy those men who are set apart as sacred ministers to serve the Church through Holy Orders [clero]

commandment a standard, or rule, for living as God wants us to live. Jesus summarized all of the commandments into two: love God and love your neighbor. [mandamiento]

common good the sum total of the social conditions that allow people, individually and as a group, to reach their full potential. It requires peace, security, respecting the rights of everyone, and meeting the spiritual and worldly needs of everyone. People have a responsibility to contribute to the good of the entire society. It is one of the basic principles at the center of Catholic Social Teaching. [bien común]

communal prayer the worship of God together with others. The Liturgy of the Hours and the Mass are the main forms of communal prayer. [oración común]

Communion of Saints the unity of all, dead or living, who have been saved in Jesus Christ. The Communion of Saints is based on our one faith, and it is nourished by our participation in the Eucharist. [Comunión de los Santos]

confession the act of telling our sins to a priest in the Sacrament of Penance. The sacrament itself is sometimes referred to as "Confession." [confesión]

Confirmation the sacrament that completes the grace we receive in Baptism. It seals, or confirms, this grace through the seven gifts of the Holy Spirit that we receive as part of Confirmation. This sacrament also makes us better able to participate in the worship and apostolic life of the Church. [Confirmación]

conscience the inner voice that helps each of us to judge the morality of our own actions. It guides us to follow God's law by doing good and avoiding evil. [conciencia]

consecration the making of a thing or a person to be special to God through a prayer or blessing. At Mass the words of the priest are a consecration that makes Jesus Christ's Body and Blood present in the bread and wine. People or objects set apart for God in a special way are also consecrated. For example, churches and altars are consecrated for use in liturgy, and bishops

are consecrated as they receive the fullness of the Sacrament of Holy Orders. [consagración]

contrition the sorrow we feel when we know that we have sinned, followed by the decision not to sin again. Perfect contrition arises from a love that loves God above all else. Imperfect contrition arises on other motives. Contrition is the most important act of the penitent preparing to celebrate the Sacrament of Penance. [contrición]

conversion a radical or serious change of the whole life, away from sin and toward God. The call to change of heart is a key part of the preaching of Jesus. Throughout our entire lives, Jesus calls us to change in this way. [conversión]

Corporal Works of Mercy kind acts by which we help our neighbors with their everyday, material needs. Corporal Works of Mercy include feeding the hungry, finding a home for the homeless, clothing the naked, visiting the sick and those in prison, giving alms to the poor, and burying the dead. [obras corporales de misericordia]

Council of Jerusalem the name of the meeting that happened about 50 A.D. that is described in chapter 15 of the Acts of the Apostles. The meeting was the result of a disagreement between Paul and his followers and the Jewish Christian followers of James, the leader of the Jerusalem Church. James felt that those who became Christians should also observe the rules of traditional Judaism and that the men should be circumcised. Paul said that there should be no such necessity. It was finally agreed that circumcision was not necessary for Gentiles who became Christians. [Concilio de Jerusalén]

counsel one of the seven Gifts of the Holy Spirit. Counsel helps us to make correct choices in life through reflection, discernment, consulting, and the advising of others. [consejo]

covenant a solemn agreement between people or between people and God. God made covenants with humanity through agreements with Noah, Abraham, and Moses. These covenants offered salvation. God's new and final covenant was established through Jesus' life, death, and resurrection. Testament is another word for covenant. [alianza]

creation God's act of making everything that exists outside himself. Creation is everything that exists. God said that all of creation is good. [creación]

Creator God, who made everything that is and whom we can come to know through everything he created [Creador]

creed a brief summary of what people believe. The word *creed* comes from the Latin credo, "I believe." The Nicene Creed is the most important summary of Christian beliefs. [credo]

crozier the staff carried by a bishop that shows he cares for us in the same way that a shepherd cares for his sheep. It also reminds us that he represents Jesus, the Good Shepherd. [báculo]

crucifixion an ancient method of execution in which the victim was tied or nailed to a wooden cross and left to hang until dead, usually from suffocation. It was the method used by the Romans to put Jesus to death. The cross with an image of the crucified Jesus on it is called a crucifix. [crucifixión]

culture the activity of a group of people that includes their music, art, language, and celebrations. Culture is one of the ways people experience God in their lives. [cultura]

D

deacon a man ordained through the Sacrament of Holy Orders to the ministry of service in the Church. Deacons help the bishop and priests by serving in the various charitable ministries of the Church. They also help by proclaiming the gospel, preaching, and assisting at the Liturgy of the Eucharist. Deacons can also celebrate Baptisms, witness marriages, and preside at funerals. [diácono]

detraction the act of talking about the faults and sins of another person to someone who has no reason to hear this and cannot help the person. Detraction damages the reputation of another person without any intent to help that person. [detracción]

dignity of the human person a basic principle at the center of Catholic Social Teaching. It is the starting point of a moral vision for society because human life is sacred and should be treated with great respect. The human person is the clearest reflection of God among us. [dignidad de la persona humana]

dignity of work a basic principle at the center of Catholic Social Teaching. Since work is done by people created in the image of God, it is not only a way to make a living but an important way we participate in God's creation. In work, people fulfill part of their potential given to them by God. All workers have a right to productive work, to decent and fair wages, and to safe working conditions. [dignidad del trabajo]

diocese the members of the Church in a particular area, united in faith and the sacraments, and gathered under the leadership of a bishop [diócesis]

disciple a person who has accepted Jesus' message and tries to live as he did, sharing his mission, his suffering, and his joys [discípulo]

discrimination the act of mistreating other people because of how they look or act, or just because they are different [discriminación]

Divine Providence the guidance of God over all he has created. Divine Providence exercises care for all creation and guides it toward its final perfection. [Divina Providencia]

Doctor of the Church a man or a woman recognized as a model teacher of the Christian faith [Doctor de la Iglesia]

Doctor of the Church, Teresa of Ávila

domestic church the Christian home, which is a community of grace and prayer and a school of human virtues and Christian charity [Iglesia doméstica]

E

Easter the celebration of the bodily raising of Jesus Christ from the dead. Easter is the festival of our redemption and the central Christian feast, the one from which other feasts arise. [Pascua]

Easter Vigil the celebration of the first and greatest Christian feast, the Resurrection of Jesus. It occurs on the first Saturday evening after the first full moon of spring. During this night watch before Easter morning, catechumens are baptized, confirmed, and receive Eucharist for the first time. [Vigilia Pascual]

Epiphany

Eastern Catholic Churches a group of churches that developed in the East (in countries such as Lebanon) that are in union with the Roman Catholic Church but have their own liturgical, theological, and administrative traditions. They show the truly catholic nature of the Church, which takes root in many cultures. [Iglesias Católicas Orientales]

ecumenical council a gathering of Catholic bishops from the entire world meeting under the leadership of the pope or his delegates. Ecumenical councils discuss pastoral, legal, and doctrinal issues. There have been 21 ecumenical councils recognized by the Catholic Church. The first was the First Council of Nicaea in 325. The most recent was the Second Vatican Council, which took place between 1962 and 1965. [concilio ecuménico]

ecumenism the movement for unity among Christians. Christ gave the Church the gift of unity from the beginning, but over the centuries that unity has been broken. All Christians are called by their common Baptism to pray and to work to maintain, reinforce, and perfect the unity Christ wants for the Church. [ecumenismo]

Emmanuel a Hebrew name from the Old Testament that means "God with us." In Matthew's Gospel, Jesus is called Emmanuel. [Emmanuel]

encyclical a letter written by the pope and sent to the whole Church and sometimes to the whole world. It expresses Church teaching on some specific and important issue. [encíclica]

envy a feeling of resentment or sadness because someone has a quality, a talent, or a possession that we want. Envy is one of the seven capital sins, and it is contrary to the tenth commandment. [envidia]

Epiphany the day on which we celebrate the visit of the Magi to Jesus after his birth. This is the day that Jesus was revealed as the savior of the whole world. [Epifanía]

epistle a letter written by Saint Paul or another leader to a group of Christians in the early Church. Twenty-one of the twenty-seven books of the New Testament are epistles. The second reading at Mass on Sundays and holy days is always from one of these books. [epistola]

eternal life the never-ending life after death with God, granted to those who die as God's friends, with the grace of God alive in them [vida eterna]

Eucharist the sacrament in which we give thanks to God for the Body and Blood of Christ, which we receive in the form of bread and wine. The risen Jesus Christ has Real Presence in the Eucharist. This means his body, blood, soul, and divinity are wholly and entirely present. [Eucaristía]

Eucharistic liturgy the public worship, held by the Church, in which bread and wine is consecrated to become the Body and Blood of Jesus Christ. The Sunday celebration of the Eucharistic liturgy is at the heart of Church life. [celebración eucarística]

Exile ordered by King Nebuchadnezzar

euthanasia an act with the intent to cause the death of a handicapped, sick, or dying person. Euthanasia is considered murder and is gravely contrary to the dignity of the human person and to the respect due to the living God, our Creator. [eutanasia]

evangelist anyone engaged in spreading the gospel. Letters in the New Testament, along with the Acts of the Apostles, list evangelists along with apostles and prophets as ministers in the Church. The term is principally used to describe the writers of the four Gospels: Matthew, Mark, Luke, and John. [evangelista]

evangelization the declaration by word or example of the good news of salvation we have received in Jesus Christ. It is directed both to those who do not know Jesus and to those who have become indifferent about him. Those who have become indifferent are the focus of what is called the New Evangelization. [evangelización]

examination of conscience the act of prayerfully thinking about what we have said or done in light of what the gospel asks of us. We also think about how our actions may have hurt our relationship with God or others. An examination of conscience is an important part of our preparing to celebrate the Sacrament of Penance. [examen de conciencia]

Exile the period in the history of Israel between the destruction of Jerusalem in 587 b.c. and the return to Jerusalem in 537 b.c. During this time, many of the Jewish people were forced to live in Babylon, far from home. [exilio]

Exodus God's liberation of the Hebrew people from slavery in Egypt and his leading them to the Promised Land [Éxodo]

F

faith a gift of God that helps us to believe in him. We profess our faith in the creed, celebrate it in the sacraments, live by it through our good conduct of loving God and our neighbor, and express it in prayer. It is a personal adherence of the whole person to God, who has revealed himself to us through words and actions throughout history. [fe]

fasting limiting the amount we eat for a period of time to express sorrow for sin and to make ourselves more aware of God's action in our lives. Adults 18 years old and older fast on Ash Wednesday and Good Friday. The practice is also encouraged as a private devotion at other times of penitence. [ayuno]

fear of the Lord one of the seven Gifts of the Holy Spirit. This gift leads us to a sense of wonder and awe in the presence of God because we recognize his greatness. [temor de Dios]

forgiveness the willingness to be kind to those who have hurt us but have then shown that they are sorry. In the Lord's Prayer, we pray that since God will forgive us for our sins, we are able to forgive those who have hurt us. [perdón]

fortitude the strength to choose to do the right thing even when that is difficult. Fortitude is one of the four central human virtues, called the Cardinal Virtues, by which we guide our conduct through faith and the use of reason. It is also one of the Gifts of the Holy Spirit. [fortaleza]

free will the ability to choose to do good because God has made us like him. Our free will is what makes us truly human. Our exercise of free will to do good increases our freedom. Using free will to choose sin makes us slaves to sin. [libre albedrío]

Fruits of the Holy Spirit the demonstration through our actions that God is alive in us. Saint Paul lists the Fruits of the Holy Spirit in Galatians 5:22–23: love, joy, peace, patience, kindness, generosity, faithfulness, gentleness, and self-control. Church tradition has added goodness, modesty, and chastity to make a total of twelve. [frutos del Espíritu Santo]

fundamentalism believing that what the Bible says is always factually true. It fails to recognize that the inspired Word of God has been expressed in human language, under divine inspiration, by human authors possessed of limited capacities and resources. [fundamentalismo]

G

Gentiles the name given to a foreign people by the Jews after the Exile. They were nonbelievers who worshipped false gods. They stand in contrast to the Jewish people who received God's law. [gentiles]

genuflect to show respect in church by touching a knee to the ground, especially before the Blessed Sacrament in the tabernacle [genuflexión, hacer la]

Gifts of the Holy Spirit the permanent willingness, given to us by the Holy Spirit, that makes it possible for us to do what God asks of us. The Gifts of the Holy Spirit are drawn from Isaiah 11:1–3. They include wisdom, understanding, right judgment, courage, knowledge, and wonder and awe. Church Tradition has added reverence to make a total seven. [dones del Espíritu Santo]

God the Father, Son, and Holy Spirit, one God in three distinct persons. God created all that exists. He is the source of salvation, and he is truth and love. [Dios]

godparent a witness to Baptism who assumes the responsibility for helping the baptized person along the road of Christian life [padrino/madrina de Bautismo]

gospel the good news of God's mercy and love that we experience by hearing the story of Jesus' life, death, and resurrection. The story is passed on in the teaching ministry of the Church as the source of all truth and right living. It is presented to us in four books in the New Testament, the Gospels of Matthew, Mark, Luke, and John. [Evangelio]

grace the gift of God, given to us without our meriting it. Grace is the Holy Spirit alive in us, helping us to live our Christian vocation. Grace helps us to live as God wants us to. (*See* actual grace *and* sanctifying grace) [gracia]

Great Commandment Jesus' commandment that we are to love both God and our neighbor as we love ourselves. Jesus tells us that this commandment sums up everything taught in the Old Testament. [El Mandamiento Mayor]

H

heaven union with God the Father, Son, and Holy Spirit in life and love that never ends. Heaven is a state of complete happiness and the goal of the deepest wishes of the human heart. [cielo]

Hebrews the descendants of Abraham, Isaac, and Jacob, who were enslaved in Egypt. God helped Moses lead these people out of slavery. [hebreos]

hell a life of total separation from God forever. In his infinite love for us, God can only desire our salvation. Hell is the result of the free choice of a person to reject God's love and forgiveness once and for all. [infierno]

holiness the fullness of Christian life and love. All people are called to holiness, which is made possible by cooperating with God's grace to do his will. As we do God's will, we are transformed more and more into the image of the Son, Jesus Christ. [santidad]

holy one of the four Marks of the Church. It is the kind of life we live when we share in the life of God, who is all holiness. The Church is holy because it is united with Jesus Christ. [santa]

Holy Communion the consecrated bread and wine that we receive at Mass, which is the Body and Blood of Jesus Christ. It brings us into union with Jesus and his saving death and resurrection. [Sagrada comunión]

Holy Days of Obligation the principal feast days, other than Sundays, of the Church. On Holy Days of Obligation, we celebrate the great things that God has done for us through Jesus and the Saints. Catholics are obliged to participate in the Eucharist on these days, just as we are on Sundays. [días de precepto]

Holy Family the family of Jesus as he grew up in Nazareth. It included Jesus; his mother, Mary; and his foster father, Joseph. [Sagrada Familia]

Holy Family

Holy of Holies the holiest part of the Temple in Jerusalem. The high priest entered this part of the Temple once a year to address God and ask God's forgiveness for the sins of the people. [lugar santísimo]

Holy Orders the sacrament through which the mission given by Jesus to his apostles continues in the Church. The sacrament has three degrees: deacon, priest, and bishop. Through the laying on of hands in the Sacrament of Holy Orders, men receive a permanent sacramental mark that calls them to minister to the Church. [Orden sagrado]

Holy Spirit the third person of the Trinity, who is sent to us as our helper and, through Baptism and Confirmation, fills us with God's life. Together with the Father and the Son, the Holy Spirit brings the divine plan of salvation to completion. [Espíritu Santo]

holy water water that has been blessed and is used as a sacramental to remind us of our Baptism [agua bendita]

Holy Week the celebration of the events surrounding Jesus' suffering, death, resurrection, and establishment of the Eucharist. Holy Week commemorates Jesus' triumphal entry into Jerusalem on Palm Sunday, the gift of himself in the Eucharist on Holy Thursday, his death on Good Friday, and his resurrection at the Easter Vigil on Holy Saturday. [Semana Santa]

homily the explanation by a bishop, a priest, or a deacon of the Word of God in the liturgy. The homily relates the Word of God to our life as Christians today. [homilía]

hope the confidence that God will always be with us, make us happy now and forever, and help us to live so that we will be with him forever [esperanza]

I

Immaculate Conception the Church teaching that Mary was free from original sin from the first moment of her conception. She was preserved through the merits of her Son, Jesus, the Savior of the human race. It was declared a belief of the Catholic Church by Pope Pius IX in 1854 and is celebrated on December 8. [Inmaculada Concepción]

Incarnation the Son of God, Jesus, being born as a full human being in order to save us. The Son of God, the second person of the Trinity, is both true God and true man. [Encarnación]

indulgence a lessening of the punishment due for sins that have been forgiven. Indulgences move us toward our final purification, when we will live with God forever. [indulgencia]

Holy Week celebration

inerrancy the teaching of the Church that the Bible teaches the truths of the faith necessary for our salvation without error. Because God inspired the human authors, he is the author of the Sacred Scriptures. This gives us the assurance that they teach his saving truth without error even though certain historical and scientific information may not be accurate. With the help of the Holy Spirit and the Church, we interpret what God wants to reveal to us about our salvation through the sacred authors. [inerrancia]

infallibility the gift the Holy Spirit has given to the Church that assures that the pope and the bishops in union with the pope can proclaim as true the doctrines that involve faith or morals. It is an extension of the fact that the whole body of believers cannot be in error when it comes to questions of faith and morals. [infalibilidad]

Infancy Narrative accounts of the infancy and childhood of Jesus that appear in the first two chapters of Matthew's and Luke's Gospels. Each Gospel contains a different series of events. They have in common that Jesus was born in Bethlehem through the virginal conception of Mary. The intention of these stories is to proclaim Jesus as Messiah and Savior. [evangelio de la infancia]

inspiration the influence of the Holy Spirit on the human authors of Scripture. The creative inspiration of the Holy Spirit makes sure that the Scripture is taught according to the truth God wants us to know for our salvation. [inspiración]

interpretation explanation of the words of Scripture, combining human knowledge and the teaching office of the Church under the guidance of the Holy Spirit [interpretación]

interreligious dialogue the work to build a relationship of openness with the followers of non-Christian religions. The Church's bond with non-Christian religions comes from our common bond as children of God. The purpose of this dialogue is to increase understanding of each other, to work for the common good of humanity, and to establish peace. [diálogo interreligioso]

Islam the third great religion, along with Judaism and Christianity, professing belief in one God. *Islam* means "submission" to that one God. [islamismo]

Israelites the descendants of Abraham, Isaac, and Jacob. God changed Jacob's name to "Israel," and Jacob's twelve sons and their children became the leaders of the twelve tribes of Israel. (See Hebrews.) [israelitas]

J

Jesus the Son of God, who was born of the Virgin Mary and who died and was raised from the dead for our salvation. He returned to God and will come again to judge the living and the dead. His name means "God saves." [Jesús]

Jews the name given to the Hebrew people, from the time of the exile to the present. The name means "the people who live in the territory of Judah," the area of Palestine surrounding Jerusalem. [judíos]

Joseph the foster father of Jesus, who was engaged to Mary when the angel announced that Mary would have a child through the power of the Holy Spirit. In the Old Testament, Joseph was the son of Jacob who was sold into slavery in Egypt by his brothers and then saved them from starvation when famine came. [José]

Judaism the name of the religion of Jesus and all of the people of Israel after they returned from exile in Babylon and built the second Temple [judaísmo]

justice the virtue that guides us to give to God and others what is due them. Justice is one of the four central human virtues, called the Cardinal Virtues, by which we guide our Christian life. [justicia]

K

Kingdom of God God's rule over us, announced in the gospel and present in the Eucharist. The beginning of the Kingdom here on earth is mysteriously present in the Church, and it will come in completeness at the end of time. [Reino de Dios]

knowledge one of the seven Gifts of the Holy Spirit. This gift helps us to know what God asks of us and how we should respond. [conocimiento]

L

laity those who have been made members of Christ in Baptism and who participate in the priestly, prophetic, and kingly functions of Christ in his mission to the whole world. The laity is distinct from the clergy, whose members are set apart as ministers to serve the Church. [laicado]

Last Judgment the final judgment of all human beings that will occur when Christ returns in glory and all appear in their own bodies before him to give an account of all their deeds in life. In the presence of Christ, the truth of each person's relationship with God will be laid bare, as will the good each person had done or failed to do during his or her earthly life. At that time God's kingdom will come in its fullness. [Juicio Final]

Last Supper the last meal Jesus ate with his disciples on the night before he died. At the Last Supper, Jesus took bread and wine, blessed it, and said that it was his Body and Blood. Jesus' death and resurrection, which we celebrate in the Eucharist, was anticipated in this meal. [Última Cena]

lectio divina a reflective way of praying with Scripture. *Lectio divina* is Latin for "sacred reading" and is an ancient form of Christian prayer. It involves four steps: sacred reading of a Scripture passage, meditation on the passage, speaking to God, and contemplation or resting in God's presence. [lectio divina]

Lectionary the official book that contains all of the Scripture readings used in the Liturgy of the Word [Leccionario]

Lent the 40 days before Easter (not counting Sundays) during which we prepare, through prayer, fasting, and giving aid to the poor, to change our lives and live the gospel more completely [Cuaresma]

liturgical year the celebrations throughout the year of all of the mysteries of Jesus' birth, life, death, and resurrection. The celebration of Easter is at the heart of the liturgical year. The other feasts celebrated throughout the year make up the basic rhythm of the Christian's life of prayer. [Año Litúrgico]

liturgy the public prayer of the Church that celebrates the wonderful things God has done for us in Jesus Christ, our high priest, and the way in which he continues the work of our salvation. The original meaning of *liturgy* was "a public work or service done for the people." [liturgia]

Liturgy of the Eucharist the second half of the Mass, in which the bread and wine are blessed and become the Body and Blood of Jesus Christ, which we then receive in Holy Communion [Liturgia Eucarística]

Last Supper

Liturgy of the Hours the public prayer of the Church to praise God and sanctify the day. It includes an office of readings before sunrise, morning prayer at dawn, evening prayer at sunset, and prayer before going to bed. The chanting of psalms makes up a major portion of each of these services. [Liturgia de las Horas]

Liturgy of the Word the first half of the Mass, in which we listen to God's Word from the Bible and consider what it means for us today. The Liturgy of the Word can also be a public prayer and proclamation of God's Word that is not followed by the Liturgy of the Eucharist. [Liturgia de la Palabra]

Lord the name used for God to replace the name he revealed to Moses, Yahweh, which was considered too sacred to pronounce. It indicates the divinity of Israel's God. The New Testament uses the title Lord for both the Father and for Jesus, recognizing him as God himself. (*See* Yahweh.) [Señor]

M

Magisterium the living, teaching office of the Church. This office, through the bishops and with the pope, provides an authentic interpretation of the Word of God. It ensures faithfulness to the teaching of the Apostles in matters of faith and morals. [Magisterio]

Magnificat Mary's song of praise to God for the great things he has done for her and planned for us through Jesus [Magníficat]

Marks of the Church the four most important aspects of the Church found in the Nicene Creed. According to the Nicene Creed, the Church is one, holy, catholic, and apostolic. [calificativos de la Iglesia]

martyrs those who have given their lives for the faith. It comes from the Greek word for "witness." A martyr is the supreme witness to the truth of the faith and to Christ to whom he or she is united. The seventh chapter of the Acts of the Apostles recounts the death of the first martyr, the deacon Stephen. [mártires]

Mary the mother of Jesus. She is called blessed and "full of grace" because God chose her to be the mother of the Son of God, the second person of the Trinity. [María]

Mass the most important sacramental celebration of the Church, established by Jesus at the Last Supper as a remembrance of his death and resurrection. At Mass we listen to God's Word from the Bible and receive Jesus Christ in the bread and wine that has been blessed to become his Body and Blood. [misa]

Matrimony a solemn agreement between a woman and a man to be partners for life, both for their own good and for bringing up children. Marriage is a sacrament when the agreement is properly made between baptized Christians. [Matrimonio]

meditation a form of prayer using silence and listening that seeks through imagination, emotion, and desire to understand how to adhere and respond to what God is asking. By concentrating on a word or an image, we move beyond thoughts, empty the mind of contents that get in the way of our experience of God, and rest in simple awareness of God. It is one of the three major expressions of the life of prayer. [meditación]

Mary, Queen of Heaven

memorial a remembrance of events that have taken place in the past. We recall these events because they continue to affect us because they are part of God's saving plan for us. Every time we remember these events, we make God's saving action present. [conmemoración]

Mendicant Order a unique variety of religious order that developed in the 13th century. Unlike monks who remain inside a monastery, members of Mendicant Orders have ministries of preaching, teaching, and witnessing within cities. They are called *mendicant* from the Latin word for "begging," which is their main means of supporting themselves. The two main Mendicant Orders are the Dominicans, founded by Saint Dominick de Guzman, and the Franciscans, founded by Saint Francis of Assisi. [orden mendicante]

Messiah a title that means "anointed one." It is from a Hebrew word that means the same thing as the Greek word *Christ*. Messiah is the title that was given to Jesus as priest, prophet, and king. [Mesías]

ministry service or work done for others. Ministry is done by bishops, priests, and deacons, who are all ordained to ministry in the celebration of the sacraments. All those baptized are called to a variety of ministries in the liturgy and in service to the needs of others. [ministerio]

miracle signs or acts of wonder that cannot be explained by natural causes but are works of God. In the Gospels, Jesus works miracles as a sign that the Kingdom of God is present in his ministry. [milagro]

mission the work of Jesus Christ that is continued in the Church through the Holy Spirit. The mission of the Church is to proclaim salvation in Jesus' life, death, Resurrection, and glorious Ascension. Missionaries are ordained, lay, and religious people engaged in mission. [misión]

monastery a place where men or women live out their solemn vows of poverty, chastity, and obedience in a stable community life. They spend their days in public prayer, work, and meditation. [monasterio]

monasticism a form of religious life in which men and women live out their vows of poverty, chastity, and obedience in a stable community life. The goal of monasticism is to pursue, under the guidance of a rule, a life of public prayer, work, and meditation for the glory of God. Saint Benedict of Nursia, who died about 550, is considered the father of Western monasticism. [monacato]

moral choice a choice to do what is right or not do what is wrong. We make moral choices because they are what we believe God wants and because we have the freedom to choose what is right and avoid what is wrong. [opción moral]

moral law a rule for living that has been established by God and people in authority who are concerned about the good of all. Moral laws are based on God's direction to us to do what is right and avoid what is wrong. Some moral laws are "written" in the human heart and can be known through our own reasoning. Other moral laws have been revealed to us by God in the Old Testament and in the new law given by Jesus. [ley moral]

mortal sin a serious decision to turn away from God by doing something that we know is wrong. For a sin to be mortal it must be a very serious offense, the person must know how serious the sin is, and freely chose to do it anyway. [pecado mortal]

Mother of God the title for Mary proclaimed at the Council of Ephesus in 431. The council declared that Mary was not just the mother of Jesus, the man. She became the Mother of God by the conception of the Son of God in her womb. Because Jesus' humanity is one with his divinity, Mary is the mother of the eternal Son of God made man, who is God himself. [Madre de Dios]

Muslim a follower of the religion of Islam. *Muslim* means "one who submits to God." [musulmán]

mystery a religious truth that we can know only through God's revelation and that we cannot fully understand. Our faith is a mystery that we profess in the creed and celebrate in the liturgy and sacraments. [misterio]

Mystical Body of Christ the members of the Church formed into a spiritual body and bound together by the life communicated by Jesus Christ through the sacraments. Christ is the center and source of the life of this body. In it, we are all are united. Each member of the body receives from Christ gifts fitting for him or her. [Cuerpo Místico de Cristo]

N

natural law the moral law that is "written" in the human heart. We can know natural law through our own reason because the Creator has placed the knowledge of it in our hearts. It can provide the solid foundation on which we can make rules to guide our choices in life. Natural law forms the basis of our fundamental rights and duties and is the foundation for the work of the Holy Spirit in guiding our moral choices. [ley natural]

New Testament the 27 books of the second part of the Bible which tell of the teaching, ministry, and saving events of the life of Jesus. The four Gospels present Jesus' life, death, and resurrection. The Acts of the Apostles tells the story of the message of salvation as it spread through the growth of the Church. Various letters instruct us in how to live as followers of Jesus Christ. The Book of Revelation offers encouragement to Christians living through persecution. [Nuevo Testamento]

New Testament

Nicene Creed the summary of Christian beliefs developed by the bishops at the first two councils of the Church, held in a.d. 325 and 381. It is the creed shared by most Christians, in the East and in the West. [Credo Niceno constantinopolitano]

O

obedience the act of willingly following what God asks us to do for our salvation. The fourth commandment requires children to obey their parents, and all people are required to obey civil authority when it acts for the good of all. To imitate the obedience of Jesus, members of religious communities make a special vow of obedience. [obediencia]

oil of catechumens the oil blessed by the bishop during Holy Week and used to anoint catechumens. This anointing strengthens them on their path to initiation into the Church. Infants are anointed with this oil right before they are baptized. [óleo de los catecúmenos]

oil of the sick the oil blessed by the bishop during Holy Week and used in the Sacrament of Anointing of the Sick, which brings spiritual and, if it is God's will, physical healing as well [óleo de los enfermos]

Old Testament the first 46 books of the Bible, which tell of God's covenant with the people of Israel and his plan for the salvation of all people. The first five books are known as the Torah. The Old Testament is fulfilled in the New Testament, but God's covenant presented in the Old Testament has permanent value and has never been revoked. [Antiguo Testamento]

one one of the four Marks of the Church. The Church is one because of its source in the one God and because of its founder, Jesus Christ. Jesus, through his death on the cross, united all to God in one body. Within the unity of the Church, there is great diversity because of the variety of the gifts given to its members. [una]

option for the poor the moral choice to address the needs of the poor. Their condition places an urgent claim on our consciences. Public policymakers need to first consider how their decisions affect the poor. The powerlessness of the poor wounds the entire community. A just society can be achieved only if its members give special attention to those who are poor and on the margins of society. It is a basic principle at the center of Catholic Social Teaching. [opción por los pobres]

Order of Penitents an order in the early Church consisting of baptized Christians who, because of sin, were in need of reconciliation with the community of the faithful. Those who had committed one of the three most serious sins—denying the faith, breaking the marriage bond, or committing murder—were required to spend a period of time in public repentance until the community was convinced of their sincerity. [orden de penitentes]

ordination the rite of the Sacrament of Holy Orders, by which a bishop gives to men, through the laying on of hands, the ability to minister to the Church as bishops, priests, and deacons [ordinación]

original sin the consequence of the disobedience of the first human beings. They disobeyed God and chose to follow their own will rather than God's will. As a result, human beings lost the original blessing God had intended and became subject to sin and death. In Baptism we are restored to life with God through Jesus Christ although we still experience the effects of original sin. [pecado original]

P

Palm Sunday the celebration of Jesus' triumphant entry into Jerusalem on the Sunday before Easter. It begins a week-long commemoration of the saving events of Holy Week. [Domingo de Ramos]

Palm Sunday

parable one of the simple stories that Jesus told to show us what the Kingdom of God is like. Parables present images drawn from everyday life. These images show us the radical choice we make when we respond to the invitation to enter the Kingdom of God. [parábola]

parish a stable community of believers in Jesus Christ who meet regularly in a specific area to worship God under the leadership of a pastor [parroquia]

participation one of the seven principles of Catholic Social Teaching. All people have a right to participate in the economic, political, and cultural life of society. It is a requirement for human dignity and a demand of justice that all people have a minimum level of participation in the community. [participación]

particular judgment a judgment made by Christ received by every person at the moment of death that offers either entrance into heaven (after a period of purification, if needed) or immediate and eternal separation from God in hell. At the moment of death, each person is rewarded by Christ in accordance with his or her works and faith. [juicio particular]

Paschal Mystery the work of salvation accomplished by Jesus Christ through his passion, death, Resurrection, and Ascension. The Paschal Mystery is celebrated in the liturgy of the Church, and we experience its saving effects in the sacraments. In every liturgy of the Church, God the Father is blessed and adored as the source of all blessings we have received through his Son in order to make us his children through the Holy Spirit. [Misterio Pascual]

Passover the Jewish festival that commemorates the delivery of the Hebrew people from slavery in Egypt. In the Eucharist we celebrate our passover from death to life through Jesus' death and resurrection. [Pascua Judía]

Passover plate

pastor a priest who is responsible for the spiritual care of the members of a parish community. It is the job of the pastor to see that the Word of God is preached, the faith is taught, and sacraments are celebrated. [párroco]

penance the turning away from sin with a desire to change our life and more closely live the way God wants us to live. We express our penance externally by praying, fasting, and helping the poor. This is also the name of the action that the priest asks us take or the prayers that he asks us to pray after he absolves us in the Sacrament of Penance. (See Sacrament of Penance.) [penitencia]

Pentecost the 50th day after Jesus was raised from the dead. On this day the Holy Spirit was sent from heaven, and the Church was born. It is also the Jewish feast that celebrated the giving of the Ten Commandments on Mount Sinai 50 days after the Exodus. [Pentecostés]

People of God another name for the Church. In the same way that the people of Israel were God's people through the Covenant he made with them, the Church is a priestly, prophetic, and royal people through the new and eternal Covenant with Jesus Christ. [Pueblo de Dios]

personal prayer the kind of prayer that rises up in us in everyday life. We pray with others in the liturgy, but in addition we can listen and respond to God through personal prayer every moment of our lives. [oración personal]

personal sin a sin we choose to commit, whether serious (mortal) or less serious (venial). Although the consequences of original sin leave us with a tendency to sin, God's grace, especially through the sacraments, helps us to choose good over sin. [pecado personal]

petition a request to God asking him to fulfill a need. When we share in God's saving love, we understand that every need is one that we can ask God to help us with through petition. [petición]

Pharisees a party or sect in Judaism that began more than 100 years before Jesus. They saw Judaism as a religion centered on the observance of the Law. The Gospels present a picture of mutual hostility between Jesus and the Pharisees. Pharisees were later found in the Christian community in Jerusalem. (Acts of the Apostles 15:5) Paul was proud to call himself a Pharisee. [fariseos]

piety one of the seven Gifts of the Holy Spirit. It calls us to be faithful in our relationships both with God and with others. Piety helps us to love God and to behave responsibly and with generosity and affection toward others. [piedad]

pope the bishop of Rome, successor of Saint Peter, and leader of the Roman Catholic Church. Because he has the authority to act in the name of Christ, the pope is called the Vicar of Christ. The pope and all of the bishops together make up the living, teaching office of the Church, the Magisterium. [Papa]

Pentecost

praise the expression of our response to God, not only for what he does, but simply because he is. In the Eucharist the whole Church joins with Jesus Christ in expressing praise and thanksgiving to the Father. [alabanza]

prayer the raising of our hearts and minds to God. We are able to speak to and listen to God in prayer because he teaches us how to pray. [oración]

prayers of intercession a prayer of petition in which we pray as Jesus did to the Father on behalf of people. Asking on behalf of others is a characteristic of a heart attuned to God's mercy. Christian intercession recognizes no boundaries. We pray for all people—for the rich, for political leaders, for those in need, and even for persecutors. [oración de intersección]

Precepts of the Church those positive requirements that the pastoral authority of the Church has determined are necessary to provide a minimum effort in prayer and the moral life. The Precepts of the Church ensure that all Catholics move beyond the minimum by growing in love of God and love of neighbor. [preceptos de la Iglesia]

presbyter a word that originally meant "an elder or trusted advisor to the bishop." From this word comes the English word *priest*, one of the three degrees of the Sacrament of Holy Orders. All the priests of a diocese under the bishop form the presbyterate. [presbítero]

pride a false image of ourselves that goes beyond what we deserve as God's creation. Pride puts us in competition with God. It is one of the seven capital sins. [soberbia]

priest a man who has accepted God's special call to serve the Church by guiding it and building it up through the ministry of the Word and the celebration of the sacraments [sacerdote]

priesthood all the people of God who have been given a share of the one mission of Christ through the Sacraments of Baptism and Confirmation. The ministerial priesthood, which is made up of those men who have been ordained bishops and priests in Holy Orders, is essentially different from the priesthood of all the faithful because its work is to build up and guide the Church in the name of Christ. [sacerdocio]

Promised Land the land first promised by God to Abraham. It was to this land that God told Moses to lead the Chosen People after they were freed from slavery in Egypt and received the Ten Commandments at Mount Sinai. [Tierra Prometida]

the prophet Isaiah

prophet one called to speak for God and call the people to be faithful to the covenant. A major section of the Old Testament presents, in eighteen books, the messages and actions of the prophets. [profeta]

prudence the virtue that directs us toward the good and helps us to choose the correct means to achieve that good. When we act with prudence, we carefully and thoughtfully consider our actions. Prudence is one of the cardinal moral virtues that guide our conscience and influence us to live according to the law of Christ. [prudencia]

psalm a prayer in the form of a poem, written to be sung in public worship. Each psalm expresses an aspect of the depth of human prayer. Over several centuries 150 psalms were assembled into the Book of Psalms in the Old Testament. Psalms were used in worship in the Temple in Jerusalem, and they have been used in the public worship of the Church since its beginning. [salmo]

purgatory a state of final cleansing after death of all of our human imperfections to prepare us to enter into the joy of God's presence in heaven [purgatorio]

R

racism the opinion that race determines human traits and capacities and that a particular race has an inherent, or inborn, superiority. Discrimination based on a person's race is a violation of human dignity and a sin against justice. [racismo]

rationalism an approach to philosophy developed by René Descartes. It dominated European thought in the 17th and 18th Centuries. The main belief of rationalism was that human reason is the principle source of all knowledge. It stresses confidence in the orderly character of the world and in the mind's ability to make sense of this order. Rationalism recognizes as true only those religious beliefs that can be rationally explained. [racionalismo]

Real Presence the way in which the risen Jesus Christ is present in the Eucharist under the form of bread and wine. Jesus Christ's presence is called real because in the Eucharist his body and blood, soul and divinity, are wholly and entirely present. [Presencia real]

reconciliation the renewal of friendship after that friendship has been broken by some action or lack of action. In the Sacrament of Penance, through God's mercy and forgiveness, we are reconciled with God, the Church, and others. [reconciliación]

Redeemer Jesus Christ, whose life, sacrificial death on the cross, and resurrection from the dead set us free from the slavery of sin and bring us redemption [Redentor]

redemption our being set free from the slavery of sin through the life, sacrificial death on the cross, and resurrection from the dead of Jesus Christ [redención]

reform to put an end to a wrong by introducing a better or changed course of action. The prophets called people to reform their lives by returning to being faithful to their covenant with God. [reformarse]

religious life a state of life recognized by the Church. In the religious life, men and women freely respond to a call to follow Jesus by living the vows of poverty, chastity, and obedience in community with others. [vida religiosa]

repentance our turning away from sin, with a desire to change our lives and live more closely as God wants us to live. We express our penance externally by prayer, fasting, and helping the poor. [arrepentimiento]

Resurrection the bodily raising of Jesus Christ from the dead on the third day after his death on the cross. The Resurrection is the crowning truth of our faith. [Resurrección]

Revelation God's communication of himself to us through the words and deeds he has used throughout history to show us the mystery of his plan for our salvation. This Revelation reaches its completion in his sending of his Son, Jesus Christ. [revelación]

righteousness an attribute of God used to describe his justice, his faithfulness to the covenant, and his holiness in the Old Testament. As an attribute of humans, righteousness means being in a right relationship with God through moral conduct and observance of the Law. We have merit in God's sight and are able to do this because of the work of God's grace in us. Paul speaks of righteousness in a new way that is no longer dependent on observance of the Law. It comes through faith in Jesus and his saving death and Resurrection. To be made righteous in Jesus is to be saved, vindicated, and put right with God through his grace. [Justicia]

rights and responsibilities the fundamental right to life and a right to those things required to live in a decent manner. This right belongs to every person. It includes the right to food, shelter, clothing, employment, health care, and education. Corresponding to these rights are responsibilities to one another, to our families, and to the larger society. As Catholics we have a responsibility to protect these basic human rights in order to achieve a healthy society. It is one of the seven themes of Catholic Social Teaching. [derechos y deberes]

rite one of the many forms followed in celebrating liturgy in the Church. A rite may differ according to the culture or country where it is celebrated. Rite also means the special form for celebrating each sacrament. [rito]

Rosary a prayer in honor of the Blessed Virgin Mary. When we pray the Rosary, we meditate on the mysteries of Jesus Christ's life while praying the Hail Mary on five sets of ten beads and the Lord's Prayer on the beads in between. In the Latin Church, praying the Rosary became a way for ordinary people to reflect on the mysteries of Christ's life. [rosario]

S

Sabbath the seventh day, when God rested after finishing the work of creation. The third commandment requires us to keep the Sabbath holy. For Christians the Sabbath became Sunday, the Lord's Day, because it was the day Jesus rose from the dead and the new creation in Jesus Christ began. [sabat]

sacrament one of seven official rites through which God's life enters our lives in the liturgy through the work of the Holy Spirit. Christ's work in the liturgy is sacramental because his mystery is made present there by the power of the Holy Spirit. Jesus gave us three sacraments that bring us into the Church: Baptism, Confirmation, and the Eucharist. He gave us two sacraments that bring us healing: Penance and Anointing of the Sick. He also gave us two sacraments that help members serve the community: Matrimony and Holy Orders. (*See* also sacramental.) [sacramento]

Sacrament of Penance the sacrament in which we celebrate God's forgiveness of sin and our reconciliation with God and the Church. Penance includes sorrow for the sins we have committed, confession of sins, absolution by the priest, and doing the penance that shows our willingness to amend our ways. [Sacramento de la penitencia]

sacramental an object, a prayer, or a blessing given by the Church to help us grow in our spiritual life [sacramental]

Sacraments at the Service of Communion the Sacraments of Holy Orders and Matrimony. These two sacraments contribute to the personal salvation of individuals by giving them a way to serve others. [sacramentos al servicio de la comunidad]

Sacraments of Healing the Sacraments of Penance and Anointing of the Sick, by which the Church continues the healing ministry of Jesus for soul and body [sacramentos de sanación]

oils used in sacraments

Sacraments of Initiation the sacraments that are the foundation of our Christian life. We are born anew in Baptism, strengthened by Confirmation, and receive in the Eucharist the food of eternal life. By means of these sacraments, we receive an increasing measure of divine life and advance toward the perfection of charity. [sacramentos de iniciación]

sacrifice a ritual offering of animals or produce made to God by the priest in the Temple in Jerusalem. Sacrifice was a sign of the people's adoration of God, giving thanks to God, or asking for his forgiveness. Sacrifice also showed union with God. The great high priest, Christ, accomplished our redemption through the perfect sacrifice of his death on the cross. [sacrificio]

Sacrifice of the Mass the sacrifice of Jesus on the cross, which is remembered and mysteriously made present in the Eucharist. It is offered in reparation for the sins of the living and the dead and to obtain spiritual or temporal blessings from God. [sacrificio de la misa]

saint a holy person who has died united with God. The Church has said that this person is now with God forever in heaven. [santo]

salvation the gift, which God alone can give, of forgiveness of sin and the restoration of friendship with him [salvación]

sanctifying grace the gift of God, given to us without our earning it, that introduces us to the intimacy of the Trinity, unites us with its life, and heals our human nature, wounded by sin. Sanctifying grace helps us respond to our vocation as God's adopted children, and it continues the work of making us holy that began at our Baptism. (*See* actual grace *and* grace) [gracia santificante]

Satan a fallen angel. The enemy of anyone attempting to follow God's will. Satan tempts Jesus in the Gospels and opposes his ministry. In Jewish, Christian, and Muslim thought, Satan is associated with those angels who refused to bow down before human beings and serve them as God commanded. They refused to serve God and were thrown out of heaven as a punishment. Satan and the other demons tempt human beings to join them in their revolt against God. [Satanás]

Savior Jesus, the Son of God, who became human to forgive our sins and restore our friendship with God. *Jesus* means "God saves." [Salvador]

scriptorium the room in a monastery in which books were copied by hand. Often, beautiful art was created on the page to illustrate the story. [scriptorium]

Scriptures the holy writings of Jews and Christians collected in the Old and New Testaments of the Bible [Sagrada Escritura]

Second Vatican Council the 21st and most recent ecumenical council of the Catholic Church. It met from October 11, 1962 to December 8, 1965. Its purpose, according to Blessed Pope John XXIII, was to renew the Church and to help it promote peace and unity among Christians and all humanity. [Concilio Vaticano Segundo]

seraphim the heavenly beings who worship before the throne of God. One of them purified the lips of Isaiah with a burning coal so that he could speak for God. [seraphines]

Sermon on the Mount the words of Jesus, written in Chapters 5 through 7 of the Gospel of Matthew, in which Jesus reveals how he has fulfilled God's law given to Moses. The Sermon on the Mount begins with the eight Beatitudes and includes the Lord's Prayer. [Sermón de la Montaña]

sexism a prejudice or discrimination based on sex, especially discrimination against women. Sexism leads to behaviors and attitudes that foster a view of social roles based only on sex. [sexismo]

sin a deliberate thought, word, deed, or failure to act that offends God and hurts our relationships with other people. Some sin is mortal and needs to be confessed in the Sacrament of Penance. Other sin is venial, or less serious. [pecado]

sloth a carelessness of heart that leads a person to ignore his or her development as a person, especially spiritual development and a relationship with God. Sloth is one of the seven capital sins, and it is contrary to the first commandment. [pereza]

social justice the fair and equal treatment of every member of society. It is required by the dignity and freedom of every person. The Catholic Church has developed a body of social principles and moral teachings described in papal and other official documents issued since the late 19th century. This teaching deals with the economic, political, and social order of the world. It is rooted in the Bible as well as in the traditional theological teachings of the Church. [justicia social]

social sin social situations and institutions that are against the will of God. Because of the personal sins of individuals, entire societies can develop structures that are sinful in and of themselves. Social sins include racism, sexism, structures that deny people access

Sermon on the Mount

to adequate health care, and the destruction of the environment for the benefit of a few. [pecado social]

solidarity the attitude of strength and unity that leads to the sharing of spiritual and material goods. Solidarity unites rich and poor, weak and strong, to create a society in which all give what they can and receive what they need. The idea of solidarity is based on the common origin of all humanity. [solidaridad]

Son of God the title revealed by Jesus that indicates his unique relationship to God the Father. The revelation of Jesus' divine sonship is the main dramatic development of the story of Jesus of Nazareth as it unfolds in the Gospels. [Hijo de Dios]

soul the part of us that makes us human and an image of God. Body and soul together form one unique human nature. The soul is responsible for our consciousness and for our freedom. The soul does not die and is reunited with the body in the final resurrection. [alma]

spirituality our growing, loving relationship with God. Spirituality is our way of expressing our experience of God in both the way we pray and the way we love our neighbor. There are many different schools of spirituality. Some examples of these schools are the monastic, Franciscan, Jesuit, and lay. These are guides for the spiritual life and have enriched the traditions of prayer, worship, and living in Christianity. [espiritualidad]

Spiritual Works of Mercy the kind acts through which we help our neighbors meet the needs that are more than material. The Spiritual Works of Mercy include instructing, advising, consoling, comforting, forgiving, and bearing wrongs with patience. [obras espirituales de misericordia]

Stations of the Cross a tool for meditating on the final hours of Jesus' life, from his condemnation by Pilate to his death and burial. We do this by moving to representations of 14 incidents, each one based on the traditional sites in Jerusalem where these incidents took place. [Estaciones del Vía crucis]

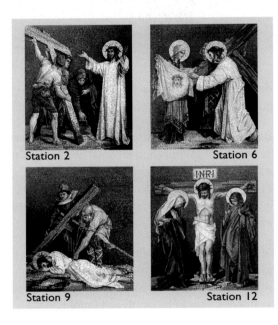

Station 2
Station 6
Station 9
Station 12

stewardship the careful and responsible management of something entrusted to one's care, especially the goods of creation, which are intended for the whole human race. The sixth precept of the Church makes clear our part in this stewardship by requiring us to provide for the material needs of the Church according to our abilities. [mayordomía]

subsidiarity the principle that the best institutions for responding to a particular social task are those closest to it. It is the responsibility of the closest political or private institution to assist those in need. Only when issues cannot be resolved at the lower local level should they be resolved at a higher level. [subsidiaridad]

Summa Theologiae the major work of Saint Thomas Aquinas that organized and clarified thinking on many religious topics in the 13th century. In it Thomas addressed topics such as proofs for the existence of God, the nature of the human soul, making moral decisions, the Incarnation, and transubstantiation. [Suma Teológica]

synagogue the Jewish place of assembly for prayer, instruction, and study of the Law. After the destruction of the Temple in 587 B.C. synagogues were organized as places to maintain Jewish faith and worship. Jesus attended the synagogue regularly for prayer and to teach. Paul went to the synagogue first in every city he visited. The synagogue played an important role in the development of Christian worship and in the structure of Christian communities. [sinagoga]

Synoptic from the Greek word meaning to "see together" that describes the Gospels of Matthew, Mark, and Luke. These are called the Synoptic Gospels because although they are different from one another, there are similarities that can be seen by looking at them together. Most Scripture scholars agree that Mark was the first Gospel written and that Matthew and Luke used Mark as the pattern for their Gospels. [sinópticos]

T

tabernacle the container in which the Blessed Sacrament is kept so that Holy Communion can be taken to the sick and the dying. *Tabernacle* is also the name of the tent sanctuary in which the Israelites kept the Ark of the Covenant from the time of the Exodus to the construction of Solomon's temple. [sagrario]

temperance the cardinal virtue that helps us to control our attraction to pleasure so that our natural desires are kept within proper limits. This moral virtue helps us choose to use created goods in moderation. [templanza]

Temple the house of worship of God, first built by Solomon. The Temple provided a place for the priests to offer sacrifice, to adore and give thanks to God, and to ask for forgiveness. It was destroyed and rebuilt. The second Temple was also destroyed, this time by the Romans in a.d. 70, and was never rebuilt. Part of the outer wall of the Temple mount remains to this day in Jerusalem. [templo]

temptation an attraction, from outside us or inside us, that can lead us to disobey God's commands. Everyone is tempted, but the Holy Spirit helps us to resist temptation and choose to do good. [tentación]

Ten Commandments the ten rules given by God to Moses on Mount Sinai that sum up God's law and show us what is required to love God and our neighbor. By following the Ten Commandments, the Hebrews accepted their covenant with God. [Diez Mandamientos]

Theological Virtues those virtues given us by God and not by human effort. They are faith, hope, and charity. [virtudes teologales]

Torah the Hebrew word for "instruction" or "law." It is also the name of the first five books of the Old Testament: Genesis, Exodus, Leviticus, Numbers, and Deuteronomy. [Torá]

Torah

Tradition the beliefs and practices of the Church that are passed down from one generation to the next under the guidance of the Holy Spirit. What Christ entrusted to the apostles was handed on to others both orally and in writing. Tradition and Scripture together make up the single deposit of faith, which remains present and active in the Church. [Tradición]

transubstantiation the unique change of the bread and wine in the Eucharist into the body and blood of the risen Jesus Christ, while retaining its physical appearance as bread and wine [transubstanciación]

trespasses unlawful acts committed against the property or rights of another person or acts that physically harm a person [ofensas]

Trinity the mystery of the existence of God in three Persons, the Father, the Son, and the Holy Spirit. Each Person is God, whole and entire. Each is distinct only in relationship of each to the others. [Trinidad]

Trinity

U

understanding one of the seven Gifts of the Holy Spirit. This gift helps us make the right choices in life and in our relationships with God and others. [entendimiento]

universal Church the entire Church as it exists throughout the world. The people of every diocese, along with their bishops and the pope, make up the universal Church. [Iglesia universal]

V

venial sin a choice we make that weakens our relationship with God or other people. Venial sin wounds and lessens the divine life in us. If we make no effort to do better, venial sin can lead to more serious sin. Through our participation in the Eucharist, venial sin is forgiven when we are repentant, strengthening our relationship with God and others. [pecado venial]

viaticum the Eucharist that a dying person receives. It is spiritual food for the last journey we make as Christians, the journey through death to eternal life. [viático]

Vicar of Christ the title given to the pope who, as the successor of Saint Peter, has the authority to act in Christ's place. A vicar is someone who stands in for and acts for another. [Vicario de Cristo]

virtue an attitude or way of acting that enables us do good [virtud]

Visitation Mary's visit to Elizabeth to share the good news that Mary is to be the mother of Jesus. Elizabeth's greeting of Mary forms part of the Hail Mary. During this visit, Mary sings the Magnificat, her praise of God. [Visitación]

vocation the call each of us has in life to be the person God wants each to be and the way we each serve the Church and the Kingdom of God. Each of us can live out his or her vocation as a layperson, as a member of a religious community, or as a member of the clergy. [vocación]

vow a deliberate and free promise made to God by people who want especially to dedicate their lives to God. The vows give witness now to the kingdom that is to come. [voto]

Vulgate the Latin translation of the Bible by Saint Jerome from the Hebrew and Greek it was originally written in. Most Christians of Saint Jerome's day no longer spoke Hebrew or Greek. The common language, or vulgate, was Latin. [Vulgata]

illumination
from a 7th century
calfskin Vulgate

W

wisdom one of the seven Gifts of the Holy Spirit. Wisdom helps us to understand the purpose and plan of God and to live in a way that helps to bring about this plan. It begins in wonder and awe at God's greatness. [sabiduría]

Wisdom Literature the Old Testament books of Job, Proverbs, Ecclesiastes, the Song of Songs, Wisdom, and Sirach. The purpose of these books is to give instruction on ways to live and how to understand and cope with the problems of life. [Libros sapienciales]

witness the passing on to others, by our words and by our actions, the faith that we have been given. Every Christian has the duty to give witness to the good news about Jesus Christ that he or she has come to know. [testimonio]

worship the adoration and honor given to God in public prayer [culto]

Y

Yahweh the name of God in Hebrew, which God told Moses from the burning bush. Yahweh means "I am who am" or "I cause to be all that is." [Yavé]

Glosario

A

Abba vocablo familiar que significa *"padre"* en arameo, idioma que hablaba Jesús. Viene a ser como "papá" en español. Al hablar con Dios Padre, Jesús le decía *Abba*. [Abba]

aborto terminación deliberada de un embarazo, resultando en la muerte de la criatura no nacida. La Iglesia enseña que la vida comienza en el momento de la concepción, por tanto el aborto es un serio crimen contra la vida y contrario a la ley moral. [abortion]

Abraham modelo de fe en Dios en el Antiguo Testamento. Por su fe, dejó su hogar y se trasladó a Canán, donde Dios hizo una alianza con él y le prometió tierra y muchos descendientes. Abraham se convirtió en el padre del pueblo escogido. [Abraham]

absolución perdón que recibimos de Dios por medio del sacerdote en el sacramento de la penitencia. [absolution]

adulterio un agravio a los votos matrimoniales. Ocurre cuando dos personas tienen relaciones amorosas y una de ellas está casada con otra persona. El sexto mandamiento prohíbe el adulterio porque menoscaba la institución del matrimonio y hace mucho daño a los niños para quienes la estabilidad del compromiso matrimonial de sus padres es muy importante. [adultery]

Adviento las cuatro semanas antes de la Navidad. Es una época de jubilosa preparación para la celebración de la Encarnación, el nacimiento de Jesús como nuestro salvador, y la espera de la venida de Jesucristo en el fin de los tiempos. [Advent]

agua bendita agua que ha sido bendecida y que se usa como sacramental para recordarnos nuestro bautismo. [holy water]

alabanza la expresión de nuestra respuesta a Dios no sólo por lo que hace sino por quien es. En la Eucaristía, la Iglesia entera se une a Jesucristo para alabar y dar gracias al Padre. [praise]

alianza pacto solemne que hacen las personas entre sí o que hacen las personas con Dios. Dios hizo alianzas con la humanidad mediante los pactos hechos con Noé, Abraham y Moisés. Estas alianzas ofrecían salvación. La nueva y definitiva alianza de Dios fue pactada mediante la vida, muerte y resurrección de Jesús. *Testamento* es sinónimo de *alianza*. [covenant]

alma parte de la persona que la hace humana e imagen de Dios. Juntos, el cuerpo y el alma forman una naturaleza humana única. El alma es responsable de nuestra conciencia y de nuestra libertad. El alma no muere y se reune con el cuerpo en la resurrección final. [soul]

altar mesa que tienen las iglesias en la que el sacerdote celebra la Misa. En la Misa, el sacrificio de Cristo en la cruz se hace presente en el sacramento de la Eucaristía. El altar representa dos aspectos del misterio de la Eucaristía: en primer lugar, es el sitio donde Jesucristo se ofrece a sí mismo por nuestros pecados; y, en segundo, es el sitio donde Él se da a nosotros como alimento de vida eterna. [altar]

ambón plataforma elevada desde donde una persona proclama la Palabra de Dios durante la Misa. [ambo]

Amén vocablo hebreo usado al final de las oraciones judías y cristianas que quiere decir "es verdad", "así es", o "así sea". Al terminar nuestras oraciones, decimos *Amén* para dar a entender que lo que acabamos de decir va en serio. [Amen]

ángel criatura espiritual que adora a Dios en el cielo. Los ángeles sirven a Dios como mensajeros y nos cuentan los planes que Él tiene para nuestra salvación. [angel]

Año litúrgico las celebraciones en el transcurso del año de todos los misterios del nacimiento, vida, muerte, y resurrección de Jesús. La Pascua es la celebración central del Año litúrgico. Las otras fiestas celebradas a lo largo del año constituyen el ritmo básico de la vida de oración del cristiano. [liturgical year]

Antiguo Testamento los primeros 46 libros de la Biblia que hablan de la alianza de Dios con el pueblo de Israel y su plan de salvación para todas las gentes. Los cinco primeros libros se conocen como la Torá. El Antiguo Testamento se cumple en el Nuevo Testamento, pero la alianza de Dios presentada en la escritura del Antiguo Testamento sigue teniendo un valor permanente y nunca ha sido revocada. [Old Testament]

anulación conclusiòn a la que llega un tribunal de la Iglesia de que al menos un elemento esencial para un verdadero matrimonio no estaba presente el día de la boda. La Iglesia puede declarar que el sacramento del Matrimonio no tuvo lugar si al menos una de las partes no escogió libremente casarse, había estado casada antes y el matrimonio no fue anulado o no estaba dispuesta a tener hijos. La anulación no puede iniciarse hasta que la persona esté divorciada. Los católicos que reciben una anulación quedan en libertad de casarse por la Iglesia y pueden recibir la Comunión. [annulment]

Anunciación anuncio traído a María por el ángel Gabriel de que Dios la había elegido para ser madre de Jesús. Al aceptar María, el Hijo de Dios se hizo hombre dentro de ella. La solemnidad de la Anunciación se celebra el 25 de marzo, nueve meses antes de la Navidad. [Annunciation]

apóstol uno de doce hombres singulares que acompañaron a Jesús en su ministerio y fueron testigos de su resurrección. *Apóstol* quiere decir "enviado". Los apóstoles fueron los enviados a predicar el Evangelio al mundo entero. [apostle]

apostólica uno de los cuatro calificativos de la Iglesia. La Iglesia es apostólica porque sigue transmitiendo las enseñanzas de los apóstoles a través de sus sucesores, los obispos, en unión con el sucesor de San Pedro, el Papa. [apostolic]

Arca de la Alianza caja portátil donde se guardaban las tablas de los Diez Mandamientos. El Arca, objeto más importante del santuario, fue transportada por todo el desierto y luego colocada en la parte más sagrada del Templo de Jerusalén. Sobre la tapa del Arca de la Alianza se encontraban dos ángeles cuyas alas se curvaban hacia arriba, representando el sitio donde Dios se acercó a Israel y le reveló su voluntad. [Ark of the Covenant]

arrepentimiento el apartarnos del pecado con el deseo de cambiar nuestra vida y acercarnos más a la forma de vida que Dios quiere que vivamos. Expresamos externamente nuestra penitencia mediante la oración, el ayuno, y ayudando a los pobres. [repentance]

asamblea pueblo de Dios congregado para rendirle culto. [assembly]

Ascensión entrada de Jesús a la gloria divina junto al Padre. En los Hechos de los Apóstoles, se escribe que, después de la resurrección, Jesús estuvo 40 días en la tierra instruyendo a sus seguidores, y luego volvió al cielo junto a su Padre. [Ascension]

Asunción el momento en que María fue elevada al cielo en cuerpo y alma. María tuvo una relación especial con su Hijo Jesús, desde el momento en que fue concebido en su seno. A causa de esta relación, ella disfruta de una participación especial en la resurrección de Jesús y fue llevada al cielo donde ahora vive con Él. Este acontecimiento lo celebramos en la solemnidad de la Asunción, el 15 de agosto. [Assumption]

ayuno limitar la cantidad de alimento que comemos por un tiempo determinado para expresar arrepentimiento por nuestros pecados y hacernos más conscientes de la acción de Dios en nuestra vida. Los adultos, de dieciocho años o más, ayunan el Miércoles de Ceniza y Viernes Santo. Se fomenta también esta práctica como devoción privada en otras ocasiones de penitencia. [fasting]

B

báculo cayado o vara que lleva el Obispo. Al llevar este cayado, el Obispo muestra que vela por nosotros de la misma forma en que el pastor cuida sus ovejas. También nos recuerda que él representa a Jesús, el Buen Pastor. [crozier]

Bautismo el primero de los siete sacramentos. El Bautismo nos libera del pecado original y es necesario para la salvación. El Bautismo nos da una vida nueva en Jesucristo por medio del Espíritu Santo. La celebración del bautismo consiste en sumergir en agua a la persona diciendo que es bautizado ". . . en el nombre del Padre, del Hijo, y del Espíritu Santo". [Baptism]

bendición oración que invoca el poder y amparo de Dios por una persona, lugar, cosa, o una actividad específica. [blessing]

Biblia la colección de libros que contienen las verdades de la revelación hecha a nosotros por Dios. Estos libros fueron inspirados por el Espíritu Santo y escritos por seres humanos. La Biblia se compone de 46 libros del Antiguo Testamento y 27 del Nuevo Testamento. [Bible]

Bienaventuranzas enseñanzas de Jesús en el Sermón de la Montaña del Evangelio de san Mateo. Las Bienaventuranzas son ocho formas de llevar una vida cristiana y son la culminación de los mandamientos dados por medio de Moisés. Estas enseñanzas nos presentan el camino a la verdadera felicidad. [Beatitudes]

bien común suma total de condiciones sociales que permiten a las personas, individualmente y como grupo, alcanzar su pleno potencial. Esto requiere paz, seguridad, respeto a los derechos de cada uno y satisfacer las necesidades espirituales y materiales individuales. Las personas tienen la responsabilidad de contribuir al bien de toda la sociedad. Es uno de los principios básicos de la Doctrina Social Católica. [common good]

blasfemia cualquier acción, palabra o pensamiento de odio o rebeldía contra Dios. Incluye palabras que son irrespetuosas hacia la Iglesia, los santos o las cosas sagradas. También es una blasfemia usar el nombre de Dios como excusa para esclavizar a la gente, torturarla o matarla. Cuando se usa el nombre de Dios para hacer esas cosas, puede ser la causa de que otros rechacen la religión. [blasphemy]

budismo religión basada en las enseñanzas de Siddhartha Gautama, conocido como Buda, nombre que significa "El Iluminado". Buda nació en una familia de la nobleza en el norte de la India unos 550 años antes de Jesús. A la edad de 29 años se sintió desilusionado con la vida y abandonó la comodidad de su hogar para buscar una respuesta a la pregunta de por qué los seres humanos sufren. [Buddhism]

C

calificativos de la Iglesia las cuatro características más importantes de la Iglesia que se hallan en el Credo Niceno constantinopolitano. Según este credo, la Iglesia es una, santa, católica y apostólica. [Marks of the Church]

calumnia declaración falsa acerca de la reputación de alguien, que hace al resto de las personas pensar mal de esa persona. La calumnia, también llamada difamación, es un pecado contra el Octavo Mandamiento. [calumny]

canonizar declaración hecha por la Iglesia de que un cristiano difunto está ya en el cielo y puede servir de ejemplo de vida cristiana e interceder por nosotros como santo. [canonize]

carácter señal espiritual permanente. El carácter muestra que la persona ha entablado una nueva relación con Jesús y ha llegado a un nivel especial en la Iglesia. El Bautismo, la Confirmación y el Orden sagrado imprimen un carácter permanente; y, por eso, sólo pueden ser recibidos una sola vez. [character]

caridad virtud dada a nosotros por Dios. La caridad nos permite amar a Dios sobre todas las cosas y al prójimo como a nosotros mismos. [charity]

castidad la integración de nuestra sexualidad física con nuestra naturaleza espiritual. La castidad permite que seamos completamente humanos, capaces de dar a otros por entero nuestra vida y amor. Todos, casados o solteros, somos llamados a observar la castidad. [chastity]

catecúmeno persona que está recibiendo formación cristiana mediante instrucción y el ejemplo de la comunidad. Por medio de la conversión y madurez de fe, el catecúmeno se prepara para ser recibido en el seno de la Iglesia en la Pascua a través de los sacramentos del Bautismo, Confirmación y Eucaristía. [catechumen]

católica una de los cuatro calificativos de la Iglesia. La Iglesia es católica porque Jesús se halla plenamente presente en ella, porque proclama la plenitud de la fe y porque Jesús ha dicho que la misión de la Iglesia es para toda la tierra. [catholic]

celebración eucarística culto público rendido por la Iglesia en el cual se consagran el pan y el vino para que se conviertan en Cuerpo y Sangre de Jesucristo. La celebración dominical de la liturgia eucarística es el eje central de la vida eclesial. [Eucharistic liturgy]

cielo unión con Dios Padre, Hijo y Espíritu Santo en vida y amor que nunca acaba. El cielo es el estado de felicidad completa y es la meta de los deseos más profundos del corazón humano. [heaven]

clero varones elegidos como ministros sagrados para servir a la Iglesia a través del orden sagrado. [clergy]

Comunión de los Santos unidad de todos los que se han salvado en Jesucristo, vivos o muertos. La Comunión de los Santos se basa en nuestra fe única y se nutre de nuestra participación en la Eucaristía. [Communion of Saints]

conciencia voz interior que nos ayuda a cada uno a conocer la ley de Dios para que cada persona pueda juzgar las cualidades morales de sus acciones. La conciencia nos guía a hacer el bien y evitar el mal. [conscience]

Concilio de Jerusalén nombre de la reunión que tuvo lugar en el año 50 D.C., descrita en el capítulo 15 de los Hechos de los Apóstoles. La reunión se produjo como resultado de un desacuerdo entre Pablo y sus seguidores con los cristianos de origen judío, seguidores de Santiago, dirigente de la Iglesia en Jerusalén. Santiago pensaba que aquellos que se hacían cristianos debían también observar las reglas del judaísmo tradicional y que, por lo tanto, los hombres debían ser circuncidados. Pablo decía que esto no era necesario. Finalmente, se acordó que la circuncisión no era necesaria para los gentiles que se hacían cristianos. [Council of Jerusalem]

concilio ecuménico reunión de los obispos católicos del mundo entero bajo el liderazgo del Papa o sus legados. Los concilios ecuménicos tratan asuntos pastorales, legales y doctrinales. La Iglesia Católica reconoce 21 concilios ecuménicos. El primero fue el Concilio de Nicea, que tuvo lugar en el año 325. El más reciente fue el Concilio Vaticano Segundo que tuvo lugar entre 1962 y 1965. [ecumenical council]

Concilio Vaticano Segundo el vigésimo primero y más reciente concilio ecuménico de la Iglesia Católica. Se reunió del 11 de octubre de 1962 al 8 de diciembre de 1965. Sus propósitos, de acuerdo al Beato Juan XXIII, fueron renovar la Iglesia y ayudarla a promover la paz y la unidad entre los cristianos y toda la humanidad. [Second Vatican Council]

confesión acto de contar nuestros pecados al sacerdote en el sacramento de la penitencia. Al sacramento mismo se le suele llamar "confesión". [confession]

Confirmación sacramento que da plenitud a la gracia que recibimos en el Bautismo. La confirmación sella, o confirma esta gracia a través de los siete dones del Espíritu Santo que recibimos como parte de la confirmación. Este sacramento también nos hace más capaces de participar en la Liturgia y en la vida apostólica de la Iglesia. [Confirmation]

conmemoración recuerdo de sucesos ocurridos en el pasado. Recordamos estos sucesos porque nos siguen afectando en el presente ya que son parte del plan de salvación que Dios tiene para nosotros. Cada vez que recordamos estos acontecimientos, hacemos presente la acción redentora de Dios. [memorial]

conocimiento uno de los siete dones del Espíritu Santo que nos permite saber lo que Dios nos pide y cómo debemos responder. [knowledge]

consagración el hacer a una cosa o persona especial ante los ojos de Dios por medio de una oración o bendición. En la Misa, las palabras del sacerdote son una consagración que hace que el Cuerpo y Sangre de Cristo se hagan presentes en el pan y el vino. Las personas y objetos dedicados a Dios de forma especial también son consagrados. Por ejemplo, las iglesias y altares son consagrados para su uso en la liturgia. Del mismo modo, los obispos son consagrados al recibir la plenitud del sacerdocio. [consecration]

consejo uno de los siete dones del Espíritu Santo. El consejo nos ayuda a reflexionar sobre cómo tomar decisiones apropiadas en la vida, a través de la reflexión, el discernimiento, la consulta, y el consejo de otros. [counsel]

consolador nombre dado por Jesús al Espíritu Santo. El Espíritu Santo nos conforta, nos habla en tiempos difíciles, y nos manifiesta la presencia de Jesús. [Advocate]

contrición pesar que sentimos cuando sabemos que hemos pecado, seguido por la decisión de no volver a pecar. La contrición perfecta brota de un amor que ama a Dios sobre todas las cosas. La contrición imperfecta está basada en otros motivos. La contrición es el acto más importante del penitente que se prepara a celebrar el sacramento de la penitencia. [contrition]

conversión cambio radical o cambio serio y extremo, de nuestra vida, que nos aparta del pecado y nos dirige a Dios. Este llamado a cambiar de vida es parte fundamental de las enseñanzas de Jesús. A lo largo de nuestra vida, Jesús nos llama a cambiar de esta forma. [conversion]

creación El acto en que Dios hace todo lo que existe fuera de Él. La creación es todo lo que existe. Dios dijo que todo lo creado es bueno. [creation]

Creador Dios, quien hizo todo lo que existe y a quien podemos llegar a conocer a través de todo lo que creó. [Creator]

credo breve resumen de lo que la gente cree. *Credo* proviene del verbo latino *credo,* que significa "creo". El Credo Niceno es el resumen más importante de lo que creemos como cristianos. [creed]

Credo de los Apóstoles declaración de la creencia cristiana, originada de un credo usado en los bautismos en Roma. El Credo de los Apóstoles enumera sencillas declaraciones de la creencia en Dios Padre, su Hijo Jesucristo y el Espíritu Santo. La profesión de fe usada actualmente en el Bautismo se basa en este credo. [Apostles' Creed]

Credo Niceno constantinopolitano resumen de las creencias cristianas desarrolladas por los obispos en los dos primeros concilios de la Iglesia, llevados a cabo en 325 y 381 d.c. Éste es el credo que comparten todos los cristianos de oriente y occidente. [Nicene Creed]

crisma óleo perfumado que se utiliza en los sacramentos del Bautismo, Confirmación y Orden sagrado. La unción con el crisma significa el llamado a los bautizados al triple ministerio de sacerdote, profeta, y rey. [chrism]

cristiano nombre dado a todos los que han sido ungidos por medio del don del Espíritu Santo en el Bautismo y se han convertido en seguidores de Jesucristo. [Christian]

Cristo título que significa "El Ungido". Proviene de una palabra griega que tiene el mismo significado que el hebreo *Mesías,* o "ungido". Es el nombre dado a Jesús como sacerdote, profeta y rey. [Christ]

crucifixión antiguo método de ejecución en el cual la víctima era atada o clavada a una cruz de madera donde se dejaba colgada hasta morir, usualmente de sofocación. Fue la forma de muerte a la que Jesús fue condenado por los romanos. La cruz con una imagen de Jesús crucificado se llama crucifijo. [crucifixion]

Cuaresma los cuarenta días antes de la Pascua (sin contar domingos), durante los cuales nos preparamos, por medio de la oración, el ayuno, y ayudando a los pobres, a cambiar nuestra vida y a vivir el Evangelio más plenamente. [Lent]

Cuerpo Místico de Cristo miembros de la Iglesia que forman un cuerpo espiritual y están unidos por la vida comunicada por Jesucristo por medio de los sacramentos. Cristo es el centro y la fuente de la vida de este cuerpo en el cual todos estamos unidos. Cada miembro de este cuerpo recibe de Cristo los dones que más convienen a esa persona. [Mystical Body of Christ]

Cuerpo y Sangre de Cristo pan y vino que han sido consagrados por el sacerdote en la Misa. En el sacramento de la Eucaristía, Nuestro Señor Jesucristo—todo cuerpo, sangre, alma, y divinidad— está presente en forma de pan y vino. [Body and Blood of Christ]

culto adoración y honor que se le rinde a Dios en oración pública. [worship]

cultura actividad de un grupo de personas que incluye su música, arte, lengua y celebraciones. La cultura es una de las maneras en que las personas conocen a Dios en sus vidas. [culture]

D

derechos y deberes el derecho fundamental a la vida y a aquellas cosas que se requieren para vivir dignamente. Este derecho es inherente a cada persona. Incluye el derecho a alimentación, vivienda, vestido, empleo, salud y educación. Correspondiendo a estos derechos hay deberes mutuos hacia nuestras familias y hacia la sociedad en general. Como católicos, tenemos el deber de proteger estos derechos humanos básicos a fin de lograr una sociedad justa. Es uno de los siete temas de la Doctrina Social Católica. [rights and responsibilities]

detracción el hablar de las faltas y pecados de alguien a otro que no tiene por qué enterarse de ello y que no puede ayudar a esa persona. La detracción daña la reputación de una persona sin que se tenga intención alguna de ayudarla. [detraction]

Día de los Muertos el 2 de noviembre, día en que la Iglesia ora por el eterno descanso de todos los que han muerto estando en amistad con Dios. Algunos de estos necesitan purificación en el purgatorio antes de pasar a vivir en presencia total de Dios; y con nuestras plegarias y buenas obras les ayudamos en este proceso. Junto al Día de Todos los Santos, esta fiesta nos recuerda que todos los que aman a Dios, vivos o muertos, están unidos en comunión viva con Jesucristo y entre sí. [All Souls Day]

Día de Todos los Santos el 1° de noviembre, día en que la Iglesia conmemora a todos los muertos que pasaron a ser santos y ahora viven con Dios en el cielo. Entre estos figuran aquéllos que han sido declarados santos de forma oficial por la Iglesia así como muchos otros desconocidos que han muerto tras haber llevado una vida recta y ahora viven en presencia de Dios. Esta fiesta celebra nuestra unión con aquéllos que se han ido antes que nosotros y nos señala nuestra meta final de unión con Dios. [All Saints Day]

diácono un hombre que recibe el Sacramento del Orden Sagrado para servir a la Iglesia. Los diáconos asisten al obispo y los sacerdotes en diversos ministerios de la Iglesia. También ayudan a proclamar el Evangelio, predicar y asistir en la Liturgia de la Eucaristía. Los diáconos también pueden celebrar bautizos, ser testigos de matrimonios y presidir en funerales. [deacon]

diálogo interreligioso la labor de construir una relación de apertura con los seguidores de religiones no cristianas. El vínculo de la Iglesia con las religiones no cristianas proviene de nuestro vínculo común como hijos de Dios. El propósito de este diálogo es incrementar el entendimiento mutuo, trabajar por el bien común de la humanidad y establecer la paz. [interreligious dialogue]

días de precepto principales días de fiesta de la Iglesia, exceptuando los domingos. En los días de precepto celebramos las grandes cosas que Dios ha hecho por nosotros por medio de Jesucristo y los Santos. Es obligación de los católicos participar de la Eucaristía en estos días, al igual que lo es los domingos. [Holy Days of Obligation]

Diez Mandamientos diez reglas que Dios dio a Moisés en el Monte Sinaí que resumen la ley de Dios y nos muestran lo que hay que hacer para amar a Dios y al prójimo. Al seguir los Diez Mandamientos, los hebreos aceptaron su alianza con Dios. [Ten Commandments]

dignidad de la persona humana principio básico y eje central de la Doctrina Social Católica. Es el punto de partida de una visión moral de la sociedad, porque la vida humana es sagrada y debe ser tratada con gran respeto. El ser humano es el más claro reflejo de Dios entre nosotros. [dignity of the human person]

dignidad del trabajo principio básico en el centro de la Doctrina Social Católica. Como el trabajo es realizado por personas creadas a imagen y semejanza de Dios, no es sólo un medio de vida sino también una manera importante de participar en la creación divina. En el trabajo, las personas alcanzan parte del potencial que Dios les ha otorgado. Todos los trabajadores tienen derecho a un empleo productivo, a salarios decentes y justos y a condiciones laborales satisfactorias. [dignity of work]

diócesis miembros de la Iglesia de una zona determinada, unidos en la fe y los sacramentos, y congregados bajo la guía de un obispo. [diocese]

Dios Padre, Hijo y Espíritu Santo: un sólo Dios en tres personas distintas. Dios creó todo lo que es; Él es la fuente de la salvación, verdad y amor. [God]

discípulo persona que ha aceptado el mensaje de Jesús y trata de vivir de la misma forma en que Él, compartiendo su misión, sufrimiento, y alegrías. [disciple]

discriminación acto de tratar mal a otros en razón de su apariencia o comportamiento, o sencillamente porque son distintos a nosotros. [discrimination]

Divina Providencia guía que da Dios a todo lo creado por Él. La Divina Providencia vela por toda la creación y la guía hacia su perfección final. [Divine Providence]

Doctor de la Iglesia persona declarada como maestro ejemplar de la fe cristiana. [Doctor of the Church]

doctrina social católica cuerpo de enseñanzas sobre justicia social, acción a favor de la justicia y obras para crear un mundo más justo. La Iglesia emite juicios sobre asuntos económicos y sociales que se relacionan con los derechos básicos de los individuos y las comunidades. La doctrina social de la Iglesia es un tesoro de sabiduría para construir una sociedad justa. [Catholic Social Teaching]

Domingo de Ramos celebración de la entrada triunfal de Jesús en Jerusalén que se hace el domingo antes de la Pascua. Esta celebración inicia una semana de conmemoración de los eventos de salvación de la Semana Santa. [Palm Sunday]

dones del Espíritu Santo disposición permanente, recibida del Espíritu Santo, que nos permite adherirnos a lo que Dios quiere de nosotros. Los dones del Espíritu Santo son tomados de Isaías 11:1–3. Incluyen sabiduría, entendimiento, consejo, fortaleza, ciencia y piedad. La Tradición de la Iglesia ha añadido temor de Dios, para sumar un total de siete. [Gifts of the Holy Spirit]

E

ecumenismo movimiento por la unidad entre los cristianos. Cristo dio a la Iglesia el don de la unidad desde el principio, pero esa unidad se ha roto a lo largo de los siglos. Todos los cristianos son llamados por su bautismo a orar y trabajar para mantener, reforzar y perfeccionar la unidad que Cristo quiere para la Iglesia. [ecumenism]

Emanuel nombre hebreo del Antiguo Testamento que significa "Dios con nosotros". En el Evangelio de san Mateo, se le llama *Emanuel* a Jesús. [Emmanuel]

Encarnación acto por el que el Hijo de Dios, Jesús, se hace plenamente hombre para salvarnos. El Hijo de Dios, segunda persona de la Trinidad, es tanto verdadero Dios, como verdadero hombre. [Incarnation]

encíclica carta escrita por el Papa y enviada a toda la Iglesia y a veces a todo el mundo. Expresa la doctrina de la Iglesia sobre un asunto determinado e importante. [encyclical]

entendimiento uno de los siete dones del Espíritu Santo. Este don nos ayuda a tomar decisiones apropiadas en la vida, y en nuestra relación con Dios y los demás. [understanding]

envidia sentimiento de resentimiento o tristeza debido a que alguien tiene una cualidad, talento o pertenencia que deseamos. La envidia es uno de los siete pecados capitales y va en contra del décimo mandamiento. [envy]

Epifanía día en que se celebra la visita de los Reyes Magos a Jesús recién nacido. Éste es el día en que se reveló a Jesús como salvador del mundo entero. [Epiphany]

epístola carta escrita por San Pablo u otro líder espiritual a un grupo de cristianos en los primeros tiempos de la Iglesia. Veintiuno de los veintisiete libros del Nuevo Testamento son Epístolas. En la Misa de los domingos y días santos, la segunda lectura se hace siempre de uno de estos libros. [epistle]

esperanza confianza de que Dios estará siempre con nosotros, nos dará felicidad ahora y siempre, y nos ayudará a vivir de forma que vivamos con Él para siempre. [hope]

Espíritu Santo tercera persona de la Trinidad, que es enviada a nosotros para asistirnos y, mediante el Bautismo y la Confirmación, nos llena de la vida de Dios. Junto con el Padre y el Hijo, el Espíritu Santo da plenitud al plan divino de salvación. [Holy Spirit]

espiritualidad nuestra creciente y amorosa relación con Dios. La espiritualidad es la manera de expresar nuestra experiencia de Dios, en la oración y en el amor a nuestro prójimo. Hay muchas diferentes escuelas de espiritualidad. Algunos ejemplos son la espiritualidad monástica, la franciscana, la jesuita y la laica. Son guías para la vida espiritual y han enriquecido las tradiciones de la oración, la liturgia y la vida de los cristianos. [spirituality]

Estaciones del Vía crucis forma de meditar las horas finales de la vida de Jesús, desde su condena a muerte por Pilatos hasta su muerte y sepultura. Consiste en recorrer representaciones de catorce incidentes distintos, cada uno de ellos basado en los sitios tradicionales de Jerusalén donde tuvieron lugar estos hechos. [Stations of the Cross]

Eucaristía el sacramento mediante el cual damos gracias a Dios por el Cuerpo y la Sangre de Cristo y que recibimos en la forma de pan y vino. Jesucristo resucitado está realmente presente en la Eucaristía. Esto significa que su cuerpo, sangre, alma y divinidad están total y enteramente presentes en el sacramento. [Eucharist]

eutanasia acto con la intención de causar la muerte de una persona discapacitada, enferma o agonizante. La eutanasia se considera asesinato y es gravemente contraria a la dignidad de la persona humana y al respeto debido al Dios vivo, nuestro Creador. [euthanasia]

Evangelio buena nueva de la misericordia y amor de Dios que experimentamos al oír la historia de la vida, muerte y resurrección de Jesús. Esta historia es transmitida en el ministerio de enseñanza de la Iglesia como fuente de toda verdad y de vida recta. Se nos presenta en el Nuevo Testamento en cuatro libros: los Evangelios de San Mateo, San Marcos, San Lucas, y San Juan. [gospel]

evangelio de la infancia relato de la infancia y niñez de Jesús, que aparece en los primeros dos capítulos de los Evangelios de San Mateo y de San Lucas. Cada evangelio contiene diferentes series de acontecimientos. Tienen en común que Jesús fue concebido virginalmente en María y que nació en Belén. La intención de estos relatos es proclamar a Jesús como Mesías y Salvador. [Infancy Narrative]

evangelista cualquier persona comprometida con la difusión del Evangelio. Las cartas del Nuevo Testamento y los Hechos de los Apóstoles, mencionan a los evangelistas junto con los apóstoles y profetas como ministros de la Iglesia. El término es usado principalmente para describir a los escritores de los cuatro Evangelios: Mateo, Marcos, Lucas y Juan. [evangelist]

evangelización declaración de la Buena Nueva de salvación recibida de Jesucristo, por la palabra o el ejemplo. Va dirigida tanto a aquellos que no conocen a Jesús como a aquellos que se han alejado de él. Aquellos que se han vuelto indiferentes son el foco de lo que se ha venido llamando la Nueva Evangelización. [evangelization]

examen de conciencia acto de reflexionar en oración sobre aquello que hemos dicho o hecho considerando lo que el Evangelio pide de nosotros. Es también reflexionar en cómo nuestras acciones pudieron haber dañado nuestra amistad con Dios y con otras personas. El examen de conciencia es una parte importante de la preparación para la celebración del sacramento de la penitencia. [examination of conscience]

exilio período de la historia de Israel comprendido entre la destrucción de Jerusalén en 587 a.c. y el regreso a Jerusalén en 537 a.c. Durante este tiempo, muchos de los judíos fueron obligados a vivir en Babilonia, lejos de su tierra. [Exile]

Éxodo liberación del pueblo hebreo de la esclavitud de Egipto dada por Dios y el haberlos guiado a la tierra prometida. [Exodus]

F

fariseos el partido o secta en el judaísmo que comenzó más de 100 años antes de Jesús. Los fariseos veían el judaísmo como una religión centrada en la observancia de la Ley. Los Evangelios presentan una imagen de mutua hostilidad entre Jesús y los fariseos. Más tarde había fariseos en la comunidad cristiana de Jerusalén (Hechos de los Apóstoles 15:5). Pablo estaba orgulloso de llamarse fariseo. [Pharisees]

fe don de Dios que nos ayuda a creer en Él. Profesamos nuestra fe en el Credo, la celebramos en los sacramentos, la vivimos por nuestra buena conducta de amar a Dios y a nuestro prójimo y la

expresamos en la oración. Es la fidelidad de todo nuestro ser, al Dios que se nos ha revelado con palabras y hechos a lo largo de la historia. [faith]

fortaleza fuerza que nos ayuda a obrar bien aun cuando sea difícil hacerlo. La fortaleza es una de las cuatro virtudes humanas centrales, llamadas virtudes cardinales, por las cuales guiamos nuestra conducta mediante el uso de la razón y la fe. Es también uno de los dones del Espíritu Santo. [fortitude]

frutos del Espíritu Santo forma en que actuamos porque Dios está vivo en nosotros. San Pablo enumera los frutos del Espíritu Santo en Gálatas 5:22–23: amor, gozo, paz, paciencia, benignidad, generosidad, fe, mansedumbre, y continencia. La Tradición eclesial ha agregado bondad, modestia, y castidad, lo que hace un total de doce. [Fruits of the Holy Spirit]

fundamentalismo creer que lo que la Biblia dice se debe interpretar al pie de la letra. Falla en reconocer que la palabra inspirada de Dios ha sido expresada en lenguaje humano, bajo inspiración divina, por autores humanos poseedores de capacidades y recursos limitados. [fundamentalism]

G

gentiles calificativo que los judíos dieron a los extranjeros después del Exilio. Eran no creyentes, y adoraban dioses falsos. Eran lo contrario del pueblo judío, que recibió la Ley de Dios. [Gentiles]

genuflexión, hacer la forma de mostrar respeto en la iglesia doblando una rodilla y haciéndola tocar el suelo, sobre todo cuando estamos ante el Santísimo Sacramento presente en el sagrario. [genuflect]

gracia don de Dios que se nos da gratuitamente. La gracia santificante nos llena de su vida y permite que seamos siempre amigos suyos. La gracia es el Espíritu Santo que habita en nosotros, ayudándonos a vivir nuestra vocación cristiana. La gracia también nos ayuda a vivir de la forma en que Dios quiere que vivamos. [grace]

gracia actual don de Dios, otorgado gratuitamente a todos nosotros, que nos une con la vida de la Trinidad. La gracia actual se nos da para ayudarnos a decidir las opciones que conforman nuestras vidas de acuerdo a la voluntad de Dios. (*Ver* gracia y gracia santificante.) [actual grace]

gracia santificante don que Dios nos da gratuitamente, que nos introduce a la intimidad de la Trinidad, nos une con su vida y cura nuestra naturaleza humana herida por el pecado. La gracia santificante responde a nuestra vocación como hijos adoptivos de Dios y continúa la obra de santificarnos iniciada en el Bautismo. [sanctifying grace]

H

hebreos descendientes de Abraham, Isaac y Jacob que fueron esclavizados en Egipto. Dios ayudó a Moisés a liberar a este pueblo de la esclavitud. [Hebrews]

Hechos de los Apóstoles el segundo volúmen escrito por Lucas a una comunidad greco-cristiana, que continúa el relato de la resurrección y ascensión de Jesús e informa sobre los comienzos de la Iglesia en Pentecostés. Pasa luego a describir cómo la Iglesia se expandió desde Jerusalén hasta los confines del mundo conocido entonces. [Acts of the Apostles]

Hijo de Dios título revelado por Jesús que indica su relación única con Dios Padre. La revelación de Jesús como Hijo de Dios es el principal suceso de la historia de Jesús de Nazaret según la relatan los Evangelios. [Son of God]

homilía explicación de la Palabra de Dios en la liturgia hecha por el obispo, sacerdote o diácono. La homilía explica de qué forma se relaciona hoy la Palabra de Dios con nuestra vida cristiana. [homily]

I

Iglesia pueblo de Dios congregado en todo el mundo, la diócesis, la Iglesia local o la asamblea de los convocados a rendirle culto a Dios. La Iglesia es una, santa, católica, y apostólica. [Church]

Iglesia doméstica el hogar cristiano, el cual es una comunidad de gracia y oración, escuela de virtudes humanas y caridad cristiana. [domestic church]

Iglesia universal toda la Iglesia tal como existe en el mundo entero. La gente de cada diócesis, junto con sus Obispos y el Papa forman la Iglesia universal. [universal Church]

Iglesias Católicas Orientales grupo de Iglesias que se desarrollaron en el oriente (en países como el Líbano) que están en unión con la Iglesia Católica Romana pero tienen sus propias tradiciones litúrgicas, teológicas, y administrativas. Éstas muestran la verdadera naturaleza católica de la Iglesia, que se arraiga en numerosas culturas distintas. [Eastern Catholic Churches]

indulgencia reducción del castigo debido a pecados que han sido perdonados. Nos conduce hacia nuestra purificación final, cuando habremos de vivir con Dios para siempre. [indulgence]

inerrancia la doctrina de la Iglesia de que la Biblia enseña sin error las verdades de la fe necesarias para nuestra salvación. Dios inspiró a los autores humanos, y por lo tanto Él es el autor de las Sagradas Escrituras. Esto nos asegura que ellas enseñan la verdad salvadora sin error, aunque ciertas informaciones históricas y científicas puedan no ser exactas. Con la ayuda del Espíritu Santo y de la Iglesia, interpretamos lo que Dios quiere revelarnos acerca de nuestra salvación, por medio de los autores sagrados. [inerrancy]

infalibilidad el don del Espíritu Santo que la Iglesia ha recibido y que asegura que el Papa, y los Obispos en unión con el Papa, pueden proclamar como verdaderas las doctrinas relacionadas con la fe y la moral. Es una extensión de la realización de que todo el cuerpo de creyentes no puede errar en asuntos de fe y moral. [infallibility]

infierno vida total y eternamente apartada de Dios. En su infinito amor hacia nosotros, Dios sólo puede desear nuestra salvación. El infierno es el resultado de la libre elección de la persona de rechazar el amor y perdón Dios de forma definitiva. [hell]

Inmaculada Concepción la Iglesia enseña que María estuvo libre de pecado original desde el primer momento de su concepción. Ella fue preservada por los méritos de su Hijo, Jesús, el Salvador del género humano. Fue declarada creencia de la Iglesia Católica por el Papa Pío IX en 1854, y se celebra el 8 de diciembre. [Immaculate Conception]

inspiración la influencia del Espíritu Santo sobre los autores humanos de la Escritura. La inspiración creativa del Espíritu Santo asegura que la Escritura sea enseñada de acuerdo con la verdad que Dios quiere que conozcamos para nuestra salvación. [inspiration]

interpretación explicación de las palabras de la Sagrada Escritura que combina el conocimiento humano con el oficio de enseñanza de la Iglesia bajo la guía del Espíritu Santo. [interpretation]

islamismo La tercera gran religión, con el judaísmo y el cristianismo, que profesa creencia en un sólo Dios. *Islam* quiere decir "sumisión" a ese Dios único. [Islam]

israelitas descendientes de Abraham, Isaac y Jacob. Dios cambió el nombre de Jacob a "Israel"; y los doce hijos de Jacob junto con los hijos de estos hijos se convirtieron en jefes de las doce tribus de Israel. (*Véase* hebreos.) [Israelites]

J

Jesús hijo de Dios, que nació de la Virgen María, murió y fue resucitado de entre los muertos para nuestra salvación. Jesús volvió a Dios y vendrá de nuevo a juzgar a vivos y a muertos. Su nombre significa "Dios salva". [Jesus]

José padre adoptivo de Jesús, que estaba desposado con María cuando el ángel anunció que ella tendría un hijo por obra del poder del Espíritu Santo. En el Antiguo Testamento, José era el hijo de Jacob que fue vendido como esclavo en Egipto por sus hermanos y que luego los salvó de morir de hambre cuando hubo escasez de comida en la región. [Joseph]

judaísmo nombre de la religión de Jesús y de todo el pueblo de Israel después de su regreso del exilio en Babilonia y la construcción del segundo Templo. [Judaism]

judíos nombre dado al pueblo hebreo, desde el tiempo del exilio al presente. Este nombre quiere decir "pueblo del territorio de Judea", zona de Palestina en torno a Jerusalén. [Jews]

Juicio Final el juicio que ocurrirá al fin de los tiempos para todos los seres humanos, cuando Cristo regrese en gloria y todos se presenten ante él con sus cuerpos físicos para dar cuenta de sus acciones en la vida. En la presencia de Cristo, quedará al descubierto la verdadera relación de cada persona con Dios, así como el bien que cada persona haya hecho o dejado de hacer durante su vida terrenal. En ese momento, el Reino de Dios vendrá en toda su plenitud. [Last Judgment]

juicio particular el juicio que Cristo realiza al recibir a cada persona al momento de su muerte, ofreciéndole entrada al cielo (después de un periodo de purificación, si es necesario) o inmediata y eterna separación de Dios en el infierno. Al momento de la muerte, cada persona es recompensada por Cristo de acuerdo con sus obras y su fe. [particular judgment]

justicia deseo firme y poderoso de dar a Dios y a los demás lo que les corresponde. Es una de las cuatro virtudes humanas centrales, llamadas virtudes cardinales, por las cuales guiamos nuestra vida cristiana. [justice]

Justicia el atributo de Dios que en el Antiguo Testamento describe su rectitud, su fidelidad a la Alianza y su santidad. Como atributo humano, la justicia significa estar en correcta relación con Dios mediante la conducta moral y el cumplimiento de la Ley. Tenemos mérito a los ojos de Dios y podemos hacerlo por la obra de Su gracia en nosotros. San Pablo habla de la justificación de una manera que no depende del cumplimiento de la Ley, sino de la fe en Jesús, y por su muerte y Resurrección salvadoras. Ser justificados en Jesús significa ser salvados, reivindicados y restablecidos en Dios mediante su gracia. [righteousness]

justicia social el trato justo y equitativo de cada miembro de la sociedad. Lo exige la dignidad y libertad de cada persona. La Iglesia Católica ha desarrollado un cuerpo de principios sociales y enseñanzas morales descritos en documentos pontificios y otros emitidos desde finales del siglo XIX. Estas enseñanzas tratan sobre el orden económico, político y social del mundo. Están fundamentadas en la Biblia así como en las enseñanzas teológicas tradicionales de la Iglesia. [social justice]

L

laicado los que se han convertido en miembros de Cristo en el Bautismo y que participan en las funciones sacerdotales, proféticas y regias de Cristo en su misión destinada al mundo entero. El laicado es distinto al clero, cuyos miembros están dedicados a servir a la Iglesia como ministros suyos. [laity]

Leccionario libro oficial que contiene todas las lecturas de la Sagrada Escritura utilizadas en la Liturgia de la Palabra. [Lectionary]

lectio divina una manera de orar meditativamente con la Escritura. La *lectio divina* es una expresión en latín que significa "lectura sagrada" y es una forma antigua de oración cristiana. Incluye cuatro pasos: lectura sagrada de un pasaje de la Escritura, meditación sobre el texto leído, hablarle a Dios y contemplación o descanso en la presencia divina. [lectio divina]

ley moral regla de vida establecida por Dios y por personas de autoridad que se preocupan por el bien de todos. Las leyes morales se basan en la directiva que nos dio Dios de hacer el bien y evitar el mal. Algunas leyes morales están escritas en el corazón humano y pueden conocerse por medio de la razón. Otras nos han sido reveladas por Dios en el Antiguo Testamento y en la nueva ley dada por Jesús. [moral law]

ley natural ley moral que está escrita en el corazón de la persona. Podemos conocer la ley natural mediante la razón porque el Creador ha puesto en nuestros corazones el conocimiento de ella. Esta ley puede brindarnos una base sólida sobre la cual podemos crear las reglas para guiar nuestras decisiones en la vida. La ley natural representa la base de nuestros derechos y deberes fundamentales y es el cimiento de la obra del Espíritu Santo al guiar nuestras opciones morales. [natural law]

libre albedrío capacidad de optar por hacer el bien porque Dios nos ha hecho semejantes a Él. Nuestro libre albedrío es lo que nos hace verdaderamente humanos. Al ejercer nuestro libre albedrío para hacer el bien, nuestra libertad aumenta; pero, si lo usamos para elegir el pecado, nos hace esclavos de ese pecado. [free will]

Libros sapienciales libros siguientes del Antiguo Testamento: Job, Proverbios, Eclesiastés, Cantar de los Cantares, Sabiduría y Eclesiástico. Su objetivo es instruir acerca de cómo vivir y cómo entender y sobrellevar los problemas de la vida. [Wisdom Literature]

liturgia oración pública de la Iglesia que celebra las maravillas que Dios ha hecho por nosotros en Jesucristo, nuestro Sumo Sacerdote, y cómo Él continúa la obra de nuestra salvación. El sentido original de *liturgia* era "obra pública o servicio prestado al pueblo". [liturgy]

Liturgia Eucarística la segunda de las dos partes de la Misa. En esta parte, se bendice el pan y el vino, que se convierten en Cuerpo y Sangre de Jesucristo, que luego recibimos en la Sagrada Comunión. [Liturgy of the Eucharist]

Liturgia de la Palabra la primera de las dos partes de la Misa. Durante esta parte, escuchamos la Palabra de Dios en la Biblia y reflexionamos sobre lo que significa hoy para nosotros. La Liturgia de la Palabra también puede ser una oración pública y proclamación de la Palabra de Dios que no va seguida de la Liturgia Eucarística. [Liturgy of the Word]

Liturgia de las Horas oración pública de la Iglesia para alabar a Dios y santificar el día. Consiste de: un Oficio de Lecturas antes del alba, los Laudes al amanecer, las Vísperas al anochecer, y una oración antes de acostarse. La recitación de los salmos conforma la mayor parte de cada uno de estos oficios. [Liturgy of the Hours]

lugar santísimo parte más sagrada del Templo de Jerusalén. El sumo sacerdote entraba a este recinto una vez al año para dirigirse a Dios y pedirle su perdón por los pecados del pueblo. [Holy of Holies]

M

Madre de Dios el título de María proclamado en el Concilio de Éfeso, en el año 431. El Concilio declaró que María no era sólo madre de Jesús hombre, sino también Madre de Dios al concebir al Hijo de Dios en su vientre. Como la humanidad de Jesús es una con su divinidad, María es madre del eterno Hijo de Dios hecho hombre, quien es Dios mismo. [Mother of God]

Magisterio oficio de enseñanza viviente de la Iglesia. Este oficio, a través de los obispos y junto con el Papa, ofrece una interpretación auténtica de la Palabra de Dios. Su objetivo es mantenerse fiel a las enseñanzas de los apóstoles en cuestiones de fe y moral. [Magisterium]

Magníficat canto de María de alabanza a Dios. Ella lo alaba por las grandes cosas que ha hecho por ella y los grandes planes que ha hecho para nosotros a través de Jesús. [Magnificat]

mandamiento norma, o regla, para vivir de la forma en que Dios quiere que vivamos. Jesús resumió todos los mandamientos en dos: amar a Dios y amar al prójimo. [commandment]

El Mandamiento Mayor enseñanza esencial de Jesús de amar a Dios y al prójimo como a nosotros mismos. Jesús nos dice que su mandamiento resume todo lo enseñado en el Antiguo Testamento. [Great Commandment]

María Madre de Jesús. Se le dice bendita y "llena de gracia" porque Dios la eligió para ser madre de su Hijo, segunda persona de la Trinidad. [Mary]

mártires aquellos que han dado su vida por la fe. Proviene de la palabra griega para "testigo". Un mártir es el supremo testigo de la verdad de la fe y de Cristo a quien él o ella están unidos. El capítulo 7 de los Hechos de los Apóstoles relata la muerte del primer mártir, el diácono Esteban. [martyrs]

Matrimonio contrato solemne entre un varón y una mujer para ser compañeros por toda la vida, tanto para su bien propio como para procrear hijos. El Matrimonio es un sacramento cuando el contrato se hace de forma apropiada entre cristianos bautizados. [Matrimony]

mayordomía administración cuidadosa y responsable de algo que ha sido confiado a nuestro cuidado, en particular los bienes de la creación que han sido destinados a toda la raza humana. El sexto precepto de la Iglesia deja clara nuestra participación en la administración al exigirnos que respondamos a las necesidades materiales de la Iglesia según nuestras capacidades. [stewardship]

meditación una forma de rezar y escuchar en silencio que mediante la imaginación, los sentimientos y el deseo de comprender, busca responder a la voluntad de Dios y cumplirla. Al concentrarnos en una palabra o una imagen, nos colocamos más allá de los pensamientos, vaciando la mente de contenidos que impiden nuestra experiencia de Dios, y descansamos en la simple conciencia de Dios. Es una de las tres expresiones principales de la vida de oración. [meditation]

Mesías título que significa "el ungido". Proviene de la palabra hebrea que tiene el mismo significado de la palabra griega *Cristo*. Mesías es el nombre dado a Jesús como sacerdote, profeta y rey. [Messiah]

Miércoles de Ceniza primer día de Cuaresma, en el que se nos coloca ceniza en la frente para que recordemos la necesidad de prepararnos para la Pascua, debemos mostrar arrepentimiento por decisiones que hemos tomado que ofenden a Dios y dañan nuestra relación con los demás. [Ash Wednesday]

milagro señales o actos maravillosos que no pueden ser explicados por causas naturales pero que son obras de Dios. En los Evangelios, Jesús obra milagros como señal de que el Reino de Dios está presente en su ministerio. [miracle]

ministerio servicio, u obra que se hace a favor de los demás. Lo hacen los obispos, sacerdotes y diáconos ordenados al ministerio en la celebración de los sacramentos. Todos los bautizados son llamados a una variedad de ministerios en la liturgia y en el servicio a las necesidades de los demás. [ministry]

misa la celebración sacramental más importante de la Iglesia. La celebración de la misa fue instituida por Jesús en la Última Cena para que fuera un recordatorio de su muerte y resurrección. En la misa, escuchamos la Palabra de Dios en la Biblia y recibimos a Jesucristo en el pan y el vino que han sido consagrados para convertirse en su Cuerpo y Sangre. [Mass]

misión la obra continúa de Jesucristo en la Iglesia por medio del Espíritu Santo. La misión de la Iglesia es proclamar la salvación por la vida, muerte, resurrección, y gloriosa ascensión de Jesús. Los misioneros son personas ordenadas, laicas o religiosas, que se dedican a la misión. [mission]

misterio verdad religiosa que sólo podemos conocer por revelación de Dios y que no podemos comprender totalmente. Nuestra fe es un misterio que profesamos en el credo y que celebramos en la liturgia y los sacramentos. [mystery]

Misterio Pascual la obra de salvación realizada por Jesucristo con su pasión, muerte, resurrección y Ascensión. El Misterio Pascual se celebra en la liturgia de la Iglesia, y nos beneficiamos de sus efectos salvadores en los sacramentos. En cada liturgia de la Iglesia, Dios Padre es adorado como fuente de todas las bendiciones que hemos recibido mediante su Hijo, con el fin de convertirnos en hijos suyos por el Espíritu Santo. [Paschal Mystery]

monacato (monasticismo) forma de vida religiosa en la cual hombres y mujeres viven sus votos de pobreza, castidad y obediencia dentro de una comunidad estable. El objetivo del monacato es buscar, bajo la guía de una regla, una vida de oración pública, trabajo y meditación para la gloria de Dios. San Benito de Nursia, quien murió cerca del año 550, es considerado padre del monasticismo de Occidente. [monasticism]

monasterio lugar donde residen varones o mujeres cumpliendo sus votos de pobreza, castidad y obediencia en una vida de comunidad estable. Éstos pasan sus días en oración pública, trabajo, y meditación. [monastery]

musulmán seguidor de la religión islámica. *Musulmán* quiere decir "que se somete a Dios". [Muslim]

N

Navidad fiesta del nacimiento de Jesús (el 25 de diciembre). [Christmas]

Nuevo Testamento los 27 libros de la segunda parte de la Biblia, que relatan las enseñanzas, ministerio, y acontecimientos de salvación de la vida de Jesús. El Nuevo Testamento se compone de: cuatro Evangelios, que presentan la vida, muerte y resurrección de Jesús; los Hechos de los Apóstoles, que narran la historia del mensaje de salvación al irse extendiendo con el crecimiento de la Iglesia; varias cartas que nos instruyen sobre cómo vivir como seguidores de Jesucristo; y el libro del Apocalipsis, que da ánimo a los cristianos que sufren persecución. [New Testament]

O

obediencia acto de seguir por voluntad propia lo que Dios nos pide que hagamos para nuestra salvación. Según el cuarto mandamiento, los niños deben obedecer a sus padres y todas las personas deben obedecer a la autoridad civil cuando obra en beneficio de todos. Imitando la obediencia de Jesús, los miembros de las comunidades religiosas hacen un voto especial de obediencia. [obedience]

Obispo varón que ha recibido el orden sagrado en su totalidad. Como sucesor de los primeros apóstoles, el Obispo vela por la Iglesia y es un educador importante dentro de la misma. [bishop]

obras corporales de misericordia buenas acciones con las que ayudamos a nuestro prójimo a cubrir sus necesidades materiales cotidianas. Las obras corporales de misericordia son: dar de comer al hambriento, dar techo al que no lo tiene, vestir al desnudo, visitar a los enfermos y a los presos, dar limosna a los pobres y enterrar a los muertos. [Corporal Works of Mercy]

obras espirituales de misericordia acciones caritativas mediante las cuales socorremos al prójimo en sus necesidades que van más allá de lo material. Las obras espirituales de misericordia son: instruir, aconsejar, consolar, confortar, perdonar y sufrir con paciencia las flaquezas ajenas. [Spiritual Works of Mercy]

ofensas actos contrarios a la ley cometidos contra la propiedad o los derechos de otra persona, o actos que físicamente lastiman a esa persona. [trespasses]

óleo de los catecúmenos óleo consagrado por el Obispo durante la Semana Santa y usado para ungir a los catecúmenos. Esta unción los afianza en su camino de iniciación en la Iglesia. Los bebés son ungidos con este óleo momentos antes de ser bautizados. [oil of catechumens]

óleo de los enfermos óleo consagrado por el obispo durante la Semana Santa y usado en el sacramento de la Unción de los enfermos, el cual brinda sanación espiritual y, si Dios quiere, sanación física también. [oil of the sick]

opción moral el elegir hacer lo que está bien o no hacer lo que está mal. Elegimos opciones morales porque son lo que creemos que Dios quiere y porque tenemos la libertad de escoger lo que está bien y evitar lo que está mal. [moral choice]

opción por los pobres la obligación moral de atender las necesidades de los pobres. Su condición de impotencia hace un reclamo urgente a nuestra conciencia. Los que formulan las políticas públicas deben considerar cómo sus decisiones afectarían a los pobres. La vulnerabilidad de los pobres hiere a la comunidad entera. Una sociedad justa puede alcanzarse sólo si sus miembros prestan especial atención a los pobres y marginados. Es un principio básico en el corazón de la Doctrina Social Católica. [option for the poor]

oración el levantar el corazón y la mente a Dios. Podemos hablar y escuchar a Dios porque Él nos enseña a orar. [prayer]

oración de intersección oración de petición en la que rezamos por otras personas al igual que Jesús lo hizo ante el Padre. Pedir por los demás es característico de un corazón en armonía con la misericordia de Dios. La intersección cristiana no reconoce fronteras. Rezamos por todos –los ricos, los líderes políticos, aquellos en necesidad e incluso, los perseguidores. [prayers of intercession]

oración común culto a Dios que se rinde junto con otras personas. La Liturgia de las Horas y la Misa son las principales formas de oración común. [communal prayer]

orden mendicante forma peculiar de orden religiosa desarrollada en el siglo XIII. A diferencia de los monjes que permanecen dentro de un monasterio, los miembros de las órdenes mendicantes desempeñan ministerios de predicación, enseñanza y testimonio en las ciudades. Se llaman *mendicantes,* del latín "mendigar", porque es su principal medio de sustento. Las dos órdenes mendicantes de mayor importancia son los dominicos, fundados por Santo Domingo de Guzmán y los franciscanos, fundados por San Francisco de Asís. [Mendicant Order]

orden de penitentes orden que existió en la Iglesia antigua, consistente en cristianos bautizados quienes, debido a su pecado, estaban en necesidad de reconciliación con la comunidad de creyentes. Aquellos que habían cometido alguno de los tres pecados más serios –renegar de la fe, romper el vínculo del matrimonio o asesinar– se les requería un periodo de tiempo en penitencia pública, hasta que la comunidad estuviera convencida de su sinceridad. [Order of Penitents]

oración personal tipo de oración que surge en nosotros en la vida cotidiana. Oramos junto con otras personas en la liturgia; pero, además, cada momento de nuestra vida es una ocasión para escuchar y responder a Dios por medìc de la oración personal. [personal prayer]

Orden sagrado sacramento mediante el cual la misión o deber, dado por Jesús a sus apóstoles continúa en la Iglesia. Tiene tres grados: diaconado, presbiterado y episcopado. Mediante la imposición de manos en el sacramento del Orden sagrado, los varones reciben una marca o carácter sacramental permanente que los llama a servir a la Iglesia como ministros suyos. [Holy Orders]

ordenación rito del sacramento del orden sagrado, mediante el cual el Obispo da a los varones a través de la imposición de manos la capacidad de servir en el ministerio a la Iglesia como obispos, sacerdotes, y diáconos. [ordination]

P

padrino/madrina de Bautismo testigo que asume la responsabilidad de ayudar al bautizado a seguir el camino de la vida cristiana. [godparent]

Papa el obispo de Roma, sucesor de San Pedro, y cabeza de la Iglesia Católica Romana. Como tiene autoridad de actuar en nombre de Cristo, al Papa se le llama Vicario de Cristo. El Papa junto a todos los obispos conforma el oficio de enseñanza viviente de la Iglesia: el Magisterio. [pope]

parábola una de las sencillas narraciones que Jesús contaba que nos muestran cómo es el Reino de Dios. Las parábolas nos presentan imágenes, o escenas, tomadas de la vida cotidiana. Estas imágenes nos muestran la decisión radical, o seria, que tomamos cuando respondemos a la invitación de entrar en el Reino de Dios. [parable]

párroco sacerdote responsable del cuidado espiritual de los miembros de una comunidad parroquial. El deber del sacerdote es velar por que se predique la Palabra de Dios, se enseñe la fe y se celebren los sacramentos. [pastor]

parroquia comunidad de creyentes en Jesucristo que se reúne regularmente en una zona determinada para rendirle culto a Dios bajo la guía de un pastor. [parish]

participación uno de los siete principios de la Doctrina Social Católica. Todas las personas tienen derecho a participar en la vida económica, política y cultural de la sociedad. Es un requisito de la dignidad humana y una exigencia de la justicia que todas las personas tengan al menos un grado mínimo de participación en la comunidad. [participation]

Pascua celebración de la resurrección corporal de Jesucristo de entre los muertos. La Pascua festeja nuestra redención y es la fiesta cristiana central de la que se originan otras fiestas. [Easter]

Pascua judía festival judío que conmemora la liberación del pueblo hebreo de la esclavitud de Egipto. *Pascua* viene de una palabra hebrea que significa "tránsito" o "pasaje". En la Eucaristía, celebramos nuestro "tránsito" de la muerte a la vida por medio de la muerte y resurrección de Jesús. [Passover]

pecado pensamiento, palabra, acción, o falta de acción deliberados que ofenden a Dios y dañan nuestra relación con otras personas. Algunos pecados son mortales y deben ser confesados en el Sacramento de la penitencia. Otros son veniales o menos graves. [sin]

pecado mortal decisión grave de apartarnos de Dios haciendo algo que sabemos que está mal. Para que un pecado sea mortal, debe ser una falta muy grave, la persona debe saber lo grave que es el pecado, y, a pesar de ello, decidir libremente cometerlo. [mortal sin]

pecado original consecuencia de la desobediencia de los primeros seres humanos, que desobedecieron a Dios y decidieron seguir su propia voluntad y no la de Dios. A raíz de esto, los seres humanos perdieron la bendición original que Dios les había destinado y se sometieron al pecado y la muerte. En el Bautismo, se nos restaura la vida con Dios a través de Jesucristo, aunque aún seguimos sufriendo los efectos del pecado original. [original sin]

pecado personal pecado que decidimos cometer. Puede ser grave (mortal) o menos grave (venial). Aunque las consecuencias del pecado original nos dejan con una tendencia al pecado, la gracia de Dios, sobre todo por medio de los sacramentos, nos ayuda a elegir el bien sobre el mal. [personal sin]

pecado social situaciones e instituciones sociales que van contra la voluntad de Dios. A causa de los pecados individuales de algunas personas, sociedades enteras pueden desarrollar estructuras pecaminosas. Los pecados sociales incluyen el racismo, el sexismo, y las estructuras que niegan a las personas el acceso a servicios de salud adecuados, así como la destrucción del medio ambiente para beneficio de unos pocos. [social sin]

pecado venial decisión que tomamos y que debilita nuestra relación con Dios u otra persona. Los pecados veniales lastiman y disminuyen la vida divina en nosotros. Si no hacemos esfuerzos para mejorar, el pecado venial puede conducir a pecados más serios. Mediante nuestra participación en la Eucaristía, el pecado venial es perdonado cuando nos arrepentimos, fortaleciendo nuestra relación con Dios y los demás. [venial sin]

pecados capitales aquellos pecados que pueden llevarnos a cometer pecados más graves. Los pecados capitales son: soberbia, avaricia, envidia, ira, gula, lujuria y pereza. [capital sins]

penitencia el apartarnos del pecado con el deseo de cambiar nuestra vida y acercarnos más a la forma de vida que Dios quiere que vivamos. Expresamos externamente nuestra penitencia mediante la oración, el ayuno y ayudando a los pobres. También se le llama penitencia a la acción que el sacerdote nos pide hacer o a las oraciones que nos pide rezar después de que él nos absuelve en el Sacramento de la penitencia. (*Véase* Sacramento de la penitencia). [penance]

Pentecostés cincuenta días después de la resurrección de Jesús. En este día, el Espíritu Santo fue enviado del cielo y nació la Iglesia. También es el día de la fiesta judía que celebraba el recibimiento de los Diez Mandamientos en el Monte Sinaí, cincuenta días después del Éxodo. [Pentecost]

perdón voluntad de ser benignos con una persona que nos ha hecho daño pero que después dice que está arrepentida. En la oración del Padrenuestro, rogamos que, al igual que Dios siempre nos ha de perdonar nuestros pecados, nosotros también sepamos perdonar a los que nos han hecho daño. [forgiveness]

pereza dejadez de corazón que lleva a una persona a no hacer caso de su desarrollo como persona, en particular de su desarrollo espiritual y su relación con Dios. La pereza es uno de los siete pecados capitales, y va en contra del primer mandamiento. [sloth]

petición el pedir a Dios lo que necesitamos porque Él nos ha creado y quiere darnos lo que necesitamos. Cuando participamos del amor redentor de Dios, entendemos que para cada una de nuestras necesidades podemos pedirle a Dios que nos ayude mediante una petición. [petition]

piedad uno de los siete dones del Espíritu Santo. Nos llama a ser fieles en nuestras relaciones con Dios y los demás. Nos ayuda a amar a Dios y a comportarnos de una manera responsable y con generosa y afectuosa en nuestra relación con los demás. [piety]

preceptos de la Iglesia aquellos requisitos positivos que la autoridad pastoral de la Iglesia ha determinado como necesarios. Estos requisitos representan el esfuerzo mínimo que debemos hacer en la oración y en la vida moral. Los preceptos de la Iglesia se aseguran de que todos los católicos progresemos más allá del mínimo, creciendo en amor a Dios y en amor al prójimo. [Precepts of the Church]

presbítero palabra que originalmente quería decir "anciano" o "consejero de confianza del Obispo". De esta palabra deriva el vocablo inglés *priest* o "sacerdote" en español, uno de los tres grados del sacramento del orden sagrado. Todos los sacerdotes de una diócesis que están bajo la guía de un Obispo forman el presbiterio. [presbyter]

Presencia real modo en que Cristo resucitado está realmente presente en la Eucaristía en forma de pan y vino. Se le llama "real" a la presencia de Jesucristo porque en la Eucaristía su cuerpo y sangre, alma y divinidad, están total y enteramente presentes. [Real Presence]

profeta persona llamada a hablar por Dios y a llamar a la gente a ser fiel a la alianza. Una sección importante del Antiguo Testamento presenta en dieciocho libros los mensajes y acciones de los profetas. [prophet]

prudencia virtud que nos orienta al bien. También nos ayuda a escoger los medios apropiados para alcanzar ese bien. Cuando actuamos con prudencia consideramos nuestros acciones con cuidado. La prudencia es una de las virtudes cardinales morales que guía nuestra conciencia e influye en nosotros para que vivamos según la ley de Cristo. [prudence]

Pueblo de Dios otro de los nombres de la Iglesia. Al igual que el pueblo de Israel era el pueblo de Dios debido a la alianza que Él hizo con ellos, la Iglesia es un pueblo sacerdotal, profético y regio gracias a la nueva y eterna alianza en Jesucristo. [people of God]

Pueblo Elegido pueblo escogido por Dios para que mantuviera con Él una relación especial. La primera vez que Dios formó un pueblo elegido fue cuando hizo una alianza o pacto solemne con Abraham. Más tarde, reafirmó esa alianza a través de Moisés en el Monte Sinaí. Esta alianza ha alcanzado su plenitud en Jesús y su Iglesia. [Chosen People]

purgatorio estado que viene después de la muerte de purificación final de todas las imperfecciones humanas antes de entrar a gozar la presencia de Dios en el cielo. [purgatory]

R

racionalismo corriente filosófica desarrollada por René Descartes. Dominó el pensamiento europeo durante los siglos XVII y XVIII. La principal creencia del racionalismo es que la razón humana es la fuente principal de todo conocimiento. Enfatiza la confianza en el carácter ordenado del mundo y la habilidad de la mente para hacer sentido de este orden. El Racionalismo solamente reconoce como ciertas aquellas creencias religiosas que pueden ser explicadas racionalmente. [rationalism]

racismo creencia de que la raza determina rasgos y capacidades humanas y que existe una superioridad inherente o innata de una raza determinada. La discriminación en razón de la raza de una persona es una violación de la dignidad humana y un pecado contra la justicia. [racism]

reconciliación reanudar la amistad que se había roto por alguna acción o falta de acción. En el sacramento de la penitencia, mediante la misericordia y perdón de Dios, nos reconciliamos con Él, la Iglesia y los demás. [reconciliation]

redención el liberación de la esclavitud del pecado mediante la vida, el sacrificio de la muerte en la cruz y la resurrección de Jesucristo de entre los muertos. [redemption]

Redentor Jesucristo, cuya vida, sacrificio de su muerte en la cruz y resurrección de entre los muertos, nos libró de la esclavitud del pecado y nos trajo la redención. [Redeemer]

reformarse poner fin a un error tomando un curso de acción mejor o distinto. Los profetas llamaban a la gente a reformar su vida volviendo a ser fieles a la alianza con Dios. [reform]

Reino de Dios el dominio de Dios sobre nosotros anunciado en el Evangelio y está presente en la Eucaristía. El principio del Reino aquí en la tierra está presente en forma misteriosa en la Iglesia, y vendrá en su plenitud al final de los tiempos. [Kingdom of God]

Resurrección el volver a la vida el cuerpo de Jesucristo el tercer día después de haber muerto en la cruz. La Resurrección es la verdad culminante de nuestra fe. [Resurrection]

revelación comunicación que nos hace Dios de sí por medio de las palabras y hechos que ha usado a lo largo de la historia para mostrarnos el misterio del plan de salvación que tiene para nosotros. Esta revelación llega a su plenitud con el envío de su Hijo, Jesucristo. [Revelation]

rito una de diversas formas de celebrar la liturgia en la Iglesia. Los ritos pueden ser distintos según la cultura o el país donde se celebren. *Rito* también quiere decir el modo especial en que celebramos cada sacramento. [rite]

rosario oración en honor a la Virgen María. En el rezo del rosario, meditamos los misterios de la vida de Jesucristo rezando el Avemaría en los cinco grupos de diez cuentas y el Padrenuestro en las cuentas que van en medio. En la Iglesia del Rito Latino, el rezo del rosario se convirtió en una manera en que la gente común podía reflexionar sobre los misterios de la vida de Jesús. [Rosary]

S

sabat séptimo día, en el que Dios, habiendo terminado su obra de creación, descansó. El tercer mandamiento nos exige que consideremos santo el sabat. Para los cristianos, el sabat se convirtió en domingo, día del señor, porque era el día en que resucitó Jesús y se inició la nueva creación en Jesucristo. [Sabbath]

sabiduría uno de los siete dones del Espíritu Santo. Nos ayuda a entender el propósito y el plan de Dios, y a vivir de una forma que ayude a realizar este plan. La sabiduría se inicia con la admiración y portento ante la grandeza de Dios. [wisdom]

sacerdocio todo el pueblo de Dios que ha sido hecho partícipe de la misión de Cristo por medio de los sacramentos del Bautismo y la Confirmación. El sacerdocio ministerial, compuesto de aquellos varones que han sido ordenados obispos y sacerdotes por medio del orden sagrado, es en esencia distinto del sacerdocio de todos los fieles porque su labor es la de edificar y guiar a la Iglesia en nombre de Cristo. [priesthood]

sacerdote varón que ha aceptado el llamado especial de Dios para servir a la Iglesia guiándola y edificándola mediante el ministerio de la Palabra y la celebración de los sacramentos. [priest]

sacramental objeto, oración o bendición dados por la Iglesia que nos ayudan a crecer en nuestra vida espiritual. [sacramental]

sacramento uno de los siete ritos mediante los cuales compartimos la vida divina por obra del Espíritu Santo y nuestra participación en la liturgia. La obra de Cristo en la liturgia es sacramental porque su misterio se hace presente allí por obra del Espíritu Santo. Jesús nos dejó tres sacramentos que nos inician en la Iglesia: el Bautismo, la Confirmación y la Eucaristía. Nos dejó dos sacramentos que nos sanan: la Penitencia y la Unción de los Enfermos. Dejó otros dos sacramentos que ayudan a los miembros a servir a la comunidad: el Matrimonio y el Orden sagrado. (*Vea* también sacramental.)
[sacrament]

Sacramento de la penitencia sacramento en el cual celebramos el perdón de Dios a nuestros pecados y nuestra reconciliación con Él y la Iglesia. La penitencia consiste en el arrepentimiento de los pecados cometidos, la confesión de los pecados, la absolución por el sacerdote, y el cumplimiento de la penitencia para mostrar que estamos dispuestos a enderezar nuestra vida. [Sacrament of Penance]

sacramentos al servicio de la comunidad sacramentos que contribuyen a la salvación personal de los individuos dándoles un modo de servir a los demás. Son dos: Orden sacerdotal y Matrimonio. [Sacraments at the Service of Communion]

sacramentos de iniciación sacramentos que son los cimientos de nuestra vida cristiana. Volvemos a nacer en el Bautismo, nos fortalecemos en la Confirmación, y recibimos en la Eucaristía el alimento de la vida eterna. Por medio de estos sacramentos, recibimos una creciente medida de vida divina y avanzamos hacia la perfección de la caridad. [Sacraments of Initiation]

sacramentos de sanación sacramentos mediante los cuales la Iglesia continúa el ministerio de Jesús de sanación del alma y del cuerpo. Son dos: Penitencia y Unción de los enfermos. [Sacraments of Healing]

sacrificio ritual en que el sacerdote en el Templo de Jerusalén ofrecía animales u hortalizas a Dios para dar muestra de la adoración del pueblo a Dios, para dar gracias a Dios, o para pedir su perdón. El sacrificio también mostraba la unión con Dios. Cristo, el gran Sumo Sacerdote, alcanzó nuestra redención por medio del sacrificio perfecto de su muerte en la cruz. [sacrifice]

sacrificio de la misa sacrificio de Jesús en la cruz, el cual se recuerda y se hace presente de forma misteriosa en la Eucaristía. Es ofrecida en reparación de los pecados de los vivos y los difuntos y para obtener de Dios beneficios espirituales o temporales. [Sacrifice of the Mass]

Sagrada comunión pan y vino consagrados que recibimos en la misa, los cuales son el Cuerpo y Sangre de Jesucristo. La Sagrada comunión nos hace entrar en unión con Jesucristo y su muerte y resurrección redentoras. [Holy Communion]

Sagrada Escritura escritos sagrados de los judíos y cristianos recopilados en el Antiguo y Nuevo Testamento de la Biblia. [Scriptures]

Sagrada Familia familia de Jesús en la que creció Jesús en Nazaret. Estaba formada por Jesús, su madre María y su padre adoptivo José. [Holy Family]

sagrario vaso sagrado donde se reserva el Santísimo Sacramento para que la Sagrada comunión pueda ser llevada a los enfermos y moribundos. Se le llama también tabernáculo. Para los israelitas, el tabernáculo es el nombre de la tienda de campaña usada como santuario para guardar el Arca de la alianza desde la época del éxodo hasta la construcción del templo de Salomón. [tabernacle]

salmo oración en forma de poema. Los salmos estaban destinados para ser cantados en el culto público. Cada salmo expresa un aspecto, o característica de la profundidad de la oración humana. A lo largo de varios siglos, se han recolectado 150 salmos que forman el Libro de los Salmos en el Antiguo Testamento. Estos salmos se usaban en el culto a Dios en el Templo de Jerusalén, y han sido usados en el culto público de la Iglesia desde sus orígenes. [psalm]

salvación don, que sólo Dios puede darnos, del perdón del pecado y la reanudación de la amistad con Él. [salvation]

Salvador Jesús, el Hijo de Dios, que se hizo hombre para perdonar nuestros pecados y reanudar nuestra amistad con Dios. *Jesús* quiere decir "Dios salva". [Savior]

santa uno de los cuatro calificativos de la Iglesia. Es el tipo de vida que vivimos cuando participamos de la vida de Dios, que es todo santidad. La Iglesia es santa por su unión con Jesucristo. [holy]

santidad plenitud de la vida y el amor cristianos. Todos somos llamados a la santidad, la cual, al cooperar con la gracia de Dios, hace posible que se haga la voluntad de Dios en todas las cosas. Al hacer la voluntad de Dios, nos transformamos cada vez más en la imagen de su Hijo, Jesucristo. [holiness]

Santísimo Sacramento pan que ha sido consagrado por el sacerdote en la Misa. Se guarda en el sagrario para su adoración y para ser llevado a los enfermos. [Blessed Sacrament]

santo persona virtuosa y ejemplar que ha muerto en unión con Dios. Además, la Iglesia ha declarado que esta persona está con Dios en el cielo ahora y para siempre. [saint]

Satanás Un ángel caído. Enemigo de todo aquel que intente cumplir la voluntad de Dios. En el Evangelio, Satanás tienta a Jesús y se opone a su ministerio. En las tradiciones judía, cristiana y musulmana, Satanás se asocia con aquellos ángeles que rehusaron inclinarse ante seres humanos y servirles, como Dios ordenó. Dado que se negaron a servir a Dios, fueron expulsados del cielo. Satanás y los otros demonios tientan a los humanos para que se les unan en su rebelión contra Dios. [Satan]

scriptórium habitación que hay en los monasterios donde se hacían libros copiados a mano. Con frecuencia, se creaban bellas obras de arte en la página para ilustrar el texto. [scriptorium]

Semana Santa celebración de los sucesos relacionados a la pasión, muerte y resurrección de Jesús, y el don de la Eucaristía. Se inicia con la conmemoración de la entrada triunfal de Jesús a Jerusalén el Domingo de Ramos; sigue con la conmemoración del regalo que hace de sí mismo en la Eucaristía el Jueves Santo, su muerte el Viernes Santo y su resurrección durante la Vigilia Pascual el Sábado santo. [Holy Week]

Señor nombre que se le da a Dios para reemplazar el nombre que Él le reveló a Moisés, Yavé, que se consideraba demasiado sagrado para ser pronunciado. Indica la divinidad del Dios de Israel. El Nuevo Testamento usa el título Señor tanto para el Padre como para Jesús, reconociéndolo como Dios mismo. (*Ver* Yavé.) [Lord]

serafines seres celestiales que adoran a Dios ante su trono. Uno de ellos purificó los labios de Isaías con carbón ardiente para que pudiese hablar por Dios. [seraphim]

Sermón de la Montaña palabras de Jesús que aparecen en los capítulos 5 al 7 del Evangelio de san Mateo, en las que Jesús revela cómo Él ha dado plenitud a la ley de Dios entregada a Moisés. El Sermón de la Montaña comienza con las ocho bienaventuranzas e incluye la oración del Padrenuestro. [Sermon on the Mount]

sexismo prejuicios o discriminación en razón del sexo de una persona, especialmente discriminación contra la mujer. El sexismo crea conductas y actitudes que fomentan una visión de los roles sociales basada sólo en el sexo de la persona. [sexism]

sinagoga lugar de asamblea que usan los judíos para la oración, instrucción y estudio de la Ley. Después de la destrucción del Templo en el año 587 a.c., las sinagogas fueron organizadas como lugares para mantener la fe judía y la adoración. Jesús asistió regularmente a la sinagoga para orar y enseñar. Pablo iba primero a la sinagoga en cada ciudad que visitaba. La sinagoga desempeñó un papel importante en el desarrollo del culto y en la estructuración de las comunidades cristianas. [synagogue]

sinópticos de la palabra griega que significa "ver juntos". Describe los evangelios de Mateo, Marcos y Lucas. Son llamados evangelios sinópticos porque aunque son diferentes entre ellos, hay semejanzas que pueden observarse mirándolos en conjunto. La mayoría de los exegetas bíblicos está de acuerdo en que Marcos fue el primer evangelio escrito y que Mateo y Lucas usaron el texto de Marcos como modelo para escribir los suyos. [Synoptic]

soberbia imagen falsa de lo que somos que exagera lo que nos corresponde como seres creados por Dios. La soberbia nos pone en competencia con Dios y es uno de los siete pecados capitales. [pride]

solidaridad actitud de fuerza y unidad que conduce a compartir los bienes espirituales y materiales. La solidaridad une a ricos y pobres, débiles y poderosos, y crea una sociedad donde todos dan lo que pueden y reciben lo que necesitan. La idea de solidaridad se basa en el origen común de la humanidad. [solidarity]

subsidiaridad el principio que sostiene que las instituciones más cercanas son las más indicadas para responder a una determinada tarea social. Es responsabilidad de la institución política o privada más cercana asistir a aquellos que lo necesiten. Sólo cuando un asunto no puede ser resuelto en el ámbito local, deberá acudirse a un nivel más alto. [subsidiarity]

Suma Teológica obra principal de Santo Tomás de Aquino, quien organizó y clarificó el pensamiento sobre muchos tópicos religiosos en el siglo XIII. En esta obra, Tomás de Aquino trató temas como la existencia de Dios, la naturaleza del alma humana, la toma de decisiones morales, la Encarnación y la transustanciación. [Summa Theologiae]

T

temor de Dios uno de los siete dones del Espíritu Santo. Este don nos conduce a un sentimiento de admiración y portento ante la presencia de Dios debido a su grandeza. [fear of the Lord]

templanza virtud cardinal que nos ayuda a controlar nuestra atracción al placer de manera que nuestros deseos naturales se mantengan dentro de sus límites apropiados. Esta virtud moral nos ayuda a optar por usar con moderación los bienes creados. [temperance]

Templo casa donde se rinde culto a Dios, construida originalmente por Salomón. El templo proporcionaba un lugar donde los sacerdotes podían ofrecer sacrificios, adorar y dar gracias a Dios y pedir su perdón. Fue destruido y reconstruido. El segundo templo fue destruido por los romanos en 70 d. de C., y nunca fue reconstruido. Parte del muro exterior del monte del templo se conserva aún hoy en Jerusalén. [Temple]

tentación atracción, que viene de fuera o de nuestro interior, que puede llevarnos a no seguir los mandamientos de Dios. Todos somos tentados, pero el Espíritu Santo nos ayuda a resistir la tentación y a optar por hacer el bien. [temptation]

testimonio el transmitir a los demás, mediante nuestras palabras y acciones, la fe que se nos ha dado. Cada cristiano tiene el deber de dar testimonio de la buena nueva de Jesucristo que ha llegado a conocer. [witness]

Tierra Prometida tierra prometida originalmente por Dios a Abraham. Fue a esta tierra que Dios dijo a Moisés que llevara al Pueblo Elegido tras ser liberados de la esclavitud de Egipto y donde recibieron los Diez Mandamientos en el Monte Sinaí. [Promised Land]

Torá palabra hebrea que significa "instrucción" o "ley". Es también el nombre de los cinco primeros libros del Antiguo Testamento: Génesis, Éxodo, Levítico, Números y Deuteronomio. [Torah]

Tradición creencias y prácticas de la Iglesia transmitidas de una generación a otra bajo la guía del Espíritu Santo. Lo que Cristo confió a los apóstoles fue pasado a otros oralmente y por escrito. La Tradición y la Escritura juntas constituyen el único depósito de la fe, que permanece presente y activa en la Iglesia. [Tradition]

transubstanciación la transformación única del pan y el vino en la Eucaristía en el Cuerpo y Sangre de Cristo resucitado, aunque las apariencias de pan y vino permanecen. [transubstantiation]

Trinidad misterio de la existencia de Dios en tres personas: el Padre, el Hijo y el Espíritu Santo. Cada persona es plenamente Dios. Cada una es distinta sólo en su relación con las otras dos. [Trinity]

U

Última Cena última comida que cenaron Jesús y sus discípulos la noche antes de que muriera. En la Última Cena, Jesús tomó pan y vino, los bendijo, y dijo que eran su Cuerpo y su Sangre. La muerte y resurrección de Jesús, que celebramos en la Eucaristía fue anticipada en esta cena. [Last Supper]

una uno de los cuatro calificativos de la Iglesia. La Iglesia es una debido a su origen en un Dios único y a su fundador Jesucristo. Jesús, mediante su muerte en la cruz, unió todo a Dios en un cuerpo. Dentro de la unidad de la Iglesia, hay una gran diversidad debido a la riqueza de los dones dados a sus miembros. [one]

unción de los enfermos uno de los siete sacramentos, en el cual la persona enferma es ungida con óleo santo y recibe la fuerza, paz, y coraje para superar las dificultades que conlleva la enfermedad. A través del sacramento Jesús brinda al enfermo sanación espiritual y perdón de sus pecados y, si Dios quiere, también sanación al cuerpo. [Anointing of the Sick]

V

viático Eucaristía que recibe el moribundo. Es el alimento espiritual para el viaje final que hacemos como cristianos: el viaje a través de la muerte hacia la vida eterna. [viaticum]

Vicario de Cristo título dado al Papa, quien como sucesor de San Pedro, tiene la autoridad de actuar en representación de Cristo. Un vicario es alguien que es y está o actúa por ella. [Vicar of Christ]

vida eterna vida con Dios después de la muerte y que nunca acaba. Es concedida a quienes mueren estando en amistad con Dios, con su gracia viva en ellos. [eternal life]

vida religiosa estado de vida reconocido por la Iglesia. Dentro de la vida religiosa, varones y mujeres pueden responder libremente al llamado de seguir a Jesús viviendo sus votos de pobreza, castidad, y obediencia en comunidad. [religious life]

Vigilia Pascual celebración de la primera y más grande de las fiestas cristianas: la Resurrección de Jesús. Tiene lugar la tarde del primer sábado que sigue a la luna llena que se observa después del primer día de primavera. Es en esta noche de vigilia antes de la mañana de Pascua que los catecúmenos son bautizados, confirmados y reciben por primera vez la Eucaristía. [Easter Vigil]

virtud actitud o forma de actuar que nos ayuda a hacer el bien. [virtue]

virtudes teologales aquellas virtudes que nos fueron dadas por Dios y no alcanzadas por esfuerzo humano. Ellas son: fe, esperanza, y caridad. [Theological Virtues]

Visitación visita de María a Isabel para contarle la buena nueva de que habrá de ser la madre de Jesús. El saludo de Isabel forma parte del Avemaría. Durante esta visita, María hace su oración de alabanza a Dios: el Magníficat. [Visitation]

vocación llamado que se nos hace en la vida para que seamos las personas que Dios quiere que seamos. También es la forma en que servimos a la Iglesia y al Reino de Dios. Podemos ejercer nuestra vocación como laicos, como miembros de una comunidad religiosa, o como miembros del clero. [vocation]

voto promesa deliberada y libre hecha a Dios por aquellas personas que desean dedicar de forma especial su vida a Dios. Los votos dan ahora testimonio del reino que ha de venir. [vow]

Vulgata traducción de la Biblia al latín que hizo san Jerónimo del original hebreo y griego. En la época de san Jerónimo, la mayoría de los cristianos ya no hablaban hebreo o griego. La lengua común, o vulgata, era el latín. [Vulgate]

Y

Yavé nombre de Dios en hebreo dado por Dios a Moisés desde la zarza ardiente. *Yavé* quiere decir "Yo soy el que soy" o "Yo hago existir". [Yahweh]

Online Resources

Visit the Loyola Press Web site at **www.FindingGod.org** for more resources to help you continue to explore your Catholic faith.

There are many other reliable Catholic Web sites available on the Internet. Here are some helpful navigational hints:

- Start with official Web sites sponsored by your parish or diocese, other dioceses or religious communities, the U.S. Catholic bishops, and the Vatican.

- Check out the suggested links on those Web sites to see what they recommend.

- When exploring a Web site, read the "About Us" page to see who sponsors it and what they stand for.

- Cross-check your sources to ensure that the information is accurate or to explore a variety of perspectives.

- Avoid any Web site that contains offensive material.

Archdiocese of St. Paul and Minneapolis—Catholic Social Teaching documents and related information
www.osjspm.org/cst/

Catechism of the Catholic Church—the Catechism, including a search engine, concordance, and glossary
www.vatican.va/archive/ccc/index.htm

Catholic Campaign for Human Development—assists people to rise out of poverty through empowerment programs that foster self-sufficiency
www.usccb.org/cchd/povertyusa/index.htm

Catholic Charities—helps families and individuals overcome tragedy, poverty, and other life challenges
www.catholiccharitiesinfo.org/

Catholic Conservation Center—features Catholic writings about ecology and the environment
http://conservation.catholic.org/

Catholic Church Extension Society—works to sustain and extend the Catholic faith in poor and remote mission areas of the United States
www.catholic-extension.org/

Catholic Music Network—Catholic music online
www.catholicmusicnetwork.com/

Catholic News Service—reports the news that affects Catholics in their everyday lives
www.catholicnews.com/

Catholic Online—information about Catholicism including an online historical and biblical database
www.catholic.org/

Catholic Relief Services—the official international relief and development agency of the U.S. Catholic community
www.crs.org/

Creighton University Online Ministries—resources in the Catholic prayer tradition and in Ignatian spirituality
www.creighton.edu/CollaborativeMinistry/online.html

New American Bible—official online version
www.usccb.org/nab/bible/

Pray-As-You-Go—daily prayer and music for your MP3 and your soul.
www.pray-as-you-go.org

Religious Ministries Online Guide—database of Catholic ministries, religious and lay communities, and a guide to discerning vocations
www.religiousministries.com/

Sacred Space—daily prayer online
www.sacredspace/ie

Second Vatican Council Documents—the full text of the 16 major documents of the Second Vatican Council
www.vatican.va/archive/hist_councils/ii_vatican_council/

United States Conference of Catholic Bishops—official web site of the U.S. Catholic Bishops
www.usccb.org/index.shtml

The Vatican Web Site—official Vatican Web site which includes the Catechism and other Church documents
www.vatican.va/

Vision: The Guide to Catholic Vocations—includes links to religious communities as well as listings of discernment, service and educational opportunities
www.visionguide.org/

These Web sites are being provided as a convenience and for informational purposes only. Loyola Press neither controls nor endorses such sites, nor have we reviewed or approved any content for subsequent links made from these sites. Loyola Press is not responsible for the legality, accuracy, or inappropriate nature of any content, advertising, products, or other materials on or available from such linked sites. In addition, these sites or services, including their contents and links, may be constantly changing. Loyola Press assumes no responsibility for monitoring the content of these sites.

and Confirmation, 206–8
  Fruits of, 270, 323
  Gifts of, 303, 323
  as guide, 53, 56, 111
  and Jesus, 52–53, 194–95
  and prayer, 57, 58, 324
  symbols of, 56
  and Trinity, 37
Holy Thursday, 294
Holy Week, 279, 293–96
hope, 80–81
human life. *See* life, human
hunger, 249

I

Ignatius of Loyola, Saint, 268–70, 274
illuminations, 17
Immaculate Conception, 178
Incarnation, the, 67, 69, 70, 73
industrialism, 19, 345
Infancy Narratives, 174–76, 286–87

J

Jesuit Volunteer Corps, 207
Jesus
  ancestry of, 160
  Ascension of, 195
  birth of, 174–76, 286–87
  as carpenter, 71
  consecrated to God, 199
  Crucifixion of, 10, 64, 67, 107–8
  Emmaus story, 216–18, 220, 299
  and Eucharist, 214, 215, 217, 218, 238, 299
  and feast at Cana, 10, 26–27
  and the Father, 9, 10, 33–34, 55, 67, 68
  as healer, 42, 86, 99–100, 106, 111
  and Holy Spirit, 52–53, 194–95
  as human and divine, 67, 69–71, 73, 124
  as Messiah, 66–67, 217, 315
  names of, 120–22
  prayer in life of, 72, 219
  Resurrection of (*see* Resurrection of Jesus)
  as Savior and Redeemer, 107, 108, 176
  as Son of God, 63, 64, 66, 68, 176
  teachings of, 77–78, 141
  in the Temple, 204–5
  temptations of, 144
  and Transfiguration, 106, 152
  and Trinity, 35–37
  virtues of, 205
Jewish people, persecution of, 269
John, as apostle, 24
John the Baptist, 179
John, Gospel of, 9–10, 12–13, 23, 27, 35, 314, 316

John Bosco, Saint, 81
John Paul II, Pope, 181
John Vianney, Saint, 54–56
Joseph, 120–21, 122, 161
Jubilee years, 93
justification, 226, 229

K

Kingdom of God, 76–78, 79, 81, 82, 83, 132, 208

L

l'Arche, 110
Last Supper, 214–15, 294
leaders, 140–41
lectio divina, 28
Lent, 279, 289–92
life, human, 73, 133–35, 147, 345
lion, as symbol, 71
Little Brothers of Jesus, 88
liturgical prayer, 155
liturgy, 155
Lord's Day, 102, 215, 239–40, 244, 338
love, 81, 271–72
Luke, Gospel of, 171–72, 179, 316
  Infancy Narrative in, 174–76, 286–87
  and Jesus' journeys, 196, 218
  and the poor, 131
  on sharing meals, 217, 219

M

Magnificat, 283
Mark, Gospel of, 63–64, 67, 69, 314, 315
marriage, 161–62, 164–65, 188, 337
Mary
  and Annunciation, 177–78, 282, 286
  and birth of Jesus, 174–76, 286–87
  and Immaculate Conception, 178
  and Magnificat, 283
  as model, 27, 287
  prayers to, 180
  role of, 175, 178
  and the Visitation, 283, 286
Mass, 338–39
Matrimony, Sacrament of, 161–62, 164–65, 188, 337
Matthew, Gospel of, 117–18, 124, 131, 136, 140, 152, 174, 286, 315
meals, 219
meat, eating of, 248–50
Messiah, 66–67, 217, 315. *See also* Jesus
ministry, 150
miracles, 86, 106, 111
moral choices, 226, 248–50, 254, 255, 340, 342
mortal sins, 341

N

New Testament, 14, 312, 314, 315–17, 318. *See also* Gospels; John; Luke; Mark; Matthew
Nicodemus, 10, 32–33, 34
Noah, 121–22, 207

O

obedience, 209
Oblate Sisters of Providence, 178
Old Testament, 12–14, 311–12, 313–14
Ordinary Time, 279
Ordination, Rite of, 151
original sin, 178, 229–30, 341

P

Palm Sunday, 294
parables, 77–78, 106
  of lost coin, 184
  of lost sheep, 78, 184
  of lost son, 184–85, 190
  of mustard seed, 77, 106
  of the sower, 106, 142–43, 144, 146
parents, 205, 241, 243
Paschal Mystery, 108
Passover, 214–15, 295
pastors, 154
Paul the Apostle (Saul), Saint, 225–26, 229, 230, 248–50
  conversion of, 199, 200, 228–29, 274
  in Damascus, 232
  journeys of, 319
  letters of, 238, 239, 262, 270, 314, 317
  and prayer, 253
peace, promotion of, 137
Penance and Reconciliation, Sacrament of, 87, 88, 89–90, 337, 344
Pentecost, 206, 279, 301–4
Peter, 118, 153
Pharisees, 32
poor, the, 59, 77, 110, 131, 221, 346
pope, 153–54
poverty, 249
prayer, 172
  attitude in, 136
  as conversation with God, 28, 324
  and conversion, 234
  Daily Examen, 329
  and detachment, 273
  and discernment of spirits, 145
  and emotions, 125
  and faith, 47
  and family, 166
  forms of, 324–25
  and good works, 82
  Hail Mary, 178, 180, 326
  and Holy Spirit, 57, 58, 324

Acknowledgments

Unless otherwise acknowledged, photos are the property of Loyola Press. When there is more than one picture on a page, credits are supplied in sequence, left to right, top to bottom. Page positions are abbreviated as follows: (t) top, (c) center, (b) bottom, (l) left, (r) right.

FRONTMATTER: i(bl) Plush Studios/Getty Images. **vi**(t) colonialarts.com. **vi**(b) Hans Neleman/Getty Images. **vii**(t) "Jesus Breaking Bread" © 1993 Fr. John Giuliani • Reproductions at www.BridgeBuilding.com. **vii**(br) Michael Kelley/Getty Images.

UNIT 1: 9(t) *The Healing of the Blind Man,* 1811 (tempera and gold leaf on panel) by Bulgarian School, (17th century), Rila Monastery National Museum, Bulgaria/Archives Charmet/The Bridgeman Art Library. **9**(bl) © The Crosiers/Gene Plaisted OSC. **10**(l) SEF/Art Resource, NY. **11** © Dex Images/CORBIS. **13** The Bridgeman Art Library/Getty Images. **14** Scala/Art Resource, NY. **16** Alamy. **17** *Christ in Majesty with the Symbols of the Evangelists,* illustration from The Bible of Alcuin (735–804) completed in 801 AD/British Museum, London, UK/The Bridgeman Art Library. **18** © Arte & Immagini srl/CORBIS. **21** SW Productions/Getty Images. **22** Giraudon/Art Resource, NY. **23**(b) The St. Irenaeus icon is by the hand of Nick Papas of Greensburg, PA. It is at St. Philip Antiochian Orthodox Church, Souderton, PA. Photo is by comeandseeicons.com. **24** Scala/Art Resource, NY. **25** Phil Martin Photography. **26** Denis Felix/Getty Images. **27**(b) Juliet Coomber/Getty Images. **28** Shaun Egan/Getty Images. **30**(l) Giraudon/Art Resource, NY. **30**(r) Denis Felix/Getty Images. **31** Veer. **32** All rights reserved, Vie de Jésus MAFA, 24 rue du Maréchal Joffre, F-78000 VERSAILLES, www.jesusmafa.com. **33**(t) © The Crosiers/Gene Plaisted OSC. **33**(b) GDT/Getty Images. **34**(b) © Vittoriano Rastelli/CORBIS. **35** www.mexicanretablos.com. **36**(r) Scala/Art Resource, NY. **42**(t) © Louis Moses/zefa/CORBIS. **42**(b) Corinne Vonaesch, www.c-vonaesch.ch. **44** Scala/Art Resource, NY. **45**(t) © The Crosiers/Gene Plaisted OSC. **48** *The Healing of the Blind Man,* 1811 (tempera and gold leaf on panel), Bulgarian School, (17th century) / Rila Monastery National Museum, Bulgaria, Archives Charmet / Bridgeman Art Library. **52** Erich Lessing/Art Resource, NY. **53**(t) Veer. **53**(b) *Saint Edith Stein,* Michael D. O'Brien, www.studiobrien.com. **54** © The Crosiers/Gene Plaisted OSC. **55**(b) David Young-Wolff/Getty Images. **56**(l) *Ten symbols of the Holy Spirit,* Susan Tolonen. **57** © The Crosiers/Gene Plaisted OSC. **58** *St. John Vianney,* Michael D. O'Brien, www.studiobrien.com. **62**(tr) Dan Dalton/Getty Images.

UNIT 2: 63(b) SEF/Art Resource, NY. **65**(c) Alamy. **65**(b) Simon Battensby/Getty Images. **66** © Images.com/CORBIS. **67**(b) Alamy. **69**(t) *A Jesus Image,* Fr. Jim Hasse, S.J., Cincinnati, Ohio. **70**(b) *Madame Acarie* (1566–1618) known as *Marie de l'Incarnation* (oil on canvas), French School, (19th century), Church of Saint-Merri, Paris, France, Lauros/Giraudon / Bridgeman Art Library. **71**(t) *St. Joseph the Worker,* Michael D. O'Brien, www.studiobrien.com. **71**(b) Cameraphoto Arte, Venice/Art Resource, NY. **72** David Robinson/Getty Images. **76**(t) SEF/Art Resource, NY. **77** www.HolyLandPhotos.org. **78** Scala/Art Resource, NY. **80**(t)(c) Susan Tolonen. **80**(b) Graphic courtesy of the Muscular Dystrophy Association, www.mdausa.org. **81**(t) Susan Tolonen. **81**(c) www.blissmfg.com. **82**(l) SEF/Art Resource, NY. **82** www.colonialarts.com. **85** Stuart McClymont/Getty Images. **86** Stephen Mallon/Getty Images. **89** *Vicomte Charles Eugene de Foucauld* (1858–1916)/photo by French Photographer, Archives Larousse, Paris, France/Giraudon/The Bridgeman Art Library. **90**(l) Dimitar Dilkoff/Getty Images. **91** *Prayer Time,* M. P. Wiggins/www.thespiritsource.com. **95** Romilly Lockyer/Getty Images. **97**(t) www.iconarts.com. **98** Alamy. **99** *Christ Healing the Sick* (acrlic on canvas), James, Laura (Contemporary Artist) / Private Collection, / Bridgeman Art Library. **100**(b) Phil Martin Photography. **101** Corinne Vonaesch, www.c-vonaesch.ch. **102** Arthur Tilley/Getty Images. **106** David Leahy/Getty Images. **108**(r) *Crosier Head depicting the Paschal Lamb,* possibly 12th century with more recent mounts (ivory) © Ashmolean Museum, University of Oxford, UK/The Bridgeman Art Library. **109** *The Holy Women at the Sepulchre* (acrylic on canvas) by James, Laura (Contemporary Artist)/Private Collection/The Bridgeman Art Library. **110**(l) Knights of Columbus photo. **110**(r) © The Crosiers/Gene Plaisted OSC. **111** Ken Chernus/Getty Images. **115**(t) Alamy. **115**(cl) Alamy.

UNIT 3: 117(cl) Nick Daly/Getty Images. **117**(bl) *The Transfiguration,* Michael D. O'Brien, www.studiobrien.com. **121** © The Crosiers/Gene Plaisted OSC. **122**(t) George Bridges/Getty Images. **122**(b) Cameraphoto/Art Resource, NY. **125** Hans Neleman/Getty Images. **126** © The Crosiers/Gene Plaisted OSC. **130**(t) Scala/Art Resource, NY. **130**(b) John Stevens. **131** *St. Luke,* Michael D. O'Brien, www.studiobrien.com. **132**(t) © The Crosiers/Gene Plaisted OSC. **135** Ed Blackburn/Dallas Museum of Art, Museum League Purchase Fund. **138**(l) Scala/Art Resource, NY. **139** © The Crosiers/Gene Plaisted OSC. **140**(t) Erich Lessing/Art Resource, NY. **142** Erich Lessing/Art Resource, NY. **143**(t) Time Life Pictures/Getty Images. **143**(b) © The Crosiers/Gene Plaisted OSC. **146** Alamy. **149** Tony Anderson/Getty Images. **150** Ponkawonka Inc. **151**(t) Ponkawonka Inc. **152** *The Transfiguration,* Michael D. O'Brien, www.studiobrien.com. **153** © Vatican Pool/CORBIS. **155** *Peaceful Server,* Regina Kubelka/www.thespiritsource.com. **156** Scott Barbour/Getty Images. **160** *The Presentation,* Michael D. O'Brien, www.studiobrien.com. **161** Ghislain & Marie David de Lossy/Getty Images. **162** Andrew K. Davey/Getty Images. **163** Jupiter Images. **165**(b) Kevin Cooley/Getty Images.

UNIT 4: 171(cl) © The Crosiers/Gene Plaisted OSC. **171**(bl) Pozycinski Bronze Studios, www.pozycinskibronze.com. **172**(cl) *St. Luke,* Michael D. O'Brien, www.studiobrien.com. **174** Smithsonian American Art Museum, Washington, DC/Art Resource, NY. **175**(c) http://photos.novica.com/. **177**(t) Annunciation, mixed media on stone with gold leaf, 8"x8", 1999,© Christina Saj, www.christinasaj.com. **178**(t) © The Crosiers/Gene Plaisted OSC. **179** *John the Baptist* (acrylic on canvas), James, Laura (Contemporary Artist) / Private Collection, / Bridgeman Art Library. **184** David Perez Shadi/Getty Images. **185**(t) Alamy. **185**(c) © Archivo Iconografico, S.A./CORBIS. **186**(t) © CORBIS. **187** Fr. William Hart McNichols, http://puffin.creighton.edu/jesuit/andre/. **188**(l) Phil Martin Photography. **189** *Eucharist,* Julie Lonneman/www.thespiritsource.com. **192**(r) Fr. William Hart McNichols, http://puffin.creighton.edu/jesuit/andre/. **192**(l) David Perez Shadi/Getty Images. **194** *Pentecost,* M. P. Wiggins/www.thespiritsource.com. **198**(t) Nordic Life AS/Getty Images. **199** *The Visitation* (acrylic on canvas), James, Laura (Contemporary Artist) / Private Collection, / Bridgeman Art Library. **203** Alamy. **204** *Finding in the Temple,* Michael D. O'Brien, www.studiobrien.com. **205**(b) Marc Romanelli/Getty Images. **206** Alamy. **207**(t) Jesuit Volunteer Corps. **207**(b) Pozycinski Bronze Studios, www.pozycinskibronze.com. **208** © The Crosiers/Gene Plaisted OSC.

210 © The Crosiers/Gene Plaisted OSC. 214(t) "Jesus Breaking Bread" © 1993 Fr. John Giuliani • Reproductions at www.BridgeBuilding.com. 215(t) Scala/Art Resource, NY. 216(b) Giantstep Inc./Getty Images. 217(t) http://photos.novica.com. 220 Erich Lessing/Art Resource, NY.

UNIT 5: 225(t), 226(b) © The Crosiers/Gene Plaisted OSC. 229 Scala/Art Resource, NY. 230 Constantine Youssis, NJ (icon at St. Mary Antiochian Orthodox Church, Johnstown, PA)/www.comeandseei-cons.com. 232(t) Sean Gallup/Getty Images. 232(b) *St. Paul escapes Damascus in a basket,* 12th/13th century (mosaic), Duomo, Monreale, Sicily, Italy/Ancient Art and Architecture Collection Ltd./The Bridgeman Art Library. 238 Robin M. White/Getty Images. 240 Neo Vision/Getty Images. 242(bl) Scala/Art Resource, NY. 243(t) Yellow Dog Productions/Getty Images. 243(b) Fr. William Hart McNichols, http://puffin.creighton.edu/jesuit/andre. 244 © The Crosiers/Gene Plaisted OSC. 246(l) Robin M. White/Getty Images. 247 Hugh Musick, www.hughmusick.com. 249 Congregatio Jesu, Augsburg, Germany. 250(b) © The Crosiers/Gene Plaisted OSC. 252(t) Jean Luc Morales/Getty Images. 252(b) National Portrait Gallery, Smithsonian Institution/Art Resource, NY. 253 Elizabeth Wang, *Through Him, With Him,* © Radiant Light 2006, www.radiantlight.org.uk. 258(t) Michael Kelley/Getty Images. 258(b) National Portrait Gallery, Smithsonian Institution/Art Resource, NY. 260 Manu Sassoonian/Art Resource, NY. 261(b) Erich Lessing/Art Resource, NY. 264 http://photos.novica.com/. 267 Olivier Ribardiere/Getty Images. 268 From The Spiritual Journey of St. Ignatius Loyola by Dora Nikolova Bittau/photo by Ken Wagner © 1998 Seattle University. 269 USHMM, Courtesy of Myriam Abramowitz. 270 Michael Kelley/Getty Images. 273 Philip J. Brittan/Getty Images. 274 Réunion des Musées Nationaux/Art Resource, NY. 280 Rebecca Bradley.

SEASONALS: 279(t) Lillian Delevoryas/Getty Images. 279(c) Ponkawonka Inc. 279(b) He Qi. 280 Rebecca Bradley. 282 Fine Art Photographic Library, London/Art Resource, NY. 283 Phil Martin Photography. 285(c, b), Lillian Delevoryas/Getty Images. 288(t) Lillian Delevoryas/Getty Images. 289(c, b) © The Crosiers/Gene Plaisted OSC. 290 © Dave Bartruff/CORBIS. 291(b) Operation Rice Bowl, Catholic Relief Services. 292(t) © The Crosiers/Gene Plaisted OSC. 292(c) Mario Tama/Getty Images. 293(t) Phil Martin Photography. 293(c, b) Ponkawonka Inc. 294 © Arte & Immagini srl/CORBIS. 296(t) Ponkawonka Inc. 297(c, b) He Qi. 299 Phil Martin Photography. 300(t) He Qi. 300(c) © Dave Bartruff/CORBIS. 301(t) www.colonialarts.com. 301(c, b), 304(t) Linda S. Schmidt. 304(c) Luc Beziat/Getty Images. 305(c, b) Steve Erspamer, O.S.B. 306 *The Last Judgement* (tempera on panel) (detail) by Angelico, Fra (Guido di Pietro) (c.1387–1455) © Museo di San Marco dell'Angelico, Florence, Italy/Giraudon/The Bridgeman Art Library. 307 Phil Martin Photography. 308(t) Steve Erspamer, O.S.B. 308(c) © LE SEGRETAIN PASCAL/CORBIS SYG.

ENDMATTER: 313 © The Crosiers/Gene Plaisted OSC. 314 © Araldo de Luca/CORBIS. 315, 316(all) © Hermitage Art, Inc./Reproductions at www.BridgeBuilding.com. 318(tl) © Shai Ginott/CORBIS. 318(tr) © Bettmann/CORBIS. 318(bl, br) Bill Wood. 319(t) Bill Wood. 321 *Sermon on the Mount,* Scenes from the Life of Christ (mosaic), Byzantine School, (6th century) / Sant'Apollinare Nuovo, Ravenna, Italy, Giraudon / The Bridgeman Art Library. 323(bl) Safia Fatimi/Photonica/Getty Images. 323(br) Art Resource, NY. 331 Greg Kuepfer. 332 Alinari/Art Resource, NY. 333(t) © Andy Warhol Foundation/CORBIS. 334, 335(all) © The Crosiers/Gene Plaisted OSC. 336(lc, tc, bc) Phil Martin Photography. 339 Phil Martin Photography. 341 Alamy.

343 Alex Mares-Manton/Getty Images. 344(b) Associated Press. 345 Alamy. 346(t) © Joel Stettenheim/CORBIS.

Glossary: 348 © Assumption Abbey/Brother Elias Thienpont, OSB. 349(b) Courtesy Basilica of National Shrine of the Immaculate Conception, Washington, DC. 350 © Noehoni Harsono, Indonesia/Asian Christian Art Association. 352 Mary Evans Picture Library. 353 Collezione d'Arte, Religiosa Moderna, Vatican/Photo: A. Brachetti, Vatican Museums. 354 © Elio Ciol/CORBIS. 356 Monica Liu. 357 © Los Angeles Times. 358 Courtesy of Bryant College from the Gladys Kinoian Lujan Collection of Haitian Naive Art, Smithfield, RI. 359 National Gallery of Art, Washington, DC., Samuel H. Kress. 361 © The Crosiers/Gene Plaisted OSC. 362(l) © Stephen McBrady/PhotoEdit. 362(r) photodisc/Getty Images. 363(r) National Gallery, London/Bridgeman Art Library. 364 © MacDuff Everton/CORBIS. 366 © Anil Kapahi/Chapel of St. Ignatius, Seattle University. 367 © The Frick Collection, New York. 368 From Fourteen Mosaic Stations of the Cross, © Our Lady of the Angels Monastery, Inc., Hanceville, Alabama. All Rights Reserved. 369(l) photodisc/Getty Images. 369(r) © The Crosiers/Gene Plaisted OSC. 370(t) © Scala/Art Resource, NY.

Spoken Word and Instrumental Music CDs
All CDs were produced and developed by Loyola Press in partnership with Loyola Productions, Los Angeles, California.

Executive Producer: Loyola Press
Executive Producers for Loyola Productions: Edward J. Siebert, S.J. Paul Brian Campbell, S.J.
Producer: Javier Ruisanchez
Production Coordinator: Mirabai Rose
Instrumental music: Nathanael Lew
CDs edited, mixed & mastered by: Nathanael Lew

Dramatized Scripture Stories: Voice Over Actors
Jessica Bogart: *Ruth, Orpah, Mother*
Nathan Carlson: *Paul, Micah, Father, James*
Cam Clarke: *Onesimus, Disciple, John, Thomas, Disciple 3*
Edward Cunningham: *Jared, Boaz, Rabbi, Disciple 2*
Jennifer Darling: *Naomi, Person 2*
Abner Genece: *Peter, Worker*
Wendy K. Gray: *Narrator*
Elijah Runcorn: *Asa, Person 1*
Lloyd Sherr: *Leader, Grandfather, Disciple 1*
R. Todd Torok: *Jesus*

Guided Reflections: Narrators
Cam Clarke & Jennifer Darling